ADOLPHE GOUHENANT

Adolphe Gouhenant

French Revolutionary, Utopian Leader,
and Texas Frontier Photographer

Paula Selzer and Emmanuel Pécontal

Number 3 in the Texas Local Series

UNT PRESS

Denton, Texas

10 9 8 7 6 5 4 3 2 1

Permissions:
University of North Texas Press
1155 Union Circle #311336
Denton, TX 76203-5017

The paper used in this book meets the minimum requirements of the
American National Standard for Permanence of Paper for Printed Library
Materials, z39.48.1984. Binding materials have been chosen for durability.

Library of Congress Cataloging-in-Publication Data

Names: Selzer, Paula, 1961- author. | Pécontal, E. (Emmanuel), author.
Title: Adolphe Gouhenant : French revolutionary, utopian leader, and
    Texas frontier photographer / Paula Selzer and Emmanuel Pécontal.
Description: First edition. | Denton : University of North Texas, [2019] | Series:
Number 3 in the Texas Local Series | Includes bibliographical references and index.
Identifiers: LCCN 2019021440 | ISBN 9781574417692
    (cloth) | ISBN 9781574417791 (ebook)
Subjects: LCSH: Gouhenant, Adolphe. | Artists--Texas--Dallas--Biography.
| Photographers--Texas--Dallas--Biography. | Political activists--France--
Biography. | Socialists--Texas--Biography. | Icarian movement--France--
History--19th century. | Icarian movement--Texas--History--19th century. | Dallas
(Tex.)--Intellectual life--19th century. | Dallas (Tex.)--History--19th century.
Classification: LCC NX512.G68 S45 2019 | DDC 709.2 [B]--dc23
LC record available at https://lccn.loc.gov/2019021440

*Adolphe Gouhenant: French Revolutionary, Utopian Leader, and
Texas Frontier Photographer* is Number 3 in the Texas Local Series

Drawing on front cover is of Adolphe Gouhenant in 1843.
*Copyright Conseil Départemental de la Haute-Garonne /
Archives Départementales / 37 FI 19 / Drawing by Léon Soulié.*

The electronic edition of this book was made possible
by the support of the Vick Family Foundation.

Dedication
To my late parents, Simon Selzer and Carolyn Downey Selzer,
and to my grandmothers who all taught me to love history
—Paula Selzer
To my mother, Michelle Pécontal, and my late father, Georges
Pécontal, who raised their children in the love of reason
—Emmanuel Pécontal

TABLE OF CONTENTS

List of Illustrations

ACKNOWLEDGMENTS

Many people were consulted in researching this project over the course of several years in both the United States and France. The authors gratefully acknowledge the efforts of archivists, librarians, researchers, family, and friends who assisted with this effort. Special thanks go to the following: Richard Selcer for his support and encouragement; Marcelle Hull, Dawn Youngblood, Clay Perkins, John Lunsford, Paula Baker, Pat Crowley, Marvin and Shirley Applewhite, Alex Troup, Jim Wheat, Alexander Mendoza; and especially to Vera Guillen—a thank you will never be enough; also to Rébecca Duffeix at the Musée d'Histoire de Lyon and Pierre Crépel at the Académie des Sciences Belles Lettres et Arts de Lyon for their special help in digging through their archives; to Bernard Masson and Florence Ferraud-Masson who provided us with the self-published books of their father and grand-father containing invaluable letters of Gouhenant's nephew Ernest Humbert; to Arlette Pécontal for her constant support. Special thanks to Claire Pécontal for her thorough proofreading. Emmanuel Pécontal has made an extensive use of the French digital libraries: Gallica at the French national library, Numelyo in Lyon, and Rosalis in Toulouse. Also, many thanks to Michael Grauer, Michael Hazel, Ronald Chrisman, Karen DeVinney, Bess Whitby, the editorial board, and the staff of the University of North Texas Press.

The staff of the following organizations were extremely helpful providing suggestions and search parameters for their respective collections

In France:

Archives Nationales

Bibliothèque Nationale de France

Archives Départementales de Haute Garonne

Archives Départementales de Haute Saône

Archives Départementales du Lot-et-Garonne

Archives Départementales du Rhône

Archives Municipales de Lyon

In the U.S:

Bywaters Special Collections, Southern Methodist University

City of Dallas Municipal Archives and Historic Preservation Divisions

Dallas Historical Society

Dallas Public Library, History and Archives Division

DeGolyer Library, Southern Methodist University

Fort Worth Public Library

The Grand Lodge of Texas

Legislative Reference Library of Texas

Maine Maritime Museum

National Archives and Records Administration

Old Red Museum of Dallas County History and Culture

City of Pilot Point

Portal to Texas History

Springfield-Greene County Library

Syracuse University, Special Collections Research Center

Tarrant County Archives

Texas General Land Office

Texas State Library and Archives

University of Texas at Arlington

University of Texas at Austin Briscoe Center for American History

University of Texas Southwestern Medical Center Library

Illustration 1. Adolphe Gouhenant in 1843.

Copyright Conseil Départemental de la Haute-Garonne / Archives Départementales / 37 FI 19 / Drawing by Léon Soulié.

Introduction

The name "Adolphe Gouhenant" will be familiar to those who have studied North Texas history. Pronounced *Gounah*, he has been well documented in narratives written by Jerry Bywaters, Sam Atchinson, Julia Kathryn Garrett, A.C. Greene, Darwin Payne, Richard Selcer, and others, as the first photographer and owner of the first artistic establishment in Dallas. A French immigrant, he established a pre-doomed Icarian communist settlement in Denton County and then became friends with Fort Worth commandant, Major Ripley Arnold.

Yet, few people know that he began his life on a cold winter morning in a small village situated near the *Jura Massif*—the foothills of the Alps. Christened François-Ignace Gouhenant, he grew up in a volatile and industrial era at the dawn of the romantic age. He was a colorful and passionate character surrounded by the philosophical, artistic, and literary movements that would define his ideology as an adult, all unfolding against a backdrop of revolution.

Gouhenant was born in 1804, the same year as French writer George Sand, American industrialist John Deere, and Austrian composer Johann Strauss; the same year that Lewis and Clark set out on their expedition and Napoléon Bonaparte became the Emperor of the French. In Great

Britain, Lord Elgin was pilfering Greek treasures from the Parthenon and Alexander von Humboldt had just completed the first modern scientific and botanical study of Latin America. Thomas Jefferson was president of the United States, and had recently signed the Louisiana Purchase vastly expanding the nation's territory. Early in the century, Romantic painters like Eugène Delacroix were stunning Europeans with their emotional and dramatic images while writers like Victor Hugo and Mary Shelley were publishing works illustrating man's inhumanity to man. Gouhenant was Hugo's contemporary and at one point his daughter would correspond with Hugo.

Swept up in this kinetic environment, a young "Adolphe" Gouhenant was finding his voice amidst the dying monarchy and growing republican sentiment. In 1831, he petitioned the Duc d'Orléans requesting funds to build a monument to science, and eventually constructed a one-hundred-foot observatory high above the city of Lyon. He spent several years working as an art dealer, painter, and restorer, and fought for workers' rights during the final years of the French monarchy. In 1843, he would be imprisoned in Toulouse for his clandestine political activities where he would survive prosecution, only to emerge a few years later as a charismatic and resourceful leader of the nascent communist movement.

Gouhenant was caught up in the early days of pre-Marxist communist rhetoric. In 1848, he left his wife and two children behind and sailed across the frigid Atlantic Ocean chasing the dream of a new Utopia. When he arrived in America, Texas had only been a part of the United States for three years. Landing first in New Orleans, he led an advance guard in a march across North Texas to establish the proposed Icarian communist colony. He encountered numerous roadblocks, both natural and manufactured—some constructed by those he trusted. In short order, the colony failed, but despite betrayals and his own shortcomings, he would eventually succeed. The same year that he arrived in Texas, revolutions broke out across Europe, and the Mexican War had just come to an end. Just one month after he landed in the U.S., slavery was abolished in the French colonies—it would be another seventeen years before that would occur in the U.S. Gouhenant witnessed all these remarkable changes, and by the end of his life, industrial mechanization would make transportation more efficient and methods of communication better and faster.

The wildly creative misspellings of Adolphe Gouhenant's last name have resulted in at least two dozen documented versions, mostly by Americans struggling with an abundance of consonants and vowels in a multisyllabic French surname. Even within a single book (Bates's *History and Reminiscences of Denton County*) his family name is spelled three different ways—Gornah, Gohnor, and Gonnough—thwarting research efforts to trace his whereabouts. Ultimately, he changed the spelling of his name to better reflect the correct pronunciation, and most likely to quell his ongoing frustration at having to spell it out to itchy-headed frontiersmen who were constantly struggling to pronounce it.[1]

His accomplishments in Texas were as varied as the many versions of his name. During his first decade there, he relied upon his artistic sensibilities to create photographs of some of Dallas's first citizens. Daguerreotypes of Hord's Ridge and the first brick courthouse are among the only surviving images of early Dallas and both have been attributed to him. Gouhenant taught music, drawing, and French and Spanish languages to the earliest settlers of Fort Worth and opened the notable Arts Saloon on the courthouse square in Dallas—the town's first cultural institution.

In 1853, he became the city's first naturalized citizen. He applied for a Peters Colony land grant and patented two prime parcels of land in Tarrant County. He was among the first group of Masons in Dallas, holding office in the Tannehill Lodge and later in the Ford Lodge at Pilot Point. He had some knowledge of scientific processes and natural remedies and late in his life began to practice medicine. He lived for a while with a Texas Ranger and made numerous real estate investments in the central part of Dallas. Ultimately, he settled in Denton County where he owned an apothecary and raised cattle until the early 1870s.

The French artist and revolutionary who immigrated to Texas was a remarkable man. His actions in the 1840s offer a strong case for his concern about the evolving threat of industrial progress on his fellow artisans and craftsmen in France and the burden of repression under the monarchy. His leadership in the Icarian Communist movement made him an enigma on the frontier, where on the eve of the Civil War, many men in Texas were decidedly not committed to equal rights, and certainly not to communal living. His successful quest to retrieve a fallen friend is among the era's most romantic stories. Finally, his legal struggles to reclaim the property that he purchased in Dallas in the mid-nineteenth century, offer some of the best historical references for his unique activities. The court battles in which he fought to keep his homestead set legal precedents that were cited for years to come. A most interesting character, Gouhenant's unpredictable wanderings in both France and America, certainly tell a rare story of a French immigrant planting his historic footprint on North Texas soil.

Note: Throughout the book there are passages from archival documents, family letters, and court records that have been translated from French. The authors have tried to remain true to the tone of the nineteenth century language and to the writer's original style. Except where noted, all translations were done by the authors.

ADOLPHE GOUHENANT

Part 1

The Early Years in France (1804 - 1848)

Chapter 1

A Temple for the Arts and Sciences

I wanted to build a temple for the arts and sciences, I wanted to beautify the city where I live, I wanted to move lightning away from it. I have used all my care, my time and my money. I almost reached the end of my project I have just one step remaining: it is the most difficult.

François Ignace Gouhenant, 1831

A Boy Raised in the Shadow of Revolution: 1804–1824

The Napoleonic Empire had finally faltered under the European coalition and a military invasion erupted just as a young boy named Gouhenant was turning ten. The year was 1814. Napoléon, who had managed to channel tremendous revolutionary energy to serve his inordinate ambition, was now in disarray and leading an exhausted empire. The allied armies had invaded French territory all the way up to her pre-revolution borders. Families were weary of seeing their sons leave home for an unending war they understood less and less as the military defeats accumulated. With the enemy now occupying their land, the faith the

French once had in their emperor had evaporated, and they longed for peace. Napoléon's military genius could slow the allies' progress, but the mass uprising he sought in order to defend his empire was far less effective than in 1792, when the Revolution was young and the people were struggling to eject invaders from their borders and spread revolutionary ideas throughout continental Europe. After ten years of fighting to secure the Empire, France was exhausted.

The end of the empire actually began in the winter of 1812, when the French were forced to retreat from Russia, wiped out by a combination of the bitter winter and continued military assaults ordered by Tsar Alexander I. The Tsar wanted to take advantage of the French defeat, and he succeeded in organizing a Sixth European Coalition. Napoléon was again defeated at Leipzig in October 1813 and his armies had to retreat to France, followed by the Coalition armies. Napoléon concentrated most of his forces on the German border—paying little attention to the Swiss border which seemed protected by their neutrality. However, the Austrians decided they would enter Switzerland and sent the main invasion army, the Bohemians—an army of 200,000 Austrians, Russians, and Prussians—to invade the French province of Franche-Comté, which had remained outside the major military theater of operations since the beginning of the Revolution.[2]

After crossing the Swiss border into France, the road to Paris is straight, starting from the valley between the Vosges and Jura Mountains: first there is Basel, then Vesoul, Langres, Troyes, and finally Paris, where the allies entered in March of 1814. Meanwhile, the huge Bohemian army would occupy every territory it crossed, controlling the main strongholds like Besançon, requisitioning equipment, food, and funds necessary for such a massive concentration of men.

The Austrian authorities set up a General Government of the Franche-Comté in Vesoul, a small town along the invasion route. For several months, it became a necessary stop for almost all the sovereigns of the European coalition. From mid- to late January, Tsar Alexander I arrived followed by the Prussian King Frederick William III and then Austrian Emperor Francis I. The three monarchs remained there until the twenty-fifth when they took the road to Paris behind the Bohemian army. Louis XVI's brother, Charles X, who would later become king of France, also stopped in Vesoul where he stayed for three weeks.

During the period that these powerful figures were in Vesoul, just five miles away in the village of Flagy, François Ignace Gouhenant, who would later call himself "Adolphe," had just celebrated his tenth birthday on February 18, 1814.

An invasion of hundreds of thousands of men does not tread lightly. Although the Tsar, who was leading the coalition, claimed he waged war "against Napoléon, but not against France" and ordered his troops to respect the French people, many abuses and atrocities were committed in the conquered countries. In Haute-Saône, and particularly in the *canton* of Port-sur-Saône, where Flagy sits, cases of rape, pillaging, and murders occurred.[3] The young François Ignace and his family certainly knew about these atrocities and probably lived in fear during the long months of occupation. He saw soldiers patrolling in the countryside, and his family suffered from the requisitions. He must have read the many threatening signs posted by the occupation authorities in the villages, perhaps even casting his eyes upon words such as:

> Any armed or unarmed gathering, whether during an attack or not, is strictly forbidden: in the cities, squares, streets or doors; and in the countryside, along the roads and hedges, and within the villages or in the mountains.

> The infantry and cavalry of the Allied powers are allowed to fire without further warning, on groups of individuals proscribed by the present order.

> Every village, whose inhabitants are found gathered and with arms will be irrevocably set on fire with no other form of judgment, its residents will fall by the edge of the sword...[4]

Up until that time, François Ignace had only known life under Napoléon, who had been proclaimed emperor the same year as his birth. The Empire had ended the post-revolutionary instability, and for many it was actually the terminus of the Revolution. Certainly, it established a new dynasty and a new nobility, closely resembling the old regime. The democratic principles of the Revolution and the people's participation in political life were being abandoned. But the social evolution of each individual, almost non-existent under the monarchy, was now possible.

Adolphe's father, Jean-François Gouhenant, exemplified the rise of a humble citizen up the social ladder, at least to its first rung. Jean-François Gouhenant owned a small family farm. He had married a girl from Flagy, Jeanne Françoise Arragon, on December 18, 1795, and they had three children. Their first daughter was Marie Scholastique, born in the spring of 1798 who, sadly, died at the age of ten. A second daughter, Marguerite-Antoinette-Virginie, was born in May of 1801. She would later marry a man named Vital Humbert, a former officer of the Imperial Guard, the elite soldiers of the First Empire, and they would have a son, George Antoine Ernest Humbert who would join his uncle in Texas many years later.[5] François Ignace was their only son.

The Revolution had spurred a vast reorganization of the country's administrative structure. Initially the mayors and city council were elected by their citizens. As the spirit of the French Revolution gradually faded, selection of the local administrators became less and less democratic. By 1799 they were no longer elected, but nominated by the state representative—called the Prefect—from a list proposed by the locals, with many men of humble origin still among the mayors across France. Jean-François Gouhenant had been appointed mayor of Flagy in 1805 under that system. As the Empire evolved towards a more plutocratic regime, mayors were selected from among the richest citizens of the communes, and in 1808, Jean François Gouhenant was replaced by Guy-Claude Junot, a newcomer to Flagy and a notable from Napoléon's empire.[6]

While very little is known about Adolphe's boyhood years, information about his father is more accessible due to his term as mayor. Usually, details about the mayors of tiny rural villages are not well known. However, Jean-François's term did not go smoothly, so some insight into his personality has been left in local records.

Jean-François Gouhenant was born in the neighboring village of Colombier with a population of 940, slightly bigger than Flagy, which had just 355 people. He was nominated by the prefect because a petition was submitted that detailed complaints about his predecessor's loose admin-istration. Once he was appointed mayor, he quickly became unpopular himself, but for the exact opposite reasons. In 1807, when the prefect asked for candidates to renew the appointments for the mayor and council, petitions were submitted listing complaints against Gouhenant and his "tyranny." Still, he was reinstated in November of that a year, but protests against him started once again, this time even stronger. A string of correspondence began between Gouhenant, the prefect and his agents, and the protest instigators. It is difficult to determine if the charges against Gouhenant were due to his overbearing administration, as claimed by the complainants, or because he was only trying to enforce the laws in the village, as he wrote to the prefect. Addressing the complaints in Flagy, the agents for the prefect reported, "All the mayor's activities, all the acts of his administration are generally consistent with your orders and instructions and one would vainly seek to find any fault on any item [...] The main criticism against him, if indeed we can consider it such, would be having attracted the enmity of the entire town, and I can assure you—entire; the people who like him remain silent before the majority, who cannot stand to see, or tolerate him." The situation finally became unbearable, and the prefect took the opportunity to appoint the recently arrived Junot as the new mayor.[7]

It is evident that not only was Jean-François Gouhenant a man of strong character, but he also possessed a relatively high level of education. His correspondence shows his handwriting was very elegant, and the syntax and spelling were quite good, which was uncommon among the popular classes of his time, although Franche Comté was among the most educated provinces in France, with 45 percent of its population being able to sign their own wedding document.[8]

Jean-François Gouhenant certainly encouraged his son to obtain an education as well and he no doubt had a strong influence on the young Gouhenant. Despite his humble origins, Jean-François was generally very concerned about the education of his fellow citizens. During his mayoral term, he secured the council's vote to appoint a primary school teacher, a significant endeavor since it was the first time Flagy had a primary school. Since there was no vacant building in which to hold classes, he proposed the use of his own home to accommodate both the teacher and classroom. Among their recriminations, the population of Flagy complained that their children were being bullied by Jean-François's children during class. However, the prefect's agent, who was sent to inquire about the complaints, wrote, "these children who are aged six years for the first, and three for the other, would not be able to mistreat or hurt anyone [...] they appeared to me well behaved and very quiet." In any case, this is the first and only mention of François Ignace Gouhenant, during his early years.[9]

Gouhenant's father died in 1819, leaving behind assets estimated to be about 2,869 francs—the monetary equivalent of less than four years' wages for a low-income worker.[10] François Ignace had just turned fifteen at the time of his father's death, leaving him the only remaining male in the family. To his mother's distress, he decided to leave home, although he stayed in touch with his mother and sister over the years.[11] There are no details regarding Gouhenant's whereabouts after he left Flagy until he turns up in Lyon, the country's second largest city. He is listed in the military census working as a salesman, twenty years old, with the nickname "Poupon."Aside from the one reference, there is no evidence of Gouhenant having lived, worked, or studied anywhere else in France during his first two decades.[12]

On December 6, 1827, at the age of twenty-three, he married Jeanne Durand, a sixteen-year-old girl from Feyzin, a village of 1,000 inhabitants, on the south end of Lyon. Jeanne was the daughter of a peasant family, and her parents gave her a dowry of 3,000 francs in cash and two plots of land in the Lyon countryside, totaling four and a half acres, worth about 4,000 francs. The marriage contract clearly stated that the dowry was given by Jeanne's mother, who probably got the money and land from her own dowry or inheritance. It also stipulated that Gouhenant would sell the plots and manage the 7,000 francs for his future bride. In fact, shortly after their marriage, he actually invested the money in a wildly ambitious scheme that he concocted, one that would alter the very face of the town of Lyon.[13]

LYON

The years Gouhenant spent in Lyon undoubtedly contributed to the development of his ideology, connecting him to the emerging socialist movement. During the 1830s, Lyon was thriving from its internationally renowned silk industry and half of the 180,000 inhabitants of the urban area were making their living from the silk weaving trade. The city was considered a merchant's town, whose bourgeoisie was focused on trading, while the workers were struggling just to make a living. Between the two extremes of the mercantile bourgeoisie and the exploited laborers, their focus on industry did not leave much room for intellectual pursuits. This climate has often been depicted—and sometimes exaggerated—by contemporary artists such as Alexandre Dumas, Stendhal, George Sand, and Charles Baudelaire. Dumas, who visited Lyon in the early 1830s, summarized the situation well in his *Nouvelles impressions de voyage*:

> Lyon's genius is purely mercantile. The junction point of fourteen big roads and two rivers, which accepts the orders and exports the products, the divinity of the town is the trade; not the trade of sea ports, glorified by the dangers of a distant navigation, where the trader is a captain and the workers are sailors; not the poetic

trade of Tyr, of Venice and of Marseille, to which the Eastern sun makes a halo, to which the stars of the South make a crown, the fog of the West a veil, and the ice of the North a belt; but the stationary and pale trade, which sits behind a counter or stands at a loom; which weakens from the lack of air, and dulls from the absence of a horizon; which removes from the day sixteen hours of work, and gives hunger in exchange for only half the bread it requests. Yes, indeed, Lyon is an animated and lively city, but animated and lively like a mechanic, and the tic-tac of the loom is the only beating of her heart.[14]

The silk industry in Lyon, called *La Fabrique,* was characterized by three levels: First were the merchants, who supplied the raw silk, and lent the silk threads and patterns to the weavers, who then gave the finished piece back to the merchants; it was the merchants who determined the price to be paid for the fabric. The second level was the workshop masters who owned the looms and worked at home with their families, apprentices, and journeymen. Subsequently, they hired the laborers, who were the lowest level. The workshop masters and laborers worked on commission and were dependent upon the price fixed by the suppliers and determined by the fluctuating economy.

In 1831 and again in 1834, Lyonnais workers instigated two insurrections that historians widely credit with transforming the French working class into a political class, as they became more conscious of the power they possessed as a unified force. Gouhenant was witness to both insurrections. The first revolt of the *Canuts*—as Lyonnais silk workers were called—in 1831 was provoked by a bad economy and a resultant drop in silk prices, ultimately causing a drop in workers' wages.

In the fall of that year, in an effort just to maintain their extremely low standard of living, the workers demanded a minimum price imposed on silk. After negotiating with the manufacturer, and under the patronage of the prefect, the latter agreed to create a minimum price. However, the merchants were reluctant to implement it, and although they were supposed to pay a fine for not honoring the new agreement, the government disavowed the prefect's order, arguing that the minimum price was only a gentlemen's agreement and was not legally binding. The merchants' refusal to pay the minimum price infuriated the silk workers, who went into open revolt under the cries of "Live working or die fighting." In defiance, they seized the military arsenal and resisted both the national guard and the military in a bloody battle, resulting in 170 fatalities and more than 400 injuries from both sides, and leaving the insurgents in control of the town.[15]

Attempting to restore order, the government sent an army of 20,000 men led by Marshall Soult, a veteran of the Napoleonic wars, and the Duke of Orleans, son of King Louis Philippe. They were able to retake the town without any further bloodshed, and without having to make any compromises with the workers. Although some of the laborers were arrested, eventually they were all acquitted. The revolt ended with the minimum price abolished and with the workers no better off than before. Three years later, they would rise up again in a much bloodier riot. The events had made a national and even international impact. Karl Marx would later write in *Das Kapital* that "the town proletariat at Lyons sounded the tocsin." It left a profound mark on the people living in Lyon, including Gouhenant who was now a family man living in town.

As a newlywed, Gouhenant was working as a *droguiste* or drug seller. Historically, this meant that he sold items used for medicine or dyeing. Drug sellers were not allowed to prepare or sell pharmaceutical compositions; they could "sell drugs only to those they recognized as having a permanent residence, who needed them for their profession or for a known reason."[16]

Possibly Gouhenant had acquired some rudimentary medical knowledge that would prove useful later on, but his actual specialization was making pigments. The Lyon census from 1830 and 1831 refers to his profession using the more accurate term, *fabricant de couleur*, literally translated as color maker.

In 1827, Gouhenant's customers were probably pharmacists, like those from the central pharmacy on Tupin Street—the same street where he was living—and also silk workers who would have needed dyes, and of course, painters. One of the witnesses at his wedding was also a drug seller living on Tupin Street. The witness, Jacques Durand, happened to be the brother of the bride. It is easy to imagine that the two young men were working and living together, within their shop, or nearby. In addition to Jacques, the other witnesses at the wedding were a twenty-seven-year-old court bailiff, and a thirty-year-old *limonadier*, or bar owner, and the sixty-six-year-old uncle of the bride. Three of the witnesses, roughly the same age as Gouhenant, were probably his friends.

Judging from existing birth registrations, it appears that Gouhenant became progressively more integrated into the artistic circles of Lyon between 1827 and 1831. In June 1830, Jeanne gave birth to their first child. Newborns were required to be registered at the town hall, and the custom was for witnesses to accompany the father. When he registered his first born, Gouhenant was accompanied by Pierre Favre, an art dealer. Sadly, this child—a son he had named Adolphe—died just a few hours after his birth. Gouhenant kept his tiny son close to his heart: at some unknown point, he changed his own name from François Ignace to Adolphe.[17]

The following year, Jeanne had a daughter whom they named Anastasie. Gouhenant then went to the town hall with Étienne Douillet, a young painter, and Jean Pollet, a well-known architect in Lyon, who was about nine years older than Gouhenant. Finally, in 1832, for the birth of his son Ernest, his witnesses were Antoine Petit, the director of a private hospital, and Jacques Dulin, another architect, who was also Ernest's godfather.

On some occasions, Gouhenant also served as a witness for the birth of his friends' children. For instance, in April 1830, he and Aimé Moreaud—a genre painter—signed the birth certificate for Moreaud's brother's child.

Years earlier, between 1819, when he had become a fatherless child, and 1832, when he had his own son, Gouhenant followed an unknown path that led him from a peasant family in the deep countryside to the intellectual and artistic community in Lyon. Gouhenant was involved in a number of artistic ventures. The same year his son Ernest was born, he wrote a preface for a poem that was published in Lyon. The poem was composed by one of his friends, a young poet named Amédée Gayet de Cesena, further establishing Gouhenant in the local artistic community.

By virtue of his trade, Gouhenant was working in close proximity to artists, and he certainly considered himself to be an artist, although there is no evidence that he had any association with Victor Orsel, Paul Chenavard, Hippolyte Flandrin, and Louis Janmot—the most well-known of the Lyon school. As a color maker he was also interested in chemistry and although he was probably self-taught in science, he was profoundly interested in all scientific fields. By 1830, he would embark on a massive undertaking dedicated to both the arts and sciences in a town whose foundation was laid in antiquity.

THE OBSERVATORY TOWER, 1830-1833

Fourvière, the oldest area of Lyon, was founded as *Lugdunum* in 43 BC by the Roman general Munatius Plancus, one of Julius Ceasars officers. A few decades after its founding, the colony became an important urban center, and many monumental constructions were erected: a large forum, baths, four aqueducts, and two theaters. During the Roman Empire, Lugdunum became the capital of Gaul. It was also one of the oldest attested Christian communities in the West when forty-seven martyrs were persecuted there in 177 AD. When the Roman Empire fell, the monuments were abandoned and collapsed into ruin, their stones reused to construct new buildings and churches. In the twelfth century, in place of the long-gone Roman Forum of Fourvière, a small chapel was erected, eventually becoming a place of pilgrimage known throughout Europe. In the beginning of the nineteenth century, the character of Fourvière hill was essentially religious, with a small basilica surrounded by convents and other religious buildings that could be seen from almost every point in town. A second hill, *la Croix-Rousse*, was populated by industrious silk workers. The contrast in the character of the two Lyon hills was captured in the famous adage: *Fourvière, the hill that prays, la Croix-Rousse, the hill that works.*

By 1830, Gouhenant had initiated the first in a string of events showcasing his acumen for persuasion and risk-taking. He had conceptualized a magnificent monument for his adopted town, drawing upon his interest in science and his artistic skills. He decided to build his monument on the top of the hill that prays, much to the dismay of the local religious population.

He was not the first to build a tower in Lyon. A few years earlier, in 1827, on the slopes of the Croix-Rousse hill, a man named Horace Pitrat had undertaken the unrealistic project of building a 300-foot tower. Pitrat was a bricklayer who had made a fortune, but he was not an architect, and what should have happened, happened. In August 1828, when construction on the tower had reached two-thirds of its planned height, it collapsed, killing a little girl. In spite of the horrific accident, Pitrat was not discouraged, but proceeded to build a smaller, 100-foot tower, illustrating the lax administrative rules on construction. In fact, there was no requirement whatsoever to obtain authorization to erect such a monument. Even if a builder had no particular skill, he was allowed to build as long as he had a plot of land and enough money to lead the construction.

Both Pitrat and Gouhenant were passionate about their projects; Pitrat was wealthy but reckless with his construction methods while Gouhenant was reckless with his financial dealings. A mere colormaker, Gouhenant was unable to raise the full amount needed to finish the tower and the entire project rested on his risky debt scheme—a scheme every bit as unstable as Pitrat's construction methods.

Gouhenant embarked on his endeavor by locating a piece of land on which to erect the monument. It would be, among other things, a panoramic and astronomical observatory. Gouhenant decided the best location would be atop one of the Lyon hills, and the best choice was Fourvière hill. Fourvière was less urbanized than Croix-Rousse, and offered a sweeping view of both the town and the surrounding countryside.

Illustration 2. View of Fourvière hill before 1830.

Lithography by Samuel Prout (1783-1852).

Before the Revolution of 1789, the top of Fourvière hill was almost entirely in the possession of the Lyon clergy, which in addition to the church, also owned the housing for the priests and the grounds where they had orchards and were growing vegetables. During the Revolution, properties owned by the church were confiscated and then sold by the government. Among the vast estates seized in Lyon were two plots close to the Basilica of Fourvière. Jean-Baptiste Perreyve, a thirty-year-old draper, had purchased two plots totaling about four acres.[18]

On March 26, 1831, Perreyve sold a small portion—about 200 square yards—to Gouhenant. Initially, Gouhenant did not spend a single franc for the land. The contract between the two men called for him to pay Perreyve 12,000 francs within five years—evidently with no down payment. It is unclear how Gouhenant was able to convince a pragmatic merchant to agree to such a venture, but clearly his charismatic power of persuasion was effective. Perreyve, at the age of seventy-two and by now a very astute businessman, was at least savvy enough to secure his loan with a mortgage.[19]

Once Gouhenant possessed the plot, he had to hire an architect, purchase the building materials, and then pay the workers to construct the building. He hired his friend Jean Pollet to do the architectural drawings and to monitor the work. Subsequently, he went into debt with Pollet for over 3,000 francs. The building contractors would of course not be content with a promise of payment, so between October 1831 and July 1832, Gouhenant took out nine mortgages to secure the funding. In July and August, Perreyve finally paid off the contractors on behalf of Gouhenant and all the mortgages were then converted to his ownership.

In addition to providing land for the building, Perreyve had already lent Gouhenant 21,000 francs in September 1831—just six months after the land negotiation—then another 6,000 francs in October. Of course all the loans were secured by cumulative mortgages first on the plot, and then on the new tower, which was slowly emerging from the ground. Finally, by August of 1832, Gouhenant owed Perreyve about 75,000 francs. Debts were also piling up from many other creditors, mainly storekeepers, but also to his friend Jacques Dulin, and a young actress, Adèle Florival, to whom Gouhenant owed 150 francs. Mademoiselle Florival, a "pretty actress having a pleasant voice," had been the mistress of the soon-to-be famous writer Eugène Sue.[20] By October of 1832, the cumulative debts reached nearly 110,000 francs, a startling amount since, by comparison, the mean daily wage for a worker in Lyon was just 2.50 francs.[21]

By the end of 1831, Gouhenant was well aware of his precarious situation. In December, just after the silk workers' revolt, he had written a letter to the Duc d'Orléans, currently installed with his army in Lyon, requesting financial help to finish his monument. Gouhenant remained optimistic. The Duc d'Orléans was considered a liberal prince and a patron of the arts and science.

Duc D'Orléans:

Born in the darkness, I could not find any way to succeed under a reign that liked to crush and suppress the impulse of every aspect of science. But the accession to the throne of His Royal Highness the Duke of Orleans,[22] brought me the torch of hope; his crown was for me the halo of happiness. As a prince he cherished the fine arts, as King no doubt he will protect them. As an artist, I was imbued with this belief, and was full of confidence as I began a project a year ago, cultivated for three or four years; I raised a monument on Fourvière hill, on a base measuring ten meters on each side and a height of about fifty meters.

I matched as closely as possible the profiles and the architecture of the wind tower of Athens and devoted this monument to astronomical and terrestrial observations; painting and mathematics will also find their place there. But the biggest advantage is that an iron rod placed at its peak, soaring upward in the skies eight hundred feet above the Saône, will attract the electric fluid and protect the whole city of Lyon from the ravages of thunder.

I wanted to build a temple for the arts and sciences, I wanted to beautify the city where I live, I wanted to move lightning away from it. I've used all my care, my time and my money. I almost reached the end of my project. I have just one step remaining: it is the most difficult.

All my resources are exhausted; my property is already mortgaged by an amount far from being equal to its actual value, but it is an obstacle to finding a smaller amount that I would need. I'm missing about five thousand francs [...] Must we see the arts deprived of such a precious monument for them, and the city from one of its most beautiful ornaments?

My plan was to seek a donation from the city of Lyon to help me finish but now everything has changed; they have other expenses to meet and I would bother them unnecessarily.[23]

I therefore appeal to you my prince and I implore your assistance; you are within our walls, you are in front of the monument of which I speak. See how impressive it is, does it not deserve to be completed? And once I have placed a twelve-inch diameter achromatic telescope, will it not be worthy of the highest interest?

Nothing can stop me in the pursuit of fine arts if I am encouraged by his majesty; I will devote myself entirely to the beautification and the utility of our city, and I will soon carry out a second project more beautiful and more useful than that of my observatory.

I will be silent on my behavior during the troubles in Lyon. I think it is exemplary: while I was defending public order on one side, on the other I had doubled and tripled the wages of all my workers to keep them at work, thus none of them left my building site. If all the National Guard would have done as I did, Lyon would have never been tainted by lawlessness.

Pending a favorable response to my request, I am with an entire devotion, one of your most loyal subjects.[24]

Gouhenant revealed his ambition in the letter to the Duc, stating he desired to build "a temple for the arts and sciences." However, while he may have been familiar with artistic principles, the tone of his letter shows that his background in science was quite rudimentary.

The Duc d'Orléans was not eager to fund the project without further information. Gouhenant's letter was transmitted to the prefect of the Rhône who asked the Lyon Academy of Sciences, Arts and Humanities to report on the project. The Academy then sent a commission to inquire about the project. The commission was comprised of a small group of three experts: Antoine-Marie Chenavard, an architect and cousin of the painter Paul Chenavard, François Clerc, an astronomer and director of the Lyon observatory, and Étienne Rey, a drawing teacher. After they visited the site, Gouhenant sent them another letter giving significantly more details on his construction.[25]

Mr. President and Academy Members,

Here, gentlemen, is my purpose in building the monument in Fourvière you have honored me to visit. But first let me tell you that I did not exaggerate its height in my petition.

My construction project is 40 feet higher than it is presently and to give you a fair idea, I send you a drawing as it will look completed as soon as the necessary precautions will allow, once the foundation and walls will be stabilized.[26] This height will add nothing to the usefulness of the monument, but much to the charm of the architecture, giving it a thin and pyramidal shape, infinitely more imposing. I would not speak to you about the ornaments I want to make if I did not hope to find among you some opinion much cleverer and of better taste than mine.

Thus, I will paint a monochrome in oil, above each arched window: at the first floor, the four elements, at the 2nd floor, the four seasons, and at the 3rd floor, the four winds. Then on each angle of the string courses, I will put heads of lions in bronze which will make a ledge on the [unreadable], and on the four angles of the terrace, there will be four bronze Greek-shaped vases dedicated to each feast day celebrated by the government, to illuminations, together with fireworks that will be fired from the center of the terrace.

I will say nothing about the ornamentation of the interior, and on the ground floor salon which will just be a room for visitors to the observatory to rest and refresh.

On the first floor there will be a painting workshop equipped with all the objects and implements necessary for this art, there will be mirrors, dark rooms and other tools useful for landscape painters. This workshop will be opened freely to the Lyon artists. Without moving, they will be able to draw the buildings of Perrache, the bridge of the railway station, the monument of the Brotteaux, and the aqueducts of Chaponost. The artist will choose his point of view according to his taste and the view will extend as far as he can see.

In addition, there will be a room for geometry, geography and perspective, presenting the same advantages as those I have mentioned.

The second floor will be devoted to a permanent and free exhibition of paintings, drawings and other art items for the Lyon artists. I will sell some of them on behalf of the artists who would so desire. This will give emulation and support to the young artists who would find an income from their work.

The third floor will also be an exhibition room for objects of natural history, mineralogy etc. under the same conditions as the second floor.

The fourth floor will be the observatory, equipped with the best instruments I am able to gather, among which will be a telescope of 11 to 12 inches in diameter. I will not make a panegyric of such an observatory, since you have in your company, gentlemen, a famous artist who will be able to provide his own report. But what I will say is that because of the broad horizon one can see without any obstacles, a general could see the military movements in the plain of the Dauphiné, in the forts of Guillotière and the Brotteaux, and before these of Montessuy. What I will say as well is that in the middle of the colonnade, I will put 4 amplifying lamps which will be illuminated at night producing a dazzling light source that will be seen for more than 80 leagues. It will be a guide for the traveler, the terminus for the cart driver, the focal point of the peasant. They will not see the town, but they will see where it lies.

Finally, on the terrace, I will plant a lightning rod 30 feet high which will soar through the sky, attracting the electric fluid, which will prevent it from striking Lyon.

Here are, gentlemen, expenses made only for the public interest, and from which I ask no profit. However, due to a commitment I made with the man who provided me the instruments for the observatory in the amount of 25 thousand francs, he will place an attendant there who will ask one franc from each visitor to the observatory.

But I arrange all the other parts of which I am the only master, and I arrange it by the means of which I told you, with no other interest, no other goal than to be useful to the arts and sciences, to strike against ignorance, to exhort people to study and be instructed, and to provide to any of our schools a breeding-ground for students. I have devoted my fortune and I will devote my entire life to that cause.

It is not to be reimbursed that I ask for a few thousand francs from the government, it is because after having spent one hundred and thirty thousand francs, I have exhausted all my resources and I still have to fulfill a commitment of about ten thousand francs from which I cannot escape without destroying all my projects.

Also, if aside from this gift I ask for a badge of honor and encouragement, it is because I believe I have deserved it. A soldier is decorated when he has risked his life once to protect his country; an artist should be decorated for having risked more than twenty times his own life to build a monument to the arts and to accomplish something the boldest builder would have feared.

A rich man is honored to have given 3 or 4 thousand francs for a mutual school, and I, gentlemen, have spent more than one hundred thousand francs.

A government employee is allowed to retire for having devoted a number of years to his job, and me gentlemen, I devote all my life to the one I willingly assigned to myself. Gentlemen, please consider all these notes, and give me your support.

I am, with the most perfect consideration, your humble servant,
François Ignace Gouhenant

After their visit, Chenavard's commission wrote their report and summarily dismissed Gouhenant's explanation. With particularly harsh criticism, they disputed his claim that the main advantage of the tower would be its ability to protect the town from lightning by installing an iron rod at its summit. Concerning its possible use as an astronomical observatory, the commission admitted,

> although this tower is not perfectly well oriented, its summit will offer indeed a great facility for observing the sky and to study the movement of the celestial bodies. Equipped with good astronomical instruments, and directed by a scientist, it will increase the number of observatories in Europe, built to increase and improve astronomy, geography and navigation.[27]

It appears from the commissioners' response that Gouhenant had no contact with the astronomers from the Lyon observatory, and imagined the use of his tower for astronomical purposes independently, without the collaboration of any competent scientists. That the commission mentioned it could possibly be used for astronomical observations reflects the fact that the town observatory, built in 1703 on the banks of the Rhône and in the center of the city, was not any better suited for accurate observations. Therefore, scientists were asking the authorities to support the construction of a new observatory on one of the hills of Lyon. François Clerc, who was trying to reinvigorate astronomical science in Lyon, and who was a member of the commission, was probably better disposed towards Gouhenant's project than the others. The report continues: "The town of Lyon would deserve such an institution, but the town only, or a prince, or a Lyonnais at heart could give it to the scientists." The astronomers were interested in the tower, but they were worried they would have to share it with activities other than astronomy, and this relatively positive statement was tempered by the fact that "this building in private hands that would equip it with a telescope to attract some spectators will always be of little usefulness for the public and the sciences."

In addition to refuting Gouhenant's scientific arguments, the commission's criticism was also concerned with the tower's dimensions. The actual size was much smaller than he had claimed; it fact, it was eight meters square instead of ten, and thirty meters high instead of fifty. Referencing the wind tower of Athens, the commission claimed, "one would vainly seek any similarity even approximate between the two buildings." Again, the opinion on the tower's architecture was extremely negative; "The building is devoid of any elegance in its proportions, of charm in its shape, and far from embellishing the top of the hill, the tower would only disfigure it by its disproportion in scale with the surroundings."

None of the other arguments Gouhenant gave in his letter to the academy convinced the commission. The report stated that they did not think "a general could direct from this point the maneuver of troops in the Dauphiné plain," or that "a small light source made of four focused lamps would be of any advantage for the travelers." Even his proposal to provide a workshop and exhibition salon for the artists of Lyon was considered simply a minor advantage.

Although their words were severe, the commission concluded their report by proposing that the subsidy Gouhenant requested should be allowed "under some conditions." It was read before the academy during its session on February 6, 1832. Some members of the academy pointed out that its conclusion was much more favorable than the body of the report itself. It was proposed that "the support asked by Monsieur Gouhenant should be awarded under the condition that some modifications would be made to the building and that after adding additional height to the construction, it would have the height and the shape needed to make it better suited for a public monument." Regrettably for Gouhenant, when the minutes of the meeting were read at the next session of the academy on February 14, a new discussion followed and members came to the exact opposite conclusion from the previous one. The last sentence of the minutes was crossed out and replaced with "the support requested by Monsieur Gouhenant should be refused by the government."[28]

The names of the supporters and opponents among the academy are not given in the minutes, but certainly the assembly was quite divided about Gouhenant's project. The members attending both sessions were not the same men and opponents outnumbered supporters in the second session. Unfortunately, Clerc, the astronomer who was probably the academician who advocated most strongly for the tower, did not attend both sessions, and in the end, the absence of his vote cost Gouhenant the project.

Not surprisingly, since he was relying on the academy's recommendation, the Duke of Orléans ultimately did not grant any funds to Gouhenant, leaving him embarrassed and with a defeat from which he would not recover.

Given the absence of scientific integrity in Gouhenant's proposals, the academy's position seems appropriate. While the judgment of the tower's architecture may have been a bit too severe, in fact it reflected the opinion of many contemporaries who were deeply attached to the appearance of the existing landscape and modest chapel atop Fourvière hill. The erection of a secular tower overshadowing the small but holy chapel was considered by the religious population as a sacrilege, "putting the throne of men beside the throne of God [...] it was throwing the mud of the world on the mantle of a virgin."[29] Moreover, the conservative aesthetes viewed it as bad taste and a degradation of the picturesque and centuries-old landscape of Fourvière.

However, the religious opinion was certainly not unanimous, and a Lyon journal published a very positive article about the observatory.[30] The article describes Gouhenant as a "compatriot with a vivid imagination and an eminently artistic head," who "successfully realized the idea of one of the most beautiful natural panoramas." The tower is described as "a monumental style" where "all the accessories which would make a visit pleasant, such as paintings, instruments of physics, natural history objects, finally a very comfortable restaurant, ensure to the observatory installed in Fourvière, the visit of foreigners and of everyone who is moved by such a magnificent scene." The description is very close to the project Gouhenant outlined in his letter to the academy, showing that he did manage to realize it although he did not receive the government help he expected. The article concludes with a mischievous remark, "I warn the ladies whose windows face the observatory, and there are many in Lyon. The telescopes of M. Gouhenant are intrusive, and often, with a ray of sunshine or around the light of a candle, an inquisitive gaze for which there is no more mystery, may fall in a room once thought impenetrable."

The tower also had advocates beyond the boundaries of Lyon, and even abroad. In 1838, an unsigned article was published in the German journal *Morgenblatt für gebildete Leser* where the author defended the monument against the criticisms of a Lyon writer:

> Few cities have such a favorable place as Lyon at her new observatory that the Lyon writer Jules Janin has recently so unfairly mocked in the *Journal des Débats*.... on Fourvières a man named Gouchenant [*sic*] has created in a pleasant manner an elegant tower of three floors and a comfortable upper room, equipped with excellent instruments, and opened to the public for a modest fee.[31]

Gouhenant had chosen an experienced architect to design his monument. He had given the task to his friend Jean Pollet, who at the young age of thirty-six, already had experience working on several monuments in Lyon. Pollet had directed the restoration of several churches in Lyon, including the famous Romanesque Basilica of Ainay. In 1826 he had gained enough renown to be selected for the reconstruction of the Grand Théâtre, in collaboration with Antoine-Marie Chenavard. The project had been the greatest achievement for both architects, but it had not gone smoothly, to say the least. From the start, the relationship between the two architects became more acrimonious. Finally, with the project in its final stages, Chenavard wrote to the mayor in January 1831 asking him to choose who between them should complete the building. The municipal council decided to keep Chenavard, the more experienced of the two.[32]

Illustration 3. Gouhenant's tower by architect Jean Pollet, from an original by Auguste Flandrin.

Courtesy of Lyon, Musée Gadagne 55.82.34.

In this context, it is difficult to estimate the contribution of each architect, because as written in Pollet's obituary, "each of [them] blamed his colleague for the faults and claimed as his own the less contested aspects."[33] Chenavard, who was president of the commission sent to evaluate Gouhenant's monument, was not well disposed towards Pollet who had designed the tower, which may explain his severe criticism of its architecture.

Just sixteen months after the land was secured, the observatory was finished. In celebration of the revolution of 1830, which had placed Louis Philippe on the throne, Gouhenant allowed the authorities access to his tower on the night of July twenty-ninth for a celebratory firework display. He also printed access tickets for the public with the phrase "Entrance Fee 1 Franc" on one edge, and proudly: "Gouhenant Owner" on the other. The observatory was now a reality, visible from almost anywhere in town, and open for business.[34]

Gouhenant's dream of a monument to the arts and the sciences would soon come to a bitter end. How he ever expected to pay his huge debts is completely baffling. In his letter to the academy of Lyon, he stated that he would sell entrance tickets for one franc that would pay for the cost of the telescopes. Yet, even if he maintained the project to keep the fee in place after paying off the instruments, it is hard to imagine that this small bit of income would have been sufficient to pay off the 110,000 francs he owed.

In 1832, Gouhenant was also running a restaurant in a small building he owned next to the tower. This little restaurant could have been an additional source of revenue.[35] Though, if Perreyve felt he was rich enough to wait for a doubtful profit from the enterprise, the other creditors certainly did not feel the same way.

Illustration 4. The entrance ticket to the observatory.

Courtesy of Lyon, Musée Gadagne N 1217.1.

In October of that year, one of the creditors, a goldsmith named Philippe Mercier, petitioned to recover his money from Gouhenant, who was by now in such disarray he did not even show up for court proceedings; in his absence, he was condemned to pay 776 francs. This amount was just a drop in the ocean toward the total debt Gouhenant owed, but the verdict triggered disaster.

Gouhenant had lost his credibility. He could not secure another loan and was unable to pay Mercier. The sale of Gouhenant's assets became more probable with each passing day, and all the other small creditors started to panic. If Gouhenant's properties were indeed sold, would the proceeds from the sale be enough to cover all his debts? It was far from certain. They then began to sue him in turn. Eleven suits were registered against Gouhenant between October 26 and December 7, 1832. His response was simply to not show up in court. Thus, he was found guilty all eleven times. It was during these dramatic events for him and his family that his son Ernest was born on November 19, making the situation even more alarming. Ultimately Gouhenant declared bankruptcy on December 14, which put a stop to the prosecutors' cases against him. However, he was temporarily sent to jail and his bankruptcy initiated the process of selling off all his possessions.[36]

THE END OF A DREAM

On January 8, 1833, the bankruptcy was advertised in the *Legal Gazette*. On February 5, the furniture and other objects from the tower were sold. The announcement provided a glimpse of the décor inside the tower: "tables with marble tops, counter with marble top, chairs, striking clock in its box of mahogany wood, silk drapery and calico, table, cupboard, coffee grinder, brass scales, cast iron stove; paintings on wood and canvas, representing different subjects, engravings, a telescope of five and a half inches in diameter on a wooden foot, an achromatic telescope of twenty-four lines in diameter, an electric machine, empty bottles and beer jugs, white wine bottles, empty barrels, and other objects."[37]

Eventually, on August 6 the tower itself was offered for sale. Jean-Baptiste Perreyve, the beneficiary of the first mortgages, had priority on proceeds from the sale, up to 75,000 francs, which was Gouhenant's debt to him. He then decided to participate in the tower auction to recover the building and the plot. The bidding started at 10,000 francs, and Perreyve raised it up to 50,025 francs, knowing he would get his money back.[38] This amount was well below the actual value of the tower, which was not only bad news for Gouhenant, but also for his other creditors who realized they would never recover their money. As soon as he officially became the owner of the tower in November 1833, Perreyve rented it to a bar keeper.

Illustration 5. View of Fourvière hill in the 1840s. The Observatory now dominates the hill.

Lithography from a painting by Adrien Dauzat (1804-1868).

In April 1834, the tower became a theater of sorts in which some dramatic scenes played out during the second upheaval of the silk workers. A dozen insurgents installed a canon on the cliff at the foot of the tower and raised their black flag at the top. They fired upon the military camp that had been installed downhill on Place Bellecour, the largest town square, but lacking munitions, they were unable to benefit from this prominent situation. In turn, the government artillery shot on the insurgent's position and the church was partially damaged. The rebels remained there for two days but the army ultimately expelled them, seized the tower, and raised the tricolor.

By 1836, the tower was already becoming part of Lyon's cultural and architectural history. A guide for travelers between Paris and Algiers stated in a section regarding Lyon:

> The tower of Fourvière, built at the expense of an individual from Lyon, is extremely high; on the ground floor there is a nice café where one can buy a ticket to the tower for one franc. This building is topped by a nice belvedere where there are many telescopes of any size [...] In a small cabinet under the belvedere, where the painters and the amateurs come to create some of the most beautiful and varied points of views in the world, there is an album in which the travelers write their reflections inspired by the wonderful spectacle offered to their eyes. This album contains quite nice thoughts, mainly from artists or Italian and English travelers.[39]

It seems that while it was in the hands of Perreyve, the tower kept a bit of the artistic mission Gouhenant had envisioned. But after having dominated the hill of Fourvière and the whole city of Lyon for twenty years, it would still have to face the rancor of its initial enemies.

Illustration 6. View of the tower from the top of the hill.

Fondation de Fourvière.

The Catholic community was still outraged by the construction of the profane monument in such close proximity to the venerable chapel of Fourvière. Furthermore, the church was too small to welcome the many pilgrims, and the bell tower was in danger of collapsing. Gradually, the idea of a new, higher bell tower gained momentum. In 1850, the Lyon clergy proposed that the new bell tower should be topped by a golden statue of the Virgin Mary. The architect Alphonse Duboys, who was in charge of construction, had to deal with the continuous modification of the specifications and the result was a baroque-styled building finalized in 1852. The inauguration of the statue was planned for December 8, 1852, but a storm forced Cardinal de Bonald, Archbishop of Lyon, to postpone it until the twelfth. As a result, the local population spontaneously illuminated the windows of the town with candles to celebrate the new monument, establishing the origin of the famous Lyon festival of lights held each eighth day of December. The following day, an idea was publicly expressed for the first time to complete the victory of the faith over the secular monument by destroying it. Lyon scholar Auguste Génin sent a letter to the journal *La Gazette de Lyon*:

> Dear Editor,
> The image of the august patroness of our city shines on the pedestal that raised her to Lyon's piety. I thought it was time to give rise to an idea that we carry deep in our souls for a long time, and for which to date, a courageous initiative, has missed, I mean the acquisition and demolition either of the Observatory or the new or old buildings that disfigure this side of our holy mountain.
>
> Confident in the spirit of intelligence and faith which yesterday was so striking a demonstration, I come, as an obscure believer, to propose the work of redemption and deliverance.
>
> At work then, and may all those who love God, their city, the fine arts, join me; our triumph will be realized soon.
>
> I subscribe for a hundred francs.[40]

On March 7, 1853, Cardinal de Bonald founded the Commission de Fourvière, aiming to raise funds not only to destroy the observatory but to gain a large enough area to eventually build a much bigger church on the top of the hill.

Perreyve had passed away in 1847 and his two sons inherited the tower, but his second son having given up his succession rights, the elder became the sole owner. Shortly after inheriting it, he decided to sell the tower, but could not immediately find a buyer and the Commission de Fourvière did not have the means or the inclination to purchase it. Perhaps Perreyve's asking price was too high and there may have been intense haggling. Ultimately, eight years after he put the observatory up for sale, the Commission de Fourvière purchased it in 1857 for 40,000 francs, much less than its original cost, and even less than the price Perreyve had paid after Gouhenant's bankruptcy.[41]

Right away, the clergy decided to reduce its height by one half in order to let the bell tower alone dominate the "hill that prays." Thus, the two upper floors were destroyed in May 1858.

Finally, between 1872 and 1884, a new larger church, Notre-Dame de Fourvière, the four towers of which now rise higher than the bell tower built in 1852, was erected beside the old chapel. Today, the church sits atop Fourvière, dominating the landscape. All that remains of Gouhenant's monument is a small three-story building which in recent years has hosted a restaurant.

Gouhenant had tried to save what he could from his financial collapse. Being a married man under a regime that enforced separation of property, his wife's dowry was protected by a mortgage on Gouhenant's properties, and by law, this mortgage was made the priority. Jeanne Gouhenant should have recovered the 6,000 francs of the dowry. But Perreyve argued that the law was not applicable for a merchant's wife in case of bankruptcy. On April 10, 1835, the civil court of Lyon issued a judgment in favor of Jeanne Gouhenant, but Perreyve appealed. Then, Jeanne, Gouhenant, and Perreyve were called to another session of the court a few months later, but the Gouhenant couple did not appear and Perreyve won the case. Subsequently, Adolphe Gouhenant, his wife, and children disappeared from Lyon.

The final mention of Gouhenant in Lyon is in the 1835 census where he was living at 8 Place Louis le Grand, known today as the famous Place Bellecour. In the "Profession" column of the census table, he is enigmatically mentioned under the heading "Solar Microscope." In fact, it was not the first time these words were associated with Gouhenant's name. In 1833, the same year he declared bankruptcy, a leaflet had been published in Chalon-sur-Saône, a small town eighty miles north of Lyon, describing the "Program of Monsieur Gouhenant addressed to the people of Chalon-sur-Saône" regarding a "solar microscope magnifying ten million times."[42]

The solar microscope was an optical instrument allowing images of very small objects to be projected on a screen by putting them close to the focus of a short focal lens and illuminating them with solar light. It allowed the public to view microorganisms contained in a drop of water for instance. These exhibitions met with great success in the 1830s.

From 1833 to 1835, after the collapse of his project, Gouhenant was likely earning his living traveling from town to town around Lyon with his solar microscope attraction. It is noteworthy that at the very time Gouhenant was exhibiting experiments in Chalon-sur-Saône, five miles away, the inventor of photography, Nicéphore Niépce, was working to improve the process that had allowed him to obtain the first photograph ever made in 1827. It would finally be perfected by his collaborator Louis Daguerre between 1835 and 1839, and named *daguerreotype,* a process from which Gouhenant himself would greatly benefit a few years later in Texas.

CHAPTER 2

THE BIRTH OF A POLITICAL IDEOLOGY

[...] Masonry is not a cult; it is the free and regulated union of every sect, which is spreading in every part of the world, dedicated to the relief of our brothers, to the propagation of arts and industry, and to the freedom of all the peoples.

François Ignace Gouhenant, 1832

ÉTIENNE CABET: GOUHENANT'S FUTURE MENTOR

While Gouhenant was attempting to realize his monumental project in Lyon, another man was emerging on the scene in Paris whose ideas would alter the French political landscape. Étienne Cabet would become a significant force in the early Communist movement, Gouhenant's mentor, and the man to whom Gouhenant would devote all his energies—at one point even putting his own life at risk.

Cabet was born on New Year's Day, 1788, in Dijon, France. He was the son of a cooper, yet he received a good education under the tutelage of the revolutionary patriot and well-known educator, Joseph Jacotot. He came to socialism gradually, beginning his career as a royalist lawyer, but later participated in the July Revolution of 1830. In the early part of that decade, there were a series of democratic demonstrations, the most formidable being the outbreak at the funeral of General Lamarque, a commander under Napoléon. Lamarque was critical of Louis Philippe's monarchy for its failure to support liberty and human rights. That demonstration and its fierce repression in the summer of 1832 increased Cabet's opposition to the government and strengthened his sympathies with the working class.[43]

In France and throughout Europe, the rich numbered in the thousands, while the poor were in the millions. What began as a movement of the middle class against an absolute monarch evolved into a movement of the working class against the bourgeoisie. Over the years, Cabet had witnessed the downfall of the aristocracy and he became passionately involved in the Republican movement; in 1833 he became the secretary-general of the Free Association for the Education of the People, and he founded a new journal, *Le Populaire*, which met with immediate success among the working class.

The association organized free lessons for the workers, who were taught reading and writing, physics, chemistry, history, book-keeping, law, and drawing—all considered to be subversive by the monarchy. In 1834, the monarchy shut down all the Republican associations. Cabet himself was prosecuted for having written two articles against Louis Philippe and after being sentenced to two years in prison, he had to flee his country and take refuge in England.[44]

Illustration 7. Étienne Cabet, founder of the Icarian movement to which Gouhenant adhered around 1842.

Bibliothèque nationale de France. Used by permission.
Cabet chose Gouhenant to lead the first avant-garde for his colony in Texas in 1848.

During his exile, he spent most of his time reflecting and reading. Cabet voraciously studied the history of the ages and great nations. He came away with the observation that regardless of the country or epoch studied, every nation seemed to have excessive wealth and excessive poverty. This realization had a profound impact on him. His desire and the goal of all his efforts became to prevent the eternally poor from falling prey to the eternally rich.

After five years in exile, Cabet was allowed to return in 1839 to France where he published *Voyage en Icarie,* one of several tomes he had feverishly penned while in England. Written as a novel, it described the Utopian country of Icaria—from which the term of Icarian communism would be cast—where people live under complete equality and community of goods. Although lengthy, the book was written in a popular and romanticized style, making it accessible for the working class. *Voyage en Icarie* was enormously popular and was read throughout France and other countries as well. By 1848, it had gone through five editions.[45]

Cabet resumed printing *Le Populaire,* making it the voice for communist ideology; he also published a *Popular History of the French Revolutions from 1789 to 1830* and *Le Vrai Christianisme suivant Jesus-Christ.* In the latter, Cabet made the argument that Christ's primary mission on earth was to establish equality among men and that he was the most prominent advocate for communism. In fact, Cabet's inspiration for his communist ideas were Christian principles and throughout his life he reinforced the idea that the teachings of Christ were the basis for his theories.

By the late 1840s, Cabet counted more than 400,000 followers and many more who sympathized with his theories. His followers were "almost exclusively working people, especially the better class of artisans" in the smaller towns, a class with which Gouhenant was closely aligned. Subsequently, Gouhenant became one of Cabet's most enthusiastic followers and a devout propagator of his theories.[46]

REPUBLICANISM AND FREEMASONRY

In the 1830s, Gouhenant was probably not yet aware of Cabet's existence. He had spent the first ten years of his adult life in Lyon, where his social, spiritual, and political ideas took shape. During his stay there, he had witnessed the two silk workers' uprisings. There is no information on his behavior during the second uprising in 1834, but there is some indication regarding his position during the first period of unrest in 1831, when he claimed he kept his employees working by increasing their wages while he was defending public order as a member of the Garde Nationale.

The fact that he increased his workers' wages offers evidence that he was sensitive to the rebels' wage demands—the main cause of their uprising. On the other hand, he claimed that he had prevented civil disorder. Like all French males between twenty to sixty years of age, Gouhenant was in the National Guard reserve, which was comprised of a corps of citizens that could be used to support the regular army in case of war or riot. In November of 1831, the mobilization of the National Guard against the silk workers was ineffective and some battalions even fought on the side of the rebels. However, according to Gouhenant, he was not one of them. Since he addressed his letter to the king's son, from whom he had requested money, it was certainly in his interest to claim he was on the government's side. In any case, at the time of the first silk workers' riot, Gouhenant was completely focused on realizing his project, and even if he had sympathy for the workers' claims, he may have seen their upheaval as a threat to the completion of his observatory.

Gouhenant had claimed that one the goals of his tower was popular education, which would aim to "strike ignorance, to exhort people to study and instruction." In the 1830s this approach was one of the cornerstones of political action in liberal and republican circles as they advocated for the instruction of the working class, believing it would be key to their emancipation. Besides spreading access to basic instruction among the workers, the most radical wanted to awaken their political consciousness and to offer them the necessary education to defend their rights.

This concept was central to the spirit of the free lessons organized in Paris by the socialist intellectual Albert Laponneraye in 1831 and 1832, and also of the Free Association for the Education of the People in 1833. Both Laponneraye and Cabet would be severely repressed by the government, Laponneraye being sent to prison for two years and Cabet forced into exile. In Lyon, a young republican teacher named Auguste Savagner also organized free history lessons for the people in 1832, which were forbidden by the administration. These lessons, as well as those given by Laponneraye in Paris, had a strong political background: "M. Savagner demonstrated that the principle of general emancipation of the peoples had always progressed [...] that the republic should necessarily bloom from this large succession of historical facts, chained one after the other [...] And from the history, presented as such, M. Savagner and his auditors drew the conclusion that we just have to walk a bit to find us in the face of HER [the republic]."[47]

It is possible that Gouhenant had met Savagner. Indeed, the most favorable article about the tower had been published in Savagner's journal and was written in terms suggesting that the author knew Gouhenant personally. This fervent republican activist would later participate in the revolution of 1848 and he would be sent to prison after the workers' riots in June, where he ultimately died.[48]

For their part, the moderate liberals were not aiming to emancipate the working class as a whole from domination by the upper classes—to which they generally belonged—but sought to help the workers emancipate themselves individually by offering the possibility of enhancing their knowledge, ultimately to improve their situation. Bourgeois philanthropists were subsidizing free elementary schools for both children and adults, where no political issues were addressed. Based on his letters to the Duc d'Orléans and to the Lyon Academy, Gouhenant also claimed his educational project would make freely available to the people, "physics instruments, natural history objects," and even telescopes to observe the sky, which were luxury items at the time and completely inaccessible to the popular classes. Judging by his written statements, Gouhenant expected to be recognized as a philanthropist and significant supporter of popular education: "A rich man is honored to have given 3 or 4 thousand francs for a mutual school, and I, gentlemen, have spent more than one hundred thousand francs."

One event that probably played a major role in shaping Gouhenant's politics was his entry into Freemasonry in Lyon at the end of the 1820s, or the beginning of the 1830s. Several political streams crossed Masonry but by its very essence it was mainly liberal and it was increasing its opposition to the monarchy in the years between 1815 and 1830.

Louis XVIII, the first king of the restored monarchy after the fall of Napoléon I, had granted a kind of constitution—the Charter—preserving some of the political gains from the Revolution, such as equality before the law, religious tolerance, and freedom of the press. However, the regime became less and less liberal with time, and when Louis XVIII died in 1824, his brother Charles X succeeded him, ushering in a period of reactionary politics; many liberals were afraid that he was attempting to restore the monarchy in its absolute form. Although during the fifteen years of the Restoration the French Masons officially supported the monarchy, a dissident republican branch became increasingly more influential.[49]

One of the main opponents to the monarchy was the Marquis de La Fayette. La Fayette was a famous Freemason who was enjoying considerable prestige in France as an indefatigable advocate of freedom and liberalism ever since his involvement in America's War for Independence in 1776. He had also played a major role in the French Revolution of 1789, and had been an opponent of the authoritarian regime of Napoléon I. After the monarchic Restoration, he remained true to his republican opinions, and once elected to the Chamber of Deputies in 1818, he continuously fought against the monarchists' attempts to restore an autocratic regime.

On August 8, 1829, King Charles X attempted a show of strength by appointing an ultra-royalist minister, the Comte de Polignac, at the head of government. The event triggered a political crisis that would ultimately lead to the revolution of July 1830. During the summer 1829, La Fayette was traveling in the French provinces of Auvergne and Dauphiné, mainly for family reasons, and once the news of the nomination of Polignac became known his journey took a political turn. In each town where he stopped, La Fayette was welcomed by the local population, and during banquets held in his honor, he took the opportunity to give speeches against the government. The culmination of his journey was his arrival in Lyon on September 5, where he was triumphantly received and honored especially by the liberals of the town. During his three-day stay, the local journal *Le Précurseur* described the jubilation; a crowd of 60,000 followed him in the streets shouting "Vive La Fayette." The second day of his stay, he was invited for a trip on the river Saône, and his boat was accompanied by "a multitude of small skiffs ... on the banks, there was a living forest of heads; above, the Saint-Rambert bridge covered by a compact crowd which made an animated amphitheater."[50]

On the evening of the sixth, which was his seventy-second birthday, and just one day before the official banquet organized by the city's liberals, La Fayette and his son, George-Washington, also a Freemason, were invited to a Masonic meeting that gathered representatives from all the Masonic lodges in Lyon and also Masons from across France and Geneva. There, La Fayette claimed the prominent role of Masonry in the fight for freedom:

> They were also Masons Washington, Franklin, Warren; these men who, by founding the liberty of their country, brought the Masonic institution as the true bond of all peoples, and the basis of that moral education which ensures their independence. Happier than many of our worthy brothers born in countries where absolutism prevails, they have been able to consolidate their work, and the gratitude of peoples has immortalized their memory. Let us make

vows that the persecutions directed against Masonry in several parts of Europe should cease.[51]

After his stay in Lyon, La Fayette went back to Paris where he resumed his activities at the Chamber of Deputies, fighting against the government's authoritarian drift. When the revolution broke out at the end of July 1830, he played a primary role and was even proposed to become the president of a new Republic. He declined the proposition, and advocated for a liberal and constitutional monarchy, giving his support to the Duc d'Orléans who was ultimately crowned under the name of Louis-Philippe, King of the French—no longer known as the King of France and of Navarre.

La Fayette's visit to Lyon had served as a catalyst, warming the city's liberal movement and especially the Freemasons who would later be active among the insurgents during the July revolution. Under the new monarchy, three of the main figures in Lyon Masonry, Frédéric Charassin, César Bertholon, and Philibert Chanay, were all republicans. All born between 1800 and 1804, they were all from the same generation as Gouhenant.[52]

Gouhenant was twenty-five years old when La Fayette made his triumphal visit to Lyon. Whether or not he was himself a Freemason at the time, or if he attended the Masonic meeting with the great figure, is not known, but undoubtedly he must have been struck by this event and by the revitalization of the republican ideas discussed among the Masonic lodges in the aftermath.

À TOUS LES ORIENS DE FRANCE

Three years after La Fayctte's visit to Lyon, Gouhenant was an active Freemason and published a small booklet entitled *La Maçonnerie: À tous les Oriens de France* (Masonry: To All the Lodges of France). He actually wrote only the preface of the small work, but he put forth an ambitious proposal, which was nothing short of an attempt to convince his fellow

Masons to set aside their secrecy and bring their debates into the light of day, "Should Masonry remain invisible to all? No! Her aim would not be reached! Her mission would be unfinished! She would not be understood!" It was in the interest of Masonry, he argued, to open herself to the uninitiated, but also in the interest of the world, for which it would also be "the last hope for salvation and the strongest lever for change this century."[53]

Gouhenant possessed an artistic soul and his ideas took the form of a poem that was about 500 Alexandrine verses in length. He then asked his friend, Amédée Gayet de Cesena, to take up the pen for him. Cesena was born in 1810, in Sestri di Levante, a small Italian coastal city on the Mediterranean Sea, at the time part of the French department of the Appenins. His father was a tax collector and his mother's name was Magdeleine Rose Françoise de Cesena. Amédée Gayet would later add his mother's name to his father's surname, but ultimately would keep only his mother's as his artist name. After the fall of the Empire, the family settled down in Beaujeu, thirty miles from Lyon.[54] Thus, Cesena likely met Gouhenant in Lyon, both of them frequenting the town's intellectual circles. Up until then, Amédée Gayet de Cesena had published poems in two Lyon journals: *La Glaneuse* and *Le Papillon*, as well as a small verse work in *Hymne aux vainqueurs d'Afrique* edited in Paris.

Although Gouhenant was not the author of the verses, he was the inspiration, as he wrote in his preface: "In order to give the necessary development to these ideas, I have communicated my material to one of my friends, a young writer [...] I thought the poet's voice would be better heard." The poem contains several spiritual and political references that seem to provide early context for Gouhenant's ideological framework, well before he would become a member of the Icarian communist movement nearly a decade later.

The poem is preceded by two short phrases. The first appears as a subtitle of three single words: *Union et Confiance* (Union and Confidence). This was the name of a Masonic lodge created in 1824, probably the one to which Gouhenant belonged. Little information about this lodge has survived except the fact that its most notable members, César Bertholon and Joseph Bergier, were republicans. There is no indication that Gouhenant had a close relationship with these two republican figures, and likely, he did not. Bertholon and Bergier were wealthy bourgeois, and Bergier's correspondence shows his social circle was from the bourgeois class to which Gouhenant did not belong.[55] These men, although republicans, were far from being socialists and even if Gouhenant heard democratic addresses during the Masonic debates, he certainly did not learn the basis of the political corpus of socialism at the lodge.

The second introductory sentence of the poem is a verse from the French poet Népomucène Lemercier, written as an epigraph: *La liberté de l'homme est un décret de Dieu* (The freedom of man is a decree of God). The same verse had also been used a year before by a Lyon republican, Joseph Beuf, as an epigraph of his short-lived journal *La Sentinelle Nationale*. Beuf was a very involved activist, two years older than Gouhenant, who had been sentenced to three and a half years in prison in June 1832 for writing a pamphlet railing against the monarchy. He was sentenced again in September for an additional eighteen months for having published the text of his defense when he appeared before the court.

Joseph Beuf's two texts were extremely virulent in their opposition to the monarchic regime. The republican journals reflected these events and Beuf, who was hiding from the police after his two trials, had become a hero of the republican fight in Lyon. Gouhenant and Cesena's booklet was published in October 1832, and this epigraph might be construed as a discreet tribute to him. In fact, Beuf's brother, Pierre, a Lyon publisher, was living in the same building as Gouhenant at 38 Rue de la Reine, suggesting that Gouhenant was likely in contact with the Beuf brothers. Joseph Beuf claimed to be a proletarian—he was indeed the son of an earthenware worker—and he was closer to Gouhenant's social class than to his Masonic lodge brothers, Bergier and Bertholon. His ideas were also much more revolutionary than those of the wealthy philanthropist Masons.

The first part of Gouhenant and Cesena's poem is typical of French romanticism from the 1830s, describing a disenchanted world having lost its ideals and its spirituality and its subsequent fall into materialism and individualism. This part is not very original, but it does mirror several political events of the time. Those events were ardently discussed in the republican circles: the upheaval in Lyon, and the fiercely repressed democratic uprisings in Poland and Italy. Conversely, the last part of the poem, which proposed to widely spread the secrets of Freemasonry, belongs exclusively to this work; broadened to include all peoples, the Masonic message would lead them from disarray by throwing a beam of light to illuminate the world. But at least one literary critic wrote: "The poet has constructed five hundred Masonic verses, yet there is not a single word of Masonry."[56] Indeed, nothing is said of the "terrific secrets" of Masonry, nor of the "mysterious fruits" that stemmed from its works that Gouhenant mentions in the preface. In fact, it is not the content of the Masonic works that are important in the piece. Rather, it is the spreading of solidarity between its members to all peoples:

> Come on, join the trunk which unites us!
> We will walk farther by walking together.

Gouhenant and Cesena were dreaming of social solidarity where the one who falls is helped back to his feet by his fellow citizens:

> If at some time, one of you may fall, when he tries,
> We will help him back, we will heal his wounds.

And they ask for the foundation of a new religion, with its temples bringing the Masonic message to the people:

> We must open a big temple in every town
> Where we could gather near the fire of a single altar

The wandering tribes of the brotherly herd.

The new world that Gouhenant dreams of is a world of freedom, having broken the yokes under which the oppressed are kept, but not having drowned in an individualism which would leave them to live a solitary destiny: "We do not need irons, instead we need links!"

The poem hints at the first seeds of Gouhenant's growing political and social ideology. First, it reflects a deep mysticism, which would later lead him to adhere to the New Jerusalem church founded by Emmanuel Swedenborg. Second, it makes a strong appeal for social solidarity between people, which he would later consider to be the driver of Icarian communism. With regard to the Icarians, however, it is hard to fathom how Gouhenant could have accepted the iron discipline advocated in Cabet's communist doctrine. In the *Voyage en Icarie,* Cabet described an "ideal" society where all human activities were ruled by a ubiquitous state authority. This seemed in complete contradiction to Gouhenant's entire life, which was like a hymn sung to the praises of individual freedom: freedom of conscience and freedom of enterprise.

Further, a few characters quoted in the poem as geniuses were champions of individual freedom, certainly not socialists. For instance, General Foy, the former marshal of the Empire, had become one of the fiercest opponents of the monarchy after the Restoration; there was also Benjamin Constant, a writer and liberal politician who had been active in the July Revolution. Another contemporary character mentioned in the poem is Prosper Enfantin, the chief of the Saint-Simonian movement, who favored an economic liberalism and a strong social link between citizens— implying solidarity of the wealthiest with the poorest. In 1828, as the leader of the Saint-Simonians, Enfantin transformed their movement into an actual religion. He was called "Father Enfantin" by both his disciples and by Cesena in his poem. Ironically, ten years later, Cabet would become "Father Cabet" in the same manner. In August of 1832, only two months before the publication of the poem, Enfantin and his followers had been arrested because of his liberal writings, and the poem echoes the event, describing Enfantin as a martyr.

Saint-Simonians were very active in Lyon after the first silk workers' riot in 1831, and like many Lyonnais citizens, Gouhenant certainly would have seen them walking in town wearing their characteristic long hair and beards and dressed in their typical blue tunics cinched at the waist. There is no evidence that he followed this movement, but the poem clearly shows his sympathy toward it. At the beginning of the 1840s, when Gouhenant would return to center stage in Toulouse, Saint-Simonism was no longer organized as it had been in 1830. Enfantin had left for several years to go to Africa, then discreetly returned to France. By the time he came back, Cabet's doctrines had taken the lead over all the socialist ideologies that were popular among the working class.

Thus, from the early 1830s Gouhenant's ideology rested on three pillars. First, was the defense of individual freedoms. Second, he supported a solidarity organized among the people. Finally, he advocated for a strong religious component.

The political movement to which he belonged, or at least which he supported, was full of religious overtones. Saint-Simonism called itself the "New Christianity," and Cabet considered his communist doctrine an application of the original Christian religion. These movements had something else in common: they all advocated for the emancipation of the poorest only by means of dialog and proselytism. After the 1831 riots in Lyon, the Saint-Simonians condemned the violence of the workers, while they still pushed for social and economic reforms that favored the working class. Cabet also always kept his movement separate from any violent action.

Conversely, the Marxists, who by the turn of twentieth century would lead socialism onto the international stage, put class struggle as the basis of their theory, and were extremely critical of the powerlessness of the other movements. Marx and Engels mocked the religiosity of these utopian socialist experiments, sarcastically comparing them to a cheap version of the New Jerusalem.[57] Religiosity was indeed a trend of the early communist movements and would completely disappear from communist philosophy after Marx, the word "communism" being then associated with a materialist atheism.

THE SWEDENBORGIAN CONVERSION

Gouhenant was never an atheist, but the Catholic church where he had been raised had not fulfilled his spiritual needs since it sided with the bourgeois government and was strongly resistant to the emancipation of the working class. Sometime before 1843, Gouhenant had become a disciple of the New Jerusalem church, a theology to which he would continue to subscribe until the end of his life.[58] Cabet reported that Gouhenant had a desire to establish a Swedenborgian church in Toulouse modeled after the one that existed in the small town of Saint-Amand.[59] The new religion had caught Cabet's attention so much that he wrote a letter to Gouhenant requesting "some details about Swedembourg [sic], his system, his progress, etc."[60]

The Swedenborgian doctrines, which had been quite secretive in France, gained a renewed attraction among some of the population during the 1830s. They had been spotlighted by Honoré de Balzac, who published two novels, *Louis Lambert* in 1832, and then again more prominently in *Séraphîta* in 1835, where he set forth the ideas of the Swedish philosopher. The second of these novels met with some degree of success, judging by the number of editions. But Balzac, as well as many Swedenborgians of the era, was more interested in the mystic and esoteric content of Emmanuel Swedenborg's writings than in the settlement of an actual church. Gouhenant may have discovered the Swedenborgian philosophy by reading Balzac's books, or through discussions with some of his artist friends who followed mysticism—and there were many in Lyon—but his efforts to establish a Swedenborgian church obviously originated from the one founded by Jacques-François-Étienne Le Boys des Guays in Saint-Amand in 1837.

Le Boys des Guays was initiated into Swedenborgianism in 1834, and was quite critical towards Balzac's "unintelligible mysticism." After the founding of the church in Saint-Amand he was seen as the organizer of the Swedenborgian cult in France, gleaning out the esoteric and spiritualist practices that had become dominant in the French Swedenborgian circles before him. An ardent republican, he was also listening to the new social doctrines and in 1838, he had welcomed some Fourierists who wanted to create a link between their movement and the new church.[61]

The new religion certainly must have appealed to Gouhenant. Le Boys des Guays described the basic principles of the theology in a letter he wrote to the mayor of Saint-Amand, informing him that he was opening a Swedenborgian church in his house:

> 1st The religion that we profess is not the result of a human conception, it is Christianity brought back to its primitive purity and putting itself in relationship with the progress of the Lumières [...]

> 2nd Our religion is only spiritual and has absolutely nothing temporal or political [...] if Christianity has been diverted for fifteen hundred years from its true way, it is because one has overused the spiritual things by applying them to terrestrial things.

> 3rd Our religion put the largest tolerance principle [...] Any man, being Christian, Mahometan, Jewish, Hindu or Idolatrous, can be saved. He just needs to have lived well, the Divinity could not impute to the man the errors in which he was born and raised.

> 4th The practice of our religion does not consist in living in the contemplation and mysticism [...] it consists in living in the world a life full of activity [...] God does not need praises and benedictions for his glory; he wants us to produce works, and then spread the goodness of charity [...] Loving God is, in all circumstances, to prefer whole men or human kind to the homeland, the homeland to the family, and the family to oneself.[62]

For a liberal and religious-minded man like Gouhenant, such a religion—tolerant, ecumenical, separated from the temporal power and for which free individual activity was a tribute to the Divinity—would have been a revelation.

The period corresponding with the foundation of the New Jerusalem church in Saint-Amand coincides with the few years, from 1835 to 1840, during which Gouhenant's whereabouts and his activities are completely unknown. It is possible, although not confirmed, that he met Le Boys des Guays during this time, although they were from very different social backgrounds. Le Boys des Guays had been born in a family of noble magistrates, and Gouhenant was a peasant's son. In any case there is no mention of Gouhenant in the archives of the French Swedenborgian church, yet the same archive have kept all the correspondence of Le Boys des Guays.[63]

Gouhenant finally left Lyon around 1835. Although his bankruptcy and the sale of all his possessions had protected him from prosecution by his many creditors, his reputation and credibility were probably heavily tarnished. The daily contemplation of his monument dominating the city, now left in other hands, may have also been a painful ordeal. He was twenty when he arrived in Lyon, full of ambition, and just six years later, he would undertake his gigantic and somewhat unrealistic project. What would have happened if he had met with success? In his letter to the Duc d'Orléans he speaks about another project "even more beautiful and useful than [his] observatory," and although he claimed in his letters that he did not aim to draw any benefit from his establishments, he obviously needed to earn money from them, at least to reimburse his creditors, but also to improve his family's situation. In the fall of 1832, a few weeks after his observatory was opened to the public, and when he published his booklet on Masonry advocating for individual freedom and social solidarity, Gouhenant's political ideology could certainly have been called socialist, but it was definitely not communist nor revolutionary, and had his project been successful, he would probably have become one of the wealthy philanthropists of the city.

The bitter end of his dream in 1835, aside from ruining him, may have led Gouhenant to radicalize his political ideas. In any case, within five years he would become the leader of the working-class activists in Toulouse and when Cabet later returned to the forefront of the political scene with his Icarian communism, Gouhenant would become his correspondent there. Yet, a critical difference would emerge in the two men's philosophies. While Cabet wanted to promote his doctrine only by way of proselytism, Gouhenant would be tempted by violent revolutionary action.

CHAPTER 3

A Conspiracy in Toulouse

The doctrine of M. Cabet, propagated in the Journal, Le Populaire, with cart loads of pamphlets and by crowds of traveling agents, had created proselytes in the departments of the Haute-Garonne, Aude, and Dordogne. In Toulouse especially, there was a church of exemplary fervor, too exemplary, perhaps, since it deviated from the dogmas in contemplating an appeal to the musket in aid of precept."[64]

Lucien Delahodde, 1850

A Revolutionary Banquet

At 7:00 pm, on January 15, 1843, four groups of about ten men each marched quietly toward Toulouse's Lafayette Square, a nice oval space surrounded by small, uniform two-story buildings, with curved brick walls. One of the liveliest areas of town, it attracted travelers who would come to stay in the hotels, sit at one of the café tables, or see a play in one of the neighboring theaters. From the square, four narrow streets radiated toward the cardinal points.

The mysterious walkers came from the four streets. From the west, the first group gathered in one of the many bars lining the Royal Square below the Capitol, the emblematic monument of the town and the seat of local power, which the writer Stendhal had described in *Voyage dans le midi de la France,* as being painted a shade of *café au lait,* but now known for its two-color brick and limestone façade.

Two other groups arrived, one from Wood Market Square to the north, and another from Saint-George Square to the south. From the east, the last group of men departed from Gouhenant's home, where he was now living at the Toulouse Circus.[65] The evening was dark; a heavy rain had fallen on the town over the past few days and the light from the gas street lamps barely pierced through the cloudy night. All the men comprising the small bands knew the aim of the meeting, but only a few knew where it would take place. Each group was under the command of an appointed chief who had kept the secret. One after the other, they arrived at the Hôtel Capoul on Lafayette Square.

Illustration 8. Lafayette Square in Toulouse (second half of 19th century).

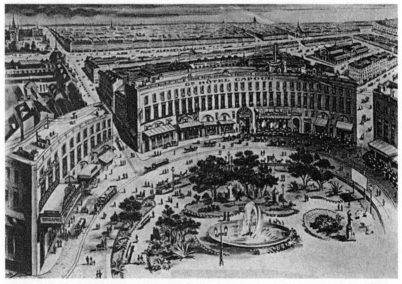

Postcard by Labouche Frères, Toulouse.
The Hotel Capoul is center, where the January 1843 banquet was held.

Gouhenant had booked the main room, accessible by crossing through an inner courtyard, explaining to the owner that he would host a Masonic banquet. As the guests arrived, they were all wearing their Masonic emblems, and the lodge's statute book was placed conspicuously upon the table. Curiously, many non-Masons also came to the meeting. Recently passed legislation restricted unauthorized meetings of more than twenty persons, although a few exceptions were tolerated, including Masonic meetings. The *mise en scène* would make it easier to face an untimely police raid should one occur; a Masonic gathering could have an aura of secrecy without arousing the suspicion of hotel staff. Once everyone had gathered, the doors of the room were closed and would only be opened from time to time to allow waiters to pass the meal through to banquet participants without entering the room.

The majority of the forty men were from Toulouse. Ten men came from southern towns: Agen, Condom, Albi, Béziers, Agde, and several smaller villages. Among the guests of honor were three Spanish men, only one of whom, Abdon Terradas, spoke French. The most illustrious of the guests was the famous revolutionary thinker from Paris, Albert Laponneraye, who would quickly become the center of attention. Gouhenant was chairing the meeting seated at the center of the table across from Laponneraye and Terradas. As silence fell over the room, he stood to propose a toast to Terradas, and then yielded the floor to him. Terradas informed the men about his recent fight in Barcelona where he had served as the head of the republican insurgents who had managed to take control of the city. He described how his men forced Spanish Regent Bardomero Espartero's soldiers to flee. He then recounted the brutal repression that fell on Barcelona with bombing for several days causing countless casualties among the local population. Finally, he said that he and his men had to flee and take refuge in France. Terradas's speech was perfectly timed since the riots in Spain had fired the imagination of the French republicans, especially those from the south who had dreamed of a simultaneous revolutionary uprising on both sides of the Pyrenees.

Terradas's attendance at the banquet was actually illegal. Since taking refuge in France, he had been residing in Perpignan close to the Spanish border, against the orders of the French government. They had commanded him to reside in the small town of Tulle, where they could keep him under observation. His goal in Toulouse was to raise funds and hire men to reinvigorate the fight in Spain. In Gouhenant's mind, however, his presence was mostly an opportunity to galvanize the assembly, who were in reality planning an insurrection in the south of France—an insurrection that would spread, igniting a general uprising across the country.

In fact, that was the real reason for the meeting that evening. For several months prior to the banquet, Gouhenant had worked tirelessly to make his mark as the leader of the Toulouse republicans, building trust among the working class. He had organized a southern division, recruiting section leaders in Toulouse and in several towns in the area. In turn, the leaders were each in charge of finding ten men they would command, and of convincing others to become section leaders themselves. During the banquet the revolutionary congress would review the forces: each delegate would provide an organizational update of his men, and Gouhenant would unveil the plan of action. He had claimed the plan was not his own, but that of a member of a Parisian steering committee with whom he had been corresponding for two years, and who had asked to remain anonymous until the division was ready to act. Once the banquet commenced, Gouhenant announced that the time had come. He was ready at last to introduce the Parisian leader of their organization. As it turned out, everyone there knew his name and his work already. It was Albert Laponneraye.

Gouhenant then proceeded to launch into a long speech wherein he told the story of his life. He disclosed how, after having sacrificed his fortune and risked his life in Paris and Lyon, he arrived in Toulouse in 1836 and since that time, had focused solely on the revolutionary organization of the south. He continued to draw an enthusiastic picture of the Toulouse forces. He told them that the national guard in Toulouse had been recently disarmed by the authorities. However, many citizens still had two weapons, and they would give one to others who had none. The blacksmiths had made pikes, and some also possessed bombs that would be thrown at the troops; during the attack, the armed men would march first on the garrison, followed by others who would seize the soldiers' weapons. Finally, he concluded his rousing speech by giving the date of the planned action in April, and with his characteristic lyricism, he described the "crown plaited with oak leaves" that would then be set atop the heads of the Nation's Liberators!

Laponneraye, born of aristocratic parents, had a much finer and complete education than his host, yet as a pale and sickly thirty-five-year-old man, his frail health would not allow him to match Gouhenant's brilliant oratory. As Gouhenant concluded his speech, Laponneraye rose from his chair and began to describe his political life, his pain, and the imprisonment he suffered for several years because of his republican opinions. Most importantly, he described the revolutionary party in Paris as perfectly organized, and led by a central committee that was coordinating with all the regions of France as they planned the insurrection. It was the central committee that had sent him to Toulouse to see for himself the strengths of the party in the south.

Just as Gouhenant had exclaimed, Laponneraye further insisted that the time had come for the uprising and that the monarchy would be over-thrown in the spring. The guests, completely familiar with Laponneraye's name, saw his face for the first time and realized that he was the long-hidden leader who had been guiding the plan. The seemingly far-fetched plan proposed by Gouhenant and delivered with his usual bombast, now appeared to have an originator more credible than their local leader. And what an originator! Enthusiasm was welling up within the assembly. Still, discretion was required and while the energy in the room was palpable, no one raised his voice or cheered as Gouhenant stood and proposed a toast to Laponneraye and to the unity of the revolutionary movement.

Illustration 9. Albert Laponneraye, communist thinker.

Bibliothèque nationale de France. Used by permission.
Laponneraye was one of the top minds of the first French communist movement in the 1830s. Although he was no longer at the forefront of the revolutionary movement by 1842, Gouhenant pledged allegiance to him and placed his organization under his orders.

After the speeches, Gouhenant read a letter from the Lyon committee announcing that the organization there was not yet complete and that they were unable to send someone to the meeting. Next, the delegates reported out. Each delegate stood up, one after the other: Maurice Dupuy, a bookseller from Albi; then Lucien Lamarque, a lawyer from Condom; Jean Marie Dubor, a print worker from Agen; Jules Balguerie, a student from Agde; Étienne Rolland, a Toulouse stonecutter; Joseph Sagansan, a carpenter in the same city; and others. Each described the organization in the cities or areas under their command. They spoke about the forces they had engaged for the movement: two hundred men here, three hundred there, five hundred elsewhere. Some of them even claimed that the garrison soldiers were prepared to support the movement when the time arose.

Balguerie, the son of wealthy merchants, said twenty-four dedicated men were with him—free, independent, and rich enough to make sacrifices for the cause. Some delegates were a little more circumspect, saying that their sections were not ready to act first, but that when the time came, they would seize guns in town halls to join the movement. It was Rolland, the sturdy stonecutter, who closed the meeting haranguing his friends from Toulouse, "Citizens, it is you, the section leaders of the city of Toulouse, I am talking to. The time to act cannot be delayed, do not do as we did in 1830, do not lay down arms before having conquered all our rights. My motto is: Live working or die fighting!"

Their clandestine meeting lasted eight hours: speeches following toasts, and toasts following speeches. By the end of the evening, Gouhenant had reached his goal; he had succeeded in rousing the ardor of the southern revolutionary movement establishing his authority (which had been questioned over the last few months). He closed the banquet by advising the delegates to speak only to the members of their local committees about what had just happened, and in order to remain hidden from police, he further advised them not to stay in Toulouse. He told them that both he and Laponneraye would leave town the next day to review the committees in Agen, Auch, and Bordeaux. From there, the Parisian leader would go back to the capital to give an account of what he saw and to finalize details for the large insurrection envisioned for the following spring.

At 3:00 am, the men left the hotel in the cold, dark night, still lit by the glow of the street lamps. Those from Toulouse returned home, the others back to their hotels. Gouhenant was satisfied with the results. Unbeknownst to him, in just a few hours the police would know everything that was discussed, and in less than two weeks he would be behind bars.[66]

GOUHENANT: LEADER OF THE TOULOUSE WORKERS

The situation in France, and specifically in Toulouse just a few years earlier, would set the tone for Gouhenant's leadership role in the southern revolutionary movement sometime between the mid-1830s and 1841.

The revolution of July 1830 had created a constitutional regime—the July monarchy—that was able to maintain its existence for eighteen years, despite being shaken by numerous insurrections. In 1831 and again in 1834, Lyon was the epicenter of the tremors, while in 1832, 1837, and 1839, Paris was the site of the most violent uprisings. Although the government had been caught off-guard by the riots at the beginning of the 1830s, it became gradually more effective at confining and repressing them. In 1830, the working class, who had fought for an improvement of their living conditions, soon realized that the bourgeoisie was the only winner in the revolution. Still, the new regime under the July monarchy was more liberal than the previous one, and although tightly reined in, freedom of expression and freedom to publish did allow some committed intellectuals to propagate liberal and socialist ideas, which spread through the working class.

Republican organizations in France became very active in the early 1830s. In 1837, Auguste Blanqui and Armand Barbès, two of the most prominent revolutionary leaders of the republican party, founded the

Société des Saisons, which remained the main revolutionary association until 1839, when they led a new, but severely repressed insurrection. Both Blanqui and Barbès were sentenced to death in 1840, although their sentence would ultimately be commuted to life in prison. After their imprisonment, revolutionary activities weakened. During the 1840s, up until the revolution of 1848, activities were either of little importance, or they were aborted before they even got started. The police were unceasingly infiltrating the associations, and particularly the Nouvelle Société des Saisons now led by a man named Henri Dourille, a much less charismatic leader than either Blanqui or Barbès.

Gouhenant, living in Lyon during the first half of the 1830s, not far from the revolutionary turmoil, was likely not actively engaged in planning. In 1831 he was just a sympathetic witness, but the silk worker revolt had affected his business. He was still living in Lyon during the much more violent riot of 1834, but if he had any role in that riot, no traces of his involvement remain.

By 1841, he was in Toulouse when a new rebellion broke out, spreading to the provinces. This time he was at the heart of the social movement that agitated the city, and even became a major player—until events would take a nasty turn in January 1843.

The 1841 riots were triggered by a tax reform put into place by the Minister of Finance Jean-George Humann to address a serious deficit in the public coffers. The reform was complex, but the most visible and controversial measure was to make the existing tax, which counted doors and windows, more efficient by taking a rigorous inventory of every home. Prior to Humann's reforms, the census had been led by the municipal authorities, but Humann suspected the locals of corrupt practices and he decided that federal officers should now collect the taxes with assistance from municipal agents.

Humann's authoritarian personality, the unpopularity of a more rigorous tax collection system, and the State's newly implemented role in conducting an asset inventory, were the key ingredients that revived the revolt in a large part of the country. All opposition parties united to denounce the reform. In Toulouse, the mayor refused to allow the municipal agents to assist the tax officers. The prefect himself, who was also opposed to the reform, did not intervene to facilitate the census and finally ordered the operations to be suspended. In response, the government revoked his authority and appointed a new prefect.

In protest of the new appointment, the entire city council resigned on July 3, and a crowd of several thousand people gathered in the center of the city. By July 7 and 8, barricades were erected near the prefecture. The action escalated emotions and led to a week of violent confrontations between the citizens and the army, culminating on the twelfth when a young man named Chavardès was killed by a soldier.

The events that had started in Toulouse spread with varying intensity throughout the country, lasting until October.[67]

A year later, on the anniversary of Chavardès's death, Gouhenant led a group of workers who wanted to hold a mass to honor his memory, and to erect a memorial stone on his grave. On July 10, 1842, the prefect of Haute-Garonne—the department to which Toulouse belongs—wrote to the attorney general of Toulouse:

> The newspaper *l'Émancipation* announced a few days ago that a funeral service would be held for the anniversary of Chavardès death .... A so-called Goualand, painter worker who recently arrived from Paris showed up at the priest's home at La Daurade, requesting the service tomorrow.[68] The priest vehemently refused on behalf of himself and his vicars; Goualand replied that they would break down the doors and then go to the cemetery to place a tombstone in honor of Chavardès.
>
> Secret meetings were held last night. It is said that the workers belonging to the association numbered 1500 to 2000. I believe this figure is nevertheless exaggerated. It is certain, however, that 60 workers met last night near the column and drafted a plan for a

violent attack. Goualand said above all, it was necessary to obtain weapons by all possible means.[69]

By the summer of that year, it was clear that the authorities considered Gouhenant to be a leader of the workers. The details given by the prefect about a secret meeting held in Toulouse show that his association had already been infiltrated by police at that time. However, aside from the secret activities, Gouhenant also orchestrated visible actions that he took care to keep within the boundaries of the law. Thus, the prefect's statement regarding the conversation with the priest may be qualified. The priest himself would later give a much less inflammatory version than the one reported by the prefect of Haute-Garonne.

> The first time Monsieur Gouhenant did me the honor to come to me (I say the honor because everything that happened between him and me was perfectly respectful and I was very pleased about my relationship with him), he came to ask me permission to hold a mass for the repose of the soul of Chavardès, killed during the turmoil in Toulouse in 1841. Monsieur Gouhenant spoke of these sad events as a perfectly wise man. I was impressed by his good feelings, and his religious language touched me. But the Archbishop was opposed to the ceremony. Monsieur Gouhenant piqued my interest, and I told him that perhaps he would be better off by not putting himself at the head of the workers. He always replied with exquisite politeness. Having left a few moments later, I found myself in a crowd of workers, without arms or sticks, but they dispersed soon with Gouhenant's exhortation and I did not have to regret having been among the gathering.[70]

The testimony suggests a portrait of a more subdued and even thoughtful leader than the one drawn by the prefect. It also reveals that Gouhenant clearly enjoyed a great popularity among the workers. His leadership is confirmed by the police commissioner Lemarquois who had been charged to disperse the crowds around the church of La Daurade in July 1842. Lemarquois claimed that there were between 1000 to 1200 workers and that many of the protestors refused to leave until they were commanded to by Gouhenant.[71]

Ultimately, the authorities banned any celebration of the anniversary of Chavardès's death. Still, Gouhenant insisted upon placing a headstone on his grave, a gesture for which he personally bore the costs. The tribute he had planned to engrave, "To Jean Chavardès, killed July 12, 1841. Erected by the workers of Toulouse," was ordered to be changed. Instead, the authorities insisted that the word *killed* be replaced by the word *dead* and *workers* by *citizens*. Finally, the stone was inaugurated without any ceremony except by Gouhenant himself who was in the company of a police commissioner, the stonecutter, Felix Lafoy, and the stonecutter's apprentice.[72]

About the same time, Gouhenant was also involved with the Icarian communists and had even become Cabet's correspondent in Toulouse. It is unclear when or how the two men came into contact, but according to Cabet, Gouhenant was not yet familiar with the Icarian doctrines during the tumultuous events of 1841.[73]

Gouhenant became a convert to Icarian ideology sometime between July 1841 and July 1842. Working as a painter, and more specifically as an art restorer, permitted him to travel extensively in the Toulouse region. Thus, he came into contact with the working population in the area and spread Cabet's writings among them. Gouhenant had become quite a prolific artist. From the period when he began working as a colorist, then in describing his plans for painting monochromatic scenes above the windows of the tower in Lyon, to sometime in 1840s, he continued to paint and restore paintings throughout his political evolution and he would later draw upon this skill in an attempt to fund his endeavors.

There are no sources that reveal Gouhenant's secret actions—or even his more visible ones—in the summer and fall of 1842, but the surveillance record from the prefect's archive has survived, making it possible to follow almost all of his political activities from October 1842 up to the secret banquet of January 15, 1843.[74] It appears that the police were extremely effective in infiltrating the revolutionary movement. The police commissioner regularly sent the prefect his report summarizing the information provided by his informer. In addition, the archive also contains the reports of another informer who sent his updates directly to the prefect. The latter was not as productive as the police informer, so his reports are less detailed and much less prolific. Furthermore, the minister of justice himself, whom the prefect kept informed on a frequent basis, had his own informer, who was well trusted among the conspirators.

DISSENSION AMONG THE TOULOUSIAN REVOLUTIONARIES

In the three months leading up to the banquet at Capoul's, the revolutionaries were divided in Toulouse, as well as in Paris. In the capital, Dourille, who considered himself to be Blanqui and Barbès's heir apparent, had tried to unify the revolutionary movement under the authority of the *Nouvelle Société des Saisons*, and to curb the rising communist influence among the republicans. The communists themselves were split between those in favor of violent action, and the Icarians who were openly opposed to any armed insurrection and who believed only in the virtues of proselytizing.

Dourille had also kept an eye on the evolution of the republican party in other big cities, especially in Toulouse where the situation was unclear to him. In Toulouse, Jean-Baptiste Raulet, manager of the newspaper *l'Émancipation,* led the non-communist republicans. Raulet was highly critical of the Icarian ideological orientation that Gouhenant had contributed to the republican movement. The Parisian leaders did not understand how Gouhenant could present himself as an apostle of Icarianism, and at the same time, advocate for armed rebellion. They also wondered from which Parisian leader he took his orders.

In October of 1842, Dourille sent a young man by the name of Moëns to Toulouse to bring the southern republicans back under his authority and lure them away from the Icarian influence. On the fifteenth of the month,

Gouhenant convened a meeting of delegates from neighboring towns to provide an overview of the current organization. Twelve delegates were gathered, and Gouhenant wanted to show Moëns that not only was the revolutionary movement very organized and advanced in the South, it was also unified under the Icarian banner. He opened the meeting with a speech claiming he received his orders from a mysterious leader from Paris:[75]

> Two years ago, a delegate from Paris came to give us the sacrament of his correspondence in an official manner, with the very explicit instruction never to name him... I kept my word; [...]
>
> The time is coming when we can realize our dearest hopes. [...]
>
> The plan of action concerning the southern division (which embraces the area inclusive of Bordeaux to Marseilles and from Bayonne to Clermont) was given to me with all the necessary details. I wish I could share it with you today, but the time has not yet come, and to abide by the orders that were given to me, I have to restrict myself in the statement of the purpose for this meeting.
>
> Here is, my brethren, the agenda for this meeting, that I copied literally, and that I burned soon after:
>
> "Citizens, you are ordered to convene on October 15, a third of your division, represented by the smallest possible number of delegates to avoid too large a meeting... You can add 12 members from your area, so that you do not exceed the total number of 20. Each delegate will make an accurate report to me of the localities he represents, the number of brothers and their means of action... Let it be done with the utmost discretion and before you part, make all the participants promise never to reveal what they have seen and heard, except to those they are representing... immediately after, give us the report of the results by the means you know, and wait for further orders."

Here is, my brethren, what motivated the notifications you received, what explains the purpose of our meeting.

We will hear the reports later, but first we need to make our own profession of faith, and ask if this is also yours; because without the unity of principles, all our efforts and our acts would only be a path towards division, hatred and civil war.

We studied long enough different political and socialist systems to summarize and formulate briefly our profession of faith...

We are revolutionaries... But we are not revolutionaries first; we are not only political revolutionaries; we are not revolutionaries by temperament, nor hatred, nor ambition!... We are revolutionaries by the duties imposed on us by charity and brotherhood.

We want universal suffrage, we want the abolition of all privileges of birth and fortune; We want equal rights; public and free education, and the organization of work, in a word, we are Icarians... That tells you enough that we do not want a change of persons, but a change of institutions.

Determine if these are your principles and to convince us, please respond to our call.

Gouhenant proposed a very clear line—install Icarian communism, but unlike Cabet's peaceful approach, he proposed installing it by force. Moëns reacted to Gouhenant's speech, leaping to his feet and confronting Gouhenant and shouting, "What committee do you represent? Who is your organizer? ... Dourille is the only man who can give orders." The discussion became more heated, but Gouhenant stood firmly by his position, claiming that men did not matter; only principles did. Moëns was finally ejected from the meeting and the delegates' reports continued.

The delegates were highly motivated. Some spoke about two or three thousand men in Albi, another about six hundred in Agen. When Gouhenant reported these figures to his Parisian leader—Albert Laponneraye—he took great care to say that these were "preparatory reports," and that he "made clear the importance of the absolute truth," realizing there may have been some exaggeration fueled by the delegate's excitement.

Following the meeting, the Toulouse revolutionary committee was split. The split lasted only a short time however, and Gouhenant's opponents did not seem to garner much support. For a few weeks, the opponents led by Raulet and Moëns tried to recruit followers from the working class, but without much success. On November 7, the Toulouse commissioner wrote to the prefect: "Gouhenant has regained the confidence of his party. He is still fighting Raulet but has resumed a very active role."

JACQUES IMBERT: THE TRAVELING SALESMAN OF THE REVOLUTION

About the same time, during the fall of 1842, another man arrived in Toulouse to meet with Gouhenant. A wine salesman named Jacques Imbert had come from Lyon, where he claimed he had inspected the forces of the revolutionary party and had come to Toulouse for the same purpose.

Imbert was well known in revolutionary circles and was among the most ardent soldiers in the clandestine struggle. He had entered the political arena in Marseille at the beginning of the 1820s, when the ultra-royalists took over the head of the government against the old moderate king Louis XVIII.

He was on the front lines of the fight in Paris during the revolution of 1830, and was disappointed by the new regime. Imbert was also strongly involved in the insurrections of 1832 and 1834. Imprisoned with many others that year, he helped organize the escape of twenty-eight political prisoners in 1835.

Illustration 10. Jacques Imbert, a fiercely dedicated French socialist.

Bibliothèque nationale de France. Used by permission.
Imbert met Gouhenant in 1842 to discuss a planned insurrection and was co-accused in the communist trial in 1843. He left France to take refuge in Belgium.

Imbert then fled to Brussels, where he remained even after an amnesty was offered in 1837. While his political activities subsided during his first years in Belgium, he gradually did go back to the French political fight. As a salesman, his many travels in France allowed him to visit the local republican leaders.[76]

In November 1842, Imbert met Gouhenant for the first time. While the interaction with Dourille's envoy in Toulouse had been awkward, the meeting with Imbert was very positive and Gouhenant relished his endorsement. Gouhenant found Imbert's character to be of a much higher caliber than that of the young Moëns. Gouhenant wrote to Laponneraye about the meeting:

> My Dear Fellow Citizen,
>
> I write to you under the strongest impression that can arise from unrelenting joy, happiness and hope!... Listen:
>
> The moment I received your last letter acknowledging receipt of my reports, the door of my office opened. It was the citizen Imbert accompanied by the citizen Tayac of our city. We knew each other well by name and by reputation but we had never met [...]
>
> Frank explanations were given on my part and on his, always with some reservation (you understand). He did attend one of our meetings. I showed him some of our forces and he was convinced of our power. He agreed throughout his tour he had never seen so much zeal and ability to act. We talked about you and Dour[ille]. He presented Dour[ille] as the leader in Paris, and without mentioning our correspondence, or anything about what I knew, I made him understand that this citizen had no influence on us, that we do not deny his good qualities, but that we had our correspondent without whom we would do nothing, and from whom we would be separated only by death. He understood that it was you. Oh, then! When he saw our strength and determination, he could not do better than to agree with us. He promised to see you when he arrives in Paris, where he will be in a fortnight. I hope you will perfectly agree together [...]
>
> He left our town to go to Agen, and since we had appointed two delegates in the previous days to organize the com...[77] in the cities between Bordeaux and Toulouse, they took the opportunity to travel together.

[...] They spent two days visiting our friends, and parted more convinced than ever of the influence we have in the whole south. In a word, Imbert cannot restrain his joy at having been in touch with us. You will have an interview together in Paris. Try to conciliate [...]

Three delegations, of two citizens each, should leave next week, one on the Montpellier side, the other on the Bayonne side, and the third on the Limoges side to announce and prepare the congress we have set for December 20. If however this date does not suit you, please let me know quickly. We won a huge victory by organizing all the compagnons. The line from Marseille to Bordeaux is ours. And what men! These compagnons! Strong, discreet, numerous, disciplined...

So far we have succeeded in what we have undertaken. Our desires are met, our happiness does not rely on hope alone, we almost possess a reality. How shall I not be drunk with joy!... Now that everything is ready in our division, your work is done, ask your colleagues who represent other divisions of France, if they are as advanced. The very serious matter to decide is when to act [...] You must proceed on a grand scale as we proceed on a small one in our area, that means 5 or 6 of you should leave Paris the same day to visit various parts of France and when you are back from your journey, if you are sure that all the regions are ready, you will order what you think best, we will execute your orders on time [...]

Farewell. A handshake and sincere hug,

Adolphe Gouhenant

Gouhenant's writing rarely lacked verbosity and he was never short of exuberance. Yet in this case, it seems his enthusiasm was warranted; Imbert was impressed by the revolutionary organization in the south and he actually visited the surrounding towns with two of Gouhenant's agents, the stonecutter Rolland and the carpenter Sagansan. Rolland and Sagansan were important cogs in the revolutionary wheel. They were compagnons, the very special class of workers whom Gouhenant mentions in his letter. The *compagnonnages* were associations of skilled workers that had existed for several centuries. During the first part of the nineteenth century, industrialization, and the subsequent rise of jobs not requiring skilled labor, resulted in a reduction of the influence of these associations. They developed into groups of elite worker communities, typically one per trade, each one having its own organization and rites, quite similar to the Masons. The recruits for the revolution were expected to stand together and be disciplined. So, the homogeneous communities like the *compagnons*, already close-knit, provided excellent men for the movement; Rolland was in charge of organizing the stonecutters, and Sagansan, the carpenters.

A Plot in Lyon: The Summer Before the Banquet

Before going to the inspection with Rolland and Sagansan, Imbert had attended an association meeting in Toulouse, as Gouhenant mentioned. Gouhenant had explained his plan of action, and Imbert had suggested the use of incendiary bombs. Invented in Lyon, the bombs were small lead grenades about the size of an apple that were filled with powder and flammable material, with which Imbert himself had experimented.[78]

In Imbert's mind, Lyon was called upon to play a major role in the insurrection.[79] However, since they did not feel they were ready, no delegates from Lyon attended the banquet. As shown in a letter sent to Gouhenant dated January 6, and later seized from him by police, the committee expected to be on the frontline of the uprising by July 1842, but apparently an indiscretion or betrayal had aborted the action.

My dear friend

In the month of December, we received a letter from our friend I[mbert] in which he told us about your plans.

For some time now, we had suspended our work in order to be highly cautious. I[mbert] when he was in your city should have informed you about our business.

Before writing to you, we wanted to reconstruct our association on a new foundation. We succeeded, and now although we cannot be on the forefront, as we expected to be in July, we will be present when necessary. I[mbert] told us about an upcoming congress. This event that we joyfully welcomed made us think that you were ready. If so, walk slowly! Especially take extra precaution and make sure that your projects do not leave your committee. This is what lost Lyon in 1842. Write us often (at least once a month), give us the names of the cities with which you are corresponding, we will send ours [...] Anyway don't worry, we never keep any letter, and we ask you that you also burn ours.

Receive, citizen, the fraternal greetings of the members of the Lyon committee[80]

Although the letter was quite evasive about the action envisioned in Lyon, another source gives more details. There was a police informer named Lucien Delahodde, who had infiltrated the very highest levels of the Paris revolutionaries. A few years later, he would publish a book detailing the activities within the revolutionary circles.[81] He would write,

Around June 1842, a letter from Lyon to Mr. Dourille, caused the immediate meeting of the four lieutenants of the association. Once the letter was read, we learned that the content was of the utmost importance. The Lyon committee had made an insurrection plan that they considered decisive, and that they were ready to carry out; but before doing so, they wanted the approval of the main towns, in order to spread the uprising. For that reason, a congress was to be held in Lyon, to which the delegates of the revolutionary centers were called. Paris was especially requested to come evaluate the state of things and to give their opinion which would have great weight. The letter was from a silk lace manufacturer, named Callès.[82]

The Paris committee, unaware of course that Delahodde was an informer, then sent him to Lyon, where he was welcomed by Callès's wife Françoise Planche. Callès took him "to a hotel, rue du Bât d'argent, where most of the congress members were staying." There he met Imbert, who was representing the northern towns of Lille and Valenciennes and three other representatives from Marseille, Toulouse, and Grenoble.

During the meeting, Callès and other Lyon leaders described the plan:"During the July celebrations, while the authorities will be in the Cathedral for mass, take all the forts; from that of Fourvière, bring two cannons loaded with grapeshot, to a plateau overlooking the gate of the church; wait until the end of the service, and when the authorities exit, shoot them and make mincemeat out of all the chiefs, civil authorities, and military. This massacre should be the signal of the insurrection."[83] In the following days, Callès gave more details about the plan. Finally, they met one last time to summarize and confirm the resolutions and made plans for a meeting to be held in Lyon on July 26. All the towns were to send a representative for the insurrection. The plan was set.

Just two weeks prior to the scheduled revolt, however, fate intervened. On July 13, the Duc d'Orleans, Prince Ferdinand Philippe, was near Paris preparing to leave for the north of France. On the way to say goodbye to his family, he fell from his carriage, hit his head on the cobblestones, and died. The young prince's untimely death led to a wave of sympathy for the monarchy and in the midst of a nation in mourning, the men postponed the insurrection.

As a result, the insurrection in Lyon never happened. In fact, the police commissioner in Lyon was aware of the project and made several searches to find the weapons that Callès had mentioned. Although he did not find them before 1844, the search warrant indicated to Callès that they had been betrayed.[84] This explains his remarks in his letter to Gouhenant telling him to "take extra precautions and make sure that [his] project plans do not leave [his] committee. This is what lost Lyon in 1842."

Callès was no doubt a rabid revolutionary, and Delahodde claimed he had also been one of the fighters during the silk workers' riot of 1834.[85] Callès and Planche's address was later found in a portfolio on Gouhenant, proving that he knew the couple. Moreover, the name of Bonnardel, one of the leaders of the Lyon committee, and the address of the hotel *rue du Bât d'argent* where the representatives stayed in June of 1842, also appeared in the portfolio leaving absolutely no doubt that Adolphe Gouhenant was associated with these revolutionaries.

The planned insurrection in Lyon shows that the revolutionaries largely overestimated their power to act. The police were so well informed of all their intrigues they could afford to launch arrests only when the threat was considered sufficiently serious. In Lyon, although the authorities were aware of the project, no arrest was attempted before the weapons were located. Similarly, in Toulouse, the commissioners asked that arrests or searches not be made in haste to increase the chances of destroying the revolutionary groups.

THE SPANISH INSURRECTION: A FEW WEEKS PRIOR TO THE BANQUET

In November 1842, revolutionary activity in the south was gaining momentum and a recent event had fired up local enthusiasm: For several years, neighboring Spain had been torn apart by wars of succession to the throne, creating divisive movements quite similar to the lines drawn in France. Two monarchist parties were in opposition, one ultra-conservative, like the French Legitimists, and the other more liberal, ideologically close to the King of France Louis Philippe. As in France, there was also a Republican Party in Spain, which was especially active in Catalonia. In mid-November of 1842, the Catalan Republicans succeeded in taking control of Barcelona, driving out troops under the command of the Spanish Regent, Baldomero Espartero.

The French republicans, especially those in the southern part of the country, were highly supportive because French revolutionaries were fighting alongside the Spanish. A famous and elusive French Republican leader, Théophile Kersausie, was trying to recruit men to join the fight in Spain. The minister of the interior himself had written to the Toulouse prefect to ask him to monitor "this dangerous man, true to his habit of hiding his travels from the authorities as much as possible."[86]

The triumph of the Spanish insurgents was short-lived, and on December 4, they had to abandon Barcelona after Espartero bombed the city for a harrowing thirteen hours. Meanwhile, in Toulouse, the revolutionaries remained optimistic; a police informer reported comments from their December 7 meeting: "There is a lot of hope about the movement in Barcelona where Kersausie, in agreement with Torreno (this is a Spanish name which is uncertain) organized secret societies.[87] It is the French Republicans, recently arrived in Barcelona, who raised the tricolor. The latest news received offers hope that the insurgency is gaining ground outside Barcelona, Espartero could be surrounded and then the insurgents will march on France." The Toulouse revolutionaries' optimism was unfailing. Certainly, the Catalan republicans' fate was sealed by Espartero's brutal repression. But at the time, there was great hope in Kersausie's action to redress the situation in Spain, and later to unite the Spanish and French revolutions.

Theophile-Joachim-René Guillard de Kersausie was a Republican from the beginning who had been, and who would remain involved in all the insurrectionary movements that shook France from 1830 to 1851. He also fought alongside the European revolutionary movements, and he traveled occasionally to France. During these trips, he visited the industrial cities and inquired about the fate of the workers. He lived successively in Bordeaux, Toulouse, Nantes, Perpignan, and Marseille.[88] In 1842, he took up the cause of the Catalan Republicans.[89] The memoirs of the writer Eugene Sue, who knew him during his exile in Switzerland, state that "he fought with such temerity during the first insurrections of Catalonia that it is almost incomprehensible that he was not killed in the fight or shot after the defeat."[90]

Kersausie remained true to his republican convictions throughout his life, and was again involved in the 1848 revolution. Later, both Karl Marx and Friedrich Engels claimed that he had been the military organizer of the popular uprising in June 1848, although recent research has shown this was unlikely.[91] He took part in the last revolutionary day of the second Republic in June 13, 1849, led by the extreme-left Republicans against the military intervention of President Louis Napoléon Bonaparte in Italy, and was sentenced in absentia. He spent the rest of his life in exile in other parts of Europe, where he died August 13, 1874.

Kersausie was not a communist, but like Imbert, a fervent revolutionary, and if he was interested in the Toulouse organization, it was to recruit fighters. In one of his letters to Laponneraye, Gouhenant boasted of having impressed Kersausie with the organization and discipline of his association.[92] However, Kersausie's links with the Toulouse revolutionaries were especially bound with Raulet's faction.

Raulet was the one who established the first direct link with the Catalan insurgents by secretly bringing Abdon Terradas to Toulouse in the first days of January.[93] The thirty-year-old Terradas was the alcalde of Figueras and one of the principal leaders of the Catalan insurrection. Contrary to the ambitions of the most exalted revolutionaries of Toulouse, Terradas had other, more pressing concerns than joining his movement to theirs. He came to Toulouse to discuss a way of raising funds in France to resume the fight in his own country. Although the revolutionary movement in the south had many men ready to fight, it also faced serious financial problems, and could not offer Terradas anything but good will.

Illustration 11. Joachim-René-Théophile Gaillard de Kersausie, a Republican revolutionary.

Bibliothèque nationale de France. Used by permission.
Gaillard de Kersausie organized secret societies during the July monarchy. In 1842 he was fighting alongside the Spanish revolutionaries in Barcelona and later met Gouhenant, who was expecting the French and Spanish movements to become unified.

It was during his initial stay in Toulouse that Terradas met Gouhenant for the first time, a young man having told him that Gouhenant had wealthy acquaintances.[94] In reality, all Gouhenant could promise was that he could help him to obtain a loan. Gouhenant invited Terradas to the January 15 banquet and promised to discuss the potential loan with him at that time.

> My dear fellow citizen
>
> I hasten to inform you that on January 15th, the General Congress of the southern division shall be held in Toulouse. We have already convened all delegates who must attend. Each city sends a representative, the delegate from Paris must arrive by the 14th.
>
> If you have two or three days, we would be pleased if you could come here at that time, in one day, you could meet the leading citizens of our division, communicate your plans to them, and immediately see the results of your efforts.
>
> I had the opportunity to see two or three friends with whom I shall put you in touch. They still seem well disposed towards you. On our side we sincerely wish you success.
>
> Do you have any news of Ker[sausie]? Is he near you? Will he come with you? If you cannot come, at least provide us with some details for our friends.
>
> Meanwhile receive the assurance of our sympathies and our entire devotion.[95]

Terradas would accept the invitation and return to Toulouse on January 15, where he would become one of the guests of honor.

THE SINEWS OF WAR

The question of financing the insurrection haunted the revolutionary movement in Toulouse during the last weeks of 1842. On November 18, it was decided that each section head should pay two francs monthly and each member, fifty centimes. But this "tax" quickly proved inadequate, especially as the emissaries sent to the southern departments to recruit militants and collect funds did not meet with great success, and their travel was quite costly.[96] Furthermore, it was difficult to collect from a wider base than the activists themselves, without drawing attention from the authorities.

At the end of November, Gouhenant decided to raise funds by holding a raffle of his paintings. The law prohibited raffles without control or supervision of the administration, but those encouraging the arts were exempted from the severe restrictions.[97] Therefore, the insurgents could legally distribute tickets and raise additional funds under the guise of being patrons of the arts. In an effort to raise 4,000 francs, Gouhenant printed forty sets of one hundred tickets at the cost of one franc per ticket. Unfortunately, the paintings were perhaps not quite attractive enough, and the fundraising efforts were a failure. Gouhenant became very agitated, as shown in this report from a police informant:

> Gouhenant is furious that the cash flow is so bad. He could sell very few tickets in Toulouse. He quarreled with Dupin who could sell only one of the hundred he had taken, telling him he had to run around the town, grabbing them by the collar and not allowing them to depart before receiving money from them; that he [Dupin] had enough influence with Toulouse Patriots to make them give some money as soon as he told them how it would be used. That he should absolutely get ready to go to Pau, that time was precious, adding that he [Gouhenant] had made enough sacrifices, he sacrificed his paintings and if no money was raised, the emissaries who left would be in trouble.[98]

The days passed and the emissaries continued their travels, but money did not arrive fast enough. The movement could count on some wealthy agents like Balguerie who could pay the expenses without relying on subsidies from the party, but it was not as easy for the workers. For instance, Rolland and Sagansan, who were to accompany Balguerie to

Marseille, could follow him only up to Nîmes and were then forced to return to Toulouse. They had sold 100 raffle tickets, but it was not enough, and Gouhenant could not wait. The date of the big congress was approaching and he desperately needed money to bring both the delegates from neighboring departments, and the great Parisian leader whom he wanted to present to his men with much fanfare. So, he proceeded to organize an auction of all his paintings.[99]

The auction was scheduled to take place every day of the week at six o'clock in the evening, beginning on Monday the nineteenth, but it also was a failure, and the situation became very difficult for Gouhenant.

On December 29, four members of Raulet's faction went to his home asking him to justify spending 500 francs from the party's fund and they spread a rumor that he would soon leave Toulouse. The police, who knew of course about this whole affair, were also concerned about Gouhenant's possible flight. Police Commissioner Louis Aumont, who had been monitoring him from the beginning, suggested that his home should be searched immediately. The Central Commissioner of Toulouse Eugène Boissonneau preferred to wait and "let things run their course and continue monitoring, and allow them to put themselves in the oven." On January 5, Boissonneau wrote to the prefect, "Gouhenant is sick in bed; he is being monitored but nothing indicates he wants to leave Toulouse. He is still penniless."[100]

At the beginning of January, the only thing Gouhenant had in mind was to organize the congress. On January 13, he called several section leaders to come to his home and he asked for a contribution of twenty francs each, which represented the sacrifice of a month's salary for many of the activists who belonged to the working class. The commissioner wrote to the prefect to ask him to quickly release the money for his informer, who was not eager to provide it from his own pocket.[101]

The price was steep, but they were immensely impatient to finally know who the leader was and learn about his plan of action, and Gouhenant had no trouble finding volunteers to pay the price. On Friday the thirteenth, he had collected nearly 600 francs, enough money to organize the conference to be held the following Sunday.

Sunday was chosen specifically because the police would be busy monitoring the theaters and balls. Commissioner Boissonneau, being aware of all the details, sent the prefect a secret drawing that would appear on cards that guests would have to show to obtain entrance to the room. With a bit of luck, Gouhenant might have discovered that he was being closely monitored; the day before the banquet, a man came to warn one of the members of the association that the prefecture was aware all their actions. Unfortunately for Gouhenant, the man who received the warning was the informer himself.[102]

Illustration 12. The secret drawing required to enter the January 1843 banquet.

Copyright Conseil Départemental de la Haute-Garonne / Archives Départementales / 1M 346.

Chapter 4

Caught in the Dragnet

The conspirators are constantly in touch with the police, they come into conflict with them all the time; they hunt the mouchards, just as the mouchards hunt them. Spying is one of their main occupations. It is no wonder therefore that the short step from being a conspirator by trade to being a paid police spy is so frequently made, facilitated as it is by poverty and prison, by threats and promises. Hence the web of limitless suspicion within the conspiracies, which completely blinds their members and makes them see mouchards in their best people and their most trustworthy people in the real mouchards.[103]

Karl Marx, 1850

Albert Laponneraye: Dubious Revolutionary

An extreme division existed within the Republican Party in the early 1840s. Those national leaders who were not under arrest were trying to unite the workers, each under the banner of their own doctrine. It is difficult to measure the practical impact of their varying ideologies, but during the first half of the 1840s, through tireless proselytism and the ardor of his representatives' network, Cabet had gained significant influence among the working class in major industrial cities. In Toulouse, according to Lucien Delahodde, Laponneraye was trying to take over as the leader of the communists.

Delahodde had not been directly involved in the events in Toulouse, but his position had allowed him to follow them from afar and he would later write about them rather sarcastically.

> The doctrine of M. Cabet, propagated in the Journal, *Le Populaire*, with cart loads of pamphlets and by crowds of traveling agents, had created proselytes in the departments of the Haute-Garonne, Aude, and Dordogne. At Toulouse especially, there was a church of exemplary fervor, too exemplary, perhaps, since it deviated from the dogmas in calling for the use of guns to help the cause. There was no spirit of revolt shown against the master [Cabet]; but quite to the contrary, a very natural impatience for the triumph of the cause, and the endowment of France and the world with the felicities of Icaria. The chief of these rather eager communists was a painter by the name of Gouhenaus [*sic*], a fine speaker, ardent and extravagant, a type of enthusiast from the South. He had been led to override the rules from an intimacy obtained with M. Laponneraye, who had arrived from Paris saying that he was authorized to give new instructions.[104]

From the way Delahodde describes the republican leaders, it is evident that he did not go to Toulouse, nor did he ever even meet the revolutionaries from this city. His characterization of Gouhenant as "a type of the enthusiast from the South" is not a realistic description. Gouhenant was from the northeast of France, and he certainly did not have the characteristic lilting accent of the south.

The competition between Cabet and Laponneraye has been well documented.[105] In fact, Cabet considered himself to be in competition with every other communist leader. When he came back from exile in England in 1839, he found a communist movement in Paris called Neo-Babouvists, in honor of the last radical leader of the great French Revolution, Gracchus Babeuf.[106]

Among the Neo-Babouvists, Laponneraye was the most active propagandist. In 1831, before the authorities stopped his activities, his popular lessons entitled *History of France since 1789* gave him important visibility among the working class.

At that time, the conservatives in power considered Laponneraye's ideas to be highly subversive, and he was sentenced to two years in jail for "having incited the hate of the workers against the bourgeois." From prison, he managed to publish other writings supporting the working class, and during his detention he was tried several times, and remained in jail until 1837.[107]

When he regained his freedom in 1837, all these activities made him very popular among the republicans. He then published a journal entitled *l'Intelligence*, which historians consider to be the first communist periodical.

It had an impact not only on the Parisian workers, but also on the working class in larger cities like Lyon.[108] Joseph Benoit, a Lyon revolutionary, wrote in his memoirs, "There was at that time in the Lyon population, and especially among the proletarians, an insatiable need to know and to learn about the political and social sciences [...] The study of history and mainly that of the 1789 Revolution was their favorite subject. Finally, a journal, *L'Intelligence,* written by Laponneraye and Lahautière completed a series of publications each week that were circulated in the workshops where they spread the most advanced ideas."[109] The final years of the 1830s were the apex of Laponneraye's political career. When Barbès and Blanqui, the leaders of the Société des Saison, started the insurrection on May 12, 1839, they wrote a proclamation, "Aux armes citoyens," signed by a so-called provisional government consisting of seven revolutionaries with Laponneraye among them. Although he was not involved in this effort, the authors included him in their proclamation in order to take advantage of his popularity.[110]

After the failed insurrection of 1839, when the main republican leaders were arrested, Laponneraye's light began to fade. He ceased publishing his journal for financial reasons, and his influence grew dim. Cabet, on the contrary, was back in France, having written his famous *Voyage en Icarie* during his exile, and two years later, in 1841 he had debuted the first issue of the new *Le Populaire*. Both publications would become very popular among the working class. Laponneraye collaborated for a time with Cabet on *Le Populaire*, but soon the two colleagues parted ways because Cabet was upset that Laponneraye had traveled to Toulouse without informing him.[111] Cabet himself alluded to a competition with Laponneraye in *Les masques arrachés*, claiming that hawkers who were sent to Toulouse to sell Laponneraye's book on the French Revolution were systematically denigrating his own book on the same subject, and moreover, slandering the Icarian doctrine.[112]

Laponneraye had indeed taken over the leadership of the communists in Toulouse, but the sad reality that emerges from the analysis of archival documents is that he was a government informer.

On February 6, 1843, the general prosecutor of Toulouse wrote a letter to his minister: "I have every reason to believe that the Minister of the Interior was not ignorant of M. Laponneraye's trip [to Toulouse] and that this man, at first and for too long associated with the criminal intrigues of the parties, sincerely and on his own account remains or has since reentered among them, as a secret agent of the superior administration."[113] The letter mentions only a hint from the prosecutor, but the documents found in the prefecture archives overwhelmingly point to Laponneraye's betrayal. They include an unsigned report about the activities of the southern revolutionary organization—the author boasting of being the leader—and three letters he received and transcribed from Gouhenant. The report clearly shows that its author is the leader to whom Gouhenant had pledged allegiance, Albert Laponneraye:

To the Minister State Secretary of the Interior

Mr. Minister,

> I have the honor to transmit three letters that reached me succes-
> sively from Toulouse, which are very important, especially the 3rd.
>
> You will see by these letters, the southern organization yields
> a formidable extension. It has branches in many cities, and its
> leaders say: Victory will be ours when we will want it (word-for-
> word). You will also see that this organization is mine, and it will
> act, according to the impulse I give to it. What is most strange
> is that Gouhenant and his friends have taken me as their leader
> without me making any advance to them, and only because they
> believe I have a great influence in the revolutionary party.[114]

Laponneraye's betrayal seems inconceivable since he was a strong
supporter of the revolution although he had never taken part in any armed
insurrection. Perhaps he had adhered to Cabet's nonviolent doctrine
to such a point that he would have sabotaged those who wanted to
install Icarian communism by force. Conversely, he may have wanted
to discredit Cabet by inciting his followers to violent action that would
compromise their mentor. Or, more prosaically, was he in such dire
straits financially after the collapse of his newspaper that he had to
use this shameful expedient to survive? At that time, he had to support
not only his wife and daughter, but also his mother and sister, and the
letters seized from his sister show that the family was facing serious
financial worries.[115]

Despite the fact that Laponneraye was no longer very influential in the
revolutionary milieu, he had been one of the mentors of the Republican
Party, and was still undoubtedly a big catch for the government.

AFTER THE BANQUET: A WAVE OF ARRESTS

Just as he had planned, Gouhenant left Toulouse after the banquet at
Capoul's, accompanied by Laponneraye and Dubor, the print worker and
delegate to the banquet from the neighboring town of Agen. The purpose
of their trip was to continue the inspection of cities in the southwest

before Laponneraye returned to Paris. The three men's trip lasted three days until they arrived in Agen, and from there, Laponneraye left for Paris alone, while Dubor and Gouhenant continued their inspections in other southern cities.

Aside from the informer's numerous reports, the police had no material evidence of the existence of a plot, and it was too soon to launch arrests of the revolutionary leaders in Toulouse. Meanwhile, Spanish revolutionary Abdon Terradas was in a precarious situation because he had circumvented the obligation imposed by the French government to remain temporarily in Perpignan.

The day after the banquet, police lost his trail, and it was not until January 18 that Commissioner Boissonneau learned from his spy that Terradas was still in Toulouse. Finally, by order of the prefect, he was arrested on January 26 at the home of a man named Soulès, with the other two Spanish refugees who accompanied him.

His arrest initiated a wide dragnet that would suddenly ensnare the southern revolutionaries. When police searched Terradas, they found the letter from Gouhenant inviting him to the banquet.

The contents of the letter were incriminating due to the fact that they revealed the existence of the "southern division," and of "delegates" from the neighboring municipalities and also from Paris. Yet, the letter could only be used as one piece of evidence to support a charge of illegal association. The police were well aware that they did not have enough substantial evidence to prove a conspiracy, but once they made the first arrest, they had no choice but to order additional arrests of the main leaders before they would have time to hide or destroy more incriminating documents. Still, Gouhenant was their primary target and arrest warrants were issued for him in all the cities he was visiting. Police subsequently searched his apartment in Toulouse.

Once the revolutionaries learned of Terradas's arrest they immediately sent an envoy to Auch, to intercept Gouhenant on his way back to

Toulouse. They were hoping to find him before the police did. Unfortunately for Gouhenant, the authorities had at their disposal an effective means of communication—the Chappe telegraph. The electric telegraph was still in development and not yet used in France. The Chappe telegraph however, was available and it utilized a network of towers bearing hinged wings at their top. The position of the wings represented a kind of alphabet for transmitting a message from one tower to the other, then deciphered once it reached its final destination. The transmission was not as close to instantaneous as Samuel Morse's electric telegraph would be just a few years later. Still, the authorities used it to send a message to Toulouse and it was received less than a quarter of hour later in Agen. By comparison, it would have taken twelve hours for the same trip by coach.

The envoy did not have enough time to warn Gouhenant. On the twenty-seventh, at two in the morning, the police broke into his hotel room in Agen and arrested him before he had time to destroy incriminating documents, including the letter from the revolutionary committee in Lyon and a list of individuals, which would subsequently be used to target searches of the other men.

Even before the announcement of the arrest, panic spread among the revolutionaries in Toulouse. The police report from January 29 stated:

> The whole party is in turmoil and they are continuously running, meeting at every moment to communicate the news [...] Emissaries went last night and some others are still leaving this morning. The delegates have been warned. The arrest of Gouhenant was not known last night, but it will be today, with the emissary sent to Agen being back soon. Everyone is trying to get away, section leaders burned all the papers they had at home. There was one hope that Gouhenant might have been met in time to make him destroy important and compromising papers he had on him.[116]

Anxiety gripped not only the Republicans; the police were also worried about the course of events. The police report further urged the prefect to accelerate the searches: "The speed in such affairs is everything, do not

waste time, march forward, otherwise we will lose half our opportunities."
In many previous reports to the prefect, Commissioners Boissonneau
and Aumont had insisted that searches of the main protagonists should
commence simultaneously. Yet news of Terradas's arrest had traveled
quickly in Toulouse. Before police had time to analyze the documents
seized from him and to initiate massive searches, the Toulouse revolutionaries had destroyed or concealed evidence of the plot. Some of them
had fled, including Rolland, one of the most active of the revolutionary
agents.

The prefect had also ordered searches of the delegates' homes in
the neighboring department, but authorities were disappointed with
the results. The law required that arrest warrants or search orders be
issued by the judicial authority—the royal prosecutor, attorney general,
or investigating judge. In Toulouse, the prefect overrode the law and
launched his own order without waiting for the warrants. Following his
lead, the prefect of Agen then immediately ordered Gouhenant's arrest
before he received the proper legal authorization.[117]

In other departments, the authorities were more scrupulous in
respecting the law—especially when the suspects were from notable
families—and they were reluctant to act. This allowed the revolutionaries
to destroy or conceal incriminating documents. The dragnet did not
provide any truly tangible evidence to support the charges, apart from
the documents seized from Gouhenant. Still, one important detail from
the search of Gouhenant's residence revealed that he was receiving
some of his mail in envelopes addressed to an illiterate widow and the
mother of one of the organization's members, Hyppolite Resplandy. The
police intercepted all the letters arriving at her address and seized a new
letter from Lyon dated January 26 that was even more troublesome for
Gouhenant than the one the police had seized from him:

My dear friend,

Since our letter of the 9th, we are surprised not to have heard from you. Yet it was urgent before bringing together the delegates from various cities to decide such important things, to take all possible precautions so that all matters can be settled at this meeting.

We longed for this congress, for the benefit of general harmony, especially in the south on which Revolutionary France today particularly relies [...]

The Isère department is good and can assist with a movement, but we do not know its resources exactly, its main leader being in Paris.

Lyon has almost as many soldiers as people, but new theories have changed everything, factions are numerous, three associations are organized, we could unite with only one. Young Europe is headed by moderates, Communists, propagandists, and above all, Cabetists.

Thus Lyon, which six months ago was willing to be the vanguard, can only assist, or if something good was about somewhere, to send men (note that with its fortifications Lyon is in a unique position) [...]

Keep us informed of what will be decided, taking care to follow what we said earlier about the important things, dates and addresses.

Receive, citizens, the assurance of our sincere friendship.[118]

Both letters from Lyon were highly compromising for Gouhenant, and possibly for his correspondent although he had not signed them. The prefect of Toulouse wrote to his Lyon colleague who knew the revolutionary underground of his town well through his own informers, but their searches turned up nothing in Lyon. The main suspect there was Callès, who was "accustomed to the precautions required for his own security" according to the Rhône prefect.[119]

It would be difficult to support a conspiracy charge against one man, even if the letters from Lyon explicitly mentioned the existence of an association with subversive activities ready for action. In order to make their case, the prosecution needed to accuse more men.

Police sought the suspects with varying degrees of zeal. It is possible that not much effort was made to find one of the men, Balguerie, given his family's influence. The prefect of Bouches-du-Rhône even wrote to his colleague from Toulouse: "The parents of that young student are living in the town of Agde (Hérault) and from what I am told, are far from sharing his political principles. They want to force him to break off his bad relationships, to make him travel for some time abroad and request a passport to Italy. May I, without inconvenience, issue the passport if he appears in my office."[120]

One search that should have been made was at Laponneraye's home in Paris. It was of particular importance in the eyes of the investigating judge. The attorney general suspected that Laponneraye was a government informer but the investigating judge considered him to be an important suspect and wanted to hold off on a search.[121] Understandably, the minister of interior was not eager to worry his informer, and he wrote to the prefect on February 2: "I do not think there is at present any need to make house searches in Paris. The case of Toulouse and the southern departments should be limited, if possible, to these locations, and I think it is prudent not to link it to an overall conspiracy whose center would be in Paris. I would dread contributing to an already serious incident, and proceeding this way would not be without inconvenience."[122] But the judge persevered and police visited Laponneraye's home on February 25. By that time, he had disappeared, and his sister Zoé received the police. It had been almost a month since Gouhenant's arrest, and not surprisingly nothing very interesting came out of their search, except they did find a series of letters Laponneraye had written to his mother and sister between January 12 and 22 from his journey in the south. The correspondence contained nothing about a plot; it mainly stated that the trip was very tiring and boring. For investigators, however, it did provide samples of Laponneraye's handwriting that identified him as the author of a letter fragment found on Gouhenant.[123]

In that letter, Gouhenant was asked to send Sagansan and Rolland to Bordeaux to organize the *compagnonnage*. Up until that point, Gouhenant had denied everything and claimed that the letter had been written by a worker of one of his friends who had "thrown his ideas on that sheet of paper describing how to organize and normalize the *compagnonnage* in Bordeaux to address the interests of the working class."

After Laponneraye was identified as the author of the fragment, Gouhenant finally adopted what would become his line of defense:

> The truth is that I had called about thirty people from various cities to expose them to a system of compagnonnage and to organize it on a large scale, with their help. This compagnonnage was the merging of different workers' corporations, who do not get along, under a single patronage to thereby ensure harmony between them, work for the unemployed, relief provided for those who are unfortunate among them. This system was very charitable and would have even been approved by the government.[124]

But investigators saw the "organization of *compagnonnage*" as more conspiratorial than a mere workers' defense. Gouhenant's letter to Laponneraye dated November 15 was unequivocal about this: "We have won a huge victory by organizing all the *compagnons*. The line from Marseille to Bordeaux is ours. And what men! These *compagnons*! Strong, discreet, numerous, disciplined." This letter—provided by a police informant—could not be used in court proceedings because it would reveal the informant's identity. But the letter fragment that was seized on Gouhenant discussing the *compagnonnage* referenced Rolland and Sagansan, which ultimately led to their arrest as well.

Ten days after Gouhenant's arrest, commissioners Boissonneau and Aumont were far from the vast haul they had expected, and they were furious at the slow pace of justice: "It is really surprising, Mr. Prefect, that the investigating judge, having the names of the most prominent individuals (I have given him the list with observations) and the names of those who were part of the banquet ... has ordered no other arrests than these of Resplandy, Sagansan and Rolland."[125]

In fact, Rolland had also fled and was being aggressively pursued. Commissioner Boissonneau wrote to the prefect that he "attached great importance and self-esteem" to his arrest. But the prosecutors could not order arrests based on information given by the police alone. They did not know who the informers were, since Boissonneau and Aumont refused to disclose their names.[126]

A WITNESS FOR THE PROSECUTION

Since there was no progress on the arrests of suspected revolutionaries, the judge used another strategy to guide his investigation. One of the documents that had been seized on Gouhenant was a sheet of paper bearing the names of several cities in the south, each with a list of people's names followed by a few notes. The document seemed pretty innocuous, but many of the names in question were those of revolutionaries that the police had given to the judge and the prosecutor as being the "most prominent." So, the names were considered to be members of the conspiracy, and the prosecutor ordered searches of the homes of many of these men, without there being any additional evidence.

During the interrogations that followed, Gouhenant sarcastically said, "If the judge intends to pursue all those with whom I had more or less direct relationships, it should be feared that he will indefinitely prolong the investigation based on non-punishable facts."[127]

Some of the suspects on Gouhenant's list would later become witnesses themselves. The most important of these witnesses was Henry Dufaur. During the entire investigation and the trial, he was called Dufaur from Lombez, the name of his hometown, in order to avoid confusion between him and his distant cousin Pierre Dufaur. Pierre, one of the accused, was from Saint Frajou and was thus referred to as Dufaur from Saint Frajou.

Dufaur from Lombez was an activist for electoral reform, a movement that aimed to amend suffrage laws and expand the electorate by lowering or even canceling the required income threshold.[128] As such, he was already considered a potential revolutionary, but when his name was discovered on Gouhenant's list, it led to his indictment in the conspiracy case. Police searched his home on February 4. Dufaur was a private lawyer in Lombez and was seeking the lucrative office of attorney. The incident therefore created difficulties for him, and his democratic convictions were not strong enough to risk sacrificing his social ascent. In addition, two of his uncles were notables in Lombez; one was a sub prefect, and the other an investigating judge. Perhaps under his family's influence, he decided to cooperate with investigators, becoming the main witness for the prosecution.[129] In his testimony before the investigating judge, he described his meeting with Gouhenant, whom he presented as a revolutionary ready for violent action:

> Dufaur from Saint Frajou had received a copy of a petition from me for electoral reform in 1841, with a letter asking him to distribute the petition; this fact was known by Adolphe Gouhenant and was probably an opportunity for him to get in touch with me ... Dufaur from Saint Frajou gave me a letter from Adolphe Gouhenant ... It spoke about the need to use violence, on the grounds that the compact majority gained by the government did not allow hope for concessions on electoral reform. Gouhenant urged me to visit him, since he couldn't tell me everything in this letter ...

> My cousin told me about Gouhenant being a very important man sent from Paris. He called him General ... Dufaur himself hoped to become a captain. He belonged to a secret society which possessed weapons and ammunition he said, and spoke to me of an uprising being imminent. I made comments to Dufaur on the impossibility of success by these means. Dufaur's responses proved to me that he was a blind instrument. However I wanted to see Gouhenant, who as I said, spoke of violence, of overthrow as immediately

forthcoming, and for which the men he led in Toulouse were ready to act. They would seize the Armory in Toulouse and the powder store. Troops would be overwhelmed by this action and once the power was in the hands of the insurgents, they would march on Lyon and Bordeaux spreading the movement from city to city until Paris. Adolphe Gouhenant's language expressed faith in the success of the operation, and his determination.[130]

Gouhenant, questioned by the investigating judge on February 10, 1843 —just two weeks after his arrest—did not deny the statement made by Dufaur from Lombez. However, he attempted to minimize its importance by presenting his calls for violence as a subterfuge to maintain his influence with the most extreme revolutionaries. He claimed,

> At the time of the Toulouse turmoil, I was as today, animated by the purest feelings for improving the lot of the working class, and for many years I had created an influential position for myself among this class. In this moment of excitement, all enemies of the government got restless and there were many opinions on how to take advantage of these circumstances. Some proposed to act openly. In order to satisfy impatient men I had to entertain their ideas, yet without adopting them, and without losing the influence I exerted.

> Thus I had to write some letters that were seen in Toulouse where I may have asked influential men from nearby locations if they were willing to assist with a movement where Toulouse would be the center. ... When I saw Mr. Dufaur, the lawyer in Toulouse, I may have talked to him in the same way in order that my words would be repeated.[131]

Both the interrogations—the one conducted during the preliminary investigation, as well as the one during the trial—show that Dufaur of St. Frajou, was a simple, uneducated man, "a tiny intelligence in a robust body," as Cabet described him. He had only been an intermediary between his cousin and Gouhenant, who had mainly used him for distributing subscriptions to the newspaper *Le Populaire* spreading

Cabetist propaganda to the working class. Dufaur was certainly not a clever conspirator, and several witnesses said they heard him claiming openly that the government would soon be overthrown, and that he belonged to a communist organization that would install the Republic. Faced with this evidence during the investigation, poor Dufaur would only say, "If I said those things, I was wrong, but I do not remember." He was nevertheless accused, without any other charges against him other than his braggart statements and his role as a propagator of the Icarian doctrine.

A QUESTIONABLE OFFER

At the conclusion of the investigation, the prosecution had some very incriminating documents and testimony against Gouhenant, and he was well aware of it. Although he continued to deny any plot, during the interrogations he eventually began to oblige investigators by confessing to facts he had previously denied, such as the existence of the January 15 banquet and using the widow Resplandy as the cover for his mail. He did remain firm on the most serious charges; he claimed he was not the leader of any organization and that letters from Lyon arrived by chance. He testified that he did not know the author nor did he understand their meaning.

Feeling the noose tighten around his neck, he began a puzzling correspondence with the investigating judge and even the prefect. It was possibly an offer to serve as an informant, but the style of his correspondence is so convoluted that the revelations Gouhenant was prepared to impart to authorities are completely beyond reach. It might also have been a way to divert the judge's attention away from the actual case, as Gouhenant would argue much later, when he told his story to Victor Considerant.[132]

The first of his letters was dated February 11, 1843, and was addressed to the judge. Gouhenant had reached his boiling point.

Mr. Investigating Judge,

Before limiting myself to the consideration of being a burden to
you, I have a duty to fulfill; I must fulfill it. Justice is presently
like a blind man who is abandoned in the middle of a vast plain
who after spinning around three times, goes to the north to find
his cottage which is actually to the south, the more he walks the
more he is lost.

I do not have the heart to see with indifference the prosecution you
are leading against completely innocent people, and yet I would
not stop an evil from occurring by committing a worse one myself.

But thank God I found a way to reconcile it all; it is a way that
I must tell you. Perfidy and betrayal have no place in it, you
can be sure, I would rather die than cause any pain even to my
worst enemy. However if you think it would be compromising
to the dignity of your character to give me a private interview I
would not object if the Royal prosecutor and the Prefect would
accompany you. I will even be glad to speak before you all [...]
After hearing me, you will tell me if my proposal should be taken
into account or if you believe it to be useless. In the first case your
task will be fulfilled, the investigation will end in one day and
the broken order will be restored. In the second, I would leave
Justice groping and cut from the social body its healthier and more
valid member, while the sick member will have time to carry its
fatal gangrene to the heart, because the truth is, the social body is
suffering. It is given neither to you nor to the most active police
nor to the strongest and most skillful government to find the
illness and cure it. Only I know the sickness and the remedy, I
repeat that everything can be reconciled without hurting anyone
and by making good to everyone. The main basis of my proposal
is the utmost discretion. If you three were to hear me you will
understand the importance of my secret. If it was known that I had
a meeting with the Prefect, that would be enough to take away all
the means in my power and that I want to give to the State, and
it would be a great misfortune, a very great misfortune, within
six months, I would not be surprised to see the land covered in

blood and smoke!... My goal is also to make the investigations and prosecutions against people who have something to do with me stop immediately. A second condition is that you do not let one day pass without hearing me. So, have the kindness to warn the prefect, the Royal prosecutor or the Attorney General; come together to the prosecutor's or the court's office but please, without the assistance of the clerk or the police commissioner [...][133]

Of course the judge rejected the extravagant request to speak to the prefect; he conducted the interview himself, accompanied by the royal prosecutor and the attorney general. Gouhenant was very upset and he confided to the police commissioner Aumont, knowing his words would be reported to the prefect:

[The attorney general] approached me with these words: "Oh Gouhenant! You are a great criminal! Remember that you are in the presence of your judges, speak, all your words will be recorded"; And since I could not make a written denunciation I confined myself to discuss the situation in France in general terms, taking care to say something occasionally to persuade these gentlemen to accept the goal I had set for myself when I summoned them; but they did not understand me. The Attorney General told me that I was like all the guilty ones, who once they are caught, try to escape by making disclosures etc. etc. Now they put me in the position of not being able to talk to the Prefect and having to wait until the judgment is pronounced to be able to do so. This is unfortunate; he alone, I believe, would have understood!... I alone know everything and can inform on the rich and highly placed persons who are in the revolutionary movement in Marseille, Bordeaux, Lyon, Nîmes, etc. I alone can finally disclose the whereabouts of the 500 guns from the factory of Saint-Étienne and two barrels of gunpowder that were gathered by partial purchases of one and two kilograms at a time.[134]

The proposal to provide the names of rich revolutionaries and disclose the cache of weapons could have lured the prefect into an agreement, but he did not take Gouhenant's words seriously, and his request to speak with him was denied yet again. Gouhenant then gave the commissioner Aumont another letter on March 2, which he passed on to the prefect:

Mr Prefect

You probably know the reason why I was arrested, and the status of the investigation; so you must already see that Justice has missed its mark. I, who know better than these gentlemen how the things of Society are going, and where the seat of evil lies, my heart bled with pain when I saw Justice striking so many innocent people.

So I thought I fulfilled a holy duty to protest against the measures taken, and I would even have wanted to take upon myself the responsibility of everything but I have not been understood.

About a fortnight has passed since I wrote a letter to the judge asking him to put me in touch with you, and as a courtesy to the Bench, I added the royal prosecutor or the attorney general. But my astonishment was great when, instead of seeing you, I found myself in the presence of Mr. Attorney General, the royal prosecutor and the investigating judge. I was even puzzled by their presence, not wanting to communicate what I wanted to say to you alone, and besides, the way they talked to me has completely removed any desire for me to enlighten them.

Today I address myself directly to you to ask you to grant me an interview.

I have to tell you things of the highest importance for the security of the State. It is only you that I want to tell, relying on the well-known loyalty of your character to be able to recognize the services I am going to provide to the government, and those who are even more important that I will provide later.

Not daring to trust to any in the house to give you this letter, fearing another disappointment, and considering the deep secret that must be kept from our interview, I gave it to Mr. Aumont who promised me he would deliver it to you only. I hope for a positive answer.[135]

French judicial archives do not contain other letters, but in a report to the prefect dated July 25, 1843, Commissioner Aumont stated, "I have the honor to send you a letter that Gouhenant handed me this morning." Aumont's words indicate that historically, there were more letters. Once the revolution of 1848 broke out, some of Gouhenant's letters were published in *L'Émancipation* in an attempt to prove his betrayal. Unfortunately, there is no comprehensive collection of the newspaper in French libraries and the issue containing the transcription of these letters is not available.

The prefect never answered any of Gouhenant's proposals, which he considered worthless. He later wrote to the minister of the interior long after the case was over,

> Upset by the isolation in which he was left, [Gouhenant] would have offered his services, and would have urged me to accept them. But the isolation itself made these services useless, though he claimed he had close ties with the committees of Lyon and Paris. This is not a man that we should take on faith, and I could dismiss these advances without inconvenience. Your Excellency knows Gouhenant; he is active, clever, resourceful; he knows the art of simulating every feeling, inventing facts that could serve his purposes, concealing those that might hurt them. Thus, endowed with the spirit of intrigue, existing only through that, he could successfully serve a rich and powerful party if he put himself at its disposal. He would then be a man to watch carefully.[136]

THE END OF A LANGUISHING INVESTIGATION

During the months of February and March, the investigation progressed very slowly. The young Hippolyte Resplandy, one of the first arrested after police discovered he had given his mother's address to Gouhenant to use for correspondence, admitted to having participated in the banquet, corroborating Gouhenant's claim that it was only a Masonic meeting. This would be the only evidence against Resplandy. On March 1, Rolland was finally arrested at an inn in a small village near Toulouse. He and Sagansan were two hardened men, not easily intimidated, and their interviews provided no evidence for the prosecution. Nothing had been found on them or in their home, and they would be accused on just two pieces of very flimsy evidence: the presence of their names on Laponneraye's letter fragment, and their many trips to different cities in the southwest.

The judge continued to question people whose names were on Gouhenant's list including a young student named Piquemal, more malleable than the two robust *compagnons*. Piquemal quickly denounced Balguerie, who was still at large, and also a man named Bruno Cucsac, a lithographer and painter from Toulouse. Both had allegedly proposed that Piquemal become a section leader in the Communist Association of Toulouse. Although there was no question of conspiracy in Piquemal's confession, Cucsac was immediately arrested. He denied any involvement, but would later be charged based solely on Piquemal's incriminating statement.

Stagecoach records had shown that a young twenty-four-year-old shoemaker named Bertrand Perpignan, whose name also appeared on Gouhenant's list, had made a trip to Auch the day of Terradas's arrest. The prosecutor needed no more evidence to accuse him of having been the emissary sent to warn Gouhenant and he was arrested on March 15. Police found a revolutionary leaflet in his home that was similar to those the informers had already provided to the police, and also a draft of a naive and convoluted letter to Cabet. While the content had nothing compromising, it would be entered into evidence and mocked during the trial.

The prosecution was so scattered that they hunted for the smallest piece of evidence, such as the number 61, hand-written on the leaflet. The same leaflet had been found on Terradas, but numbered 81. Further, a handwriting expert tried to prove that the two numbers were from the same hand, and pronounced it was none other than Gouhenant's.

Another month passed before one of the fugitives, Dubor, was arrested in Condom on April 17. During searches of his home, police found nothing significant, apart from a few subversive songs. In police custody en route to Toulouse, he spent a night in jail in the small town of L'Isle Jourdain. Several days later, authorities found a few scribbled lines in his cell ending with the words, "Louis Philippe you will die!" He denied being the author, but the prosecution seized upon the opportunity and used the graffiti as evidence against him.

The other fugitives would never be arrested. Three of them, Lamarque, Manein, and Balguerie, presented themselves to the police in August a few weeks before the trial was scheduled to begin. Imbert, meanwhile, had fled to Belgium beyond the reach of police, where he would live for many years. Shortly before the trial, Imbert wrote a letter to *L'Émancipation* in which he denied any revolutionary project:

> Having been away from Brussels for a long time, it is only now that I read in your valorous newspaper, the 8th of this month, the charges that the prosecutor in Toulouse imposes on me, an alleged communist plot. Not willing to get into a discussion of principles that would lead me too far, I will only tell you what everyone who knows me already knows, that Mr. Cabet never counted me among his followers. One of my letters to Mr. Gouhenant was indeed seized, but what did this letter contain to agitate prosecutors? [...] Is it because, in this letter, I asked him if he wanted to walk with us or with Mr. Lap...? The silence that Mr. Gouhenant has kept proves that he preferred the communism of Messr. Cabet and Lap... to the political and social principles I was charged to make known to him; but I repeat, there was no question of association or conspiracy between us; it was only to distribute brochures among the people for their moral and political education.
>
> [...] I deeply regret that the business of the company I represent keeps me in this country, and does not allow me to sit next to

my political friends on the benches of your circuit Court. I would have been proud to share in their captivity, being confident that the informed jury of Haute-Garonne will bring justice against the monstrous accusation led against us.[137]

In the letter seized on Gouhenant, there is no instance of Imbert asking "if he wanted to walk with [them] or with Mr. Lap...."[138] This phrase reveals that Gouhenant and Imbert had probably exchanged several letters, but Imbert did not know which one was seized. It also shows that after Imbert's trip to Toulouse there must have been some ideological discussions between the two men. Imbert was not a communist and all he cared about was the republican organization in Toulouse that Gouhenant had set up. It is clear from the police reports that the purpose of their activities was significantly more than "to distribute brochures among the people for their moral and political education."

Imbert and Laponneraye would ultimately be tried in absentia in March 1844 and sentenced to five years in prison.[139] Imbert, forced into exile, continued to promote socialism internationally, and became vice president of the *Association Démocratique ayant pour but l'union et la fraternité de tous les peuples*, founded in 1847. The other vice president was Karl Marx.

Once the revolution broke out in 1848, Imbert finally went back to France and participated in the fight. However, the democratic spirit of the revolution rapidly faded away, and the most zealous republicans entered in resistance against the authoritarian president Louis Napoléon Bonaparte. Imbert was arrested on January 15, 1851, and put in jail in Lyon with several other republicans. There he fell sick and died after three weeks in prison. His funeral in Lyon was attended by several thousand.[140]

As for Laponneraye, it is unclear how he managed to evade his sentence in 1844, but he probably had the government's protection. He retired from politics and devoted himself to his historical work. His whereabouts are unknown until the revolution of 1848 when he eagerly jumped into the revolutionary fray, becoming the director of the journal *La Voix du*

Peuple in Marseille. Due to his poor health, however, he was unable to sustain his journalistic efforts and he died on September 1, 1849. A huge procession accompanied him to the cemetery; and if there were "slanders" printed about him in the obituaries, the republican newspapers did not contest his status as "veteran of the democracy." Imbert himself, who had been closely involved with the Toulouse conspiracy, and whom Laponneraye had exposed in another letter to the Minister of Interior, paid a warm tribute to him in *La Voix du Peuple*.[141]

On June 5, 1843, after an investigation lasting more than four months, the attorney general ordered the prosecution of seventeen out of fifty-one men who were more or less involved in the case and a date for the trial was set. Ultimately, the indictment chamber held twelve men who were brought before the Circuit Court: Gouhenant, Terradas, Rolland, Sagansan, Dubor, Resplandy, Dufaur of Saint-Frajou, Perpignan, Cucsac (all of whom were already detained), and Manein, Lamarque, and Balguerie, who would turn themselves in later that summer.

CHAPTER 5

THE TRIAL

The circuit court was opened on August 1843 to try the accused. It was presided over by Mr. Justice Moynier, whose outspoken language, wooden leg, impatient and irascible mood was legendary within the courthouse at the time.[142]

Jean Baptiste Dubédat, 1889

IMPRISONED ARTIST

In 1843, Etienne Cabet described Gouhenant as "a painter, art dealer, 38 years old. His face is stern and impressive, his long curly hair, his thick blond beard, his moving eyes, indicate an artistic and impressionable nature. His big, pale and calm forehead reveals passions that are now extinct. His speech is elegant, easy and accurate, like a man who studied and thinks much. His costume of black velvet, with its smooth cuffs and its white collar, gives him the appearance of a character from the Middle Ages."[143] Gouhenant had been imprisoned for six long, agonizing months before he and his codefendants were finally brought to trial. During the time between his arrest on January 27 and the trial, which began on August 21, he claimed he was held mostly incommunicado. This was likely an exaggeration. Gouhenant was a strategist and he was quite clever in his use of the press to bring attention to his plight. On March 30, having already spent two months in prison, he somehow managed to get a letter published in *L'Emancipation* describing his detention in very dark terms. His verbose, rambling tirade was at least successful in triggering a discussion among officials.

> After sixty days in jail... under the most rigorous confinement... without any kind of communication... no news... without a quill, without a pencil... nothing that could stop my ardent imagination, which is a thousand times more active in isolation than in the midst of the world; absolutely deprived of air, and almost of light, forced to endure the cold or to be choked to death, and in a small room of six by seven square feet, one half occupied by the bed, and the other by a simple chair, a table and a small jug of water; my strength was exhausted.

> A few more days and you would have accompanied one more martyr to the field of rest; not that I lacked the courage and resignation, I have never found so much energy in my soul.

> Just two days ago, I returned to life, I was able to get out into the courtyard, but alone, always alone. I only have the pleasure of seeing my child and the young man who is managing my workshop. I use this opportunity to dedicate my first words to those who care about me. If you have been told that I was complaining about my suffering, you have been deceived. It is a lie ...

> Oh! I am not complaining, I do not blame anyone, I ask for mercy! Mercy at the foot of the desolate mother who grieves to see her only son torn away from her. I ask for mercy to the young bride who has seen her husband caught the very day the hand of the Lord was to unite them. Mercy to the father, snatched from his five children he left destitute. Mercy to all of you who have been persecuted!...

> I too have suffered much; because I am also the only son of an old mother who may have died of grief after the news of my arrest! I am also the father of young children, who are now orphaned and

under the care of some charitable souls, my industry suddenly stopped, my workshop... ruined...

Finally, the days of darkness are almost gone, and the shock is over. Do not cry good mother, or you grandchildren, always pray fervently for our Master, and soon He will return, I hope, dearest ones.

Don't blame me anymore, because I am not guilty, give me back your esteem and friendship, I will devote my whole life to becoming worthy, and make you forget if I can, all the evil you have suffered!... In this sweet hope I have the privilege of being yours truly.[144]

In response to Gouhenant's impassioned letter, the attorney general in Toulouse flatly denied the harshness of his confinement. Nevertheless, he did request the judge and royal prosecutor to investigate the circumstances of his detention.[145]

Police reports show that the police commissioner made statements to the royal prosecutor, the prosecutor to the attorney general, and the attorney general to the minister of justice. Their letters indicate that after the allegations were investigated, they all more or less came to the same conclusion denying before the minister of justice that Gouhenant had been locked in a dungeon for sixty days.

The officials' description of his conditions, at least from April when the attorney general ordered the inspection, differ from Gouhenant's description. Gouhenant conceded that by the time the inspections were carried out, his situation had improved. However, the prison keeper as well as the judge, said that as early as February Gouhenant had already been allowed to communicate with his son and his employee in the presence of the police commissioner.

It is impossible to know the precise conditions of Gouhenant's imprisonment in Toulouse during the first few weeks. Nevertheless, it is almost certain that from the end of March he was confined to a small cell of

approximately thirteen by eight feet, with an eight-foot ceiling and a
large window measuring about five by two feet.

CABET ENTERS THE SCENE

It is surprising that Gouhenant was able to get his letter published
in *l'Émancipation*. Jean-Baptiste Raulet, the manager of the journal, had
been his rival for leading the Toulouse revolutionaries, and he might not
have been so eager to help his adversary. However, Gouhenant's arrest
was followed by many others and the republicans needed to unite. Raulet
and Jean-Baptiste Paya—another republican leader and the editor-in-chief
of *l'Émancipation*—both had ulterior motives in defending Gouhenant.
According to the prefect, their goal was to ask the famous Toulouse
lawyer and republican Chamber representative, Henri Joly, to defend all
the accused including their leader, Gouhenant. Joly was a non-communist
republican, and if he had taken the defense of a notorious Icarian, it would
have weakened the communist influence on the republican movement
in Toulouse.[146]

As early as February 1843, although the inquiry had just begun, the
national newspapers were talking about a communist plot and Cabet
decided to defend Gouhenant and the Icarian doctrine. Gouhenant then
refused Joly as his defense lawyer. The same day he sent his letter to
l'Émancipation, he wrote another one to Cabet that was subsequently
published in *Le Populaire*.

> Monsieur Cabet, I have before me, only since yesterday, the last
> two issues of *Le Populaire*. In one of them you say: If Mr. Gouhenant
> deceived us, we would disown him. — No, sir, I did not deceive you,
> the following will prove it: I have never compromised your name
> nor your writings. My arrest is a mistake, or a pretext, which was
> used to lead prosecutions against some honorable citizens, who
> were probably offending some statesmen. I have neither known
> nor helped any secret society, nor plot, nor violent project. I never
> said: "You have 4 francs set aside: buy a pound of powder! You

have 10 francs set aside: buy a gun" — But I said: "You have 4 francs set aside: buy a copy of Travel in Icaria! You have 10 francs set aside: take subscription to *Le Populaire.*" This is the whole truth. Among twenty or thirty thousand people I know, and who have known me for twelve or fifteen years, you will not find one who would dare to testify against me. I fear no one, the truth is too strong not to overcome. Do not disown me, Mr. Cabet, for that would be striking the strongest of your children![147]

Cabet answered immediately, "If there is, as I believe, no conspiracy and no secret society, if you are just persecuted, whatever the appearances and whatever the persecution, I will support you." However, he was not eager to get involved in such a cause that might compromise his doctrine without Gouhenant's complete confession.

Over time, Gouhenant gradually sent Cabet a series of letters that ultimately made "a large volume containing accurate details of his religious and socialist opinions, the accusation, the procedure, the evidence, the interviews, the answers, etc."[148] This "large volume" has unfortunately been lost, but Gouhenant did convince Cabet of his innocence. After his explanation Cabet was still a bit hesitant, and on July 4, he wrote a letter claiming he was "convinced that there is no plot," but "if, during the debate, a conspiring secret society was proven [he] would not defend him."

Gouhenant answered,

> No, my dear citizen, there is no plot, there is no secret society. I told you all the charges against me; I have omitted nothing, hidden nothing, and even forgotten nothing; but you should be completely comfortable because once you see the court proceedings, if you find something that repels you, you will always have to defend our doctrine ... I have requested you because I know that Icarian Communism will be vigorously attacked by the public prosecutor, and that it could not be well defended by an anti-Communist or even a non-Communist lawyer, however clever he may be; I want you because, although I have courage, heart, energy, perseverance, and though Dubor is motivated by the same feelings as me, we

are not strong enough. Not learned enough to fight against our enemies ...

Do not believe it ever entered our minds to justify ourselves at the expense of the truth: I would rather be condemned as Communist Icarian than be discharged as a propagator of subversive ideas who would repent what he might have done.[149]

Gouhenant had convinced Cabet of his innocence. But Cabet also saw the trial as a potential forum for his doctrine. On July 14, he convened a general assembly of the shareholders of Le Populaire. They approved his decision to go to Toulouse and act as Gouhenant's counsel and to represent two other accused men: Dubor and Perpignan. They also voted unanimously to solicit funds among the Icarians to bear all the expenses of his travel and stay in Toulouse. This solicitation met with a great deal of success in France and abroad, collecting the significant amount of 1,272 francs.[150] By the beginning of August, Cabet was ready to leave Paris for Toulouse.

The non-communist Republicans in Toulouse, led by the l'Émancipation owner and manager, Paya and Raulet respectively, were also raising funds to support all the imprisoned men, but because Gouhenant had refused to be defended by Joly, they decided to stop supporting him.[151] Furthermore, just prior to the trial on August 5, the president of the circuit courts, François Joseph Jean Moynier, met the accused. Moynier was an imposing figure. A former officer in the Napoléon Great Army, he had been wounded in 1813 during a battle in Saxony and his leg was amputated.[152] Moynier asked Gouhenant the name of his counsel, and when he answered "Cabet!" the president cautioned him: "I must point out to you that according to Article 295 of the Code of Criminal Procedure your counsel should be chosen by you or appointed by us, among the lawyers or attorneys of the Royal court of Toulouse and its jurisdiction, and since it is important that you are able to communicate at the earliest possible time with your counsel, I appointed Mr. Gasc to defend you."[153]

Moynier's decision struck Gouhenant like a thunderbolt, seeing his defense suddenly compromised. His idea was to take advantage of the court's approach to attack communism, which would relegate the conspiracy plot to the background. From Cabet's perspective, he had lost access to the forum that such a trial offered for promoting his Icarian doctrine. He told Gouhenant that the judge could not apply the clause that prohibited the choice of a defender from outside Toulouse, because the article was outdated and no longer in use. The legal newspaper *La Gazette des Tribunaux* shared Cabet's opinion on the outdated clause.[154] But Moynier did not wish to see the trial become a political platform, and when he later wrote to his minister, he justified his decision by explaining that he had used "the power that the law gives the president to remove everything he considers unnecessary in order to discover the truth."[155]

Cabet was an experienced lawyer, and when Gouhenant wrote to warn him about Moynier's decision, he replied in a reassuring letter, "Do not be afraid ... this is obviously the President's mistake ... do not doubt, the President and the Court will serve justice."[156]

Cabet finally arrived in Toulouse on the evening of August 19, to discover that two opposing parties were hostile to him: the president of the court, whom he knew, but also the non-communist Republicans from Toulouse. The latter argued that the communist doctrines would scare the jurors and the accused men would be lost. According to Cabet, the local Republicans had pressured the accused families to give up choosing him as their defender.

The same night he arrived, Cabet went to Moynier, accompanied by Republican lawyer Jean Gasc, who had been assigned to replace him. Despite several meetings between the three men, Moynier persisted in his decision forbidding Cabet to defend Gouhenant.

Cabet then visited Gouhenant in prison to give him the text of a protest to read at the beginning of the trial. For the press, it was not yet clear that Cabet would be prohibited from serving as Gouhenant's counsel, and on the twenty-first, the *Journal de Toulouse* announced that Gouhenant, Dubor, and Perpignan would have two counsels: "Gasc, Carivenc and Beautes for the question of the facts, Mr. Cabet for the question of principles."

While it was not clear what the "question of principle" would legally mean, the prefect did not hesitate to repeat this expression in a letter to the minister of the interior.[157]

The Trial

At 11:00 am, on August 21, 1843, in a densely packed and uncomfortable court room, the trial commenced. The *Gazette des Tribunaux* had reported on the atmosphere surrounding the trail,

> The public, at first indifferent to the plot, the existence of which they have long ignored, and who do not understand much more its extent and nature today, have discussed for several days the new drama that will unfold before them. On walks, in cafes, as well as in private meetings, it is all about communism, community system, and about the high priest of the doctrine, Mr. Cabet, who arrived within our walls yesterday ...
>
> In the morning the area around the courthouse is cluttered with a crowd more curious than excited. Two elite companies of the 14th line regiment serve to provide order inside and outside.[158]

During the trial, Léon Soulié, a painter and one of Gouhenant's friends who had been briefly interrogated during the investigation, made two drawings, one depicting the twelve accused, and the other showing the part of the room where all the interested parties were installed. The public does not appear in his drawing, but if the number of characters, magistrates, lawyers, jurors, defendants, soldiers, and gendarmes are counted, it is clear that there is a crowd of about one hundred people packed into the back of the room. The oppressive heat of August was stifling. In fact, within the first hours, Terradas's sister, whose charm

struck the journalists, fainted and had to be carried out. The same would
happen to the robust Sagansan, just a few days later.

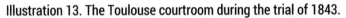

Illustration 13. The Toulouse courtroom during the trial of 1843.

Copyright Conseil Départemental de la Haute-Garonne / Archives Départementales / 37 FI 17 / Drawing by Léon Soulié.

Adding to the already densely packed room, pieces of evidence piled
up at the foot of the president's chair: "2 guns seized in Gouhenant's
workshop, one rusty and without the firing mechanism, that he used
to draw with charcoal, the other, with a bayonet, which he used for
his paintings; 2 hunting rifles seized from Dubor; 2 national guard
swords!!!"[159] The rest of the physical evidence consisted of brochures,
books, and communist newspapers—all published legally—scattered about
on display for upcoming arguments.

Cabet ignored the president's orders and appeared in court the first
day of the trial wearing his judicial robe and sitting with the defense. The
president made no comment and the debate began by reading the lengthy
indictment, followed by the president's address to the lawyers, "I warn
you that you cannot say anything that goes against your conscience,

and you should express yourselves with decency and moderation." In making these comments, the president addressed the defenders' bench where Cabet sat, being sworn to the Court along with the other lawyers.

Gouhenant misunderstood the situation and believed that his counsel was finally accepted. In response, he abandoned his resolution to read the protest Cabet had given him earlier that morning, and instead answered the president's interrogation. His defense was the same he had adopted throughout the investigation: The January 15 banquet was purely Masonic, and his actions had never been anything other than to promote the *compagnonnage*. It did not take long for the debate to focus on the most compromising documents, the letters from Lyon that had alluded to the plot. The attorney general then led the attack. Gouhenant could of course deny neither the existence of the letters nor their content, but never being short of aplomb, he invented a story to explain how he could have received such correspondence without being complicit in what it expressed. "I would have great difficulty giving you an explanation. I have never corresponded with the Lyon committee, and I do not know why such letters were addressed to me, unless they came to me from some enemy. Here is what I can only assume: while in Toulouse some time ago, I met a young man who was from Lyon. We talked much about socialism; I also spoke about Icarian communism, to which I belong. I may have been misunderstood; it is perhaps the origin of the letters which were sent to me from Lyon."[160] The prosecutor tried to back him into a corner by citing excerpts from the letters showing collusion between him and the author, but Gouhenant held fast to his position and persisted in his defense stating, "I have never been able to understand from where these letters came." The battle between the two men did not last long and was interrupted by an incident that would have a decisive impact on the course of the trial.

Continuing his attack, the prosecutor read an excerpt of the second letter from Lyon in which they complained that in their town, the Cabetists were only propagandists and were paralyzing the revolutionary action. This was precisely the phrase that Cabet had hoped the prosecutor would introduce: If the revolutionaries had written that the Cabetists paralyzed their planned violent action, then how could they have been moving forward with a violent conspiracy? At that point, he sprang to his feet, launching his argument, but the president interrupted, admonishing him sharply: "You are not the counsel Mr. Cabet. When you came to me, I told you I thought it inappropriate to allow you to offer your support to the accused Gouhenant who requested you, and I gave you the reason. I have not changed my mind since yesterday. Therefore, I invite you to leave your place on the bench."[161]

A legal debate then followed between President Moynier and Mr. Gasc, the counsel assigned to Gouhenant. Gasc embarked upon a passionate diatribe, showing that the application of the clause invoked by the president was contrary to the spirit of the law, and that the two other lawyers who were admitted to the defense bench, Joly and Rousseau, were no more registered with the Toulouse Bar than Cabet. The audience immediately sided with Cabet and within minutes the overheated judicial hall erupted in near-unanimous applause.

The attorney general entered the fray, asking the court to clear the room and to close the remainder of the trial to observers. But the president responded by merely threatening to empty the room, and the debate resumed. Aware of his fragile position, he then presented another argument: after having read an article in which Cabet stated, "If any trace of conspiracy or association was shown in the course of the debate, he would desert the cause of the accused, regardless of the consequences," Moynier could not risk leaving Gouhenant without legal defense, and thus officially assigned Mr. Gasc, one of the most experienced lawyers in Toulouse as his primary lawyer.

Gasc easily countered President Moynier's argument; if Cabet were to abandon Gouhenant's defense, then he would take over, but in the meantime, since the prosecution had decided to focus on the communist aspect of the conspiracy, he argued that Cabet alone should be allowed to defend Gouhenant. Cabet tried to argue in turn, but the president interrupted him, and with a scathing rebuttal shouted, "Sir, you are nothing here!" Gouhenant, who was silent until then abruptly raised his objection: "I ask for Mr. Cabet. I request him only. For four months I have corresponded with him on my case. Only he knows it in its entirety with all the details. He alone therefore can take my full defense. So, if I am refused to be represented by both him and Mr. Gasc, whose talent I honor as well, I declare that I will not answer, I consider myself therefore as forced and coerced, and I solemnly protest against this abuse of authority."[162] Gouhenant's declaration made a strong impression on the public, and when the court retired to deliberate for a moment on the incident, agitation reigned in the room.

Once the court returned, it was announced that the president's decision was approved and the incident was closed. The president told Cabet he would allow him to attend the arguments: "I will see later if there is any need to let you speak in Gouhenant's interest." But the head of the Icarian Communists could not accept being relegated to second chair. "It is a right to which I claim use, not a tolerance. Consequently, I protest, and I retire."

Despite his outburst, Cabet was not yet ready to give up his platform. The president, while denying him the opportunity to serve as the defender, inadvertently provided him with a powerful weapon. For the duration of the trial, Cabet sent the attorney general a series of open letters published in the Toulouse press, discussing the case point by point, but also defending his doctrines. He would never have had such a public forum if he had simply acted as Gouhenant's counsel.

The prosecutor tried to resume questioning Gouhenant, but just as he had proclaimed, Gouhenant refused to answer. The prosecution was then completely disarmed. The only really incriminating documents and testimony were related to Gouhenant alone. The examination of Dubor, the only other one interrogated the first day, was a prelude to the insanity of the debates ahead.

Illustration 14. Portraits of the accused during the trial of 1843.

Copyright Conseil Départemental de la Haute-Garonne / Archives Départementales / 37_FI_17 / Drawing by Léon Soulié.
Gouhenant is bottom left.

The next morning, the judge tried to convince Gouhenant to reconsider
his position, but he held steadfast, "I will be silent. I am not a man to
change his resolution in twenty-four hours, and I beg you not to even
bother to question me." The day's inquiries brought no new elements to
light, and none of the accused was compromised in the least.

On the third day, Gouhenant adopted an even more provocative
attitude, ostentatiously reading a newspaper during the trial and earning
a reprimand from the president. Indeed, the judicial session was almost
as dull as that of the previous day. Only the testimony of the main
prosecution witness, Dufaur from Lombez, might have been able to
destabilize Gouhenant, but since he still refused to speak, there could be
no debate, and the testimony fell flat. In the minutes of the following
session, it seems boredom was beginning to overtake the audience. The
Journal de Toulouse reported, "The most important witnesses have already
been heard, and public attendance decreases. The defense pleadings
that will start in a few days will probably present greater interest."

The monotonous litany of interrogations and testimonies continued. Public emotion was aroused only for a moment when the priest of La Daurade parish in Toulouse testified on behalf of Gouhenant's peaceful behavior during the case advocating for Chavardès tombstone in July 1842. Gouhenant himself seemed very moved, and the president took this opportunity to try to get him out of his silence, but got only these few words, "I would answer in any other circumstance, and I feel the deepest regret not being able to do it today. I thank the priest for everything he has said in my favor; moreover, his story is perfectly true."

On the fourth day, witnesses only said that the accused "dealt with communism." Perpignan acknowledged having written a letter to Cabet. It was a naive letter full of misspellings and poor syntax, which the attorney general took pleasure in reading, triggering laughter from the room. On the fifth day, the examination of witnesses continued, revealing nothing new. The attorney general questioned the witnesses essentially on ideological issues that had no direct connection with the alleged plot.

The next day, the crowd returned to the trial, which had progressively languished, and in the sweltering heat, the prosecutor read his indictment for a staggering seven hours over a period of two days! After a long political preamble, he insisted upon focusing on Gouhenant's path of "wandering." He described the collapse of his business venture, the observatory in Lyon, and the financial assistance he had requested from the Duke of Orleans to finalize its construction. The prosecutor then proceeded to attack Gouhenant's character. He insisted upon criticizing "the fluidity of his opinions, which left him relying on the luck of the draw," of his "power to fascinate and his authority, [his] great facility of speech, and [his] proven calm." He recalled the revolutionary past of the two accused in absentia, Laponneraye and Imbert, whom he presented as friends of Gouhenant. Before turning to the actual facts, he focused on the subversive content of Laponneraye's works that dared to call Robespierre a "Martyr!" He finally attacked the Icarian doctrine itself.

During the second part of the indictment he tried to prove the reality of the conspiracy and especially Gouhenant's guilt as its organizer, citing the flimsy evidence provided during the investigation.

The arguments grew weaker against the other defendants, who were essentially accused of having been in touch with Gouhenant, having participated in the banquet, and of being subscribers to *Le Populaire.*

Cabet, white hot during those long hours, stood up as soon as the general attorney finished reading the indictment, and asked once again to speak. But the president would of course not reverse his decision. In a theatrical move, Cabet then requested to be seated with the accused, stating, "My name was mentioned several times; false accusations were made against my principles!" When he was refused once again, he stormed from the room to write another letter of protest that would be published the next day in all the Toulouse newspapers.

Cabet had won the battle of public opinion. He had managed to turn the case into a forum for his ideas, and in his open letters, he jumped at the opportunity to respond to the attorney general's attacks on the Icarian doctrine and the president's refusal to let him speak. The conclusion of Cabet's last letter confronted the judge and the attorney general with their contradictions:

> But be consistent! if the doctrine is criminal, I am the first to be guilty, the main one who is guilty, the most dreadful and inexcusable guilty one. Why did you not arrest me from the beginning? Is it fair, moral, exemplary, to indict my victims, and allow me to be free and unpunished? Set them all free, and accuse me alone with Gouhenant! I asked earlier, and I ask you again! I will answer you, we will answer! This doctrine that you do not know, and that is nothing other than Christianity in its most primitive purity, may captivate you as it has already captivated many, as strong as you!...
>
> But you are backing down, Mr. Attorney General, before the discussion, before the light, before the truth! You shrink before

the Icarian doctrine! Well! I tell you, the doctrine will overcome you! It has already overcome you!

By refusing to hear me as a counsel, you condemn yourself. Refusing to prosecute me and hear me as the accused, you bring death to your own accusation.[163]

After Cabet's exit, the assistant attorney, Ressigeac, finished reading the indictment.

The prosecutors had presented their case over a two-day period and it would take another three days for the eleven defense lawyers to present their arguments on behalf of each of the accused. It was Gasc who spoke first. He was officially responsible for both Gouhenant's and Dubor's defense but after the surprising turn taken by the debate, he stepped into the breach Cabet had opened:

Mr. Cabet was constantly accused during the debates, and still he was denied the floor to defend himself; Mister Gouhenant is accused, and he was denied the right that all the other accused had to choose his own counsel. I have no mission to advocate for either one or the other; but associated with the cause for Dubor, my client, could not I speak of them, when the first is the soul of the defense, when the interest of the second is the interest of all the accused? Yes, I speak for those who do not, who cannot, defend themselves because their innocence is ours, their freedom is ours.[164]

The remainder of Gasc's argument was a long defense of the Icarian doctrine until the end when he "demolished the prosecution in an impassioned improvisation that captured everyone's emotions."[165] At the end of Gasc's plea, applause broke out in the room and the attorney general again requested the room be cleared, which the judge denied.

The die was cast, there was nothing left to defend, other than secondary characters of the alleged conspiracy, upon whom no significant charges had been weighed. The arguments followed one after another, presenting one as a "young man, brave, open to the new ideas, but not letting his zeal overcome him," the other as a "simple man, strong and rough, father of a family dreaming of a better future for his children." One of the defense counsels mocked the accusation of possessing weapons of war, showing the two swords and broken guns, "Ah! I am not surprised if the conspirators wanted to seize the arsenal. Obviously, it was not without need!"

Finally, on August 31—ten days after the trial began—at five in the afternoon, the jury retired to deliberate. Jurors had to answer forty-one questions regarding the partial or complete guilt of the accused on four crimes: conspiracy against the security of the state, proposal to participate in a conspiracy, unauthorized association, and unauthorized possession of war weapons. After two and a half hours of deliberation, the Court returned and the jury foreman broke the silence in the courtroom, reciting the same answer to each question and responding forty-one times with the answer "no" —not guilty.

The room erupted in applause one last time, and the "considerable" crowd that had gathered outside the courthouse welcomed the decision with shouts of joy. Apart from Terradas, who was held in custody by order of the prefect, all the prisoners were released immediately.[166] The attorney general could not hide his bitterness when he reported this conclusion to the minister of justice: "We had to hear the bravos of the crowd gathered near the palace and attend, defeated, to the triumph of the wicked devices and most pernicious doctrines."[167] The president, who also wrote to the minister of justice, admitted the weakness of the conspiracy charge, which he considered indefensible. On the other hand, he regretted that the charge of unauthorized association was not upheld. In fact, he told the minister that five of the twelve jurors had actually answered "yes" to that question, and it was a close call that Gouhenant was not condemned. Had he been found guilty of this single offense, the penalty would have been a sentence of two months to one year in prison, and a fine of fifty to one thousand francs, a sum he would undoubtedly not have been able to pay.

AFTER THE TRIAL

According to a letter from the prefect of Haute Garonne to the minister of justice, Gouhenant ended his misadventure completely discredited among the revolutionary circles in Toulouse and "in the most awful misery."[168]

The reports of Commissioners Boissonneau and Aumont do not mention Gouhenant at all after the trial. It seems from these reports that the revolutionary party of Toulouse remained divided into rival factions in which several accused from the trial were still very active. For instance, Balguerie and Rolland took the lead of the non-Icarian communists opposed to the bourgeois republicans as well as to the orthodox followers of Cabet.[169] The names of Perpignan and Sagansan also appear in the reports as having participated in secret republican meetings.

The police reports concerning the political surveillance in the department of Lot-et-Garonne, to which Nérac belongs, have not been kept. It is thus not possible to know for certain whether or not Gouhenant had any revolutionary activity there. However, there is no doubt that he remained close to Dubor,[170] who was still politically involved in revolutionary circles. Commissioner Boissonneau's report from March 7, 1847, claims that Dubor had been sent by some revolutionary committee from Nérac and Agen to visit Toulouse to inquire on the organization in this city, and that he had been told there were one thousand men of action ready to fight in Toulouse.[171]

Gouhenant may have kept in contact with the revolutionary movement along with Dubor, and certainly the authorities considered him a suspect. The central commissioner Segon from Agen—the very one who had arrested Gouhenant in January 1843—wrote a letter to his counterpart in Toulouse in August 1845, leaving no doubt about this fact: "The communists do not fear us at all here, more than once I have been able to show them that I knew them well and that I was watching them. The arrests of Gouhenant and Dubor proved it to them. However, if you learn of any attempt of their part, which should raise my suspicion, I beg you to let me know it."[172] Gouhenant's wife would later claim in a letter to Cabet that after his release, Gouhenant had been "persecuted by police harassment."

Even though Gouhenant may have been tempted to continue his revolutionary activism like Dubor, he officially adopted the "orthodox" line of Icarian communism. After the trial, Cabet claimed that Gouhenant had "publicly expressed his appreciation to [him] and called [him] his guide, his first judge, his venerated father."[173] There are very few sources on Gouhenant's Icarian activity; his name was never quoted in *Le Populaire* between the end of the trial in September 1843 and the beginning of the Icarian emigration process in 1847. However, he remained so well known that a letter he sent to Cabet in 1847 was published under the title "letter from Gouhenant" without any further description of its author.[174]

The Nérac census in 1846—the only official census made during the period from 1843 to 1848—shows that Gouhenant was living alone with his son Ernest. The imprisonment and subsequent trial were likely the breaking point for Gouhenant, and perhaps for his wife as well. At some point the family had split. Just before the beginning of the trial, Gouhenant had written a letter to Cabet where he claimed that his daughter "in her boarding school was suffering as much as [himself], isolated, without support, without help, without consolation" and that his "young son, abandoned, has run the risk of falling into delinquency."[175] Of course, Gouhenant's usual hyperbole should be considered since he wrote in the same letter he had been kept "far from his octogenarian mother, who was on the verge of dying, and who asked [him] to give her the last farewell"—the same mother who would live another twelve years. Still, the fact that he mentioned his mother and his two children, but not his wife, was definitely a sign that the relationship between the two spouses was strained.

Jeanne and Anastasie's whereabouts in 1846 are a mystery. How were they surviving? Jeanne probably did not return to her parents' home in Feyzin, since the census does not mention her presence there between 1843 and 1848. Letters she would later write to Cabet in 1848 were sent from La Teste de Buch, a small town close to Bordeaux. In any case they did not fall into poverty because in 1853 Anastasie would marry Charles Houry in Paris. Houry was from a family belonging to Belgium's intellectual elite. He was a painter and also involved in a successful ceramics business with his brothers.[176]

It would have been close to impossible for Gouhenant to still support his family. In the same letter he also wrote that his collection of paintings had been auctioned off at a low price by inexperienced people while he was imprisoned, and it had been the source of his ruin. More than the sale of his own art, it was his work as an art restorer that was his major source of income. As Cabet wrote, "Gouhenant's trade as a painter-restorer required him to travel [and] buy old paintings at a low cost to restore and resell them with profit (often very great)."[177]

He resumed this profitable activity once in Nérac, and it appears that he managed to bounce back with substantial impact. During the July Monarchy, only the wealthiest citizens were able to vote, and in cities of fewer than 10,000 inhabitants like Nérac, the richest 10 percent voted in local elections. In 1843–45, Gouhenant was not among the local electors of Nérac, but his name did appear on the list in 1846. Thus, between 1843 and 1846, he rose from total ruin to the wealthiest 10 percent of Nérac's citizens, even increasing his income in 1847.[178]

Gouhenant's name also appears in the town's judiciary archives. Throughout his wanderings, wherever he went, he challenged the boundaries of the legal system. For instance, in 1846 and 1847 the register of the Nérac civil court mentions a trial between Gouhenant and David Dutilh, who was the nephew of Louis Dutilh, the representative of Nérac at the

National Assembly and one of the wealthiest citizens of the city. But, neither the cause of the case nor the result is known.[179]

One of Gouhenant's key traits was his ability to bounce back after a disaster. He had been able to recover after his bankruptcy in Lyon as well as after his ruin in Toulouse. Gouhenant's resilience would certainly be a salient criterion for Cabet when he would soon select a leader of the avant-garde for his utterly fantastic project—building a real-life Icaria in Texas.

Illustration 15. Map of France showing departments.

Copyright Emmanuel Pécontal.
The towns where Gouhenant lived (Flagy, Lyon, Toulouse, and Nérac) or where his presence was recorded (Chalon-sur-Saône, Marseille, Le Havre, Paris) are indicated. The small village of La Teste-de-Buch where his wife was living in 1848 is also shown.

Part 2

A Long Journey (1848)

CHAPTER 6

A Utopian Paradise in Texas

Robert Owen, Etienne Cabet, Thomas Hughes, and other European social reformers looked to the United States as a place where their ideal society might take root and flourish.[180]

Jyotsna Sreenivasan, 2008

THE EMIGRATION: HOPE IN A NEW LAND

For a time, Cabet had considered the idea of transforming France into a communistic society through a new constitution that he hoped would be accepted by the French people. However, at the end of the 1840s, as the monarchy was becoming more and more repressive against the republicans and socialists, Cabet became convinced that a transformation was not possible. In April 1847, he wrote a small announcement in *Le Populaire* entitled, "Great Confidence," where he said he would soon disclose a solution to address the ongoing persecutions. Then in May, headlines shouted, "Allons en Icarie!" introducing a series of papers proposing emigration to a new land to establish his utopian Icaria.

Cabet extolled the perfect conditions for the new colony, describing a "virgin land, unsoiled, which will offer us the treasures of its fertility." In the fall of that year, he traveled to London and met with the Welsh social reformer, and one of the founders of utopian socialism, Robert Owen.

Cabet needed to settle on a destination—quickly. He had inquired among his colleagues to help him find a location and the first person he turned to for assistance was Owen. The two men's ideologies were not that far apart, and since Owen had already tried to start a communist experiment in the United States—the short-lived New Harmony in Indiana —he was well acquainted with the country. So, Cabet was not the first to choose the United States for a utopian colony. In addition to Owen's attempt, there had been colonies in the Ohio Valley and on the East Coast of the United States several years earlier. Unitarian minister George Ripley established Brook Farm and Amos Bronson Alcott, father of Louisa May Alcott, had also founded a settlement in Massachusetts. There were others. But, Cabet had no intention of setting up another experimental colony. His goal was now to found a communist nation somewhere in America and to start with 10,000 to 20,000 Icarians.

Although he had spent five years in London, Cabet was far from fluent in English, and he needed an intermediary to facilitate communication between him and Owen. He approached an old companion from his days in exile, Dr. Camille Berrier-Fontaine, who had remained in England and knew the London socialist circles very well. Berrier-Fontaine introduced Cabet to Charles Sully—one of the few socialists in London who were receptive to Cabet's emigration idea. Sully not only became the intermediary, but he would also become a major player in the Icarian adventure.

Although generally described as a zealous Icarian, faithful to Cabet's doctrine, Sully was an activist in the social fight long before he met Cabet; he was an Englishman who had fled to France in the 1830s for personal reasons and once back in London after returning from exile, he started advocating for a communist emigration to North America, several years before the idea occurred to Cabet.[181] In 1844, his Democratic Co-operative Society for Emigrating to the Western States of North America met each Sunday in a coffee house in Covent Garden, London.

The spirit of this movement was radically different from Cabet's, since it was described as "the first association of its kind which had made the rejection of religion one of its principles of union."[182] Since becoming a fervent Icarian sometime between 1844 and 1847, Sully, who had once held fast to atheism in the communist doctrine, redirected his focus, and began following Cabet, who considered Christianity to be the most fundamental aspect of communism. However, it is possible that Sully was mainly attracted to Cabet's doctrine because of the Icarian emigration project—regardless of its Christian spirit.

Sully had discovered Cabet's project in the May 9, 1847, edition of *Le Populaire.* He then sent a letter that appeared in *Le Populaire* on July 4, where he offered his services to help prepare the emigration, and pledged allegiance to Cabet:

> Dear Citizen and Revered Father
>
> In the present status of Communism, your Confidence is the necessary thing; thus I had the greatest satisfaction in reading it, and I felt that my mission was to work for the achievement of your intentions ...
>
> A Communist emigration to America has been the subject of my studies for several years; for the past three years I have been convinced that it is the true means of salvation for our race and the only possible way to establish the Community. My goal was then the establishment of a Communist state in America ... I am entirely at your disposal and at your orders, as the pupil submits to his master, the soldier to his officer, the son to his father... Thus I find it is my duty to promise you fidelity and support, and I will keep my word.
>
> Charles Sully

A valuable recruit to assist Cabet with preparing an emigration to America, Sully was fluent in both English and French, he knew the challenges associated with such an endeavor, and he was a sturdy and

very devoted man. But his personality—the exact opposite of Gouhenant's
—would later lead to a dramatic confrontation between the two men.

One of his friends, socialist John Ludlow, described Sully as "spare,
gaunt, hard-featured, yet with a sweetness in his very rare smile, he
certainly looked the revolutionist he had been." Ludlow stated, "I never
knew a man upon whom one could more thoroughly rely for carrying
out any duty which he might undertake with as much discretion as
resolution."[183]

THE PETERS FAMILY: LAND SPECULATORS AND MORE

Robert Owen had talked to Sully about his discussions with a man
named William Smalling Peters regarding his proposition to settle a
community in Texas, and they decided to present it to Cabet for his
consideration.

Born in England, W.S. Peters was the co-founder of the Texas Emigration and Land Company. He had immigrated to America and was largely
responsible for bringing together a binational group of men who had
petitioned Congress to engage in a contract offering large parcels of land
to immigrants under the condition that they stay and settle the land. Cabet
traveled to London in September to meet Owen and other businessmen
who were proposing to sell tracts of land in Texas. In fact, Cabet was
close to reaching a deal on a contract for 50,000 francs for a vast parcel
of land on the Gulf of Mexico with a man named Snider de Pellegrini,
but Peters was offering a much more compelling deal: free land.[184]

When W.S. Peters met with Cabet, he was trying to fulfill the contract
obligations that he and his colleagues had first proposed to the Fifth
Congress of the Republic of Texas back in 1841. Collectively, Peters
and his group consisted of twenty American and English investors who
convened to attract settlers to the Republic of Texas. During that time,
only about 50,000-60,000 white settlers lived in Texas and the country was
in severe financial crisis. There were just a few population centers, such

as Galveston, San Augustine, Harrisburg, old Nacogdoches, San Felipe, Columbia, Bexar, and Indianola. The dubious mix of low population, lack of sufficient revenue, unrest between settlers and Native Americans, and threats from Mexico to retake Texas kept land values down. All these factors led the Texas Congress to establish the *Empresario* approach to land policy. Empresarios were immigration agents who contracted with Mexico to select colonists, allocate land, and oversee law enforcement in Texas lands. In exchange, the Empresarios received vast amounts of land for each 100 families they settled. The Peters Colony proposal, mimicking that system, emerged as a potential solution to the new Republic's settlement problems.[185]

The Peters contract with the government was complex. There were four contracts over a period of seven years and the terms and conditions changed multiple times with each iteration. Even the trustees and the name of the contracting company would change over time. As the terms of each contract were renegotiated, among other things, the size of the land grants would shrink while the boundaries of the overall colony would expand requiring the contracting agents to settle more colonists within the boundaries of Peters Colony.

The stipulations in two of the contracts would greatly impact the Icarians. First, was the stipulation set forth in the third contract signed in 1842. President Sam Houston strategically inserted a new clause reserving each alternate one-mile square section of land (640 acres) for the government. In so doing, he was investing in large reserves of land that could later be sold by the government at a premium price once the Peters Colony contract expired. This stipulation would also make it impossible for immigrants to acquire large contiguous tracts of land. In turn, the contractors would also reserve alternate sections, further expanding the practice of fragmenting land allocation. The company then went one step further and decided to give only 320 acres—half sections— to the migrants who were expected to buy the second half later at a high price once the colonization would have made the land more valuable.

The second stipulation put forth in the fourth or final contract set July 1, 1848, as the termination date of the company's agreement with Congress. So, when Peters met Cabet in the fall of 1847, very little time remained to establish the Icarians in the colony.[186]

Illustration 16. Diagram showing the distribution of the land parcels in a Peters Colony township.

Sections reserved for the Texas Government.

Half sections reserved for the Peters' Company.

Half sections opened for settlement.

In addition to land speculation, the Peters family had an interesting background in American music and river boats that would later coincidentally link to Gouhenant's story. Peters had come to America along with his family, including several of his sons and sons-in-law, who comprised most of the American petitioners of the Peters Land Company. While William Smalling Peters appears to have been chiefly responsible for promoting the colony, one of his sons, William Cumming Peters, was the most musically talented member of the family. W.C. Peters was a music teacher and composer, and he also published several songs by American composer Stephen Foster. The Peters family was acquainted with the Foster family, who were both living in the same area of the Ohio River Valley. Stephen had traveled to Cincinnati in the 1840s to take up work at the Irwin and Foster Steamboat Agency where his older brother Dunning was employed as a steamboat agent. Dunning brought Stephen on to keep the company books. During the time Stephen spent in Cincinnati, he wrote several compositions that helped to make him famous. W.C. Peters claimed he was among the first to recognize Stephen Foster's musical talent and in 1848, W.C. Peters published Stephen Foster's composition, "Oh Susanna," one of his most famous songs.[187]

The Peters group was offering the irresistible enticement of free plots of land and ultimately, Cabet was convinced. Consequently, Cabet announced his decision in Le Populaire on September 26, 1847, that the colony site would be in North America and that the final destination could be reached "by traveling first on the sea, then on a big river."[188]

Once he arrived in London, Cabet learned about the conditions of the Peters grant, specifically, the details of the awkward land distribution and the requirements for the immigrants to occupy the land by the rapidly approaching deadline of July 1, 1848.

As Cabet was negotiating with Peters, it was decided to send one or two men to Texas as soon as possible to gather information. In September, Sully was chosen for the task. Berrier-Fontaine thought it was too big a responsibility for just one man, and he proposed that another man should join Sully. However, on October 4 Cabet wrote to Berrier-Fontaine, "for all this, there is a question of money. We will be very rich someday, but in the beginning, we have many expenses and yet few resources." Cabet's goal was to send several thousand Icarians to Texas in the upcoming year. In reality, he was not successful in raising the funds for even two men for the preliminary expedition, and to the chagrin of Berrier-Fontaine, Sully had to leave alone for the exploratory mission.[189]

Sully had been working diligently since offering his services to Cabet and he had met with several people in London who were able to share potentially helpful information. Among them was American traveler and artist George Catlin, whose portraits of Native Americans were being exhibited in Europe at the time. In another letter to Cabet, Berrier-Fontaine mentioned the contact between Catlin and Sully: "you should also see with no delay mister Catlin whom Sully told you about, and ask him for letters of recommendation from persons he knows concerning America but also the Indian chiefs he has known. Sully has a good idea, it is to advise these Indians to prepare themselves for the hunt of big game which would be used to feed the first emigrants and which would put them in a relation of reciprocal interest with these Indians."[190]

It is Texas

Although negotiations between Cabet and Peters were not yet finalized, Sully eventually left for America on December 3. The goal of his mission is not entirely clear; it would have taken months for one man traveling alone to explore a new country, make the necessary preparations, and to report his findings back to Cabet. On January 16, 1848—just six weeks after Sully left—Cabet printed his startling announcement in *Le Populaire*:

C'EST AU TEXAS

After having examined all the possible countries for a big Emigration, we have selected Texas, in its north-east part, as the most preferable concerning healthiness, temperate climate, soils fertility, vastness, etc., etc. We have already more than one million acres along the Red River, a beautiful river navigable up to our establishment; and we can extend indefinitely. [191]

The Icarians were stunned to read the announcement, but due to the increased persecution in France, they quickly became receptive to the idea.[192]

In his idealized description however, Cabet kept important details such as the checkerboard distribution of the Peters Colony land plots to himself. Still, he did mention the July 1 deadline in another part of the journal, "I negotiated with M. Peters who granted me one million free acres of land, along the Red River, if I could bring emigrants there before July 1." Whether by design, or from sheer negligence, he did not mention the requirement for the colonists to build cabins upon the land plots, but only to "bring emigrants there." It is astonishing that he imagined a settlement on discontinuous land, and to build the thousands of cabins needed to take legal possession of the million acres claimed before July 1. Cabet would later claim that he believed in good faith that he had been able to navigate around these problems during his negotiations with Peters.

Cabet and Berrier-Fontaine would still be unclear about this point three years later and would contradict each other in their explanation of the contract. Cabet wrote in December 1850 that Peters "finally consented, after many discussions, to give all our half sections in a block, at the East,"[193] whereas Berrier-Fontaine claimed in July 1851, "it was agreed that M. Cabet could take all the remaining land, the sections reserved by the government and the half sections of the Company at a predetermined price."[194]

In either case, it would have been extremely difficult to acquire one million acres under such conditions and send several thousand Icarians before July 1, since the first sixty-nine men would not even leave France until February.

Furthermore, Peters and his representatives were drawing an extremely idyllic picture of the possibilities for settling a community within the colony, and the information they provided was definitely not based in fact:

> The [tract of land] is bounded on the north, by the Red River, which is navigable more than seven hundred miles from its junction with the Mississippi, about three hundred and fifty miles above the mouth of the latter .... The heat of summer, owing to the constant refreshing breezes that blow over the country from the mountains or the sea, is not more sensibly felt than in the south of England; and winter is comparatively unknown.[195]

As the members of the avant-garde would soon discover, the Red River was navigable only up to Shreveport, just 180 miles from its junction with the Mississippi. Not only that, but regardless of the differences in climate between northern Texas and southern England, no mountain range or sea exists within hundreds of miles of the Peters Colony boundaries.

PREPARING FOR THE EMIGRATION

In November, Cabet had announced the establishment of a committee that would select the members of the avant-garde. This announcement was well received and many Icarians became candidates for the great journey. Gouhenant applied, yet even before the announcement he had sent a letter where he expressed his enthusiasm for the emigration in a laudatory tone.

> Very Dear Mr. Cabet,
>
> You are right, time is pressing, time is precious, enthusiasm is at its peak, it is wide-spread. Oh! How happy am I, me, after so much suffering! We finally realize our holy doctrine of fraternity.
>
> We will be able to come together, and always live together, we, who are your children. It will no longer be fiction, this name of

father we carry in our hearts for so long, without being able to say it every day with the tender filial embrace.

You are right to rely on your disciples, to dare to undertake everything with them. We will surround you with all possible care, our most tender, most devoted solicitude.

We will lighten the strain you will face again as much as possible. We will gather around you all the power of our hearts, our spirits, our devotion. And our efforts will be even stronger as they came from the depth of our souls.

Here, we are suffering enough to see you struggling at every instant with so many werewolves, without being able to make you a rampart of our bodies.

How many struggles, persecutions, attacks, you had and you still have to bear! What courage, what resignation, what strength you have shown for fifteen years! And no rest, no respite, no breaks. Where so much strength could be found, but in a soul toughened in the divine source of the good and the truth?

Courage, the time is coming when you will find the reward. You will enjoy it with happiness. Icarie! This is the goal.

Gouhenant[196]

The selection committee worked diligently during the last months of the year, and the number of men selected was published in successive issues of *Le Populaire*: nineteen men on November 14, then fifty-eight on December 5. A first nominative list finally appeared in the December 26 issue, containing only forty men's names along with their skills. Gouhenant was among them, described as a "painter, suited to doing many jobs."

As winter approached, the Icarians were involved in contests for designing Icarian clothing and for composing a national anthem. Although the main selection committee was centralized, there were many local committees that were organizing meetings and the feverish preparations had drawn police attention. The police considered the meetings to be covert revolutionary activity. As a result, they interrogated Cabet again in mid-December, and on January 5, his office was searched and he was thrown in jail just as he was returning from negotiating with Peters in London. The accelerated persecution was strong motivation for the Icarians to commence emigration immediately.

The selection for an avant-garde continued in January. The criteria focused on the candidates' skills, but also on their ability to provide the 600 francs to finance the travel. Cabet suggested that if an Icarian did not have the money, then another should pay for him. On January 23, *Le Populaire* reported that there would be a first avant garde comprised of forty, fifty, or sixty men. Ultimately, it was determined that sixty-nine men would depart at the end of January, Cabet having named Gouhenant as their leader.

In January, when Cabet announced the final destination to his followers, Charles Sully was long gone, already sailing to Texas with 3,400 francs in hand (about 700 dollars) to prepare for the arrival of the first advance guard. Sully had left France on December 2, 1847, and would arrive in New Orleans on February 3, the exact same day that the avant-garde would embark on their own travel. So, when the Icarians left France, they had received no communication whatsoever from Sully and really had no accurate knowledge about the land they were preparing to settle.

At the time of departure, Gouhenant had in his possession only one copy of the contract between Peters and the Texas government, and one copy of the contract between Cabet and Peters—which still had not yet been finalized since Cabet would not send his acceptance letter to Peters until February 6. In addition, Gouhenant was traveling under the assurance that a second advance guard of 200 men would follow in March.[197]

By early February 1848, he and the first Icarian group of emigrants had put the issues of France behind them and were on their way to America; in their wake a revolution ensued.

CHAPTER 7

JOURNEY TO ICARIA

They are called the Icarian Colony. Where they are to land we have not heard. We trust they will have better luck in their flight hither, than Icarus from whom they appear to have descended.[198]

The Galveston News, April 27, 1848

DEPARTING LE HAVRE, 1848

On Saturday, January 29, 1848, as midnight approached, sixty-nine men made their way through the frigid darkness. Just a few weeks into the New Year they were headed to Gare du Nord on the north side of Paris to board the train to Le Havre. Despite the late hour, a packed crowd of thousands was there in the large station hall to bid them farewell.[199] Traveling on the newly built rail line, they arrived at Le Havre the following morning. They soon began making preparations for their transatlantic departure, purchasing supplies and attending to final details. Their time in Le Havre passed quickly and by Wednesday, their stay was drawing to a close.

That evening a farewell banquet was held in their honor, at the Château-Vert, a lovely sea-side villa just a few kilometers outside the city. As dinner was winding down, a young physician named Charles Leclerc raised a glass to his fellow diners to toast the impending departure of the French Icarians. They toasted to the devotion of the Icarian dream and to the happiness of humanity. Tomorrow, they would depart for a new life in America.[200]

At nine o'clock the next morning, the port of Le Havre was bustling with excitement. The *Rome*, a three-masted, square-rigged vessel, weighing nearly 700 tons and just over 142 feet long, was about to leave the harbor. Built in Bath, Maine, and barely a year old, the ship was well equipped to make the journey across the Atlantic, and the crew was preparing her to embark. The captain, Robert P. Manson, was highly competent, having been at sea since the age of fifteen, and he had become known as a man of sterling character and uprightness.[201]

Among Captain Manson's 140 passengers, half were men of the first avant-garde. A second avant-garde would follow, then a third, and finally several waves of colonists bringing their families along. Their dream of Icaria would become a reality.[202]

Their leader, Adolphe Gouhenant, was now just a few days shy of his forty-fourth birthday.

As the sun was rising in the sky, hundreds gathered to view the spectacle. As they stood in the cold morning air, Cabet took their pledge.

Are you loyal adherents without reservation to the Social Contract?

Yes!

Are you sincerely devoted to the cause of Communism?

Yes!

Are you willing to endure hardship for the benefit of humanity?

Yes!

The men bid farewell to family and friends. The gendarmes checked their passports, then left the ship. On the stern deck, each man, wearing

black velvet tunics, grey trousers, and grey felted hats proudly sang the
"Chant du Départ Icarien."

> Arise, workers stooped in the dust,
> The hour of awakening has sounded.
> To American shores the banner is going to wave,
> The banner of the holy community.
> No more vices, no more suffering,
> No more crimes, no more pain,
> The august Equality advances itself:
> Proletariat, dry your tears.
> Let us found our Icaria,
> Soldiers of Fraternity,
> Let us go to found in Icaria,
> The happiness of humanity.[203]

The men who comprised this first avant-garde represented a variety
of arts and crafts. Gouhenant's fellow Icarians on the *Rome* were Henri
Levi, Bondidier Berthet, and Joseph Therme, all weavers. Twenty-one-
year-old Dieudonné Meslier was a baker. Jean Caudron was a farmer. Luc
Bourgeois was a tailor by trade, but listed on the passengers manifest as
a farmer. He was educated and may even have spoken several languages.
Elie Drouard was a young cabinet maker. There were also merchants, a
bookbinder, a saddler, and a coachman. There was a shoemaker named
Joseph Piquée and a Spanish physician named Rovira, who had been
sent to represent the Icarians from Barcelona. There were carpenters,
quarrymen, button-makers, a watchmaker, a blacksmith, a butcher, and
a man named Pierre Petit, who was also a painter. Eugène Rougier was
a lawyer as well as the secretary for the group. Alfred Piquenard was an
architect who had studied at the Ecole Centrale des Arts et Manufactures
in Paris and would later become successful on his own. Representing a
variety of trades and experiences, the youngest man was not yet twenty,
and the oldest was nearly sixty. The average age of the avant-garde
was about thirty-four.

Although not part of the avant-garde, two additional Icarians named Sénez and Herqué were also aboard the *Rome*. Each was traveling with his wife and young child. They would stop in New Orleans and later join the first wave of colonists that was planned to arrive in September.[204]

On February 3, 1848, the *Rome* embarked. As the ship sailed slowly out of the harbor, the men were singing. For some, it would be the last time they saw France, their families, or both. The names, ages, and professions of the sixty-nine men were:[205]

Francois Barroux, 35 Smith
Jean Bellet, 48 Farmer
Jacques Berson, 50 Farmer
Bondidier Berthet, 29 Weaver
Moïse Biltz (jeune), 25 Compositor
Cerf Biltz (aîné), 31 Chaser
Guillaume Bira, 28 Carpenter
Francois Boissier, 46 Ship Carpenter
Jacques Boissonnet, 36 Seaman/Farmer
Philippe Boué, 37 Tailor
Luc Bourgeois, 31 Farmer
Charles Buisson, 33 Plasterer/Mason
Jean Jacques Buisson, 31 Farmer
Jean Baptiste Cardot, 32 Weaver
Jean Baptiste Caudron (jeune), 24 Farmer
Francois Champeau (père), 41 Gardener
Pierre Francois Champeau (fils), 17 Gardener
Joseph Chauvin, 29 Saddler
Charles Cochard, 44 Buttonmaker
Louis Collet, 36 Merchant
Jean Conefray, 41 Mechanic
Joseph Crombez, 32 Saddler
Léon André Damours, 23 Farmer
Raymond Dargelas, 34 Carpenter
Pierre Doussin, 46 Blacksmith
Élie Drouard, 21 Coachmaker
Martin Esnault, 25 Shoemaker
Adolphe Gouhenant, 43 Painter

Pierre Grillas, 47 Cabinetmaker
Claude Guerin, 34 Cabinetmaker
Guillaume Guillot, 45 Farmer
Charles Hédouix, 24 Gardener
François Pierre Hidou, 45 Carpenter
Commeral Jacob, 34 Tailor
Pierre Labrunerie, 25 Smith
Charles Lafosse, 26 Gardener
Francois Larbalestier, 26 Farmer
Francois Layaux, 29 Joiner
Charles Leclerc, 30 Physician's Surgeon
Henri Levi, 37 Weaver
Elie Lucas, 27 Machinist
George Ludwig, 34 Bookbinder
Alexis Marchand, 34 Cashkeeper-Farmer
Jean Louis Marchand, 44 Tinman
Luigi Marinelli, 34 Farmer
Francois Maurice, 45 Tailor
Raymond Mazoir, 55 Coachman
Dieudonné Meslier, 21 Baker
Louis Moity, 26 Joiner
Jean Myet, 44 Agriculturist
Nicolas Paquot, 58 Farmer
Jean Baptiste Pasquier, 57 Farmer
François Paul, 25 Carpenter
Pierre Petit, 32 Painter
Alfred Piquenard, 22 Architect
Joseph Piquée, 27 Shoemaker
Eugène Rougier
Jean Luc Rousset, 39 Butcher
Juan Rovira, 27 Physician
Pierre Sacreste, 28 Farmer
Henri Charles Saugé, 31 Farmer
Edgard Sieyes, 32 Farmer
Léon Teyssier, 19 Watchmaker
Joseph Therme, 27 Weaver
Jean Pierre Thorel, 24 Farmer
Pellagus Uker, 27 Coachman
Van den Eden [age and profession unknown]

François Viardot, 45 Quarryman
Charles Félicité Waucherpfenig, 36 Tailor [206]

FIFTY-THREE DAYS AT SEA

From the ship, Gouhenant could see Cabet standing on the pier among the many friends and families who had come to wish the Icarians a *bon voyage*.

Chosen by Cabet as the delegate and leader of the avant-garde, Gouhenant was also responsible for overseeing a board composed of Raymond Mazoir, the two doctors Charles Leclerc and Juan Rovira, Eugène Rougier, Guillaume Guillot, Jean Jacques Buisson, and Jean Myet. Alexis Marchand was the treasurer.[207]

During the crossing, from early February to late March the Icarians kept two journals: a joint one, giving factual and consensus reports of the events on board, and another one written by Gouhenant that revealed his concerns. Gouhenant's journal provided a more accurate glimpse into the situation, which deteriorated rapidly after they set sail. Between the menacing weather, the diverse personalities of the men, and prevalent illness, the journey nearly reached a flash point.[208]

Gouhenant recorded his first entry on February 3. Not yet out of the channel, he remarked on the beauty of the water. Yet from that beauty, an ugly scene would soon emerge. As the evening unfolded, so did a sudden bout of seasickness among five or six of the Icarian brothers. By the next day, all but seven or eight were ill. The following day rain, high seas and contrary winds took their toll on almost everyone, including the doctors and cooks. After three days out, the wind died down and the ship began to tack. In an attempt to address discontent, Gouhenant decided to convene a council to establish some rules of order while on board. This would be one of the countless assemblies convened to discuss every single detail of the organization. Certainly, Gouhenant had been appointed as the leader of the avant-garde, but the communist rules compelled him to let the men make decisions by consensus.

Although they were Icarian brothers, they had come from different towns and villages and they were mostly strangers to each other. In Gouhenant's mind, following onboard policies and procedures would allow for much-needed structure and discipline during the long voyage.

On February 8, the seas were high, the breezes favorable, and they were able to depart the channel, but as another day passed, the winds changed once again. The rain, wind, and heavy seas took a toll on the men and the mood became increasingly foul after only five days at sea. Anxiety became rampant, not so much among those who were bedridden, but with those who were fighting fatigue and boredom. Gouhenant noted that the men seemed to be acting selfishly and egotistically, quite a poor start for the avant-garde of a communist society.

The second week began with more favorable winds, and Gouhenant was busy developing a plan to occupy the Icarians.

February 11th

The weather is better; convening of the Board to discuss the rules of the community.

February 12th

The head-wind took many of the brothers captive once again disabling them.

Nevertheless, I convened a General Assembly in steerage to let them know the rules of the Community with all necessary instructions

February 13th

The wind, which seems to bring a little calm, gives us countenances of expressions of joy and happiness. I take this opportunity to give a little party on board, inviting the captain and five passengers from Grenoble to dinner.

By mid-February, the weather seems to have improved and it remained fair for a good length of time. It allowed Gouhenant to focus on assessing the men's strengths and skills, and the various capacities and industries represented in the group. He convened a council to communicate his plan to organize the group into sections. Again, he called for a general assembly to share his plan on February 15 and 17.

At first, Captain Manson was biased against the Icarians, but later became friendlier with them. During all their travels, the Icarians would be naively confident in their ability to convert everyone to their doctrine, and they believed they were on the verge of converting Manson, "Our doctrines seem to be very agreeable to him, and he speaks of them with the respect of an almost converted man." More likely, the captain was happy to have among his passengers a well disciplined and autonomous group creating no problems aboard his ship. The Icarians were also cautious about their hygiene, and had strict health rules. Captain Manson asked Gouhenant and the two doctors to apply their sanitary regime to all the passengers.

By Friday the eighteenth, the *Rome* was sailing between the Azores and Spain with calm seas and a gentle breeze. The men met again to finalize the organizational sections and to elect a leader for each one. Trying to keep them occupied, Gouhenant ordered an inspection of the Icarian uniforms on Sunday:

> Today has been for us a feast day; at the invitation of the Delegate, after dinner all the Icarians have dressed themselves in their uniforms and carefully groomed. Then, they climbed on the poop deck, and queued in pairs by size order.
>
> ... We have begun our maneuvers before the whole crew and the passengers.

We have stopped all our chores and put away until tomorrow the evening classes. To close the day with a party, after dinner, the sound of the flute, the violin and the accordion welcomed all the Icarians to a joyful ball which lasted until ten at night.

On Monday the twenty-first of February, waves pummeled the ship, once again sending the men back to their hammocks. Gouhenant made a note in his journal observing the way in which the men responded and their various characteristics.

About the same time a great restlessness began to erupt and spread among the Icarians. Four or five of the brothers even grew hostile. By Saturday, anger was simmering and some of the men were disgruntled and expressed disapproval of the process. Observing their agitated state, Gouhenant's response was to appoint a committee for managing the food supply, composed of his opponents: Piquenard, Therme, Biltz the elder, Rougier, and Meslier. Most of them were well educated men. In addition to Rougier, the lawyer and Piquenard the architect, Biltz spoke fluent English and served as the Icarians' interpreter. Therme was a weaver, educated, and the local leader of the Icarians of Vienne in France. Any of these men were qualified and might have been nominated as the leader of the avant-garde, and they were constantly challenging Gouhenant's leadership.

Towards the final days of the month, Gouhenant recorded that the committees continued to complete the tasks he had assigned to occupy their time. He heard their reports on the inventory of the food. Then, he had them distribute flannel vests, and even appointed nineteen-year-old watch maker Léon Teyssier to collect and manage the men's watches, which he claimed were poorly maintained.

He held another board meeting and noticed that the difficulties among the Icarians were increasing and discussions were spinning out of control as the men became more embittered. He noted, "The ghost of the old world often shows its head: it is about the redaction of our journal.

Rougier claims he was appointed with the exclusive right to write it in his own way. Some wish to designate neither people nor events, others want more uniformity, etc... finally, to reconcile everything, it was agreed that the journal would simply narrate general facts of the crossing; we would do a joint letter to reassure our families, and send [Cabet] a separate informative letter." Gouhenant insisted that the board meet every day to keep an eye out, watching for the "germs" of opposition among them. After three weeks at sea, it appeared that the tension among the Icarians and the contesting of Gouhenant's leadership were becoming fretfully high.

In addition to the Icarians' preoccupation with the ongoing divisiveness, Captain Manson also expressed his concern about the bad weather and its impact on the duration of the trip. Gouhenant then decided to appoint a food committee whose mission was to come up with a standard menu, taking into account the amount of food stock for the rest of the journey.

The second week in March was dedicated to addressing the discontent, which still had not subsided. Gouhenant believed it was due to the fact that many of the men did not know the communist doctrine well enough, so he began a course on Icarianism. Establishing a routine as a means to quiet discontent, he appointed two new committees to occupy the brothers and to boost morale, making a special effort to console and praise the most desperate.

Finally, on March 17 the *Rome's* passengers saw land for the first time since they had left Normandy. They sailed along the coast of Santo Domingo, close enough to see the trees and houses on the mountainsides. After forty-three days at sea, it was a welcome relief for the Icarians, who wrote in their journal, "this scene charmed us all the day long, and we looked away from it only once the night fell and covered it with her veil." During the rest of the journey they navigated close to the Caribbean islands, sailing along the southern edge of Cuba before entering into the Gulf of Mexico on March 23. Three days later they reached the mouth of the Mississippi, where they could see the frenetic activity of the New World as they neared their destination:

> Everywhere ships, sloops cross each other in every direction; steamboats which proudly neigh; it is the most impressive sight; in the midst of so much magnificence, our hearts are galvanized with enthusiasm; the link between them seems tighter, and we feel full of new physical and moral strength. We are already sailing fast on the majestic river; a steamer which pulls two ships, one on the right, the other on the rear, came to tow us, and chain us on its left; we sail united and vigorously head up the river. All our brothers, all the passengers visit the steam boat and are very impressed by all the various aspects.

The romantic picture described in their joint letter contradicts the last part of Gouhenant's journal which shows how difficult it was to maintain the cohesion of the avant-garde until the end of this long journey:

> March 16, 17 and 18. The food committee did not want to make a complete report which forces me to convene the general assembly. In my view it was undiplomatic but I could not avoid it.
>
> March 19. Very long discussions with the various committees.
>
> March 20. General Assembly to determine the food to buy, etc. There I saw demands expressed that were unworthy of true Icarians who should be willing to withstand anything, even deprivations.
>
> March 21. Time has come to unpack the guns, and it was also a good way, by distributing them, to keep busy and to divert all the brothers, because nothing is more harmful than idleness aboard.
>
> March 22. Same occupation.
>
> March 23. In order not to let any of our brothers rest, I make them check all our trunks, listing everything, etc.

March 24, 25 and 26. Continual meetings. Revision of the committees. Instruction about what we will have to do during our stay
in New-Orleans.

The long and tedious journey finally ended on March 27. But the fifty-
three days at sea had sowed the seeds of discord among the Icarians that
would soon germinate in their new home.

CHAPTER 8

WALKING ACROSS TEXAS

THE BONHAM ROAD

The word "route" that I am using does not at all have here the
European meaning, for that is what they call the trail that you
have to follow, even when there is no roadway from the point
of departure to that of arrival.

Henri Levi, 1848

NEW ORLEANS, SPRING 1848

Somewhere in the North Atlantic, Adolphe Gouhenant had passed
his forty-fourth birthday under a full moon. Among the discontented
and anxious travelers, there was no celebration to mark the event; any
acknowledgment there might have been was overshadowed by strong
winds and even stronger emotions.

A few weeks later, on Monday, March 27, the *Rome* finally sailed into
port. At the time the Icarians landed, New Orleans was a bustling city
of over 100,000 people—the fourth largest city in the U.S.—owing much
of its economic success to the thriving southern cotton industry. As
fast as the cotton was being loaded onto vessels for export to Europe,
newly arrived Europeans were unloading their wares to begin their new

lives in America. The city had just recovered from one of the worst yellow fever epidemics in recorded history. In previous months, more than 2,300 people had died from the mosquito-borne disease and that year, another 800 would die.[209]

There was a well-established population of French descendants already living in New Orleans and against the backdrop of exotic Gulf Coast flora, the scent of freshly brewed coffee, baked bread, and other delicacies must have been a familiar and much-welcomed pleasure for the Icarians. Yet, among the familiarity, they may also have encountered scenes that would have been especially shocking to those who believed so intensely in equality. An English woman named Rebecca Burlend had also made a transatlantic journey some months before. She was repulsed by the manner of activity occurring in town on a Sunday and justifiably outraged by the scenes she encountered.

> The shops everywhere were opened, stalls set out in all directions, and the streets thronged with lookers-on more in the manner of a fair than a Christian Sabbath... Slavery is here tolerated in its grossest forms. I observed several groups of slaves linked together in chains, and driven about the streets like oxen under the yoke... The river, which is of immense width, affords a sight not less unique than the city. No one, except eye-witnesses, can form an adequate idea of the number and variety of vessels there collected, and lining the river for miles in length... The town itself, from its low marshy situation, is very unhealthy; the yellow fever is an everlasting scourge to its inhabitants, annually carrying off great numbers. As a trading port, New Orleans is the most famous and the best situated of any in America; but whoever values a comfortable climate or a healthy situation, will not, I am sure, choose to reside here.[210]

In fact, their stay in New Orleans would be brief. Charles Sully, who had landed two months earlier to prepare for the impending arrival of the avant-garde, had noted, "the question of slavery is even more dangerous to address than we supposed," confirming that the Icarians were quite uncomfortable with slavery existing in the country they planned to colonize. Yet, slavery would not be a problem the Icarians would have to address, for their obstacles would be too numerous in the coming days, focused primarily on their own survival.[211]

Some published accounts have claimed that as the Icarians sailed into the harbor, they heard the sound of booming cannons and assumed they were hearing a welcoming salute. Whether or not they heard cannons is debatable, but the celebration underway was marking a much more significant event and the men were not yet privy to the news already being celebrated by the French expatriates.[212]

Shortly after their arrival, they discovered that the local French population had been celebrating the end of King Louis-Philippe's eighteen-year reign and the dawn of the Second French Republic. Unbeknownst to them, Louis-Philippe had abdicated the throne on February 24, a mere three weeks after they left for America; they were in the middle of crossing the ocean at the moment the last French monarchy ended. News of the French revolution had reached the U.S. on a faster ship and was published in the New Orleans *Daily Picayune* on Friday March 24—just three days prior to their arrival. As new details emerged, the paper printed several stories with increased coverage. On Tuesday, March 28 an article stated,

> There was an intense excitement among the French population on the reception of the important news from Paris on Saturday [25th] Frenchmen might be seen in various parts of the city, interchanging congratulations with each other on account of the news, which they seemed to regard as the harbinger of better days for their native land. Every countenance seemed lit up with gladness and hope, and no news could possibly give them greater joy unless it should be that la belle France had permanently established a Republic.
>
> The tri-colored flag floated gracefully from all the French ships in port, from coffee houses, and many private dwellings. We

understand that several French houses were brilliantly illuminated on Saturday night.[213]

By the time the Icarians landed in New Orleans, the local celebration may have been largely over, but the situation created a new kind of chaos for them.

Gouhenant disembarked first and alone. The city was hot, but alive with energy in the French Quarter. For two hours he walked around, then he went to check for mail or newspapers, but there was nothing. He inquired about Charles Sully but got no information. He asked around for a man named Bandelier, to whom Cabet had written earlier asking for information about Texas. Still nothing. His other contacts, a man called Dominique Tessa who was Cabet's correspondent in New Orleans, and someone named Gardès, were nowhere to be found. Frustrated, Gouhenant did not know where to look next to find someone who might be able to help him coordinate and obtain the necessary information for reaching the land concession. When he returned to the ship, he instructed the brothers to dress in the Icarian uniform so they would be seen as a group when they disembarked. His strategy worked, and an hour later, the whole town knew that they had arrived. As a result of the maneuver, Tessa soon arrived to guide the Icarians and to instruct them in how to conduct business.[214]

Gouhenant learned that Charles Sully had stayed with Tessa from the third of February to the tenth until he left and headed up the Red River to Texas. Sully wrote two successive letters on February 19 and 20 that he sent to Tessa, which Tessa then delivered to Gouhenant. Both letters were dated from Shreveport, but neither one provided much in the way of logistical information. Gouhenant was extremely upset not to find Sully in New Orleans, but later wrote, "It does not stop us."[215]

CHAOS FOR THE ICARIANS

Their first days in New Orleans did not go well. As the avant-garde learned of Louis Philippe's abdication, they debated how to proceed. At this point, most of the men were heavily invested and wanted to continue with the established plan. Still, others were anxious to abandon the Icarian dream, and some immediately made plans to return to France. Of the sixty-nine men who arrived in March, five left the group right away: the doctor Charles Leclerc, farmers Jean Myet and Jean-Baptiste Pasquier, carpenter François Boissier, and the young architect Alfred Piquenard. Piquenard left the Icarians and headed back across the Atlantic where he would reconnect with Cabet. (He would eventually return to America.) According to Gouhenant, Leclerc was the leader of the five, and he was also accused of having fled with 400 francs and taking the pharmacy and all the surgical instruments along with him. Cabet would later declare Leclerc guilty of desertion and treason towards the Icarian community "under the fallacious pretext of a few disagreements with Gouhenant."[216]

Belonging to the upper class, Leclerc had been a recent convert to Icarianism, as shown by his application letter published in *Le Populaire*. He was more a republican than a committed communist, and his newly adopted political ideology was still fluid. The announcement of the revolution in France and establishment of a Republic was likely sufficient cause for Leclerc to return. In addition, his increasing rivalry with Gouhenant during the journey probably had reached a tipping point once they arrived in New Orleans and he left for good.[217]

While a few men left, two Icarians who had been living in New Orleans joined the avant-garde, a man named Paul Levavasseur, and another, named Dondot, a furniture seller who had been living there since 1830, and who had traveled to Texas before. Aside from the five deserters, the balance of the men decided to push forward and fulfill the dream of establishing Icaria.[218]

After the dust settled, Gouhenant drew upon his skills as their leader, organizing them to make preparations for an immediate departure. He noted in his journal that his mission was becoming very difficult, but his ample self-confidence allowed him to lift the men up and carry on.

> Fortunately, today, as in all serious events in my life, I have always remained calm. I convened the General Assembly, and I said, France has made its revolution, the Republic is proclaimed... We had to expect such would occur sooner or later. Yet, since the Republic does not want the community any more than any other government, we shall nonetheless continue the devotion to our work .... We will fulfill our mission! The second avant-garde may be delayed, but it will happen, we are certain, because between men of heart such as us, the promises and commitments are sacred. There is no human power, no reason, no excuse that can stop us.[219]

They remained in New Orleans for only five days, picking up supplies and making preparations for the second leg of their expedition. On Saturday, the first day of April, they embarked at six o'clock in the evening on the steamboat *Monterey*. The *Monterey* would take them on a three-day trip up the Red River as far as Shreveport, where Sully had posted his letters—the letters that Gouhenant deemed far too insufficient to use as the basis for any informed decisions.

When he had arrived in New Orleans two months earlier, Sully had met the town's small Icarian community—probably just a handful of men. Dondot, the furniture seller, and Tessa were among them. Tessa was the owner of a general merchandise store located in the Vieux Carré on present-day Decatur Street. Wilhelm Weitling, a well-known German communist leader, who was passing through New Orleans, was also there. Sully proposed to Dondot that he join him for an exploration to Peters Colony, but Dondot had declined. Subsequently Sully recruited another guide and left New Orleans on February 10, taking a steamboat up to Shreveport. It was well known to the inhabitants of Louisiana that the Red River was not navigable year-round above Shreveport, but Sully did not discover that disappointing fact until he arrived, finding the water too low to continue any further. He therefore had no other option but to walk more than 250 miles to reach the Peters Colony.[220]

For reasons not entirely clear, Charles Sully decided not to travel all the way out to the colony. Perhaps the journey was too difficult and too long for two men alone, especially for Sully, who although he was certainly a dedicated Icarian, was also a city dweller, and unused to the wilderness he encountered in East Texas. Sully was likely sick as well, since one of the first avant-garde, Joseph Therme, would later write to his Icarian friends in Vienne, "We have lost a lot due to the illness of Sully (illness that prevented him from doing more exploration) for we have been obliged to explore the land ourselves." While Cabet's directive to Sully was to explore the country around Peters Colony and prepare for the arrival of the avant-garde, Sully ultimately decided on his own initiative to stop after traveling just one hundred miles from Shreveport.[221]

Somewhere along the way, Sully had met a Texas landowner named John Becknell who was living in Titus County near Mount Pleasant, and who owned several tracts of land in the area. The Becknells were a well-known local family. John was the son of William Becknell, a frontiersman and explorer from Missouri who had fought in the Indian wars of the 1810s and later became a trader and businessman. Recognized as the father of the Santa Fe Trail, William Becknell first explored the route in 1821, developing a major commercial trading route, making him a wealthy man in the process. In 1835 the Becknell family moved to the Clarksville area in northeast Texas. When the war for independence from Mexico broke out, Becknell led a local militia, the Red River Blues, which included his two sons, William Jr. and John. The Red River Blues never engaged in battle, but the family's active participation in supporting the war caused the Becknells to be highly regarded by their neighbors. After independence, the Republic of Texas included in the new constitution land entitlements, and as head of a family William Becknell was granted a league and one labor—under Spanish measurements—and John, as a single man aged seventeen or older, one third of a league. (Equivalent to

4605 and 1476 acres, respectively, in modern units.) William's tract, six miles west of Clarksville, was surveyed in 1838 and John's land, surveyed March 4, 1840, was twenty miles southwest where he settled a farm called Sulphur Prairie that was situated on both sides of the Sulphur River.[222]

Sully may have encountered the Becknells once he arrived in Mount Pleasant or in Clarksville, en route to Peters Colony. As a result of their meeting, John Becknell sold Sully his farm on Sulphur Prairie for four thousand dollars.[223] Sully purchased the land on credit, hoping it could be used as a base of operation, an act that would later cause problems for the Icarians.[224] The land on the Sulphur River, as described in a newspaper article was, "about six miles to the right of the road, leading from Duty's Crossing of the Sulphur to Mrs. Morton's on White Oak."[225]

Sully wrote to Cabet and sent him a sketch of the land, showing the Sulphur River running through it, and indicated that the size of the plot was about 3,000 acres. Since the acreage was twice the size of John Becknell's, the purchase may have involved other landowners in addition to Becknell.[226]

Three days after leaving New Orleans, the avant-garde arrived at Shreveport at nine o'clock in the evening. Although Gouhenant complained that Sully had given him insufficient information, the Icarians likely knew when they arrived at Shreveport that they would have to travel cross-country to reach the promised land. Sully had recommended they go to a man named Jordan in Shreveport, whom he had told about the farm. So, the Icarians discovered that the next leg of their trip would be from Shreveport to Sulphur Prairie. The turmoil was just beginning; throughout their 200-mile overland journey, they would meet with innumerable obstacles.[227]

DISTRACTED BY THE REVOLUTION

The revolution had also split the Icarians in France. A small minority wanted to carry on with the emigration, but the majority wanted to recall the avant-garde and put every effort into building a successful Icaria at home. Although Cabet himself did not take part in the first days of the revolution, he could not resist participating in the extraordinary events, and he became deeply involved in the political debate in the immediate aftermath. On February 25 he founded a club called the Société Fraternelle Centrale, aiming to promote his social ideas to the provisional government, which was composed of Republicans who were mainly resistant to communist ideas and certainly reluctant to any deep social transformation.[228]

The Société Fraternelle Centrale soon became one of the most popular of the hundreds of clubs that sprang up in Paris during the revolution. The huge success of his endeavor was decidedly a distraction for Cabet, leading him to push the emigration project into the background, and to devote most of his energy to the French revolution until June.

The most conservative Republicans considered a Democratic Republic to be much more of a threat than communism, which they viewed as a foolish utopian dream. Still, Cabet's rising influence led the conservatives to launch a massive anti-communist campaign aiming at first to undermine Cabet's credibility with the working class, while at the same time seeking to discredit the other socialist leaders, cast as communists themselves. The conservatives' campaign reached its climax on April 16 when 60,000 armed national guards, controlled by the provisional government, overwhelmed a workers' demonstration, shouting, "à mort les communistes! À mort Cabet!" The following week, panic reigned among the communists and refueled the idea that emigration was the solution to the persecutions which had now reached an unprecedented level under the Republic—even more so than during the monarchy.

Although Cabet was discouraged, he ran for the constituent assembly during the elections of April 23. The elections, however, resulted in severe defeat for the socialists, after which Cabet held very little hope of seeing a victory for a democratic republic, and although he would also run in a special election on June 3, he gradually resumed the emigration process that had been pending since the beginning of the revolution. Meanwhile, the conservative counter-revolution, which had won the political battle, fiercely suppressed a workers' uprising that occurred from June 22 to June 26. The socialist leaders, who had been divided, sought to unite but they were not able to reverse the situation. Ultimately, the conservative Republicans themselves would be crushed by the authoritarian regime of the newly elected president Louis-Napoléon Bonaparte—nephew of Napoléon I—who would later orchestrate a *coup d'État* in December 1851, making him president for life. Bonaparte would ultimately restore the imperial regime and crown himself Napoléon III exactly one year later.[229]

After the June Days uprising, most Icarians had lost all hope of seeing their ideas realized in France and on June 3, the second avant-garde left for America. However, it was not the two to three hundred men Cabet had promised. There were only nineteen men.

THE OVERLAND JOURNEY

The belief that Texas was a perfect spot for the colony was not unique to the Icarians. The untamed beauty of the North Texas landscape captivated many. Land was plentiful and cheap, and wild game, abundant. There were rivers, forests, and soil suitable for farming, and most importantly it was far from the ubiquitous monarchs of Europe; it met all of Cabet's criteria. In contrast to the urban centers of France, Texas was still very much a frontier, busting at the seams with wild men, bounteous resources, and seemingly endless opportunities. Her borders meandered northwest for miles.

But a calm spring morning can turn into a violent and deadly afternoon and many days were not so bucolic. A traveler headed south through Gainesville recorded his experience quite a bit differently. The heat was far too intense for traveling during the afternoon hours. So, he continued his journey under a harvest moon, and encountered a ghastly site.

This collection of five or six log cabins, dignified with the name of a town, was rendered celebrated in the annals of storms by a most terrific tornado, which occurred here on the twenty-eight of May... passing over the county about a mile wide... A horse was blown into a tree, where it happened to catch its fore-leg and shoulder; these were torn from the body and were still hanging there, the balance of the carcase laying in a field full a–quarter of a mile off. A sheep was blown into the top of a high tree, where we saw it as we passed... One house, also blown down to the foundations, whilst another, beyond and in a line with it, had the roof taken off.[230]

Deadly tornadic winds were perhaps the only disaster the Icarians did not encounter during their expedition, although the weather would prove to be one of their biggest hindrances.

Sully's disappearance, the Icarians' inability to communicate with Cabet, and the unanticipated revolution in France, combined to create bedlam. Nevertheless, the men moved forward on their treacherous journey with remarkable perseverance and blind trust.

One Icarian, Henri Levi, was a thirty-seven-year-old weaver from Reims, who wrote to his parents about the pilgrimage from Shreveport to Icaria. Levi's dramatic account describes weeks of torrential rains, extreme heat, sickness, fear, hunger, and aimless wandering.[231]

We spent all day on the fifth [April] unloading the boat in a driving rain. On the sixth, a great surprise was in store for me. One of our brothers went into a store to make some purchase; seeing H. Levy and Co. written on the cases, he remarked to the merchant that there was one of the same name among us. He came to look for me, and although it had been about fifteen years since he had seen me, he fell into my arms calling me cousin, which is true, for our fathers are brothers. I will not describe to you the joy that I felt at this meeting; I will tell you only that our cousins have been very valuable to us in all the transactions that we have had to make here and that I have made a good Icarian of him. It is to his house that all the letters and papers that arrive for us, either from Europe or from New Orleans, are now addressed, and he is also the one who serves as intermediary in almost all our transactions here. Besides, you will hear talk of them, for he and his wife have rendered outstanding services to the community.

The second Henry Levy had a thriving business in Shreveport with his brother Gabriel, running the H. Levy and Brother Company. Although the chance encounter was itself quite amazing, it is doubtful that Henri would have made "a good Icarian" of his cousin, the young capitalist. The Icarians continued with their enthusiastic proselytizing in Louisiana, convinced that their doctrine could convert anyone—cousins, sea captains, fellow passengers; in a collective letter they sent later, they even boasted of having converted the Peters Colony agents.[232]

Levi continued that on April 5, they decided to purchase a piece of land. They had determined that their stay in Shreveport would be long, and since rent was expensive, they resolved to build a warehouse where they could store their supplies. They were able to find only one functioning wagon, which they sent to accompany twenty-five men on the trip to Sulphur Prairie. They continued to look for wagons for another day or two, but to no avail. The Icarians concluded that they were losing time in Shreveport so they discussed their situation and on April 8 they finally decided to send a group of men ahead to meet the twenty-five who had already left. Fourteen men volunteered to continue the walk westward. Henri Levi and his friend Jean Cardot, also a weaver, were among them.

You will be surprised that we were still traveling with our supplies on our backs; but imagine a country where one can travel ten to fifteen leagues [35–50 miles] without coming across any dwelling. One or two persons can travel by horseback – the Americans do not travel any other way in these parts – and they always find something to eat, for you can enter into any farmhouse and sit down at the table. This kind of mutual hospitality is practiced everywhere in the United States, without being ridiculous or impolite. But since there were so many of us, that was not possible.

We would not have found enough to eat, and there are no inns or hotels out in the country. So, we continued on our way in a suffocating heat, sleeping in the forest, wrapped in a blanket.

Levi, Cardot, and the others did not catch up with the twenty-five men accompanying the wagon until noon on April 11. As they continued their march the next day, the wagon broke an axle. Their supplies began to diminish, yet they were still about a three-day walk from Sulphur Prairie. Many of the men were sick, tired, and had sore feet, and they were afraid of getting caught in heavy spring rains that would slow them further. After a lengthy exchange, they decided to split up once again.

On the morning of April 13, nineteen men set out, taking only their own supplies with them. They arrived in Mount Pleasant at noon on April 15. Since Levi was the only man among them who spoke a few words of English, he was designated to purchase additional food and stay with one of the men who had fallen ill while the others continued the trip ahead to Sulphur Prairie.

It seems that Gouhenant was navigating between the groups. First, he remained behind with the men repairing the broken wagon, probably to supervise the operation, then he left to catch up with the others. He passed through Mount Pleasant on April 17 where he briefly met Levi and inquired after the health of the sick man, then continued on. He was followed a day later by the twenty men who had stayed to repair the wagon.

Levi continued,

> On the twenty-first I was replaced as companion to the sick man, and I left for Sulphur Prairie, where I arrived at six o'clock in the evening. I was astonished not to find Cardot there; he had left the same day for Icaria. I found about fifteen of our brothers busy working on the cabins and in the gardens; I was obliged to remain with them until further orders. So there was our advance guard

divided into three parts: one at Shreveport, one at Sulphur Prairie, and the third on the way to Icaria.

Although we were not numerous, we worked eagerly on the cabins, the garden, and the crops, which grew with astonishing rapidity.

The Texas newspapers followed the avant-garde's progress. The *Northern Standard*, the largest newspaper in northeast Texas (and published less than twenty miles away in Clarksville), printed a story about their endeavors. The article had been originally published in the *Journal du Havre* back in February, when the men had first departed for America. The translated version that appeared in the *Standard*, on April 22, described the Icarians' march to the *Rome* stating they were, "persons, of all professions, uniformly clad... bound for New Orleans."[233]

The article continues with an update detailing the Icarians' plan for establishing the colony and several small communities, one of which they reference as John Becknell's tract of land in Titus County, "about six miles to the right of the road where building is currently taking place." The article also mentions plans to establish a town in the Cross Timbers, where another group was headed, and "throughout Texas." The newspaper writer must have spoken to the men who were working in Titus County because the story specifically mentions that they were wood and iron workers, and that they were planning to start an iron foundry in Titus. It also states that they will "clear out the Sulphur commencing this summer."[234]

There were indeed wood and iron workers among the Icarians and in a letter from Cabet, he confirms that they planned to clear the river, "If it is easy to make the Sulphur navigable between the station [Sulphur Prairie] and Shreveport, it would be a very useful operation which would be good for the public's perception of us."[235]

About two weeks later, another item appeared in the *Democratic Telegraph and Texas Register* from Houston, stating that a group of "hardy and robust" men were preparing to make their way into the wilderness. The men were observed to be "cheerful, quiet, industrious and orderly."[236]

Twenty-seven of the Icarians had arrived in Sulphur Prairie a few days before Levi. With Gouhenant as their leader, they had departed for Peters Colony on the morning of April 21. However, by the end of April, a messenger from the group had returned to Sulphur Prairie. Levi's account goes on:

> On April 30th a messenger arrived [at Sulphur Prairie] telling us to leave right away for Icaria, although when he left, those who sent him were still far from their destination. The sixteen or seventeen men, who remained at Shreveport to finish the warehouse, have finished their work and arrived one after the other at Sulphur Prairie.

Levi's journal does not offer any details of the reason why the messenger expressed a sense of urgency for the remaining Icarians to depart. In any event, the men did not comply and remained in Sulphur Prairie to continue their work there. Meanwhile, the first group finally reached Peters Colony on May 1. As soon as they arrived, Gouhenant explored the colony area alone on horseback up to the Trinity River. While most of the Icarians were resting in a vacant house, eight men later joined his search to determine the best location for the settlement, which was finally agreed upon on May 8.[237]

The surviving letters that the first group sent to their families show that it had been a very difficult journey. Pierre Grillas wrote to his wife on May 10: "We have suffered a lot from the difficulties and the deprivations, obliged to clear the passes through the rivers and forests; I have been forced several times to leap into the water to sound the path for my brothers. I also walked so much that I killed a pair of boots without taking them off my feet."[238]

Almost all of the Icarians' letters contain a few earnest sentences describing the suffering the first group endured. They likely wanted to keep morale high among their families and friends, so they also included descriptions of the beauty of the landscape, and shared their hopes of building a thriving community. Alexis Marchand wrote, "We are in one of the most beautiful countries in the world, there is nothing in France that could compare, either for the rich soil or the beauty of the sights."[239]

In the collective letter they wrote to Cabet, the first group added: "From Bonham to the source of the Trinity, it is a country of great beauty and prodigious richness, which gathers all the advantages for our colony." Despite their glowing appraisal of the Texas land, the men were extremely tired and they still had the unenviable task ahead of clearing the land and building houses in a very short time. Joseph Therme, in his letter to Icarian friends who had remained in France, warned them, "Those who would not have the courage necessary to make all the sacrifices, of being selfless for their fellow man should not come, for there still will be fatigues to endure."[240]

Aside from fatigue, the Icarians had by now also discovered the unfortunate news that the ambiguous contract between Cabet and Peters gave them no special rights with respect to any other settlers. The Peters agents applied the same standard rules for colony settlement to the Icarians as they did to all settlers, as though the unique contract with Cabet did not exist: 640 acres for the head of family and 320 for a single man, both requiring settlers to occupy and build a small house before July 1. Also, the distribution of the alternating plots stipulated by the government applied to the Icarians as much as any colonist, and the hope of acquiring a large continuous tract of free land had vanished.[241]

Gouhenant realized then that he would never be able to obtain the million acres Cabet had promised, but at least he had twenty-six men who could start to work immediately, and about forty others still back in Sulphur Prairie or Shreveport. Furthermore, he was still expecting the second avant-garde to arrive in June, adding an additional two hundred men who, even if they could not secure their own plot in such a short time, would be able to help build the cabins and increase the land acquisition for the future Icaria.

On May 13 Gouhenant was still eagerly awaiting the arrival of the Icarians from Sulphur Prairie that he had requested to join him. Instead, one of the Biltz brothers arrived, carrying word from Sully asking him to return with enough funds to purchase wagons. Gouhenant had no choice then but to return to Sulphur Prairie. He arrived on May 19. According to Henri Levi, "when [Gouhenant] explained the situation, we were all anxious to reach Icaria. The reason was that the land grant company allocates each family one square mile of land, which is 640 acres. But after July 1, we will have to pay $1 per acre, which makes the importance of our departure understandable, so that we can take free possession of the land."[242]

In fact, the events happened much less smoothly than Levi's narrative suggests. Complying with the communist rules, Gouhenant organized a general assembly to decide upon an appropriate path forward. When he arrived in Sulphur Prairie, many of the Icarians who had remained in Shreveport the first time had since joined their friends, and now a group of thirty-six men attended the assembly. Sully's annotations, captured in the minutes from the meeting, offer bitter comments on the decisions. Gouhenant had to report all his activities since leaving Shreveport, and he tactfully "accepted with gratitude the opinion of his brothers, giving them all the explanations they each requested." They discussed the possibility of traveling together to the designated land as soon as possible. After a lengthy debate they decided that five men would remain with Sully and that all the others would leave the "day after tomorrow" with all the tools and necessary supplies to continue building the cabins.[243]

Sully was convinced that Cabet's initial plan to settle Icaria in Peters Colony by the July 1 deadline was unrealistic and that the Icarians should now retreat to Sulphur Prairie. He was very irritated by the decision to proceed as planned and commented: "I was not at all satisfied by Gouhenant's explanation given in rather calculated language to distract the brothers from the original questions, rather than to enlighten them. But since those who had knowledge of the facts were satisfied, as I did not know them myself, I could say nothing. Furthermore, I already saw that everything should be sacrificed to preserve unity and Gouhenant's authority, which was being compromised."[244] And although Gouhenant agreed to leave five men behind to continue the work on Sulphur Prairie, it was decided that these five men should be replaced by five others fifteen days before July 1 to allow them to take possession of their own plot of land. Gouhenant needed all his troops to conquer Icaria. Before leaving Sulphur Prairie, he wrote an enthusiastic letter to Cabet:

> My Dear Mister Cabet,
>
> Departing from Shreveport to go to Icaria, we arrived first in Bonham. There I received the most encouraging information from the State Secretary. We were not yet in Icaria, but we were getting close, and we just acquired the confirmation that we could get there with no danger. Equipped with this information, we continued our walk, and on the sixth day we touched Icarian ground.
>
> Oh! If you could see Icaria! It is an Eden. If someone offered you to be the president of the republic, rather come to Icaria, you would be happier, wealthier and greater among us.
>
> We have been very welcomed by the agents of the Peters' company and by the State secretary. I immediately requested their assistance to survey and delimit the sections we are going to occupy. At last, we possess Icaria. We are saved.
>
> The Revolution shook some of our brothers, three or four only. I had hoped to dissuade them from going back to France; but the bulk is devoted, courageous. There is not a day without cries of "Vive Cabet! Vive l'Icarie!" being heard. We are at the height of our desires, all the descriptions of Icaria are weak, our expectations have been exceeded.
>
> Tomorrow, those of our brothers who were with Sully will join me going to Icaria, 50 leagues farther, between the Trinity and

the Red River, in Eden, a real earthly paradise. There is neither snakes, nor savages, nor Indians, all these are fables. I have been traveling for fifteen days by horse visiting every corner of our land, I saw nothing frightening, I saw only marvelous things.

If I have the time after having put everything into action, and it is possible to go to New Orleans to receive our brothers of the second avant-garde, I will do so, otherwise I will go to Shreveport. In any case, they will be guided and accompanied up to Icaria by the best route, and they will find log houses to shelter them, and nice sections to possess. We are eagerly awaiting them.

I embrace you with all my heart.

Adolphe Gouhenant[245]

Throughout the summer, *The Northern Standard* was still following the evolution of the Icarians' journey and in the June 10 issue, a small item on page two stated, "We are informed that the first comers at the colony in Titus, have all gone to Peters' Colony, to obtain grants of land, and that all who arrive before July, will also go there with the same object. By those who may arrive subsequent to that time, the work in Titus will be carried on."[246]

Illustration 17. Original map of Peters Colony in Denton County.

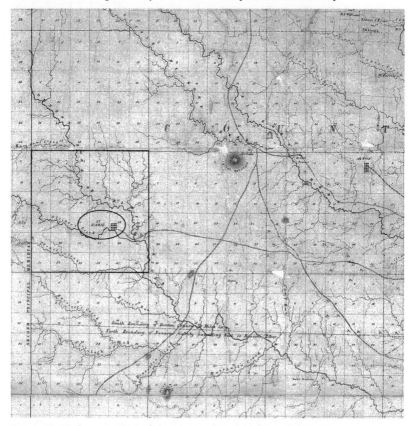

Henry O. Hedgcoxe, *Map of the Surveyed Part of Peters Colony Texas,*
Louisville, KY: Milne and Bruder Lithographers, 1852, Map #3155, Map Collection, Archives and Records Program, Texas General Land Office, Austin, TX.
Used by permission.

The land was divided into 6x6-mile townships (large square). The townships were
themselves divided in sections of one square mile. The Icarian settlement at the junction of Denton and Oliver's Creeks is shown. However, since the Icarians had secured
32 half sections, the settlement extended to a much larger area than indicated on
the map (see previous figure showing the distribution of the Icarian sub sections in a
township).

Henri Levi's chronicle of the final phase of their trek from Sulphur Prairie to Icaria is a harrowing tale. It is certainly among the worst scenarios that settlers would have had to endure in their march across the prairies and forests of North Texas. He confirms the challenges facing travelers on cross country explorations,

> Because the route through Mt. Pleasant and Bonham was very dangerous, we were shown another more practicable one. Here is a glimpse of the route we took.

> The word "route" that I am using does not at all have here the European meaning, for that is what they call the trail that you have to follow, even when there is no roadway from the point of departure to that of arrival. For this reason, the Icarians have blazed for themselves a route through a forest, and we had first to explore what is supposed to be the shortest and most practicable way, so that the Icarians who were following us could get through.

> On May twenty-first we left and spent the first night camped on a plain beside a stream. We were scarcely asleep when the thunder began to roll. We had been told that we were not very far from a farmhouse, so we got up at once and began to walk. We had just taken a few steps when the storm broke with violence and forced us to stop. After only a few minutes we were in water up to our knees. When calm returned, we continued our march across streams in water up to our arms, and we traveled like this until daylight, without the thunder stopping, guided only by the flashes of lightning. We finally arrived at a much longed-for farm, where we lit a big fire to dry us and we made tea to warm us inside. After this rest, we continued our walk through a forest cut by several ravines that we crossed through waist-high water. After two hours, we arrived at a river swollen by the storm and plunged into it. We had barely taken four steps when the water came up to our packs, we took a sounding with a pole and found there was more than 20 feet of water.

> Since several of us did not know how to swim, especially with arms and baggage, we were obliged to double back to look for

a way to get across. Finally, we came to a mill, and a man on horseback led us across the forest for more than an hour in water and mud up to our knees. At the end of this awful road, we rested for two hours and then continued on our way until evening. We camped near a farm.

The next evening, the men camped in a heavy storm and the rain extinguished their fire. Then the next morning, they walked another ten miles, stopping near a farmhouse to eat a lunch. They possessed only the remainder of supplies brought with them from Sulphur Prairie: bread, salt, tea, and a little *eau de vie.*

> When the bread ran out, we bought corn meal that the Americans use to pass through a sieve; unreasonable to overload ourselves with a sieve, we ate it with the husk, which made it taste like chopped straw. We made some bread out of it in the shape of little balls, the size of an egg, which we cooked on the coals. We also made a broth of it, which we cooked with a little bacon. I assure you that we are not enjoying Lucullan meals.

> After lunch, we set off into the woods by a frightful road and were devoured by clouds of mosquitoes, a kind of large gnat, which, each of us, walking one behind the other, chased off the back of the one in front with a branch. We got to a river whose bridge was broken down and took a sounding of the depth. It was at least thirty feet deep. We hastily built a raft with the debris from the bridge, tied together with our belts, and we attached it to a vine-like plant about thirty feet long, which we thought was the width of the river, to serve as a hauling line. One of our brothers courageously tried it first, but he was scarcely in the water before he was dragged away by the current, and we had all the difficulty imaginable to haul him back on board. We were forced to back-track for the second time through some mosquitoes, to the farmhouse in order to get information. Someone told us that four miles higher up we could pass, but we were already so tired that we put it off until the next day.

Still struggling to advance toward Icaria, one of the men became ill and they decided to leave him for a while to recuperate at the farmhouse then they backtracked to where they had tried to cross the river the previous night. By then, the water had dropped about ten feet and with the assistance of several downed trees, a bridge was created connecting both banks, and the men were able to navigate to the other side of the river.

They continued through the woods, fording streams, until they reached a massive prairie that Levi estimated to be about thirty miles wide, where there were no farmhouses or woods of any kind. "On May 27th, we left that road and turned to the right; we camped in an abandoned house, whose inhabitants had been massacred by the Comanche Indians." They finally reached the Trinity River, which they crossed on a ferry. Upon landing on the opposite side, they trudged through the underbrush in sticky mud and stagnant water, being constantly attacked by mosquitoes. They came across a man with eight oxen, his wagon bogged entirely in mud to the point where he was forced to abandon his load.

After two long days wandering, they reached a house occupied by two English women. The women sent the men to another farm, assuring them they could get accurate information on how to proceed. Once there, the men were told that two Icarians from the settlement had arrived the night before and had just left, only two hours earlier.

Knowing they would not immediately catch up with the other two men, the Icarians prepared a small meal and drank a bit of fresh milk the farmer had given them. They gathered as much information as possible and set off to reach the next farm ten miles away. They expected to arrive at the farm before nightfall, but came up short of their goal. Under the darkness of a waning moon, the black of night fell over them. They were in the woods once again, and the trail became all but invisible in the dark. One of the Icarians was able to catch a small bird weighing scarcely half a pound. They boiled it without any seasoning and split it thirteen ways, then they shared the broth among them.

On May 31, they left early in the morning and reached the farm about eight o'clock.

They learned that they still had eight miles to go to reach Icaria. One of the farmers escorted them across the hills and through the woods and left them in the middle of a vast sun-drenched prairie with only enough directions to get them lost once he had departed.

After they had walked for hours, the sun was beginning to set on the lost Icarians once again. They turned back to a river to spend another night camping on the ground. One of them turned to head back to the farm and came upon fresh wagon wheel tracks. Five of the men immediately began to walk in opposite directions, some to the east, and some to the west. Levi continued to walk, placing markers to indicate where they could meet up again when he suddenly met two soldiers who were part of an Indian-fighting troop and who showed him the right direction. He continued toward the camp, however, because his fellow Icarians could walk no more.

Two men started in the direction indicated by the soldiers and the other six stayed in camp. Wandering in the vast prairie of the frontier, Levi states that he was completely reconciled to his fate. He writes,

> We drank a little whiskey, lit a fire, and slept rather peacefully. My expectations did not prove wrong; the two brothers who went to the west soon arrived at our settlement. They wanted to return at once to look for us, but were prevented from doing so, because they were bone weary. Cardot, learning from them that I was in this unhappy position, left immediately with five other well-armed brothers to come to us in spite of a very dark night and the difficulties of the terrain, to bring us fresh bread and eau-de-vie. Scarcely had they gone a league when they met the two brothers who had left at nightfall. Cardot returned with them to the settlement. The others would have been quite willing to camp and wait for daylight, but the danger threatening their brothers gave them fresh impetus. We were sleeping quite peacefully, when about eleven o'clock, we heard a gunshot in the distance.

I answered immediately with another shot, which was answered by two shots; I answered with two more. About midnight, the five brothers got to our camp, wet and dirty, having rolled into the gullies as they marched blindly at the risk of breaking bones, in order to come to our aid. These generous brothers were Rougier, Dondot, Meslier, Terme, and Caudron, brother of the former manager of Le Populaire. I name them at the risk of violating the promise that we have made to personalize neither good nor bad actions.

We set forth in broad daylight toward Icaria, where we arrived with the greatest joy. Cardot had even come to meet us with eau-de-vie and warm bread.

Now some words about Icaria. I found there one house finished, two others nearly so, a magnificent countryside, filled with hills, cut by a stream of clear water.

It goes without saying that the climate is excellent, for if we had done in Europe what we are doing here, we would all be dead. Walking all day, sleeping on the ground, having nothing but a light blanket for shelter, drinking at every hole; finally undergoing all the inconveniences of a long journey across an uninhabited and unknown country, however no one's health has been affected.[247]

Although the house Levi mentioned was likely just a rustic cabin, the general feeling among the Icarians was almost universal happiness. Their exhaustion was overshadowed by a collective euphoria praising the land, climate, and each other, but it was a short-lived victory and their exaltation would not last the summer.

Illustration 18. Map showing the Icarian route through Texas and Gouhenant's locations, 1848-1871.

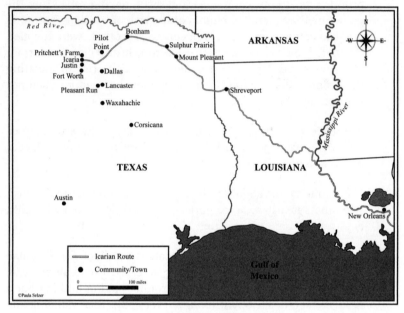

Courtesy of Alexander Mendoza, Copyright Paula Selzer.

CHAPTER 9

LETTERS AND ACCUSATIONS

One cannot judge one who is absent because he cannot defend himself.

Jeanne Durand, 1848

JEANNE'S LETTERS

Adolphe Gouhenant had left his wife and two children far behind in France when he joined the avant-garde and sailed for America. The plan was for his son Ernest to join him as soon as possible and then his wife and daughter would go later, once Icaria was established. Jeanne and Adolphe however, had already been separated from each other for a while when Gouhenant sailed from Le Havre in February.

About ten days after the *Rome* had arrived in New Orleans, Jeanne wrote to Cabet, frantic to learn more about the Icarians' situation and to ask when they might be able to travel to be with Gouhenant. In her letter to Cabet, Jeanne wrote,

Sir,

Clearly understanding how little freedom your countless occupational duties allow, I would have waited for the letter you mention in your note from March 1 before writing to you, had I not read in *Le Populaire* on April 6, that a small number of your disciples would leave during the current month. My son is so eager to join his father that it is affecting his health and precludes him from engaging in any serious occupation. As for me, before making a final decision for my daughter and me, I would like to get information for my son on the position of the emigrants in the country where they made a rendez-vous.

I hope very strongly that you would consider the wishes of Monsieur Gouhenant, by allowing his son to leave with those traveling in April. I do not see what might hinder his departure. From what M Gouhenant wrote me, he must have taken the necessary steps to cover the cost of passage for this dear child. If this departure is to occur, my intention is to take my son to you in Paris myself. I shall take the opportunity to lay before you the letters that Monsieur Gouhenant wrote to me before his departure, where he speaks of his children. I appeal sir, to your feelings of affection for M Gouhenant to get a prompt reply. Please sir, accept the assurance of my highest consideration.

Gouhenant

née JD

April 8, 1848[248]

Jeanne was desperate in her plea to secure a place for Ernest. As it happened however, the second avant-garde did not depart in April. Rather, they did not leave France until June 3. After receiving no reply to her inquiry, Jeanne wrote to Cabet a second time.

Sir,

I had the honor of writing to you on April 10, and my letter went unanswered, which I attribute to the amount and the importance of your business. To impose on your time as little as possible, I beg you to send your response to my letter with the messenger who I sent to you.

Can you allow my son to be among those who depart next? When will the next departure occur? What conditions must I fulfill to allow my son to be among those departing?

... Please accept, Sir, the assurance of my highest consideration.

Jeanne Gouhenant

née D

May 4, 1848

Post Script

Ernest, as you have seen in Toulouse, is big and strong, he appears to be 20 years old rather than 16. He is as able to endure the rigors of the crossing as well as the most robust of your disciples, and I am sure he will not be a burden for the colony you are founding.

Cabet finally responded to Jeanne's letter. Unfortunately, it was not the answer she was seeking. In his reply dated a month after her first letter he explained in a very direct manner that he no longer had much affection for his communist brother.

Madame Gouhenant, May 11, 1848

Madame,

I received your letters of April 9th and May 4th. I wanted to answer without delay, but I was so overwhelmed with business and my life was so troubled (as you probably know) that it was impossible, and I do regret it. Your letters lead me to believe that you do not know the issue of *L'Émancipation de Toulouse* of March 25th that published several letters found by Government Commissioner Joly at the Prefecture of Toulouse and attributed to Adolphe Gouhenant. [249]

It is very painful for me to have to tell you about the journal and the letters, if you do not already know—which in fact seems almost impossible to me. You understand, Madam, that my relationship with the author of these letters should change, and that I can no longer allow your son to depart since his father can no longer be with us. Besides, your husband has done nothing to ensure the journey of his son, and on the contrary left me exposed to the complaints of his creditors. Please accept the expression of my regret and my fraternal greetings.

Cabet refers to one of the letters Gouhenant had written to the prefect during his imprisonment in 1843. It had just been found by the republicans after the revolution when they took over the prefecture of Toulouse.

Jeanne was not in the least intimidated by Cabet's admonition. In fact, she responded yet again with a rational and vigorous argument, vehemently defending her husband.

Sir,

I bought the issues of the newspaper you mention and it is with the utmost indignation that I have read them. One cannot judge one who is absent because he cannot defend himself. In fact, one who is absent must be assumed innocent, more so than any accused, until sentenced by his judges.

What proof exists that the letter was written by the hand of Monsieur Gouhenant? What proof is there that it was not written by a fraud in the pay of the police who were intent on creating disunity among the opponents of the monarchy? What proves that this alleged letter speaks about Republicans or Communists?

... Finally, what proof is there that the deprivation that occurred in his prison cell did not add to the usual exaltation of Mr. Gouhenant's ideas? Doesn't the superhuman power of which he boasts in this letter look like the delusions of a sick mind? And would there be any generosity from you to condemn a moment of aberration resulting from the torture he endured for your own cause?

The passionate exchange between Jeanne Durand and Etienne Cabet provides an interesting glimpse into Jeanne's character. Although little is known about her, she appears to have been an educated and determined woman. Based on her age and the signature on the marriage certificate, she did not seem to be educated when she married Gouhenant. Yet, if her letters to Cabet were written in her own hand, they stand as sufficient evidence that by 1848, she was not only literate, but an intelligent, independent, and self-confident woman. Perhaps Gouhenant encouraged her education. After living with him for fifteen years, she would have been exposed to illuminating ideas and likely developed the ability to present her thoughts eloquently among educated men.

Jeanne argues that if in fact her husband did write the letters to the prefect, then he must have been under extreme duress to compose such inflammatory words. She continues to dissect Cabet's claim, questioning the logic of his accusation that Gouhenant was paid for selling out.

> One consideration would also seem to dominate the entire question: If M G. as he is accused, has sold out his friends to Louis Philippe's police, he undoubtedly received payment for his treason, but everyone knows he remained without fortune, even you, sir, speak about his creditors.

> The police of the deposed government have continuously persecuted and harassed the one [Gouhenant] who is now accused of having served them so well. I hope, sir, now that you have been better informed, you will change your opinion which is unjust.

> I will write to Mr Gouhenant so that he knows the charge with which he is faced, and that he wastes no time unmasking his accusers. Please sir, give me his address and let me know a safe way to send him a letter.

Please accept, Sir, the assurances of my highest consideration.

Gouhenant

née JD

Cabet likely never provided Jeanne with an address where she could write to her husband. Henri Levi mentioned in his letters that the Icarians received mail at one of his relatives' addresses in Shreveport, but if Jeanne did write to Gouhenant, he did not receive her letters.

Disappointing News

Three months after Jeanne had written to Cabet, Gouhenant also wrote to "Father Cabet," completely unaware at this point of Cabet's accusations against him. His letter described the hardships they encountered in establishing the colony, but attributed their overall success to the enthusiasm and dedication of his fellow Icarians. He drafted his heartfelt letter on July 12, 1848:

> We arrived in time to construct our cabins on every one of the sections which we were to occupy, and thus took possession. On July 1st, the agents [of Peters Colony] came to visit us, to inspect us, and to make their report to the government. The operation took two days. This formality fulfilled, we gathered again at the site of our first establishment, in order to concentrate our forces, our resources, and our labor.

> What a pity, what a loss, what bad luck that the second avant-garde did not arrive before July 1st! We would have obtained an additional half section for each family or two bachelors.... At any rate, we have 32 half sections; that is already very good, it is very large, it is enough to support 15,000-20,000 persons. Moreover, when you come or if you send a commission, or send new orders, we can obtain as much land as we want.

Thus, we have the full possession: Icaria is founded.

Now that the July 1st deadline has passed, we are turning to making our situation more comfortable. Many of the brothers are showing the effects of fatigue and privations from our long voyage. The change in climate, food, lodging, habits, etc. contributes to a general malaise. We must pay a heavy price to acclimate; but there are no serious illnesses, no danger. The majority of us are solid, and vying with each other in the zeal and ardor with which we do our work. Some go to the forest to cut down trees, some drive the wagons which transport our supplies. The carpenters are building some wooden houses; our mechanics busy themselves constructing a gristmill, others are building a kiln; the gardeners, the farmers, the terrace-builders, the charcoal-makers, all the brothers are in motion preparing the necessary things and awaiting the Second Advance Guard, which perhaps you will accompany.[250]

Had his letter stopped there, it would have given an optimistic view of the status of Icaria. The men were exhausted, yet still steadfastly devoted to the development of the colony. But the letter continues to reveal their desperation, their feeling of abandonment, and the terrible anxiety that was completely devouring them.

But when will this second avant-garde, so desired by us, arrive? We have no news of you, of them, or of our families; we appear to be abandoned by all... We only received your short letter of March 22, announcing the departure of the second advanced guard on April 15, and four issues of *Le Populaire*, the most recent from March 30.

Now our hopes are dashed, our anxiety is terrible... Also we have read American journals quoting some French journals, where we read many things which considerably increase this anxiety devouring us. What has happened, what is happening in France? And especially with you, about communism? Your life is in danger! Our brothers are persecuted, hounded, liquidated! The people are riled up against you![251]

Two weeks earlier, Eugène Rougier had also written to Cabet from Shreveport where he had returned with Chauvin to welcome and guide the second avant-garde, which they assumed had left France in April. In Shreveport, they met two Spanish Icarians, Roig and Porté, who had traveled from Paris to the United States independently, without the second avant-garde. In Rougier's short letter there is no hint of the anxiety that began to affect his brothers who remained in the colony. On the contrary he writes, "I will leave tomorrow for the colony, following the national route with our two new brothers and brother Berson. We look forward to leaving Shreveport, where the climate is unhealthy, especially in this season. Berson has been a bit sick for a few days, but he will ride our horse, and the better air in Texas will soon cure him as it has already done for several brothers who had been sick when they left Shreveport."[252]

Rougier and Chauvin had left the colony on June 4. At that time, the Icarians were fully absorbed in activities to secure as much land as possible for their settlement, and their worries about the future do not surface in Rougier's letter. During the last days of May, they had built a big cabin to shelter them and had started to work on the small forty-square-foot log houses required to take possession of as many sections as possible. Although the cabins were quite rudimentary, their construction required a monumental effort. The men had to cut the trees, saw them, carry the wood onto the sections, which were separated from each other by one mile and then transport them between sections. During the month of June, the Icarians were thus dispersed across a wide tract of land, working all day long under a blistering sun that would soon become devastating for the already exhausted men. Furthermore, the two Spaniards had brought with them some very bad news. They informed the men that when they left France on April 30, the second avant-garde was less than twenty men—not the two hundred they expected—and that they had not departed yet and were not expected to depart before May 30. That meant that the reinforcement the Icarians were eagerly awaiting would not arrive before the second half of August![253]

The Icarians learned of the disappointing news on July 19, when Rougier, Berson, and the two Spanish men rejoined them in the colony, where all the men were now suffering from fever. Adding to their despair, Porté and Roig brought back no letters from their families nor from Cabet, but only a few issues of *Le Populaire*, describing the persecutions against the communists in France.

The Icarians' desperation was palpable in letters written to their families in mid-July. Then on August 20, they penned a collective letter to Cabet that described their horrific suffering.

> For our part, we do not have good news to give you today. In the middle of June, several of us had the fever. The illness spread day by day. In July, almost all were ill; on July 30, we had the misfortune to lose our brother Guillot. By August, no one had escaped the curse, and quite a large number were severely ill. Only a few convalescents could provide care for the sick, make the bread and cook. The slightest work was enough to cause an immediate relapse. Some had the fever five different times. A gross and unvaried food source contributes to worsening our situation. We indeed have no vegetables, and except for three oxen, eight roe deer and a few turkeys, our food has consisted only of bacon, bacon soup, corn soup and corn bread mixed these last days with a quarter of wheat, tea or coffee for drinking ....

> The Americans have told us that during the months of July and August, under this climate, one should abstain from any work, that it was the most important condition the emigrant should fulfill to lessen the acclimation diseases ....

> The illness we suffer leaves a heavy languidness upon most of the brothers. All our work has remained interrupted since the first days of July, and we do not know when we will be able to resume. Until now, we have not been able to start clearing for the autumn sowing, because of our situation and due to our lack of appropriate tools and animals that are trained for ploughing (you

will find enclosed a note about the ploughing tools etc. needed by our farmers).

Even now, our housing remains insufficient for us, and before building comfortable houses for the families, establishing a mechanical sawmill, and building a mill, we will need much more time; also we defer to your wisdom to decide the most appropriate time for the first departure of the women ....

Since the beginning of May, we have been out of money, and we were obliged to use credit. We were fortunate to find some credit with M. Hedgcoxe, an agent of the Peters Company, and with several other American households in the area. Through these means, we have been able to get the necessary things, but under expensive conditions. We still have some supplies of cattle and wheat for a while, but our credit has been accepted only with the hope of seeing the second advance guard for which we are still eagerly waiting. The time we had given for their arrival expired, so we are on edge seeing the source of our credit disappear .... The amount of our debts is today of 9,454 francs 80 centimes ....

Petit, Cochard, Sjès and Paul the carpenter, who have proclaimed their desire to leave for a long time, have just broken away from us in the most improper manner. Petit left stealthily. The three others walked away with their bags without accepting the help we had promised them. Indeed, we had planned to leave with a wagon for Shreveport as soon as we had enough men to drive it, feed them on the way, and, in Shreveport, to pay for their passage to New Orleans. But they preferred to seize the moment when we were the sickest to take to the road. The others who have also expressed a desire to leave are waiting for the departure of our wagon to take advantage of our help.

We urge the selection committees for the next wave of the departure to be extremely selective in making their choice. For the moment, the men needed should be carpenters, pit sawyers, wheelwrights, ploughmen, brick makers, bricklayers and a few farriers.[254]

For the Icarians who wrote to their families in August, the abandonment was the main cause of their misfortune, but some also began to blame Sully, who, according to them, did not fulfill his exploratory mission. Joseph Therme wrote to his father on August 15:

> But this is what significantly delayed our work and increased our suffering: Charles Sully, the Englishman sent by Mr. Cabet to explore the country and serve as our guide, had regrettably stopped at Becknell's, and had quite misinformed us. He had chosen this place for the founding of Icaria. A first detachment arriving on the site, did not find it a favorable place for such an undertaking, and continued their journey to Icaria. Sully made every effort to engage our men to settle on the property he had bought at Becknell's. Put off by the difficulties of transporting our baggage, many of us stopped there, and sowed many seedlings of vegetables corn and potatoes.[255]

The Biltz brothers wrote similar thoughts in a letter to their siblings, adding that they never understood the reasons why Sully stopped in Sulphur Prairie, and "in [their] opinion, Sully had not at all accomplished his mission." In a report to Cabet written on June 15, Rougier was less critical of Sully, but he claimed that the land was much more fertile in the colony than in Sulphur Prairie, and for him there was no doubt that Icaria should be settled in Peters Colony as planned.[256]

The fiasco that consumed the first avant-garde resulted from an incredible lack of preparation and they were all but predestined to fail. Sully, who had been sent alone on a difficult mission, had taken it upon himself to buy property in Sulphur Prairie. Understandably the avant-garde could not resign themselves to settle on a small 3000-acre plot when they were under orders to secure one million acres in Peters Colony. Furthermore, they were relying on the second avant-garde who could have helped them acquire additional land had they arrived in June as expected, or at least been able to relieve them if they had arrived in July. As August was winding down, they still had not arrived.

The situation continued to grow worse. On August 21, Louis Moity wrote a letter to his friends in which he bluntly, and without much pathos, described a tragic event, "A new misfortune happened to us, the brothers Collet and Dousin were busy fixing a fence to a pen where we put our calves, the lightning fell on them, struck Collet, and extraordinarily, Dousin who was almost touching him, received the electric shock, and a few moments after he recovered. But Collet was left naked by the strike and killed instantly."[257]

In the following week, two other Icarians, Henri Charles Saugé and Claude Guérin, succumbed to the fever, and the despair was complete. Therme wrote to his father on August 22,

> Our position is now the most deplorable; we are unable to help each other. There are not enough able-bodied men for the sick, and we only have tea for medicine. Many suffer physically and morally; others are convinced that there will be no second Avant-Garde. For me, I think we will not be abandoned; nothing surprises me, even our situation. However, if by the end of the month we do not receive any money or Avant-Garde, our position will become intolerable because we owe about 9000 francs. If we cannot pay, I do not know what will happen and how we will live.[258]

THE SECOND AVANT-GARDE ARRIVES

The second avant-garde finally arrived in America on July 22 and disembarked from the *Hannibal.* Unlike their brothers they were welcomed in New Orleans; Joseph Chauvin had been waiting for three weeks to meet them.[259]

When the group arrived in Shreveport on August 2 the bad news from Icaria had not yet reached them. The leader of the second avant garde, thirty-one-year-old Pierre Favard, wrote enthusiastically to Cabet, "Everywhere the steamboat stopped, we found French men: we are known all along the road and nobody ignores our undertaking ... according to the information our brother Chauvin gave us on Icaria, it is the most beautiful country in the world: we need only patience to succeed."

However, during the trip from Shreveport to Icaria, they began to fall ill. The problem was no longer the strong spring rains and the swelling rivers that had been among the primary obstacles encountered by the first avant-garde, but the unrelenting heat of late summer. Of the nineteen men who made the overland journey towards Icaria, eight fell along the way, and were left behind to recover.[260]

The balance of the group finally reached the settlement in the last days of August, where they discovered their brothers' situation. Four days after their arrival, Favard wrote a dramatic letter to Cabet.

> Poor Father: How can I describe to you the situation where I found our brothers? Almost all the ones who remained are sick. Four are dead; the first is Guillot; the second is Collet, who was killed by lightning, the third is Guérin and the fourth is Saugé.

> The least sick prepare the food and the effort causes them to fall ill again. The sun is so hot, that if one is exposed to its rays, one is almost certain to develop fever. I did not hesitate a single moment to break camp, which pleased everyone, because several were expecting our arrival to get help to be able to leave.

> We would not be able to bring the women over these abominable roads. The wagons only made six to nine miles per day. There are no towns, only occasional farms, and none of them have beds for even four people. One cannot find any bread, because the country people only make small quantities with each meal.[261]

In addition to the dire sanitary conditions, Favard discovered their poor financial position:

> What is annoying is that there are debts for seven or eight thousand francs and we are quite embarrassed to pay them under these circumstances.

We are waiting for our creditors that we have called to hear us and if we can arrange it with them, we will only focus on our retreat to Shreveport.

The second avant-garde was lacking not only manpower, but also substantial resources. They had left France with 11,000 francs allocated to cover their own expenses and possibly to partially pay back the loan Sully had taken out to pay for the land at Sulphur Prairie, but it was far insufficient to pay any debt incurred by the first avant-garde and especially one as large as 9,000 francs.[262]

Cabet should have envisioned the possibility that the first Icarians would be short of resources after having been left on their own for five months. While the first accounts of the Icarian colonists from July were very optimistic, Cabet might have been misled about the real situation. Still, as early as May 13 they had written that their foremost need was money.

Cabet would later claim that the main reason he had decided to send such a small group during the midsummer Texas heat was the discovery of Gouhenant's 1843 letters. To Cabet's way of thinking, the main danger the first avant-garde faced was not the illness, the fatigue, the lack of resources, nor the scorching heat, but the possibility that Gouhenant might have been an agent of the police or even of the Jesuits—Cabet's longstanding imagined enemy—seeking to sabotage the Icarians. Before Favard left France, Cabet had given him several documents indicating that he considered him to be a political emissary whose mission was not to rescue the first avant-garde but mainly to investigate the dissidents, to interview Gouhenant, possibly arrest him, and bring him back to France. For the mission, Cabet had selected a trustworthy man, and practically a member of his family; Favard was the brother of his recently deceased son-in-law.[263]

CONFLICTING STORIES AND A HASTY RETREAT

For more than a century and a half, the true story of the Icarian settlement's demise has been veiled in mystery; the account has been incomplete and often misrepresented in local lore. No one can truly confirm the capricious events that transpired at the settlement near the junction of Denton and Oliver Creeks. Some accounts of Icaria paint Gouhenant as an incompetent doctor, a treacherous villain, or a double-crossing agent who betrayed his fellow Icarians. In reality, Gouhenant was none of these, and it is to his credit that he was able to hold together the men in his charge for as long as he did.

Cabet first told his version of the story shortly after the Icarians left Peters Colony. As the bad news eventually reached Paris, he began to write what would become the official Icarian version. He blamed the failure on unfortunate circumstances and pointed a finger at several people, never accepting any responsibility. As a lawyer, Cabet was adept at defending his position and he published his version of the narrative as a defense speech in the December 17 edition of *Le Populaire*. According to him, the cause of the failure was a series of events that were beyond his control: the Revolution, which upset his plans, the desertion of the doctor Leclerc in New Orleans, the inability to navigate the Red River above Shreveport, the "reckless undertaking of a long and perilous trek instead of stopping at Sulphur Prairie," and most of all, Gouhenant's alleged treason. Cabet wrote,

> An amazing fact was discovered against Gouhenant, the leader of the first avant-garde, and this fact was that letters were found in the Prefecture of Toulouse, in which this Gouhenant, at the time of the Toulouse trial of 1843, offered to sell himself to the prefect for 200,000 francs. Yes, the delegate of the first avant-garde, who inspired in us extreme confidence, who seemed to combine fidelity, devotion, intelligence and experience, was—the fact now appears definite—a traitor, in charge of the infernal mission to wreck the most useful undertaking of human kind.

And furthermore, he begged me to send him his young son!

Without shining a light on this horrible discovery, which would be more harmful than useful, I put the Delegate of the second avant-garde in charge of secretly interviewing Gouhenant, to present to him the evidence in case he would deny it, then to bring him to trial before the general Assembly.

Cabet set the scene for his readers:

When they arrive on August 29, with half of the second avant-garde ... the Delegate finds the first avant-garde ill, discouraged, demoralized, resolute against Gouhenant's advice, as well as two others to leave the settlement to retreat to Shreveport and New Orleans. He thinks he should postpone the accusation, in order to use Gouhenant during the retreat, while keeping an eye on him. But many accusing Gouhenant of huge faults and even of treason, the Delegate of the second avant-garde decides to confide everything to the general Assembly.

There is a unanimous cry against Gouhenant... He doesn't dare to deny; he confesses...

Letters are found in his trunk, brochures, ornaments or badges, which seem to prove that he is the agent of the Jesuits... He is believed to be the agent of the Jesuits!...

You can guess the general sentiment and the degree of anger!

He is condemned as a traitor... he is told, "You are proud of your nice hair and nice beard: you will be punished in your pride; your hair and your beard will be shorn."

He resigns himself without a whisper and without protest, then he is expelled and the retreat begins with Rougier, selected to replace him.

Thus, it is perhaps the hand of the police, or the hand of the Jesuits which drove a new Judas in the middle of the desert to stop the realization of fraternity.[264]

Cabet had given Favard very detailed instructions about how to interview Gouhenant, leaving him almost no autonomy to make his own decisions regardless of the situation he would find in the colony.

First, Cabet instructed Favard to ask if Gouhenant was familiar with the issue of *Le Populaire* and the facts stated therein. Second, he should inquire about the nature of his relationship with the prefect of Haute-Garonne in 1843. Then, he should show Gouhenant the issue of *L'Emancipation* from March 25, 1848, and ask him to read it. Once Gouhenant read it, he would then be required to either confirm or deny having written the letters. Favard should then ask Gouhenant for his oral answer and provide him with the sealed letter from Cabet. Finally, Favard should ask for a written response and suggest a resolution. In the event that Gouhenant were to confess to writing the letters, he would then be allowed to retire quietly and Favard should proceed to facilitate his exit as smoothly as possible. Even if Gouhenant were to deny culpability, and attempt to explain his actions, Favard would then be obliged to accommodate his request.[265]

Once Favard and his men arrived at the colony, he realized that his mission was no longer relevant since the first avant-garde were desperately in need of relief. Favard had essentially no means to help. Still, he decided to accuse Gouhenant publicly, creating the fiasco and ultimately sealing the fate of Icaria in North Texas. The balance of Icarians retreated in the final days of summer.

Favard himself would not be spared Cabet's wrath. Three years later, Cabet wrote that the Peters Colony agent had offered to continue, and even increase, his credit, and to shelter the Icarians in neighboring farms during the months of September and October. Bitterly, Cabet wrote that "If they had accepted this offer, everything would have been saved."[266]

Gouhenant's alleged treason was actually a boon for Cabet so that he could shift the blame away from his own mistakes. One member of the second avant-garde, Chambry, wrote a letter to Cabet on October 20, just a few weeks after the retreat, suggesting that not all the Icarians had been fooled by Cabet's accusatory distraction:

> I think it would be good to publish Gouhenant's treason: A striking article would be needed to condemn him and to attribute the fall of Icaria to his maneuvers. I advise you to do it as soon as possible, otherwise you are lost in public opinion .... The newspapers will sound the tocsin of mocking; the propaganda will be paralyzed; *Le Populaire* will fall, and many of your disciples will leave you if you do not exploit the treason of Gouhenant. For me, I am convinced that without treason we would still have failed: the climate, the little money we had, the number of men with no capacity and without true conviction, all prove me that we did not have the elements needed to succeed.[267]

There were several versions of the Icarian story that found their way into Texas newspapers as well. With each telling of the story, the facts became a little fuzzier, including the spelling of Gouhenant's name.

In 1891, *The Dallas Morning News* published another version of the same events, entitled "Old French Colony," highlighting memories of colonists from La Réunion, another French settlement established in 1855 (sometimes confused with the Icarian settlement). Forty-five-year-old Guillaume Guillot, one of the Icarians who died that summer, had a relative named Maxime Guillot, a wagon maker who would later open a carriage shop in Dallas. Maxime Guillot knew Gouhenant and he was also the brother-in-law of Élie Drouard. In the newspaper article, Maxime's daughter recounts a version she recalled hearing, several decades earlier:

> Sometime in the '40s a colony of French communists started for Texas. Their guide was a man named Gounant. Gounant was in the pay of the French government and was instructed to lead the colony into the wilds so that it might perish. He obeyed his instructions only too well and lost the colony somewhere about

Denton. The colonists suffered great hardships. Many of them died. Mr. Guillot had a brother-in-law in this colony and came to Texas to search for him. This colony discovered the treachery of their guide, tried him and condemned him to death. But some of them hesitated at this extreme step and determined to mitigate the punishment. Gounant had a magnificent beard, and hair of which he was very vain. The colonists in lieu of the death penalty shaved his head and face and drove him into the woods... Gounant, in spite of his treachery, was received into the Dallas colony and became book-keeper.[268]

In still another variant from 1894, Denton County resident Alex Robertson conveyed his memories of the Icarian settlement just forty-six years after the dissolution of the colony. In retelling his story for the local press, Robertson said, "In the summer and fall of 1848, the advance guard of the Socialist community, calling themselves Icarians and numbering about one hundred and fifty men under the leadership of Doctor Adolph Gonnough came from France..." Robertson claims that they made the settlement at the mouth of Oliver Creek and constructed "about thirty or forty houses," broke land, and sowed wheat. He recalls that there were one hundred and fifty men or more and that game was abundant with buffalo still roaming forty miles to the west. He mentions that the Ranger station was about eight miles away and the Icarians were on friendly terms with the Rangers.

Doctor Gonnough was not acquainted with Texas' chills and fevers, and probably did not have a sufficient supply of quinine, as it was very scarce and high. The colonists having to use creek water for drinking and cooking purposes, they all took sick. The Doctor's mode of treating fever, which was to get in the shade on the creek and remain there until the fever ended, proved ineffectual. Some of them died. The colonists lost confidence in the medical skill and leadership of Doctor Gonnough and rebelled against him. He fled in fear of his life and went to the ranger post for protection.[269]

Finally, Gouhenant himself would later share his version with the French socialist Victor Considerant during his first visit to Dallas. Considerant later wrote a letter describing his discussion with Gouhenant:

> After several months, ten or twelve Icarians sent by Mr. Cabet arrived. It was a relief. But only for assistance, they brought the proof, printed in *Le Populaire*, of the infamous treason of Gouhenans. The latter had finally fallen ill. The newcomers gave him no notice of the purpose of their mission, only he saw around him comings and goings, and an atmosphere of mystery. When his companions' minds had been secretly shaped, attuned appropriately, influenced so much by misery and fever, it was said to the poor sick man that he was the last among the wretches, an infamous traitor, and that he would be brought before his judges. Some wanted to kill him immediately.
>
> In the evening, being on his guard, he heard a conversation which concluded this way: "Well? If he asks to be judged by the citizen Cabet (who, he had been told, should have arrived in New Orleans) we will take him there. We will attach a rope around his neck behind a wagon. He will have to follow."
>
> Gouhenans understood that the sufferings had exasperated many of these unfortunate men to such a point that in the poor condition where he was himself, he was lost if he could not escape immediately. Seizing the opportunity of a drop in his fever, he went out without clothes, pretending to go wash himself in the river. Once in the woods, he went to a ranger station that was eight or ten miles away, and put himself under their protection.[270]

Considerant also added that fellow Icarian Luc Bourgeois had confirmed this version of the story. After the Icarians retreated, Bourgeois had remained within the colony with his friend Élie Drouard.

The multiple versions that have survived over one hundred and seventy years of storytelling all hold some elements of both fact and fiction. Still, Gouhenant was not a doctor; he was not in the employ of the French government; nor had he ever been aligned with Louis Philippe.

The accusations from Favard and the others left him shocked and terrified. He had been occupied with building cabins and trying to get crops started, all the while focusing on the business of the commune. He had little access to news from France and had no idea that Cabet believed him to be a traitor until Favard and his men arrived. He had no knowledge that his letters had been published several months before, nor was he aware of the correspondence between Jeanne and Cabet. Now, suddenly accused of conspiracy by his communist brothers, and his life threatened, Gouhenant was in a dire situation.

Narrowly escaping with his life, his departure from the colony was marked by frustration, anger, and despair. In less than nine months, he had left his family behind, spent hundreds of francs on his passage, and logged nearly 5,000 miles and six weeks sailing across the Atlantic on a cold, drafty ship, traveling by steam up the Red River, and walking across North Texas. Unprepared for the customs and hardships that life on the American frontier presented, he encountered dozens of challenges as he led the sixty-nine men overland to claim the oddly distributed land plots that Cabet had recklessly secured. There was sickness, near-drownings, broken equipment, injuries, lost men, and financial difficulties. Yet, for all these trials, he continued to inch forward, keenly focused on establishing Icaria. In the end, he left the colony alone, destitute once again.

Whatever actually did transpire in the summer of 1848, the outcome was the same. The August days melted into September and by the middle of the month, the settlement was completely abandoned. With Gouhenant being the first to go, the remainder of the men left as well, some heading back to New Orleans and some returning to France. The first avant-garde had been there less than four months, the second group, only two weeks. They paid the Peters Colony agent what they owed for supplies with their oxen and equipment and headed back east across the prairie in small teams, each with a gun, haversack, and six or seven dollars. Many men were still sick and scattered across North Texas. Most of those who had reached the settlement returned to Shreveport within the month.

Sadly, another four or five had died during the retreat, including Henri Levi whose journal provided the most detailed narrative of the journey of the first avant-garde.

Towards the end of 1848, a few hundred Icarians did actually arrive in New Orleans sailing over on several different vessels. They rented a large brick building on Saint Ferdinand Street and stayed a few weeks to plan their next endeavor. Cabet himself had departed France in mid-December and finally arrived around the first of January. Near the end of their wits, the Icarians confronted Cabet demanding accountability for his role in the Texas failure. Ultimately about 200 of Cabet's disillusioned disciples returned to France and gave up the Icarian dream altogether. Another 280 loyal souls remained with him and in early March steamed up the Mississippi to begin a new colony in Nauvoo, Illinois.[271]

As for Sully, the only Icarian source that addresses his fate after the retreat is a letter from St. Louis dated May 9, 1849, from a man named Gluntz, an Icarian who had arrived after the second avant-garde. The letter mentions that Sully had just been sent to Paris and London, and that he would come back to Icaria. John Ludlow claims in his memoirs that Sully participated in the revolutionary fights in Paris in 1848 and 1849. Sully was still in America in 1848, but it is possible that he was in Paris in June 1849, having just arrived from New York, when the last violent uprising of the revolution broke out. According to Ludlow, Sully told him that during June 1849, he had fought in the insurrection, "till his arms were bloody to the elbows." In any case, Sully was back in England in 1850 where he joined a Christian workers association. He went back to the United States soon after, but he did not return to be with the Icarians in Nauvoo. Instead, he went to New York where he became the manager of a large firm and remained engaged in workers associations. Finally, he went back to Europe and died in North Wales at an unknown date.[272]

A final news item concerning Icaria appeared on the front page of the *Northern Standard* on January 20, 1849, a year after the Icarians first set sail from Le Havre. One of the members of the second advance guard had ultimately abandoned his Icarian enthusiasm, turning his back on the cause and directing the full force of his anger toward Cabet:

> "Honor and glory to Pacha Cabet and his Janissaries! Icaria is founded: Icaria exists; it is an Eden, a pure Paradise on earth. Oh, if you could only see Icaria." Such are the alluring terms employed in France to entice emigration, and then fleece the poor dupes who listen to them. Blind and unbounded confidence is required, says the Pacha of Icaria. A modest disciple, like many other, I shut my eyes, and took good care not to ask what were the resources of the Icarian treasury. No account was exhibited to us of the receipts or expenditures; nor did the titles of the cession of a million acres of land ever meet our eyes. Poor victims of a misplaced confidence, we handed over our money, and embarked without asking questions... Our arrival in Icaria, however, proved the last and saddest of our many deceptions. We saw, on our arrival, not men but corpses! Not an inch of cultivated ground in this pretended paradise! The first thing we heard was a debt of ten thousand francs! The day after our arrival it was unanimously agreed that the Society was dissolved; everything abandoned, and every member at liberty to select for himself another paradise on earth.[273]

PART 3

A SECOND LIFE IN TEXAS (1848–1871)

CHAPTER 10

A REBIRTH ON THE FRONTIER

He is a genius, teaches music, drawing, dancing,—everything.
Lieutenant Samuel Henry Starr, 1850

REFUGE WITH A TEXAS RANGER

After his frightening retreat from the Icarian colony, Gouhenant embarked on a new chapter in his wildly erratic life. As it happened, he landed at the home of Texas Ranger Samuel A. Pritchett. The Pritchett farm was located roughly ten miles northeast of the Icarian settlement.[274]

Samuel's father, Edley Campbell Pritchett, had brought his family from North Carolina to Texas a few years earlier, and had received a land grant in Peters Colony. In 1847, both Edley and his son volunteered with Captain William Fitzhugh's Company of the Texas Rangers. Edley was a private; Samuel became a bugler. Just a year later, Edley was killed in an Indian battle at Hickory Creek. With Samuel's mother already deceased, that left him and his new wife, Martha Smith Pritchett, to raise Samuel's four siblings, ranging in age from seven to sixteen.[275]

The exact date of Gouhenant's arrival at the Pritchett farm is unknown, but he must have made his way there quickly after his departure from the Icarian settlement. According to Martha Pritchett's recollections, Gouhenant had stayed with the family from about September 1848 to perhaps the latter part of 1849 or early 1850. While there, he spent time resting, helping with family chores, improving his English, and traveling around North Texas. He and Samuel became good friends. In fact, Martha and Samuel had a son on August 15, 1850 and they named him William Adolphus Pritchett, presumably after their French friend. Gouhenant also developed a friendship with the neighboring Withers family.[276]

The year he spent with the Pritchetts served as a much-needed respite for Gouhenant. Now forty-five years old, he was surely weary of conflict and defeat. Fortunately, he found himself in the right place at the right time. Just about thirty miles away, Fort Worth would become a welcoming home and a perfect stage to showcase his talents.

WHERE THE DEER AND ICARIANS PLAY

During his sojourn at the Pritchetts', Gouhenant became acquainted with Mexican War veteran Major Ripley Allen Arnold. Arnold was a tall, handsome, auburn-haired soldier who had survived a stormy career at West Point and subsequent battlefield action, and was now charged with protecting settlers as they continued to encroach further onto native land. Arnold was stationed at Fort Graham when he received orders to head north to establish a new outpost near the West and Clear Forks of the Trinity River.

In May of 1849, a scouting party rode out from Fort Graham to find a site for the new fort. They settled upon a location that sat on a bluff above the West Fork of the Trinity River with woods nearby that would afford ample timber to build the structures. The river was abundant with fish, the trees flush with mockingbirds, jays, and woodpeckers, and the land boasted no shortage of game. Simon Ferrar, a young Texas

Ranger, was traveling with Colonel Middleton Tate Johnson—a man whom Gouhenant would come to know quite well—to determine the appropriate spot for the fort. Ferrar later recorded his impressions of the proposed site with approval and respect worthy of a sacred place:

> It is out of my power to describe the grandeur of the wild and beautiful scenery .... After staying about a week at Johnson's Station, we started in company with Major Arnold's command up the Trinity River .... We passed through and across timbers, crossing different creeks as best we could, through a wild, beautiful country inhabited only by Indians, wild mustang horses, innumerable deer, wolves and wild turkey ... we went until we reached the point where the Court House now stands, there halted and reviewed the scenery from all points and I thought it the most beautiful and grand country that the sun ever shone ....

> While we were at that place in view of all advantages of a natural point of defense, and our late experience at Monterrey, wherein the strategic action of General Worth had so terribly defeated the Mexicans, we there, in honor of that grand old hero, named the point Fort Worth.[277]

Major Arnold ordered his Dragoons to begin constructing the fort and the men commenced working in the heat of June. By mid-winter they had built a barracks, mess hall, commissary, infirmary, stables, and smithy. By the end of the year, the fort was suitable for Arnold's wife Kate and their children, and he sent for them to join him on the banks of the Trinity.

The circumstances surrounding how and when Gouhenant met Major Arnold are murky. An article in the *Dallas Morning News* that appeared about forty years after the founding of Fort Worth offers one clue to the possible first encounter between Gouhenant and the Fort Worth officers after he left Icaria: "Gounant remained for some months in the wood. One day a United States army officer came upon him as he was chopping wood. The officer was going to Fort Worth and was in some doubt as to the route. He inquired of Gounant, but the latter not speaking English very well could give him no information. Gounant, however, was very smart and managed to catch the officer's meaning. He was an expert draughtsman and out of the rude materials at hand soon made a sketch which gave the officer the information he wanted. The officer recognized the man's talent and took him to Fort Worth and gave him employment."[278]

This version of Gouhenant's meeting with the men of Fort Worth is likely a hybrid of local lore and actual events. The story is plausible. However, Gouhenant was known to have been staying at the Pritchett Farm thirty miles north of Fort Worth. The officer would most likely have been traveling north from Fort Graham to Fort Worth (both forts located south of the Pritchett farm). So, if this was their initial meeting, it is unclear why the officers would have encountered Gouhenant so far north, unless they were out scouting. Another version of their meeting states that Gouhenant was skinning deer when the soldiers happened upon him. In either case, it would seem that his current skills had evolved from the decades before when he passed his days in artistic circles, painting and organizing workers, to presently performing tasks that were more aptly suited to frontiersmen. Wherever they met, the encounter was the launching point for the next upswing in Gouhenant's life and the beginning of a lifelong friendship with Ripley Arnold.

Major Arnold took command of the camp in the summer of 1849, and in Fort Worth's fledgling days, he and Gouhenant quickly became friends. Daily life at the Fort was generally unexciting. The winters were miserably cold with housing that consisted of drafty canvas tents or cabins with dirt floors. The summers were unbearably hot, and the fort's proximity to the river provided ample opportunity for mosquitoes to breed, making life very uncomfortable for the soldiers stationed there. Although Major Arnold was known to keep a clean and disciplined fort, outbreaks of malaria, yellow fever, and even cholera were not uncommon; the only surgeon at the post had his hands full with sick soldiers on many occasions. In addition to the physical challenges, the boredom and isolation also proved insufferable for both soldiers and their families.

This captive audience would provide a new opportunity for Gouhenant to earn money and get back on his feet.

An educated man, Major Arnold had a deep appreciation for the arts, languages, and music. In fact, he had written a song while enrolled at West Point that was still sung years after he graduated. Since there were few amusements overall, Gouhenant's presence at the fort provided a welcome relief from the drudgery and daily military drills.

Around Christmas time 1849, a new quartermaster, Lieutenant Samuel Henry Starr, rode into Fort Worth. Starr was diligent in his correspondence with his wife Eliza, and his letters to her offer a compelling glimpse of life at the fort and the few diversions they found there. Starr wrote that he had a small deer that followed him around wherever he went.[279]

When not shooting them for food, frontier folk were apparently fascinated with deer. A traveler through Texas in 1840 describes his experience during breakfast on a wintery morning, "I was gratified and surprised to see enter the door and approach the table a beautiful female deer, having a small bell around her neck. With perfect familiarity she received her breakfast of corn bread, and departed to see its wonted pastime in the woods and prairies. The landlady remarked that it thus came every morning and disappeared till the morning following."[280]

Another traveler, renowned journalist and landscape architect Frederick Law Olmsted, passed through Texas and he too, encountered a pet doe in New Braunfels. Impressed with the "German sense of humanness," Olmsted noted that a "doe wandered around the houses of the rustic community and was docile enough to wear a collar and bell, and lick his hand."[281]

There was no shortage of fawns, turkeys, rabbits, and other amusing creatures in the verdant Texas landscape, but the men at Fort Worth were particularly fascinated by a more novel form of amusement. A French artist on the Texas prairie was infinitely more interesting. Adolphe Gouhenant presented residents at Fort Worth with one of the most artistic and intellectual sources of entertainment in the entire region—there were only a few hundred people living in Tarrant County at the time and there were only about eighty-two dwellings in the entire county.[282]

Lieutenant Starr included frequent passages about the Frenchman in his letters to Eliza. On at least three separate occasions he composed enthusiastic descriptions praising Gouhenant's talents.

On January 6, 1850, just a few days after he arrived at Fort Worth he wrote, "There is a French Gentleman here teaching all the officers, Mrs. [Arnold] and her two daughters (one 11, the other 6 years old) the French language. I shall begin to take lessons on my return from Dallas. I wish you and Kate were here to join in the study. He teaches the language after a plan very simple, requiring very little effort of the memory. He is a genius, teaches music, drawing, dancing, – everything." Again, on January 18, he writes that he himself is learning the language, "I am studying French so are all the men in the army, Mrs. A., and the Major and their children and all –." Finally, on January 25, he reiterates his desire to have his daughter begin her lessons with Gouhenant: "... I am anxious to have Kate here to benefit by the teaching of the F[r]ench master who is residing here, a very accomplished gentleman... He also teaches music, drawing, dancing, singing, embroidering, and, indeed, everything."[283]

After his arrival at Fort Worth, Gouhenant's efforts to regain lost ground ignited like a flint-borne spark in the dry Texas grass. In addition to Starr's portrayal of his artistic activities another account adds that Gouhenant's "superior swordsmanship made the off-duty hours fleeting for the officers of the garrison." And that "he engaged them in fencing, teaching them many of his dexterous tricks with the sword."[284]

Among the forty-three enlisted men at the fort in 1849, at least half were from Europe and the British Isles. While Gouhenant's ability to speak English at the time of his arrival is unknown, his proficiency surely improved during the time he spent with the Pritchetts and with fellow Europeans at the fort, an accomplishment that would benefit him greatly in the months ahead. Gouhenant was undoubtedly pleased to have regained some stature such a short time after parting with the Icarians.

By November of 1850, there were more than ninety soldiers and a handful of officers living at the fort. Gouhenant had moved on, leaving Fort Worth to strike out on his own and establish a business in Dallas, but his friendship with Starr and Arnold endured. They would both travel to spend time with him in the small village thirty miles to the east; the officers journeyed to Dallas for social events and Gouhenant rode back to Fort Worth to visit and tend to his interests near the fort.[285]

Gouhenant had left an impression on the two families. At least two years after he left Fort Worth, Eliza Starr wrote to Mrs. Arnold from New York: "I expect your little Nannie could walk long ago, and talk too by this time, do write me a long letter, I shall receive it with so much pleasure and tell me all the news, how Fort Worth looks and what changes have been made since you returned to it, the least thing will be interesting to me... How does Flor and Kitty get along, do you ever see Mr. Ganar [Gouhenant]?"[286]

320 ACRES OF PRIME TEXAS REAL ESTATE

In the spring of 1850, Gouhenant staked his claim to the land adjacent to the military compound. Because he was a married man over the age of seventeen, and had emigrated to the U.S. prior to July 1848, he was entitled to receive 320 acres under the Peters Colony contract. Just two years after arriving from France, stripped of all material goods with no resources except his own talents to sustain him, he had not only obtained a certificate for land in Texas: by the summer of that year, he had also embarked on a commercial venture securing additional property in Dallas. Regaining his momentum, Gouhenant now had to adapt to his new environment and he was apparently turning his back on the communist principles that brought him to Texas, extinguishing once and for all any smoldering Icarian embers.

Gouhenant chose a parcel of land located just north of Fort Worth (Abstract 582), not far from where the parade grounds and the flagpole were (presently the corner of Houston and Belknap Streets in downtown). He selected a second parcel (Abstract 612), located about three miles south, lying near the present-day site of the Fort Worth Zoo. Both parcels must have offered stunning views at that time; the river, teeming with fish and bordered by buffalo grasses growing alongside its banks, the post oak forests providing shelter for abundant deer, and the rolling hills that offered a westward view rising above the Trinity would have framed a panorama of endless beauty and inspiration. Perhaps it even mirrored the pastoral scene of the Flagy countryside where he was born.[287]

Acquiring the certificates was only the first step in legally obtaining the land patent. The entire process involved three steps: getting the certificate, having the land surveyed, and finally receiving the patent. The process could take several months, or even years, to complete. Complicating matters further, some men had their land surveyed by Peters Colony contractors, but when it came time to patent the land, the field notes could not be located and the land had to be resurveyed. There were ongoing legal issues with the land company.

In fact, both of Gouhenant's 160-acre parcels were surveyed several years after obtaining his certificates, and it is likely that his allocation was initially a single 320-acre plot. In April of 1855, twenty-five-year old A. M. Keen, deputy surveyor of what was then called the Denton Land District, surveyed the first parcel (582) near the fort. Two years later in April of 1857, John Peter Smith, Fort Worth's first educator, surveyed the second parcel (612) of land. (Smith had quit his job as schoolmaster to study law while simultaneously working as a surveyor.)[288]

The final step in the land acquisition process was to patent the land, which was completed a year later in May of 1856. By the spring of 1856, Gouhenant legally owned the land that is today prime real estate in the city of Fort Worth.

Illustration 19. Gouhenant's land patents in Fort Worth (A612 and A582).

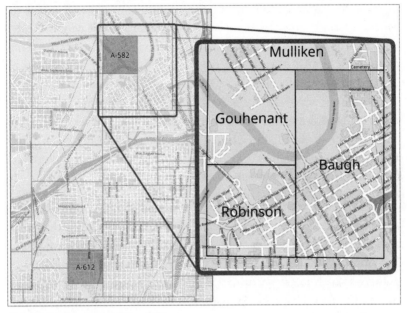

Copyright Emmanuel Pécontal.
The insert shows the re-surveyed plots of Gouhenant, Baugh, Mulliken, and Robinson, as well as the twenty-five-acre parcel of land Gouhenant purchased in 1856 (shaded area).

In recent years, the land near the fort has been the source of confusion. An historical marker states that Gouhenant set aside three acres of land for a cemetery. Although Gouhenant did not yet hold the patent in 1850, he was in possession of the land when a tragic event occurred in the Arnold home. In the summer of that year, the Arnolds' youngest children, Willis and Sophia, both died. Their premature deaths were most likely caused by cholera, or a similar illness. Gouhenant was gravely saddened by their passing. They were placed in graves under the oak trees in what would later become Pioneers Rest Cemetery.[289]

Gouhenant had not really intended for his land to become a city cemetery. Pioneers Rest sits astride two parcels granted to the original colonists under the Peters Contract. The northern portion of the cemetery occupies land granted to Felix Mulliken. South of Mulliken's land is the Mitchell Baugh (southeast) survey and Gouhenant's survey is located just west of Baugh's land. All three men received their Peters Colony certificates in 1850—Gouhenant's was issued on April 15, Baugh's on May 7 and Mulliken's on May 9. All three certificates also state that the land had been surveyed by Peters Colony contractors, but that no field notes could be found. Therefore, each man had his land surveyed again. The new survey was likely different from the one initially made by the Peters Colony contractors, which explains why the Arnold children were buried on land Gouhenant considered to be his.

Baugh's land was re-surveyed in January of 1852. He then sold it to Middleton Tate Johnson that same month for $125. Felix Mulliken's heirs surveyed his 640 acres on June 25, 1852, and then also sold it to Middleton Tate Johnson on April 1, 1853. By the time Gouhenant had his land re-surveyed much later—on April 20, 1855—Middleton Tate Johnson now owned the land formerly claimed by Baugh and Mulliken both north and east of Gouhenant, all the property that the cemetery would occupy. Later, Gouhenant would purchase twenty-five acres from Johnson where part of the cemetery now lies. Then many years later, as land around the site was increasing in value, Gouhenant's brother-in-law would argue before the city council to keep the land as a cemetery.[290]

By 1851, it was clear Gouhenant had made the decision to stay in Texas and he petitioned for American citizenship in May of that year. The French romantic whose undying devotion to Icarian communism had led him across the Atlantic to establish a utopian colony was now marching ardently down the path to frontier capitalism. Now in possession of significant land holdings, and a prime commercial lot in a growing town, he was on his way to becoming more successful than he had ever been in France. His drive was not unusual for men of his generation who ventured from Europe or the East Coast to make a life in Texas, but his artistic talents and creativity certainly were and they would propel him on to his next quest thirty-some miles east to the settlement at the Three Forks of the Trinity River.

CHAPTER 11

THE ARTS SALOON

DALLAS'S FIRST CULTURAL ESTABLISHMENT

Although some historians, going by the name, have mistaken this for a bar, the Art Saloon was something more significant. Starting as a picture gallery, it became a daguerreotype studio by 1852 and thus Monsieur Gouhenant was Dallas' first photographer. To him, we owe most of the scant surviving camera studies of the 1850s.[291]

A.C. Greene, 1973

DOCTORS, LAWYERS, AND MASONS

At mid-century, Dallas was a burgeoning county seat. In 1850, there were about 500 inhabitants in the town center—slightly more than in the village of Flagy where Gouhenant began his life—and about 2,700 people in the county. Most were farmers, but there were a few saddle makers, carpenters, blacksmiths, and several lawyers. John Neely Bryan was the town's first settler; Nathaniel (Nat) M. Burford, J.W. Latimer, and John Calvin McCoy were lawyers. Gouhenant's contemporaries were young, educated, and hard-working men who made notable contributions to Dallas in the earliest days. He counted most of them among his trusted friends, but he also had his share of adversaries. They were all neighbors, fellow Masons, and on several occasions, they would occupy the same court room, some sitting on Gouhenant's side, others on the opposing side.

John C. McCoy had come to Texas five years earlier to work as a surveyor and subagent for the Peters Colony. Before moving to Dallas, he had worked in Missouri and attended law school in Indiana. By 1846, the eloquent and fastidious McCoy was elected as Dallas's first district clerk, but resigned shortly thereafter to resume his law practice. He married his wife Cora M. McDermot in 1851 and they soon had a baby. McCoy's heart was broken a short time later when in the summer of 1853, he lost both his wife and child and buried them both on the same day. He never remarried.

McCoy served during the Civil War and in 1862, he was elected to represent Dallas County in the Texas House of Representatives. According to some, his success as a lawyer "lay in the justice of the cause he would advocate, his deep earnestness, and the truthfulness of his heart as expressed in his words, his countenance and his gestures." He was a founding member of the Tannehill Masonic Lodge and a close friend to Gouhenant.[292]

Nat Burford was born in Tennessee. He later formed a law partnership with John Reagan who would one day be elected to Congress. On the first day of February 1856, he was elected judge of the newly created Sixteenth District while McCoy was elected as District Attorney. Burford was later elected to the Texas House of Representatives, then as Speaker of the House.[293]

John M. Crockett and his wife arrived in Dallas in 1848, from Paris, Texas. He practiced law with the colorful and enigmatic George W. Guess, and also with John Jay Good, both elected as town mayors after the Civil War—Guess in 1866 and Good in 1880. Crockett himself would be elected mayor eight years later and serve three consecutive terms. He became the lieutenant governor of Texas in 1861. Crockett's interests went well beyond law and politics. He was passionate about astronomy and music; he played the violin at parties and was Dallas's own meteorological observer for the Smithsonian Institution. Certainly, he and Gouhenant had much in common.[294]

Still another lawyer came to Dallas from Tennessee. James W. Latimer had opened a law practice—also in Paris—before buying the *Texas Times* with William Wallace. In 1849, they moved to Dallas and started the *Dallas Herald.* Latimer served as justice of the peace and later chief justice of Dallas County. Latimer would later support Gouhenant in some of his legal endeavors.[295]

Adolphe Gouhenant was the *homme étrange* at Three Forks but he soon found his niche among the town leaders, most of whom were Masons. In May of 1849, McCoy, Burford, and Latimer founded the Tannehill Masonic Lodge; John Crockett was the first master and John Good was also a member. In August 1850, Gouhenant returned to his Masonic roots by becoming a member of the Tannehill Lodge in Dallas. By 1853 his name would appear among the six officers of the lodge as the "tyler." An important office, it was the tyler's duty to "guard the door of the Lodge, and to permit no one to pass in who is not duly qualified, and who has not the permission of the Master." Gouhenant had reached the rank of Master Mason and had the full confidence of his fellow Masons.[296]

Gouhenant of course had a long history with the Masons, having joined the Masonic brotherhood in Lyon at the beginning of the 1830s (probably the Union et Confiance lodge). He had achieved the 30th Masonic degree of the Scottish rite—Knight Kadosh—from the lodge Les Sept Écossais in Paris at an unknown date. In 1838 he was affiliated with Française de Saint-Louis lodge in Marseille and in Toulouse in 1843, he was affiliated with Les vrais amis réunis lodge.[297]

In December lodge members paid John Neely Bryan forty dollars for two adjoining lots on Houston Street to construct a two-story building, although they continued to meet in a building on Main and Jefferson until the building was completed a few years later. With only thirty-seven original members, financing the new construction was a challenge, but the men raised the money and by August of 1853, they had moved into the two-story structure that included a porch and a three-foot-wide staircase on the north side of the building. The second floor would be used for meetings, while "the first floor was suitable for church and school purposes. It was set on Bois d'Arc blocks about two feet above ground, and space underneath the first floor became a resting place for hogs, dogs, and other animals."[298]

As well as a number of attorneys, there were also five doctors in town including S.B. Pryor—who would become Dallas's first mayor—Samuel T. Bledsoe, Perry Dakens, S.B. McCommas, and A.D. Rice. The dentist was James B. Bryan.[299] Only three men were listed as merchants in Dallas according to the 1850 census. They were James Patterson and John W. Smith, who were business partners, and Madison M. Miller. Adam Haught was the city's first saloonkeeper (although Haught preferred the title of "ferryman" since he also operated a barge on the Trinity). Haught would later be elected sheriff. Although he had joined the Tannehill Lodge in 1850, Gouhenant's name did not appear in the Dallas County census that year. Whatever the reason for his lack of an official presence, he was well on his way to being established among Dallas's first entrepreneurs, and the men knew each other well, for better or worse.[300]

Illustration 20. John McCoy, the lawyer who claimed the Icarians' land on behalf of their heirs.

Courtesy Dallas Historical Society. Used by permission.
McCoy ultimately paid $1,000 for Gouhenant's Arts Saloon— the photograph was taken many years after he knew Gouhenant.

Illustration 21. Nathaniel Burford, the judge who oversaw *Gouhenant v. Cockrell*.

Courtesy Dallas Historical Society. Used by permission.
The photograph was taken many years after Burford knew Gouhenant.

Illustration 22. John Crockett, Gouhenant's friend and lawyer.

Courtesy Dallas Historical Society. Used by permission.
Crockett argued for the Arts Saloon as Gouhenant's homestead.

Illustration 23. Wedding portrait of John Jay Good and his wife Susan Anna
Floyd taken in 1854.

Courtesy John J. Good Family Papers. Special Collections. The University of
Texas at Arlington Libraries, Arlington, Texas.
The daguerreotype was almost certainly taken by Gouhenant.

DALLAS'S FIRST RESIDENT PHOTOGRAPHER

Gouhenant traveled the distance between Dallas and Fort Worth
frequently. There was no stagecoach line between the two small settlements in the early days; he made the arduous trip on horseback or by
wagon, enduring whatever conditions the Texas weather could throw at
him. In addition to the 320 acres he claimed in Fort Worth, Gouhenant
acquired several lots in the commercial area of Dallas. An old hand at
juggling numerous ventures simultaneously, he joined a handful of other
men who had set their sights on real estate. His first commercial lot and

certainly the most significant of his holdings was Lot 4 in Block 7, which he bought from John N. Bryan in October of 1851. It was conveniently located on the south side of the courthouse square. The spot provided a view facing the square, and light from the north sky fell through the front window, a prime space for an artist's studio. He called his place the Arts Saloon, and it would become the first cultural establishment in Dallas.[301]

The word "Saloon" befuddled travelers passing through Dallas. On several occasions visitors to the town would saunter across the square looking for a drink, but it was no barroom. Gouhenant had opened a magnificent place unique to Dallas and the only art gallery and daguerreo-type studio in the region.

He did not christen his Arts Saloon in error. It was thoughtfully named to reflect what it truly represented. Arts Saloon could have been interpreted as a literal translation of the French *salon des arts*, used for an exhibition of fine arts. Artists in New Orleans for instance, were fond of using the term "saloon" to describe their studios. New Orleans, forty times the size of Dallas County at the time, hosted a number of daguerreotypists. Edward Jacobs was one of the most prominent among them and according to the local press, he was considered to be not only the finest in the city, but among the best in the nation. Like Gouhenant, Jacobs's gallery had both a daguerreotype studio and a fine arts gallery.[302]

The word "saloon" was also used to describe some nineteenth century ice cream parlors. In the late 1840s, Eagle's Ice Cream Saloon was located on the ground floor of a Pittsburgh neighborhood. The proprietor of the Saloon offered ice cream for 12.5 cents. Coincidentally, the Odeon Theater, situated three flights up from Eagle's Ice Cream Saloon, was known as the spot where the Christy Minstrels performed some of Stephen Foster's musical compositions—the same songs that William Smalling Peters's son, W.C. Peters, published in Cincinnati.[303]

In still another instance, The *Photographic and Fine Art Journal*, which was published from 1854 to 1860, makes numerous references to *Saloons*, in the context of art galleries or studios. One item referenced a Saloon in the Louvre where the French Romantic painter, Theodore Gericault, exhibited *The Wounded Cuirassier* in 1814. An 1857 edition of the *Journal* also states, "For what saloon is more agreeable than the large room of an Academy Exhibition in the opening of a new season?"[304]

Gouhenant's studio, aptly named, is certainly less of a puzzle than is his sudden ability to create daguerreotypes. Where did he get the money to purchase the property and buy photographic equipment? One possibility is that during the time he spent with the Pritchetts and teaching the officers at Fort Worth, he was paid a small sum. The officers likely offered him some kind of financial arrangement for music and language lessons. He undoubtedly painted signs, sold drawings or paintings to earn a few dollars, and possibly secured a loan using his Fort Worth acreage as collateral (although it was not yet patented). Even if he did have a loan to purchase property on the square, where did he buy photographic materials and how did he learn to make daguerreotypes? Was he familiar with the process in France?

THE DAGUERREOTYPE: FROM FRANCE TO AMERICA

As early as 1849, suppliers in New Orleans were selling equipment to daguerreotypists and one could purchase a "New York camera" for eighteen dollars—about the same price as the fare on one of Thomas Crutchfield's four-horse stagecoaches from Clarksville to Shreveport. Competitive pricing offered plates for $2.50 per dozen, and daguerreotype cases for about the same price as plates. So, the purchase of equipment was feasible and affordable.[305]

Lieutenant Starr never made any mention of daguerreotypes in his letters to Eliza. Had Gouhenant been making photographs at the fort, surely Starr would have listed that skill among Gouhenant's many talents. The new permanent images were still enough of a novelty in 1850 that Starr would have been as impressed with Gouhenant's ability to operate such an artistic mechanism, as he was by his ability to sing, dance, sew, and teach French.

Europeans had been making daguerreotypes for a few years by the 1850s. In fact, attempts to capture an image with a camera date to the earliest days of the nineteenth century. At the end of the 1700s, it was already known that light could blacken a sheet of paper dampened with silver chloride, for instance, making it possible to register an image created by the *camera obscura*. But the image was rough, negative, and fugitive, disappearing once the paper was exposed to light. A French inventor named Joseph Nicéphore Niépce is credited with making the first fixed photographic image by a chemical process in 1826. Louis Daguerre, a painter and stage designer, learned of Niépce's achievement incidentally, and the two men collaborated to improve the process. After the death of Niépce in 1833, Daguerre continued his research alone, which ultimately led to the invention of a much more efficient chemical process. He kept the process secret for several years until the summer of 1839, when he finally made his technique public at a long-awaited joint meeting of the French Académie des Sciences in Paris. Coincidentally, Samuel Morse was presenting his electromagnetic telegraph invention to the Académie and seeking a European patent about the same time that Daguerre's invention was emerging. Morse was particularly interested in Daguerre's invention since he himself had led experiments in early photographic processes. The two men met in 1839 and Morse wrote a letter to the *New York Observer* that same year chronicling his meeting with Daguerre and expressing how impressed he was by the Daguerreotype. He wrote that "exquisite minuteness of the delineation cannot be conceived."[306]

Niépce's research had been conducted at his home at Chalon-sur-Saône, located only about seventy miles north up the Saône River from Lyon—not far from where Gouhenant was living at the time. It was even in this same town that Gouhenant had given one of his solar microscope exhibitions in August 1833, just a month after Niépce's death. However, Niépce had been quite secretive about his invention and it is unlikely that

Gouhenant knew about his work. Still, Gouhenant did know the optical part of the photographic process perfectly well, shown not only by his experiments with the solar microscope, but also by the optical devices he made available to artists in his observatory in Lyon. It is even possible that he knew how to obtain fugitive images with the camera obscura as early as 1832; in an ad for a solar microscope exhibition published in a Lyon journal that same year, it was claimed, "in the same room, there is also a small device which draws in less than a minute a profile portrait made by the sun on a sheet of paper." While it is not certain that Gouhenant was the organizer of the exhibition, it is highly probable he saw the device.[307]

Daguerre's announcement ultimately allowed individuals worldwide to capture moments in time and his process had such overwhelming momentum that it swept the U.S. with lightning speed. By the mid-1850s, thousands upon thousands of daguerreotypes had been made in the U.S., the process greatly improved upon by innovative Americans. "In 1860... the U.S. Census reported 3,154 photographers. Every major city and town had at least one...and itinerant daguerreotypists traveled to remote backwoods and frontier areas in their horse-drawn 'saloons,' or floated down the rivers in houseboats."[308]

Morse, who had trained as a painter, became a daguerreotypist as well. In fact, Morse was one of the first men to introduce the daguerreotype process to Americans in 1839; Matthew Brady, the famous Civil War photographer, became one of his students. Morse's telegraph, however, did not reach Texas until February of 1854, although the first message had been transmitted ten years earlier. Had the telegraph arrived in Texas just a few years earlier Gouhenant might have been in touch with his family much sooner than he actually was.[309]

While he may have experimented with the process in France, it is much more feasible that Gouhenant became proficient as a daguerreotypist once he settled in Texas. In fact, although no details of these travels have survived, one court reference suggests that Gouhenant spent three months in Waxahachie and Corsicana and also six months in New York pursuing his occupation as "painter and dagueman artist." He had been in contact with another daguerreotypist, Francesco N. Vassallo. Vassallo worked in Clarksville and Austin in the early 1850s. He would later loan Gouhenant money.[310] Vassallo was not only taking portraits of Texans, but also teaching the art of making daguerreotypes. In the summer of 1849, he published an advertisement in the *Northern Standard* of Clarksville:

> Signor N. Vassallo has taken the Room over Rhine's Store, and will be happy to furnish Portraits to the citizens of Clarksville and vicinity, which he will guaranty of superior quality.
>
> Sig. N. has practiced his art in Italy, France and the United States for the last ten years, and feels warranted in claiming superior skill in the taking and finishing of his portraits.
>
> He will give instruction at his Room to any person who may desire to learn the practice of the art and will insure them the necessary knowledge in fifteen days.[311]

Gouhenant may also have traveled back to New Orleans to study the procedure and purchase the chemicals and equipment necessary to set up a studio. He made at least one trip to New Orleans in 1854 to purchase equipment for another endeavor and it is likely that he traveled there on several occasions.

Gouhenant's interest in the daguerreotype would have been quite logical, and he probably had a proprietary interest in the process, both as an artist and a Frenchman. As a romantic, he would have been attracted to the medium; as a man who had an ongoing interest in science and chemistry, he would have appreciated the scientific process; and with his background working as an artist, he would have been well suited to make a living as a daguerreotypist. Wherever he learned to work with photographic chemistry, by the early 1850s, he had mastered the process with enough competence to make a success of his studio to create not only paintings and drawings, but also daguerreotypes of Dallas's first citizens. There are a few surviving daguerreotypes from Dallas's earliest days. Historians attribute the image of Dallas's first two-story brick courthouse (the third physical courthouse), built in 1856, to Gouhenant. That courthouse survived a massive town fire in 1860, but was torn down in 1871. There are photographs of Hord's Ridge (Oak Cliff), Alexander Cockrell, John Neely Bryan, Samuel Jones, and others housed in archives and private collections that survive now only as copies of long lost or broken daguerreotypes. They were in all probability taken by Gouhenant. Descendents of Dallas's first citizens may hold troves of photographed ancestors sitting on shelves, in boxes, and packed away in attics that Gouhenant made mid-century.[312]

Illustration 24. The Dallas courthouse in 1856. Daguerreotype attributed to Gouhenant.

From *Our City—Dallas: A Community Civics* by Justin F. Kimball, published by the Kessler Plan of Dallas in 1927.

Illustration 25. The daguerreotype assumed to be of Major Ripley Arnold and his wife Catherine.

Ripley Arnold Collection, Tarrant County Archives. Used by permission. The photographer is unknown; however, if it was taken between 1852 and 1853, which would be compatible with the apparent age of the man, it was likely taken by Gouhenant.

There are also several daguerreotypes believed to be of Major Arnold and his family that have survived and remain in excellent condition. Although there are no markings on the front of the daguerreotypes nor on the cases, it seems likely they were taken by Gouhenant.[313] While there were other daguerreotypists traveling around Texas about the same time Gouhenant was there, he was the only daguerreotypist with a studio in the Fort Worth/Dallas area in the early 1850s. He was a good friend of the Arnolds and he was respected for his artistic ability. If the images of the Arnolds were made in North Texas, it is reasonable to argue for Gouhenant as the photographer.[314]

THE ARTS SALOON

Ultimately, Gouhenant's photographic adventures resulted in the establishment of one of North Texas's most unique places. Not only was his Arts Saloon the first photography studio in Dallas; in a very short time it became the scene of lively conversation, dances, art shows, photographic sessions, and reunions. It quickly gained renown as the center of town activity, as a place to socialize, learn, and worship; it even served as a temporary courthouse. The distinctive identity of the business coupled with his charismatic personality were sufficient magnets to attract both the local population like John Crockett, Nat Burford, John McCoy, and Major Arnold, and travelers as they passed through Dallas.

Dallas continued to grow over the next few years. Thomas Crutchfield, a local businessman, responded to the demand for overnight accommodations and built Dallas's first permanent hotel in 1852. He constructed his building on the northwest corner of the square, across from Gouhenant's Arts Saloon. At the Crutchfield House, visitors could enjoy a square meal for twenty-five cents and room and board for $12 to $15 a month. According to lore, the dinner bell that hung outside the hotel was one of the first bells in Dallas. In addition to calling folks for meals, the bell was also used as target practice on at least one occasion by a drunk gun slinger.[315]

Crutchfield was only a month older than Gouhenant and a friendship developed between the two men. Crutchfield's son, James Oscar, would have been in his early twenties about the time the Crutchfield House and Arts Saloon opened. In 1889, James shared his fond memories of visiting the Arts Saloon and his description of the space was printed in the *Dallas Morning News*. He vividly described the Arts "Salon," which may have been how it was pronounced when he attended events there as a young man.

> [It] was a one-story frame 25x40 and was canvassed with domestics on the walls and ceiling. Here the enterprising Frenchman opened the first photograph gallery in Dallas. I have one of his pictures, taken in 1852, in my possession now. In addition to taking pictures it became a famous resort for the citizens to meet socially. Many a dance have I seen there in the old days, with Hon. A.G. Walker, the man who beat John H. Reagan for the state senate, as a musician. He would accompany his music on the violin...[316]

The younger Crutchfield claimed that Gouhenant had over $300, which he used to open the 1,000-square-foot saloon. He described the frequent dances and social events hosted by Major Arnold and the men of Fort Worth that many citizens of Dallas attended.[317]

The Arts Saloon was a multi-purpose building, and on at least one occasion it was used as the site of judicial activity. As the newly established county seat, Dallas's men answered the call of civic duty and built a 16-by 32-foot one-story frame structure in the span of one week. It served as office space, a repository for records, and for sessions of the district court. Since the tiny courthouse was only about half the size of the Arts Saloon, when the court was in session additional space was needed and the proceedings would move to space that could better accommodate such events. During the last term of the district court in 1852, Dallas residents were treated to an additional seventy-two-square-feet of judicial comfort within the walls of the Arts Saloon.[318]

The Arts Saloon was certainly well established by the spring of 1852 and Adolphe Gouhenant embodied the spirit of the place, presenting a striking image with his blond beard and long hair. He had worked tirelessly to elevate his social status in his newly adopted home and he was once again a thriving, energetic, and upstanding citizen.

One visitor to the Arts Saloon was Charles DeMorse. He was the well-known editor of the *Northern Standard* of Clarksville, the most prominent newspaper in the area. (Although the *Dallas Herald* began publishing in 1849, it remained a weekly publication until 1874.) DeMorse was actually named Charles Denny Morse at birth, and remarkably was a distant cousin of Samuel Morse, both men having descended from brothers who came to New England in the mid-1600s. DeMorse had served in the Mexican War as a young man and was taken prisoner at one point. During his imprisonment, he gave his name to one of the guards as "Charles D. Morse." The guard misunderstood and wrote it as, "Charles DeMorse." His amused friends encouraged him to keep his new moniker, and because it incorporated part of his mother's name (Denny), he made the switch and kept the name for the rest of his life.

DeMorse had been traveling during the first week of April 1852. His companions were District Judge Bennett Martin and Captain William Fitzhugh, the same Fitzhugh who had led the company that Samuel Pritchett and his father had served in a few years earlier. The travelers had journeyed south from McKinney, where they had attended recent court proceedings. During their trip, Fitzhugh entertained DeMorse and the judge with colorful stories of him and his brother herding buffalo to the East Coast in their youth. They had met up with P.T. Barnum before selling the buffalo on speculation to a buyer in Europe, and ultimately getting swindled in the process.

Illustration 26. Charles DeMorse, editor of the Clarksville Northern Standard.

DeMorse documented his visits to the Arts Saloon in 1852 and 1853— he found Gouhenant's watercolors to be "decidedly beautiful."

The good humored but weary men finally arrived in Dallas on Saturday evening to eat and rest before heading on to Denton for the next session of District Court. The three companions encountered the Arts Saloon, and DeMorse subsequently penned a front-page editorial describing his time there and his unforgettable meeting with Adolphe Gouhenant.[319]

> We reined up our beasts before the Crutchfield House, a very respectable hotel of two stories, passably well kept, and went up stairs to the room assigned us. Looking out the front window the first attraction to my eye was a building opposite, with a wide front, upon which appeared in Church text, well delineated the words, "The Arts Saloon"—looking again, I tried to read it The Ark Saloon, not understanding what a gallery of the Fine arts should be doing at the city of the Three Forks, but rather supposing that a drinkery had been so termed, to indicate its generalizing character; but the immoveable letters defied my scrutiny, and would read no other way than Arts Saloon. So, concluding that here was something to be inquired into, I proceeded with the usual ablutions, and change of dress after travel, and sallied out. The first difficulty to be encountered was to get out of a Railroad speech, for which his Honor had been involuntarily advertised, and to which your correspondent was also complimentarily invited. His Honor boldly faced the difficulty, and made the speech, daring the progress of which your correspondent, being of lesser magnitude, escaped in the smoke, and retreated to the outer confines of the square. The Arts Saloon we soon found to be the head quarters of Monsieur Gouhenant, a gentleman of education and accomplishments who had come out with the first French emigration to the Cross Timbers, and after some vicissitudes incident to life in a strange land, and the fortunes of an enterprise, had settled himself in Dallas, and between teaching French and Spanish languages, the painting of pictures and signs, and instruction upon half dozen musical instruments, had constituted himself a decided feature of the place.

After Judge Martin and DeMorse met with Gouhenant, DeMorse wandered around town enjoying the cool spring evening. Later, he and his companions returned to the Arts Saloon.

At night, attracted by the lights and sound of the violin, we proceeded to the Saloon and found a dance in full operation, in which, besides the ladies and the resident gentlemen, were participating, Maj. Arnold the gentlemanly commandant of Fort Worth, and Maj. Young, the Sutler for that Post. We found the main room of the Saloon large enough for two sets at a time, and in a little recess at one side was an Hon. Member of the legislature playing the violin, assisted by Mons. Gouhenant. The Saloon itself was draped with flesh colored canvass, and pleasantly lighted, and to the best of my ability I represented the City of Clarksville upon the floor. His Honor, not caring to dance, enjoyed himself by mixing conversationally.

DeMorse returned one last time before he left Dallas.

This morning, Sunday School was held at the Arts Saloon, and subsequently there was preaching at the same place. So my readers will perceive that the Arts Saloon occupies no mean position at "the Three Forks." During the morning Mons. G. exhibited to us some specimens of his painting, in both oil and water colors, some of the latter decidedly beautiful.

C.D.M.[320]

The following Saturday, DeMorse published another account of his trip to Dallas in a second front-page editorial, where he recounted his impression of Gouhenant's wine-making abilities: "I should mention that at Dallas, I found some wine made by Mons. Gouhenant from the native Mustang Grape, resembling in color the best claret, but sour when I tasted it, like Claret vinegar. It was said to have been originally very palatable."[321]

The minutes from the Tannehill Lodge in 1852 also describes a very picturesque event that occurred on the evening of June 24 celebrating St. John of Summer.

By order of the Worshipful Master a procession was formed under the direction of brothers R.A. Arnold and Samuel B. Pryor,

Marshalls, the brethren in their appropriate and imposing regalia, comporting themselves with elegance of order so peculiar to our noble institution, and the weather being superbly auspicious, the procession moved with well timed step to the spirit stirring strains of the solemn noted Flute, and the Violins soft mellow tones, and marched to the Dallas Inn, where a large number of Good Samaritans, Heroines of service, and Masons Daughters, together with many fair female relatives joined the procession and proceeded to the grove, where after an impressive invocation by the Chaplin, and a Masonic Ode promiscuously sung, the brethren and friends were entertained for Thirty or Forty minutes by an appropriate address by the Orator (John M. Crockett, who also wrote these minutes) from whence the procession repaired to the Arts Saloon, and sisters, brothers all united in partaking of the elegant and sumptuous dinner prepared by Bro. S.B. Pryor and ladies.[322]

DeMorse wrote about his meeting with Gouhenant once again and published it later that summer. After leaving Alton on the morning of April 8, DeMorse had ridden a while and was a few miles from Gainesville exploring the Grand Prairie when he came across a number of fossilized items he described as petrified terrapin, ammonites, buffalo bones, and even Indian monuments. He then recalls examining fossils at Gouhenant's place in Dallas. By this time, DeMorse assumes that his readers are well acquainted with Gouhenant since he provides little background for his recollection and simply mentions his name and town,

At Dallas Mons. Gouhenant showed me the petrified bark of a tree four inches through. The inner wood was gone, but the bark was perfect with pebbles adhering to it. The piece of tree that I have, was found in the open prairie— the others in a creek. The house I write this in is situated upon a hill, on the North of the Elm Fork of Trinity, which we crossed half a mile before getting here. The place is known as Fitzhugh's old station.[323]

Gouhenant had become well-known across the region and travelers were aware of his artistic endeavors. The year following DeMorse's visit to the Arts Saloon, Gouhenant was in Fort Worth and created quite a sign for his friend's hotel. Since their early days together at the fort, Gouhenant and Captain Ephraim Merrell Daggett had remained friends. After the fort closed permanently, Daggett appropriated the former cavalry stables and turned them into a dirt-floor hostelry. One time while he was away, Gouhenant painted a life-sized mural promoting his friend's hotel.[324]

> In 1853 Dr. Gounah exhibited his talent as a landscape painter on the northwest corner of the public square by painting a hotel sign for that good old patriot, Capt. E. M. Daggett, Fort Worth's first hotel keeper. While the captain was away the doctor erected a cloth canvas covering nearly half of the hotel front. On this canvas he pictured in life size toothsome game to inveigle the appetite of the itinerant cowboy. Deer were there running full tilt and bear en rampant, as they say in heraldry, and many other of the lesser tribes, to grace the captain's festive board. This was the first hotel sign ever painted in Fort Worth and the like of it has never been and will never be again. It was such a drawing card the stranger needed no invitation to feast with a pioneer in another direction.[325]

Daggett was himself a colorful individual. He had fought with the well-known ranger Jack Coffee Hays in the Mexican War and during one of their raids in Puebla, Daggett captured several souvenirs from General Santa Anna's personal stash. The Mexican general had fled his quarters at Tehuacán just moments ahead of the invading company, leaving behind not only trunks containing valuable treasures, but lighted candles still burning on the dinner table. The day after the raid, Daggett rode north with Hays's company, wearing Santa Anna's military coat.[326]

The Art Saloon was the most significant of Gouhenant's artistic efforts in Dallas, but just the beginning of his quest for prominence in Texas. It was the first of many town lots he purchased as he continued to buy and sell real estate in Dallas for the next several years. Court records are incomplete, so details of specific transactions are sketchy.

Illustration 27. Map showing the lots Gouhenant owned in 1854.

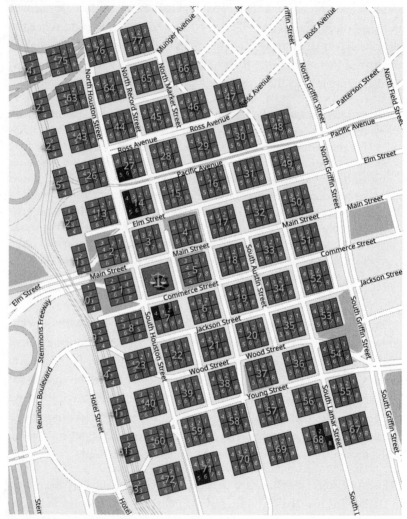

Copyright Emmanuel Pécontal.
The lots owned by Gouhenant are shown in dark gray. The original Dallas plat is in
light gray overlay. The Arts Saloon was Lot 4 Block 7, on the south side of the courthouse square.

Still, there is documentation that as early as January 15, 1852, Gouhenant paid $100 for a lot on the same side of the street and in the same block that housed the Arts Saloon. He bought the space from William and Martha Beeman (William was John Neely Bryan's brother-in-law.), but he only purchased a portion of the space: the "west half of Lot 2 in Block 7, also the south half of the east half of the same lot..."

About a year later in December 1852, he paid fifty dollars for Lot 5 in Block 14 that was owned by John Neely Bryan and Alexander Cockrell, located one block north of the courthouse square. There were four more real estate transactions in 1853. In January he bought Lots 5 and 6 in Block 71 from William H. Beeman. In March, he sold the lot he bought the previous December to his friend, Maxime Guillot. Guillot had arrived in Dallas about the same time, and opened a wagon and carriage shop on the opposite side of the square from Gouhenant's Arts Saloon. According to Victor Considerant, who arrived in Dallas that same year, Guillot was living with Gouhenant at that time along with another Icarian from the first avant-garde, Luc Bourgeois.[327] Like Gouhenant, Guillot was building a successful business. He too, continued to buy town lots and by 1859 had bought five more properties just west of Gouhenant's saloon.[328]

Then, in the spring of 1853, Gouhenant purchased Lot 4 in Block 14 from Samuel H. Beeman and Lot 6 in Block 14 from Wesley Morgan. Dallas had been voted as the permanent county seat three years earlier, and for those who were willing to speculate, there was ample opportunity for growth and even the potential to become wealthy. DeMorse returned to Dallas again a year later, and noted the development of the expanding town when he wrote, "... I notice the Masonic Hall which has been a long time under way, is now moving onward to completion, and also that Monsieur Gouhenant has a quantity of cedar frame work lying about, to create a large addition to the "Arts Saloon." Other minor improvements have been made since I was here."[329] Gouhenant was planning to enlarge the Arts Saloon and expand his growing empire. By the spring of 1853, Gouhenant had been living in America for five years. He had pulled himself up from the depths of the darkest mosquito-infested waters and escaped a nasty flogging from former Icarian brothers. He had spent time among farmers and soldiers and made new friends among the frontiersmen. Finally, he had found a means of using his artistic skills to make a living and earn a place among his new American peers.

However, competition was on the horizon. By the late 1850s, photography was becoming even more popular; by 1856 A man named O'Neill had opened a daguerreotype studio in the Odd Fellows Hall over a carpenter's shop near the town square, and during the winter of 1858, D.B. Griffin had arrived for a six-month stay in Dallas before traveling south in August, when, according to the newspaper, he intended to visit Mexico "to daguerreotype the bronzed señors and lovely señoritas of that country...." In 1859 S.A. Galleher was charging $1.50 and up for his work. Soon, the daguerreotype would disappear completely, leaving behind a broken case and a few pieces of shattered glass—a fragile and quaint novelty of the past.[330]

CHAPTER 12

TWO FRENCHMEN
AND A FUNERAL

One of our countrymen who settled in Dallas (who is no other than the brave Gouhenant, the leader of the first Icarian avant-garde), has begun last year to gather and press wild grapes. The wine he obtained brought a dollar a bottle out of the press ... and I think there is no doubt that vineyards of the finest kind could be raised on the rocky slopes of the country.[331]

Victor Considerant, 1854

LAYING DOWN PERMANENT ROOTS

The cold winter morning that he sailed from Le Havre was the last time Gouhenant would see his homeland. He likely never planned to return to France; his dream was to establish a new community in Texas built on Cabet's Icarian theories. Once the settlement had failed and he was back on his feet, he could have made an attempt to return home. His family was still there, but his marriage was likely over. There had been no communication between Adolphe and his wife Jeanne since he left France. Transatlantic letters could take weeks, perhaps months, to arrive, assuming none were lost along the way. There appeared to be no imminent plan for a reunion in Texas. So, he stayed on in Texas reinventing himself again... and again.

Jeanne and Adolphe had been living apart during the trial in 1843, and she had taken up residence elsewhere. She may have been desperate for her husband to return to France where he could thrive under the new Republic, or possibly she was angry with him for abandoning her and their children. This part of their story remains a mystery.

In her father's absence, their daughter Anastasie, or Anna as she was now known, had grown up. She had remained in France, and at the age of twenty-two, married a Belgian artist, Charles-Borromée Antoine Houry, on October 5, 1853. Like her father, Anastasie's husband was a painter and he was a pupil of Léon Cogniet, who had himself been a student of Edgar Degas, at the Ecole des Beaux-Arts in Paris. Houry painted genre scenes and portraits. He had also made a name for himself painting porcelain with his brother Jules in Anvers, Belgium. In addition, he had exhibited at the Paris Salon in 1850. Anna was also artistic. It seems she had inherited her father's love of music; she was a talented pianist and singer. Also, like Gouhenant, she got involved in politics and would become a rather vocal advocate for the women's suffrage movement a few years later.[332]

No diary or letters between Anna and Gouhenant have survived, but her feelings for her father must have been quite complicated. Her mother's letters, however, give some indication of how Jeanne felt, at least shortly after he left France. Jeanne's tone, reflected in her letters to Cabet when she requested his assistance with their son Ernest, showed every indication that she still supported her husband. Whatever financial consideration, family quarrel, physical challenge, or illness may have kept them apart, by 1853, Gouhenant had made his decision to become a U.S. citizen official.

During the 1850s, only a dozen or so men sought American citizenship in Dallas. Of those, the earliest recorded instance occurred during the 1853 term of district court. Four men appeared before Judge John H.

Reagan the third week in May. They were: John Jackson, Maxime Guillot, Francisco Bartolomus Natale Vassallo—the same itinerant daguerreotypist who probably helped Gouhenant with his daguerreotypes—and Adolphe Gouhenant. The first three all filed their intent to become citizens, while Gouhenant, who had actually declared his intent to do so two years earlier, took his final oath on May 16. He swore to "absolutely and entirely renounce and abjure all allegiance and fidelity to any foreign prince, potentate, state, or sovereignty whatsoever, and particularly to Napoléon III present Emperor of the Government of France of whom [he] was a late subject."[333] Fellow Mason Judge Reagan signed the proclamation, making Gouhenant officially the first naturalized citizen in Dallas.[334]

The process of becoming a citizen was quite simple. A naturalization law from 1802 had attempted to establish uniformity in the process; the law required, among other things, that immigrants file an "intent" to become a citizen and then wait three years before taking a final oath. In Gouhenant's case, there was only a two-year period—almost to the day —from the time he filed his intent to the day he took his final oath. The procedure to obtain citizenship seems to have been somewhat random from state to state since the federal government did not begin to oversee the process until 1906. Still, as an increasing number sought to become American citizens, there were plenty of men with experience in the matter ready to dispense advice.[335]

Viktor Bracht, one of the many German immigrants who had arrived in Texas a few years earlier, penned a helpful guide published in 1848 that was designed to assist German colonists headed to Texas. Along with detailed descriptions of flora and fauna, Bracht also directed settlers on the appropriate size to build windows in their soon-to-be-constructed cabins. On the subject of citizenship, he simply advised, "The acquisition of citizenship at the earliest possible date is very important. You simply declare before a justice of the peace or district judge at the place you have selected as your residence that you wish to become a citizen of the United States. After the expiration of a number of years, you are then a real citizen."[336] On the subject of politics and religion, Bracht was more abrasive and he certainly would not have approved of Gouhenant's Icarian background when he cautioned that "Communism and Mormonism are diseased plants that will not thrive even in the healthful west... and Communism in America need not set its expectations too high." He also sternly advised that "cowardly, stupid, and lazy people have no place in America."[337]

MORE SOCIALISTS ARRIVE IN TEXAS

Victor Prosper Considerant would likely not have been swayed by Bracht's admonition. Considerant was a French utopian socialist and an ardent follower of the early socialist philosopher, Charles Fourier.

Although Fourier was advocating for a radical societal change along with Cabet, Saint-Simon, Owen, and other utopian socialists, he considered that any new organization should take into account the differences among men. Fourier claimed to have discovered a scientific classification of human passions and the optimal way to organize the collaboration between men according to these individual passions. In his social system, private property was allowed—not abolished—and, in that respect, his philosophy was fundamentally different from Icarian communism. Another striking difference was that Fourier and his successors considered a small-scale experiment essential for the success of a global application of his principles, while Cabet ultimately decided to establish a small Icaria because he was desperate to see French society peacefully adopt his doctrine. Fourier had even theorized the organization of a small scale community which he called *phalanstery* (a combination of the words *phalanx* and *monastery*). He considered everything: the geographical situation, the architecture, and the sociological composition of the population in the proposed phalanstery. Some of his followers first attempted to establish a community in 1833 in France, but it quickly failed; several others were founded in Brazil, Algeria, and even in the U.S. between 1837 and 1847, all of which eventually failed.[338]

Illustration 28. Victor Considerant, the Utopian socialist (Fourierist).

Bibliothèque nationale de France. Used by permission.
Considerant founded La Réunion and met Gouhenant in front of the Arts Saloon in 1853.

In June 1849, Victor Considerant had been involved in an insurrection against Louis Napoléon Bonaparte, President of the Second French Republic, who later became the Emperor Napoléon III (and thanks to

Victor Hugo's scathing criticism of him, *Napoléon Le Petit*). Considerant, along with Victor Hugo and many other French activists, had been living in exile in Belgium when he met the American socialist Albert Brisbane. Brisbane, Considerant, and Gouhenant were three men whose dreams would find a shared path in Texas. They would come together based on their political philosophies. Promises would be made between them, and in time, those promises would be broken. Albert Brisbane would play a prominent role in Gouhenant's future.

Brisbane was born to a wealthy family in Batavia, a small town in western New York. As a youth, his thirst for intellectual stimulation began early.[339] Brisbane's father sent him to boarding school and he wound up in New York City, where he was exposed to new cultural experiences and embarked on an intense study of French. He was average in appearance, with brown hair that he parted on the side, a slight Hapsburg jaw, and a narrow strip of facial hair that ran down the side of his face.

By the age of nineteen, Brisbane had sailed for Europe to further his education. He remained abroad for six years, living in France and Germany and visiting a dozen other countries. A member of the privileged class, he had no trouble navigating the circle of intellectual elites. During his travels, he met with some of the most accomplished men and women of the nineteenth century. The list of his encounters included relationships— or at the very least—memorable conversations with General LaFayette, Goethe, Hegel, Felix Mendelssohn, Horatio Greenough, and Samuel Morse.

Over the years, he crossed the Atlantic several times, each trip meeting more writers, musicians, royals, and academics. He studied philosophy, architecture, art, music, anatomy, astronomy, and geology. Returning to the U.S., he worked with Horace Greenley, met Daniel Webster, debated with Senator Calhoun, and spoke with Wendall Phillips and Frederick Douglass. Yet, it was his friendship with a classmate, Jules LeChevalier, a follower of the socialist philosopher Saint-Simon and later of Charles Fourier, that had the most profound influence on him.

Illustration 29. Albert Brisbane, a Utopian Socialist and Fourierist.

New York Public Library.
Brisbane accompanied Considerant to Dallas on the scouting trip for Considerant's
colony. Gouhenant mortgaged the Arts Saloon to Brisbane in 1854.

Brisbane was so enraptured with Fourier's ideas, he pronounced, "life on earth seemed to me utterly empty. For days after I was possessed with the strongest desire to get away from this world and to be able by some means to participate in that grand, Cosmic life."[340] He was also familiar with Icarian doctrine. In April of 1849, he penned a letter to the Icarians offering them information about Nauvoo, the Illinois community where they had settled after the Texas fiasco.[341]

Brisbane's socialist views, knowledge of astronomy and science, and his proximity to the European elite, were aspects of his persona that certainly attracted Gouhenant. Brisbane, Considerant, and Gouhenant not only shared a socialist philosophy, but they also had a shared romantic and revolutionary spirit, and apparently a mutual penchant for getting arrested or tossed out of town.

While in Europe, Brisbane and Considerant would meet and have long discussions about the idea of establishing a utopian colony in America. Considerant had been an ardent disciple of Fourier for several years and had been looking for place to establish a colony to put Fourier's theories into practice. Brisbane had been pressing Considerant to accompany him to America to establish a colony there. Finally, Considerant acquiesced and in December of 1852, the two men boarded a powerful new paddle-wheel steamer, *The Arctic,* and headed to America.[342]

Just two weeks later, they arrived in New York Harbor. Considerant spent the first few weeks of his time in America exploring New York and meeting Horace Greeley—founder and editor of the *New York Tribune* —and other prominent journalists. Considerant also visited a Fourierist community in Red Bank, New Jersey. However, he was not too impressed with the colony and wrote that poverty was evident in the community and the leaders were tired and discouraged. Yet, he stayed on for a while to plan his travels and work on his English.

He visited other cities along the East Coast for the next several months. Considerant and Brisbane continued to meet and debate the best path forward for establishing a Fourierist community in America. Ruling out other areas of the country because of the price of land, or long winters that would stifle production, they finally agreed that the American West would be the most promising option for a settlement. At that time the failure of the Icarians' attempt in North Texas was well known among socialists worldwide, but it did not discourage Considerant from exploring the very same land to settle his own colony.

They left Buffalo on April 10, 1853, and headed for Cleveland, then traveled downriver for several weeks, arriving in Fort Smith, Arkansas, in mid-May. On May 19, they purchased horses and saddles and headed out for the 200-mile, eight-day journey to Preston, Texas (now a ghost town, Preston was north of present-day Sherman).[343]

They finally arrived in Texas during the last days of spring. Riding south on the Preston road, Considerant and Brisbane pulled up their horses at the home of none other than Samuel Pritchett! Meeting Mrs. Pritchett, Considerant described her as a "delicate, petite woman, recovering from a recent bout of pneumonia." He learned that her husband had died about six months earlier. Considerant also discovered that the Icarian settlement had been located about ten miles from their farm. Mrs. Pritchett told Considerant that after the colony had failed and the French had scattered, her husband had taken in one of the Frenchmen, who had "stayed with them for a little over a year."[344]

Mrs. Pritchett told Considerant that "Adolphe Gouhenant was a good man." She took out a small bag and from it, pulled out a note where he had written his thanks to the "brave people who had given him hospitality."[345]

Hearing that Gouhenant was now in Dallas, "keeping a saloon and teaching a school," they continued on their journey south toward Dallas to meet him. Forty-eight hours later, Considerant and Brisbane, weary from their travels, arrived at the Arts Saloon. They inquired about the proprietor, and were surprised when Gouhenant himself answered. Considerant spoke to Gouhenant in French, and was completely unprepared for the emotional response that he received. "Gouhenant responded with such excitement when I introduced myself that he nearly fainted, fell in my arms and broke into tears."[346] Gouhenant told Considerant that he had read about their arrival in a newspaper and was wondering how he could manage to meet them. Coincidentally, the news about Considerant's travels had appeared in the newspaper the same day as the announcement about Gouhenant's plan to enlarge the Arts Saloon. He had seen the story about his own business expansion, and read past that item to page two, where he came across the article about Considerant and Brisbane.[347]

The next day, they strolled down to a cool spot on the banks of the Trinity, situated themselves under an old cottonwood tree, and Considerant listened to Gouhenant's saga going back to his trial ten years earlier, and his affiliation with Étienne Cabet. Considerant wrote that Gouhenant's *Odyssey* would take several sessions to fully tell. It was thrilling and would fill two volumes, he wrote. The men remained in Dallas for several days before departing to complete the scouting trip for the proposed community.[348]

Considerant provides additional evidence about Gouhenant's clandestine activities in southern France plotting against the monarchy, and even offers some explanation of his supposedly selling out to police —the conspiracy his own Icarian brothers accused him of at Icaria. Considerant wrote,

> There was a secret society that was to extend throughout France. In the south, it was under his direction. This was the basis for the trial in Toulouse and the reason for his imprisonment. He had been jailed for 50 days at first in a dungeon during the coldest part of the winter, and then placed in jail for another 8-9 months. He gave me the oddest details of the conspiracy.
>
> He succeeded in getting out of jail, halting the police searches, and the unwarranted arrests using a well-conceived strategy. He wrote to the Prefect of Toulouse that prison had defeated him and that he was willing to provide information of the utmost importance in exchange for compensation. Thereafter, it was determined that the bulk of the case was solved and the investigation lost momentum. Gouhenant created diversions, always buying more time; months

passed and the investigation eventually slowed. Finally, the case was brought to trial.

Without denying the secret meetings, which had been proven, Gouhenant claimed they were only dealing with communist doctrines. Cabet's defense was clever, and all the defendants were acquitted, there was no light shed on the actual events and they never got to the real basis of the charges.[349]

Considerant writes that it was because of Gouhenant's affiliation with Cabet that he was later chosen to lead the avant-garde going from Paris to Texas with 12,000 francs and 75 men.[350]

Gouhenant told Considerant that Cabet had promised reinforcements and additional resources, but that he did not provide accurate information about the overland journey, nor the unreasonably short amount of time that they would have to construct cabins in order to comply with the Peters Colony's requirements to take possession of the land. Gouhenant further told Considerant that because they arrived during the hottest time of the year, they were exhausted, demoralized, and soon overcome with fever. Arguments erupted. Jealousy and competition took over and the men began verbally abusing Gouhenant, flinging insults and accusations while he had tried in vain to appease them. Tension finally reached a bursting point when the second avant-garde arrived accusing him of betrayal and forcing him to flee. Considerant's letter continues by stating that once Gouhenant was under the Ranger's protection, he began a new series of adventures, some of which were "fantastic." He then writes that he will not say further about Gouhenant's exploits in his letter. Regrettably, Considerant's failure to resume writing resulted in the loss of a key piece of an historic puzzle.

According to Gouhenant, he held no grudge against his companions. Not knowing at the time about the newspaper accusing him of betrayal, he was at a loss and could offer no explanation of Cabet's behavior towards him and surmised that he was distracted by the revolution of 1848, which had of course occurred only a few weeks after the advance guard left France. In addition to his unscrupulous land deal with Peters, Cabet had taken a leading role in the revolution, leaving the men of Icaria in the lurch for a longer period of time than he initially planned.

Gouhenant lamented to Considerant that during the entire time that he had been in Texas, he had received no communication from France until just two weeks before Considerant had arrived. He had finally received a letter from his sister, Marguerite—a letter marking the beginning of a renewed correspondence that would at last reunite him with some of his family.

Considerant promised Gouhenant he would carry his words back with him and respond to the slander printed in *Le Populaire*.[351] Considerant did in fact ultimately publish a very short summary of his encounter with Gouhenant in his book *Au Texas*:

> I intended to add a special note devoted to A. Gouhénans, named several times in this report. Those who read *Le Populaire* in 1848 know the accusation with which he has been charged.
>
> The narrative of the facts, able to set the record straight on his account and on the history of the first Icaria expedition sent to America, would lead us too far. I will only say that when these facts will be published, and they will be, they will allow a full rehabilitation of the accused, and the accusers will have to justify themselves if it is only possible.[352]

Considerant, who would soon face the hardships of the settlement of his own utopian community in North Texas, would never find the time to publish this promised justification of Gouhenant.

The arrival of Victor Considerant and Albert Brisbane in the spring of 1853 was significant for several reasons. The meeting between Considerant and Gouhenant documents perhaps the only meeting between the two Frenchmen, who are often linked as being together at La Réunion Colony. It also provides Gouhenant's accounts of Icaria's failure and the events that took place during the final, disastrous days and of his own role in promoting communism in southern France in the early 1840s.

Their conversation was also important to Considerant because it shed light on certain pitfalls of establishing a new colony in Texas, and it provided details about problems the colonists would likely face creating the Fourierist settlement. He now understood the need for planning everything to the last detail, and the necessity for a well-prepared avant-garde. He also became convinced, more than ever, that under the right conditions, Texas was the perfect spot to establish the colony. For Gouhenant, their arrival marked the first meeting with Albert Brisbane, a complex man who would be both Gouhenant's supporter and nemesis over the next few years.

Brisbane and Considerant left Dallas and rode west to Fort Worth to meet Brevet Major Hamilton Merrill; Major Ripley Arnold and his men had left Fort Worth the previous summer and Merrill had replaced Arnold as commandant of the fort. Coincidentially, Brisbane and Merrill had both grown up in Batavia, New York. Merrill graciously welcomed the two travelers and served as their host and guide for the duration of their scouting trip.

Their idea for establishing the new colony was to purchase 250 to 300 square leagues of land in the vicinity of Fort Worth. As the price of land was rising, they made plans to return to Europe and reinvigorate their efforts by promoting the concept for the colony in Texas. They would establish a joint-stock company to buy the land, with the goal of purchasing it inside of two years. According to their well-laid plans, the Fourierist colony in Texas would be realized.[353]

FUNERAL FOR A FRIEND

Just a few months after Considerant and Brisbane left Gouhenant, a tragedy occurred. About a year earlier, in the summer of 1852, Major Arnold and his company had departed Fort Worth. Arnold was then detached to duty in Washington for a while, but returned to Texas once again with his family to take command of Fort Graham in 1853.[354]

Arnold was known to be a strict disciplinarian and he also had a challenging temperament, both with his family and his soldiers. Once he was back at Fort Graham, he got into an argument with the post surgeon, Dr. Joseph Steiner. Steiner and Arnold were known to be adversaries. Their ongoing feud finally exploded in a violent ending on September 6, 1853.

On the evening of September 5, Steiner and another officer were involved in a loud and drunken altercation. Major Arnold tried to stop the noise and Steiner confronted him, demanding to know if he was being arrested. Arnold said he would not arrest him if he retired to his quarters immediately. The next morning, Arnold borrowed a pistol and told his first sergeant that he would be ready for Steiner and "give him the first shot." Arnold went on to say, "If he comes in my sight I will shoot him. I ought to have done so four years ago, the damn scoundrel."[355]

Arnold sent an officer to place Steiner under arrest, but Steiner rejected the order and marched across the parade yard to Arnold's quarters, where he found the major standing in the doorway, talking to a corporal. The two men exchanged words and pistols were drawn.

Eyewitnesses had conflicting statements about who drew first, but they all agreed that Major Arnold fired the first shot. He fired twice and missed. Steiner fired three times and hit Arnold with all three shots. Major Ripley Arnold died a short time later, leaving behind his wife and young children. He was thirty-six years old. Arnold was buried at Fort Graham and Mrs. Arnold decided to move her family back to Fort Worth where Sophia and Willis were buried. Dr. Joseph Steiner was ultimately acquitted.

Learning about the death of his dear friend, Gouhenant was shocked and distraught. Arnold had been one of his first friends in America. He had spent time with the Arnolds in Fort Worth and hosted them at dances at the Arts Saloon. He had also shared in the family's sadness as they buried their young children.

Time passed. The sense of loyalty and grief Gouhenant felt towards Ripley Arnold must have weighed heavily upon his soul. A year and a half after his burial, he arranged to have Major Arnold's body moved. Middleton Tate Johnson and Alphonso Freeman rode the seventy or so miles south to Fort Graham. They exhumed his body, loaded him up in a wagon, and carried him back to Fort Worth where he was buried once again, this time near the graves of his two children where they had been laid to rest a few years earlier. He was buried with Masonic rites, likely the first such burial in Fort Worth.[356]

There was a brief mention in the *Texas State Gazette* on Saturday, June 30, 1855,

> **Remains of Major R. A. Arnold**—We learn from the *Dallas Herald* that the remains of the late Major Arnold have been removed from Fort Graham, where he was killed, to Fort Worth. The ceremonies of removal were performed by the Masons under the lead of Col. M. T. Johnson. Fort Worth had been established by the deceased in 1849 and was a favorite place with him. His remains were in excellent preservation though some year and a half had elapsed.[357]

CHAPTER 13

FAMILY REUNIONS
AND MORE SOCIALISTS

What an unfortunate destiny he had! He was foolish and crazy
to abandon everything – family, relatives, friends – to go abroad
and get eaten by savages or crocodiles![358]
                                        Ernest Humbert, February 2, 1853

The economic situation in North Texas was highly volatile in the
1850s. Dallas had become the county seat in 1846 and by 1856, the small
village had been granted a town charter. Communication, transportation,
and commercialization were rising to meet the demand of the swelling
population. Telegraph lines were popping up in towns east of Dallas
and by the end of the decade, the nation would be at the brink of the
Civil War. Such was the backdrop against which Dallas businessmen
bought, sold, and litigated their way to success. Subsequently, events that
began in 1853 propelled Gouhenant into a series of property disputes
and courtroom dramas that would launch him in more directions than
an exploding firecracker.[359]

Between the spring and fall of that year, Gouhenant experienced an inordinate number of emotional events. He began selling off some of his recently acquired real estate. In March, he sold his lot on the corner of Elm and Houston Streets to carriage-maker Maxime Guillot for $150, netting a 300 percent profit on the sale. Guillot had been renting up until the purchase; he continued to operate the carriage and buggy shop for the next two decades.[360] Gouhenant had just recounted his life story during the unexpected meeting with Victor Considerant, while only a few days before, he had signed an oath of U.S. citizenship. He was once again in contact with his sister, Marguerite Antoinette Virginie, he was actively planning on expanding the Arts Saloon, he was involved in producing and selling wine made from mustang grapes, and of course, he had just learned of the death of Ripley Arnold.

FAMILY REUNION, 1853

After his father died in March of 1819, Gouhenant had left Flagy to find work and help support his mother and sister. His mother had protested this move, and he reminded her of it years later in a letter he sent her: "You may have banished me from your heart. You did. But tearing you from mine, do not think only about that. I would protest. Your mother's right does not extend that far. It allows you to ignore a son. But it does not allow you to be ignored by him."[361] Now, Gouhenant longed for his family. His sister Marguerite had remained in the little village, and married a man named Antoine Vital Humbert. They had two children, Amanda and Ernest Humbert. The family was struggling to make ends meet and once Ernest Humbert turned nineteen, he followed Gouhenant's path and left the family home in Flagy to seek work in a nearby town.

Ernest Humbert traveled to Besançon, a day's journey south, and found employment as bookkeeper at Saillard, a pipe factory. He moved into a modest pension on the other side of the river Doubs at 4 Rue de la Madeleine, just across from Sainte Madeleine's Church.[362]

He wrote to his parents and included a vivid description of his daily hardships, keeping long hours and working a half day on Sundays. He was thrifty. He saved money by not hiring a maid, rationing his meat, and building only small fires for warmth; he complained about the lack of heat, both at work and in the pension. He groused about his diet of soup, cheese, and apples, and was grateful for the occasional potatoes his family sent him. He wrote that he was *never* warm and he endured fitful nights on a bad mattress. In frequent contact with his family, he encouraged them to apply for a license to sell tobacco (the sale of tobacco was under a state monopoly in France at the time) to help make ends meet.

One frigid February evening in 1853, he received a much-welcomed letter from Amanda which completely lifted his spirits. She informed him that the family had heard from their uncle Gouhenant and that he was living in Texas and doing well! The news came as a total shock to Humbert, and he was overcome with emotion.

They had all but given up on Gouhenant and were completely taken aback to learn of his endeavors in the United States. They assumed he was dead, likely "eaten by savages or crocodiles." Humbert was beside himself with excitement and wrote back immediately,

> It's a miracle! What a surprise, what happiness, what joy! I am so excited I think I must be dreaming! When I think that Uncle Gouhenant is found! That he exists! He's still alive! What happy news! Especially with the hope that we understand him to be in a wealthy country and that he advises us, along with his son, to come meet him... I want to join him, since it is so hard to earn a living here, and you must work 15 hours a day to get a salary of 500 miserable francs a year, and only that if you are fortunate enough to do so. And even if you miss the smallest thing or miss a day or two, you can be thrown out the door.

In what must have seemed like the longest winter of his life, Humbert finished out the season at Saillards, sleeping in his uncomfortable bed, and eating the occasional tuber. Once the summer arrived, he became increasingly anxious to reunite with his uncle. Before he sailed, he made all the necessary plans to meet Gouhenant's son, Ernest-François-Marie, who was at that time completing his military service in Provins—a small town fifty miles southwest of Paris. Gouhenant's son—the other Ernest —left no record of his impressions; family letters that survive are from Ernest Humbert's perspective alone. His words indicate that the cousins may have had some difficulties between them. Ernest Gouhenant had been conscripted in the military and had transferred from one company to another. Ernest Humbert had concerns about his behavior and mentions his mother's admonitions when, at one point, he had lent his cousin some money: "You were so angry when I sent him ten francs that you could not control your anger. Ah how you moralized... I responded, laughing, saying that nothing would be lost, that his father would come back one of these days with gold bullion from California and that he would reward those who helped his children." Humbert had written detailed directions to his mother about how to reach Ernest Gouhenant while he was in the army and instructed her to purchase a stamp, because he supposed if Ernest were to receive a letter without a stamp, and he would have to buy one to take receipt of the letter, "he may prefer to drink the twenty centimes rather than read the letter." Humbert also expressed concern that if Ernest Gouhenant had his father's address, he might share it with unsavory characters and it would cause more harm than good.

Gouhenant's son would have been twenty-one years old by this time and he had not heard from his father for five years. Whatever feelings the cousins may have had between each other, they were willing to set them aside for the time being and move forward. They had experienced enough of life in the challenging climate of the French working class to take their chances together in America.

The two cousins made their way to Le Havre and by August 29, they were on their way to America beginning what would be an agonizing fifty-day passage in the ship's hold. The journey was so distressing, it made Humbert's winter stay in the pension seem palatial by comparison.

His food and wine rations were stolen, there was no privacy, and the French and German passengers kept battling with each other over food. He nearly died of thirst before he landed in New Orleans. On a positive note, Humbert reported that he was at least a sturdy seafarer. "I didn't get seasick, nor feel any discomfort until now, which is extraordinary. Almost all the other travelers got seasick. They vomited all the time. It was disgusting."

By October 21, the young men had arrived in the U.S. The ship's captain had taken a circuitous route, reaching New Orleans by way of Santo Domingo, Cuba, and Jamaica in order to avoid arriving during the peak summer months when a yellow fever epidemic was raging at full force. By fall, the worst of it had passed and Humbert recorded his first impressions of the new land, echoing some of the same sentiments as the first Icarians five years before: "When we arrived at the mouth of the Mississippi River, a steam boat came to tow us in to New Orleans. It is a distance of thirty leagues, which took us 24 hours. A ship cannot go up the river, which is very fast. The water of the Mississippi is yellowish and muddy, just like at home when the water is high. The scene along the river banks is delightful. What lovely and charming sights! You can see herds of cows and horses freely grazing in the woods and plains, large plantations of sugar cane, or orange trees, pretty houses nicely painted... It's charming!" He found the city intriguing, but he complained about the heat, still a force in late October. Once he arrived, Humbert sought assistance from Joseph Jamey, the *chargé d'affaires* at the convent, who was from the same area as Gouhenant. The cousins were in New Orleans only two days before they boarded the steamer *Mexico* and headed to Galveston.

After nearly a year of corresponding, planning, and traveling, they arrived overland in Dallas just three days before the New Year.

Humbert's description of meeting his uncle offers a few clues about Gouhenant's appearance and also affirms his version of innocence,

contradicting the Icarians' accusations of treason.[363] Humbert wrote
to his mother:

> Then I saw Poupon [Gouhenant].[364] I was longing to see him.
> How much I found of you in him. He has your eyes! I thought you
> were looking at me when he cast his eyes on me! His beard and
> his long curly hair falling on his shoulders give him an impressive
> artistic demeanor. He is in good health.
>
> He was surprised to see me so big and tall. He recognized in my
> face many features of you mother, and of himself. Especially in my
> taste for music, he says he will make me one of the best violinists
> in the world... These are his words!
>
> Nothing happened to him that was said in France. He did not sell
> himself out as it has been said. It was a political trick on his part
> to save the Society where he worked when they were under the
> burden of justice in Toulouse. Otherwise they would not have
> been released. And if his writings would have been incriminating,
> he would have withdrawn them when he was in Nérac. He is a
> respected person in Texas.

Gouhenant's son must have had wildly conflicting emotions about
the reunion with his father. He had wanted to come to Texas with him
in 1848. Apparently, Gouhenant had written to his wife Jeanne prior
to his departure from Le Havre and made some sort of arrangement
for Ernest to make the crossing with the second avant-garde. When
Jeanne had written to Cabet around the first of April requesting that
her son be allowed to accompany the second avant-garde to Texas,
Cabet had of course denied her request. Had Ernest been allowed to
accompany the Icarians to Texas that spring, the outcome for him and
his father might have been dramatically different. Now a fully grown
man, Ernest's perceptions had likely shifted and the relationship with
his father would have changed. Their reunion ushered in a new era of
unforeseen developments that would unfold over the next few years and

include new business enterprises, improvements in communication and transportation, several marriages, deaths, and even a civil war.

FRONTIER ENTREPRENEURS

By February of 1854, just fifteen months after Charles DeMorse noted the expansion of the Arts Saloon, Gouhenant entered into a fateful transaction with Albert Brisbane. He mortaged the Arts Saloon to Brisbane for $500. The agreement was intended to be a short-term loan, Gouhenant using his Saloon as collateral to obtain cash. Perhaps he felt responsible for his son and nephew, or maybe he was seeking to expand his holdings. In any event, he was juggling several projects at once and using the same suite of dubious skills he had used in France to advance his goals.

Humbert wrote to his mother summarizing his uncle's situation, which was not yet that of a wealthy man, but still full of hope:

> Concerning his material position, it is not yet a hundred times better than the one he had in France. However, he owns a dozen plots, which are 100 feet long by 50 feet in width each. They are suitable for building. They are in the town of Dallas.
>
> They may be worth 10000 francs [$2000] right now. But in several years, since Dallas is growing daily, these lands will increase more and more in value.

Gouhenant owned at least nine lots in January 1854 at the height of his small real estate empire in Dallas.[365]

In March, Gouhenant sold Lot 2, in the same block as the Arts Saloon, to William Gold and Richard Donaldson—two dry goods, grocery, and hardware merchants—for $350. He made a nice return on this investment since it was the same property he had purchased from the Beemans two years earlier for only $100.[366]

About a year after selling the lot to Guillot, Gouhenant entered into a series of negotiations with several other businessmen. Starting out as simple loans, they would soon evolve into a string of legal issues that would not easily be untangled. Humbert and Ernest had been in town for just a short time when Gouhenant decided to borrow money from a man named Solder and according to Humbert, he was now engaged in the pursuit of another solar microscope venture, harking back to his 1830s presentations in Lyon and Chalon-sur-Saône.

In July 1854, Humbert wrote to his family,

> Poupon finally left 15 days ago to find his solar microscope and other good tricks to earn more income. He was tired of waiting in vain and has been obliged to play the game. He had to pledge the art saloon as collateral to cover the large sum he borrowed from Mr. Solder.

> Then, he immediately went to New Orleans. When he is there, if he does not find what he needs he will go to New York where he will meet one of his political colleagues, Mr. Brisbane, who is very rich. Brisbane had visited him in Dallas, holding him in esteem. He must give him five or six hundred dollars. If he gets this money, it would not be impossible that Poupon would make the trip to France to see you. But it is quite unlikely to happen, because he will find what he needs in New Orleans.

> We have just written him in New Orleans, and I enclosed your letter in mine. He will receive it in 15 days. He will be quite surprised and upset by what has happened to us.

Humbert had just received his mother's letter telling him that his father had passed away in May. His response to her conveys his sorrow. He requests details about the funeral and about other family members and he asks his mother to save some of his father's sentimental items, such as his bird call devices, until he returns to France. He also inquires as to whether or not they are still keeping the tobacco shop and how they will manage it without his father. Finally, he asks about his grandmother, "Neinein Gouhenant."

In spite of his sadness, Humbert was hopeful for the future and optimistic that Gouhenant would help him get established. Gouhenant had nurtured his talent and introduced him around town: "I do not know what share of the benefits he will offer me. I think he will be generous. He finds in me all the talents and tastes that he had at my age. I do not need to see him doing anything more than once [to learn it.] I can paint signs as beautiful as you want." Gouhenant's money issues were becoming a distraction. Borrowing from Solder and Brisbane, expanding his business, buying and selling lots and solar microscopes, his financial escapades more closely resembled a frontier shell game than a legitimate business endeavor.

In March of 1855, Gouhenant sold one of his two Dallas lots in Block 68 near Calhoun and Lamar Streets to Daniel Cornwell. Just a few weeks later in Fort Worth, A.M. Keen surveyed Gouhenant's 160-acres of land near the fort. By late April, fourteen months after it was signed, the promissory note for the Art Saloon came due. In the agreement with Brisbane, Gouhenant had acknowledged receipt of the loan and agreed to pay back Brisbane. Their agreement would have given Gouhenant over a year to pay off the mortgage, thus making the sale of the Arts Saloon null and void, but there was a problem.[367]

Among all his properties in Dallas, the Art Saloon was the most improved and valuable, and the contract with Brisbane was not the first time Gouhenant had used it as collateral. In November of 1852 he had secured a loan of $244 from the daguerreotypist Francis N. Vassallo, and then in June of 1853 another loan for $211 from William Gold. Gouhenant had also mortgaged another lot and in August 1855, he lost the second lot he owned in Block 68 to Trezevant C. Hawpe after a court judgment against him—probably an unpaid debt.[368]

Gouhenant was apparently liquidating some of his assets to pay back his accumulating debts. He may also have been planning to settle in Fort Worth. In the fall of 1855, he left Dallas for a few months, and there was word around town that he was preparing to build a house on his property near the fort. He may have even been attempting to reunite his family. As he wrote to his sister in November 1856, "we wanted to build a comfortable house there, and bring you to live with us."[369] There was no mention of his wife or daughter.

In 1856, Albert Brisbane sued Gouhenant to obtain the mortgage to the Arts Saloon, now more than a year overdue. Ironically, the two socialist ideologues were locking horns over a valuable piece of downtown real estate. The problem was that Gouhenant claimed, and testified in court, that he had only received $300 and that Brisbane still owed him $200 of the $500 he had promised to loan him. Nevertheless, in July of that year, the court ruled in favor of Brisbane and subsequently ordered the sale of the Arts Saloon. The battle had just begun.[370]

LA RÉUNION 1855–1860

Considerant had high hopes for his Utopian settlement that would come to be known as "La Réunion." He published *Au Texas* upon his return to Europe in 1854, praising the land, and also Gouhenant's accomplishments. Considerant was convinced that his Fourierist colony would succeed in America in large part due to the ideal conditions of the land they would settle. He wrote, "We found there a great abundance of a vine which augured well, of lower growth and much less run of wood and leaf, than the kind that overspreads the bottoms .... One of our compatriots, established in Dallas (Who is none other than that fine fellow Gouhenant, the chief of the first Icarian avant-garde, who was supposed to be lost, and whom we discovered at the junction of the Forks of Trinity), has begun to gather those grapes for the wine press and last year sold his wine, immediately at a dollar a bottle."[371] In October of 1854, as the leaves on the Texas cottonwoods were turning bright gold, François Cantagrel, Considerant's choice to lead the scouting expedition, and a young Belgian medical student named Roger, were sailing from France to make another attempt at establishing a French socialist colony in America.

Once Cantagrel and Roger docked in New York, their journey took them towards Cincinnati, and then down the Ohio River, where they picked up two other men, John Allen and Arthur Lawrie. John Allen had been involved in the Brook Farm utopian colony in Massachusetts in the 1840s and agreed to help set up the community in Texas by hiring local laborers who would prepare the land for Considerant's colonists.

Arthur Lawrie also went along, even though he had no ties to the socialist movement. Lawrie was born in New York City, and as a young man had found work there as a photographer. More recently, he had moved with his parents and sister to Patriot, Indiana, a community sitting at a bend on the river across the border from Kentucky. He met up with Cantagrel and Dr. Roger, and probably looking for a bit of adventure, signed on to assist them during their expedition. Lawrie kept a journal of their travels on the way to Texas, providing an interesting account of their journey.[372]

The men left Patriot on a Wednesday evening in late November and boarded the newly built steamboat, *Highflyer*. They meandered down the Ohio River, eventually cutting through white churning water to Louisville, where they then boarded the *Norma,* and continued down to Memphis.

The *Norma* was well equipped to carry the young Mr. Lawrie and his companions. In fact, the same steamboat had been used to transport the expedition assigned by Congress to survey for a trans-continental railroad route just about a year earlier. Passengers in 1853 had described it in the most glowing terms and praised the sumptuous meals and stellar accommodations and were quite impressed with the ornate décor.[373] Coincidentally, the captain of the *Norma* was Dunning M. Foster, the older brother of Stephen Foster. In March of that year, Dunning was prosperous and content as captain of the *Norma,* but bouts with chronic illness were becoming more frequent and by the spring of the following year, he had expressed his frustration, growing weary of spending frigid days navigating the rivers. Lawrie traveled on the *Norma* in the fall of 1854 and was likely aboard during one of Dunning's last southward voyages.[374]

The scouting party finally arrived in Texas on December 22, after about three weeks of traveling, and crossed the Red River just before sunset. On December 29, Lawrie wrote, "We have arrived at Dallas. Allen and the Dr. left us at Bonham to pursue their journey to Sherman and Gainesville on to Alton through the Cross Timbers, we to do the same to Belknap. We are now at the house of Mr. Gouhenan[t]'s at Dallas on the Trinity, a friend of Considerant's."

Unfortunately, Lawrie made no journal entries for two days. The time he spent with Gouhenant was either too mundane, or perhaps he was too busy to write down his thoughts. As a photographer and traveler, Lawrie must have had some common interests with his host. But their conversation was not documented, and thus remains forever entombed within the walls of Gouhenant's home.

While staying at Gouhenant's place, they met former Icarian Luc Bourgeois. He was educated to some extent, and would later serve as a translator. He was currently working as a tailor—his original trade. Having resided there now for six years, Bourgeois knew the North Texas landscape well. Lawrie and the men planned to meet a surveyor, named Mr. King, in Fort Worth and ride with him to the Brazos River to examine a large tract of land for the potential colony. Bourgeois rode along to accompany them and assist during the land survey; he and his wife, Louisa would ultimately join La Réunion colony.[375]

Lawrie resumed his writing on New Year's Eve, when he arrived at Fort Worth. He was awed by the land around him and recorded his impression in very simple terms: "The country west of Dallas is most beautiful and fertile. The handsomest landscape I ever saw is just west of Elm Fork of Trinity."

In his diary, Lawrie referenced Considerant and Brisbane's trip the year before. In February of 1855, Victor Considerant returned from Europe and arrived in New York with his family, ready to head to Texas and purchase land for the colony.

Auguste Savardan, one of the La Réunion colonists, would later write his own account of the colony. He claimed that Gouhenant knew Considerant wanted to buy the land where the former fort had been built for his French colony, but once it was time to make the purchase, Gouhenant and several others had already taken the land and made a rudimentary village and it had since become the county seat of Tarrant County.[376]

In fact, Gouhenant had received the certificate for his Peters Colony land five years before Considerant's colonists arrived in Texas.[377] Moreover, just prior to Cantagrel and Roger's arrival a few years earlier, speculators were buying up land all across North Texas. Once Considerant arrived, he discovered that the Texas Legislature was planning on building a railroad across North Texas. Lawmakers had subsequently closed off a wide swath of land, preventing further settlement until the final route could be determined. Unfortunately, the territory that Considerant had explored in 1853 and chosen as the ideal site was now closed to settlement.[378]

So, the men were headed toward the Brazos because Mr. King had informed them that there was a large tract of unclaimed land that would suit their purpose. Lawrie wrote that since King was obliged to be in Austin, he was unable to accompany them to explore the potential site. They were on their own and their expedition was plagued by mishaps and false starts. They were unable to find a guide, their horses were stolen, they were delayed by rain, and their buggy broke down. Arthur Lawrie's agreement with Cantagrel must have reached its conclusion, or he was simply fed up. Either way, by the end of January 1855, he stopped writing about the expedition and returned home to the family farm in Indiana.[379]

By now, the colonists' arrival in Dallas was imminent. The price of real estate was climbing, and the first location selected for the settlement was not available. François Cantagrel therefore felt he needed to purchase the land for the colony right away. He finally settled on more than 2,000 acres just three miles west of Dallas. The colonists soon began arriving and the settlement was started.[380]

Gouhenant's association with La Réunion colonists is not well documented. There are few accounts of his involvement with the settlers. Eloise Santerre, a descendant of one of the colonists, wrote her master's thesis on La Réunion, and translated Dr. Auguste Savardan's account of La Réunion entitled, *Un Naufrage au Texas (Shipwreck in Texas)*. There is no mention of Gouhenant's involvement in the colony in her writing, nor is there any mention of him in *The White Cliffs of Dallas*, written by her father, George Santerre. Kalikst Wolski, a Polish engineer, who came with the first immigrants, stayed only a few months. He too, wrote about the colony, and offered a different perspective from Savardan. Neither of their versions mentions Gouhenant. He was known to have been involved with one colonist, however, a Swiss educator by the name of Jasper Baer.

Baer had embraced Considerant's cause enthusiastically, but his talent had not been sufficiently utilized; he was told there were not enough children in La Réunion to open a school, which had been his goal. Savardan bitterly criticized Considerant for having been unable to use the skills of the Swiss man, who he claimed was "a gift of Providence for the phalansterian works in Texas."[381] In the fall of 1855, Baer, his wife, and their four children, discouraged by the difficulty of living in the colony, left to go to Dallas. They tried to earn an income there by opening a small shop, but they soon left there as well to establish a farm near Fort Worth, which also turned out to be a failure. Ultimately, they retreated to New Orleans, almost ruined. During their stay in Dallas however, the house Baer rented was none other than Gouhenant's Arts Saloon. A document signed by the two men shows that Baer even envisioned buying the building, but Gouhenant's price of $1200 probably deterred him and the two men never reached an agreement on the sale.[382]

Gouhenant's association with Baer occurred after he left La Réunion. So, aside from his meeting with Considerant, a shared language, and one vague reference to him being a bookkeeper, no other connection between Gouhenant and the colonists is documented. Unlike Considerant, Gouhenant was not a Fourierist; the socialist ideologies of the Fourierists and Icarians did not mesh. Even if he was inclined to join La Réunion, he had moved on. While the newly arrived European colonists were struggling to make the community a success, Gouhenant was diligently working to ensure his own success. The cousins were also working. Humbert had been painting signs for six dollars each and local merchant William Gold had hired him to paint a large sign for his business, paying him seventy-five dollars for the job. Ernest, however, was apparently working with the La Réunion colonists in some capacity. A manuscript table listing men who were "present on May 16 1855," mentions "Gouhenant the son" as an assistant of some kind.[383]

Furthermore, as La Réunion colonists were settling in, Gouhenant was occupied with court battles, land patents, and family matters that kept him quite busy traveling between Dallas and Fort Worth. Humbert had written in his first letter, "he is still young, his ideas, his character have not gotten old and are the same as you have known." By the mid-1850s he was coping with the competitive environment of a growing frontier town, so his socialist ideology had to take a backseat to the necessity of making a living.

La Réunion colonists essentially shared the same fate as the Icarians. From the time of their arrival, almost nothing went as expected. In theory, Considerant had laid out a plan that seemed to be rational enough to attract numerous investors, although not the number that they had anticipated. Even Albert Brisbane had pledged $20,000, but in the end only contributed $7,000. In practice, Considerant turned out to be a poor leader. He was unprepared for the challenges the colonists faced. Both mentally and emotionally overwhelmed, he eventually turned to morphine to ease his suffering.[384]

Like most of the other communal ventures in America, La Réunion had a brief history. The summer of 1855 was one of the driest summers on record; plagues of grasshoppers, an early freeze, poor access to adequate supplies, dry wells, low morale, and the settlers' dissolution all contributed to the failure of the colony and La Réunion was officially dissolved. Most of the colonists left the area; some did stay on and their descendants remain in Dallas.

CHAPTER 14

A WANDERER BY VOCATION

He was a daguerreotypist; a wanderer by vocation...[385]
Judge John Hemphill, December, 1857

BACK IN COURT

No stranger to the courtroom, Gouhenant's financial misadventures had taken him from Lyon to volatile new financial investments in Texas. He did not shy away from begging, borrowing, and fighting for his projects, and his battles with Albert Brisbane and others would plague him for a decade.[386]

Some of Gouhenant's engagements with the judicial system were less adversarial than others. In some cases, his lawsuits were necessary to claim what was rightfully his. In others, the litigation involved bizarre situations that raise more questions than the surviving minutes of the trial disclose. Yet the brittle archival documents shed some light on his activities during the time he was in Dallas. Gouhenant's first legal battle occurred in late 1853.

Back in 1851, Gouhenant had worked for a man named J.B. McPherson, who likely ran a local tavern, or similar establishment. During the month of July, his efforts were mostly focused on upgrading McPherson's property. He painted his house, glazed the windows, canvassed the walls, and painted a couple of signs. In October, Gouhenant billed McPherson for thirty-five empty bottles and fifty corks, two kegs (forty-four gallons of mustang wine), preserved grapes, and brandy peaches. He had also loaned him seventy-two dollars in cash. In addition, Gouhenant billed him twenty-five dollars for "one fine drawing of Potiphar's wife." A year later, in November of 1852, he repainted the "front exchange" and "both signs," an indication that McPherson may not have been completely satisfied with the job. The total for all supplies and services came to $364. Gouhenant claimed that McPherson never paid him. In March of 1853, Gouhenant sued McPherson for $500 including payment and damages.

McPherson countered that if he ever did owe Gouhenant, he had long since paid him. He further claimed that Gouhenant owed him $215.17, likely some kind of tab that McPherson kept, because he presented a list that included a couple of dozen items each under one dollar. The list included several entries of twenty-five cents for "a game of billiards," seventy-five cents each for a "deck of cards" and "assorted candy," a "box of sardines," a few "drinks," a "package of tobacco," and other random diversions. McPherson also claimed that the "fine art painting of Potiphar's wife" was a "present" unsolicited by him. Adding a dramatic flair to the courtroom scene, McPherson brought the painting into the room and asked to be discharged of the cost.

Ultimately the jurors found for Gouhenant, but both men left the courtroom with less than they wanted. The jury awarded Gouhenant only $122, significantly less than his total bill to McPherson. In the spring of 1854, McPherson requested a new trial, but ultimately, he lost again.[387]

THE ICARIANS' LAND LEGACY

The peculiar dispute was an early glimpse of the many courtroom conflicts to follow. About six months after Gouhenant sued McPherson, his friend John McCoy filed petitions during the November 1853 term of the Dallas County Court on behalf of the heirs of eleven men who had made the journey with Gouhenant to Icaria; the men had died soon after they arrived—either in North Texas, New Orleans, Louisiana, or Nauvoo, Illinois.[388]

Thirty-two Icarians had fulfilled the first condition of the Peters Colony contract by building a log cabin on their land before the July 1, 1848, deadline. Only three of the thirty-two had fulfilled the second condition, which was to remain on the land for at least two years. Gouhenant, Bourgeois, and Drouard remained in Texas after the retreat, being entitled to 320 acres each. However, during the early 1850s a battle raged between the settlers, Peters Colony administrators and stockholders, and the State of Texas. As a result, the final attribution of the land patents was delayed for several years, and often decided before a judge. So, each settler's situation was unique and sometimes difficult to untangle, especially in the case of the deceased Icarians.

In January of 1850, a law had been enacted entitled, "An act to secure to all actual settlers within the limits of the colony granted to Peters and others, commonly known as Peters' Colony, the land to which they are entitled as colonists." This act reinforced the definition of a settler as any colonist settled before the first day of July 1848, who had "since continued and still remained settlers in the said colony." It further stated that the heirs of deceased settlers were "entitled to the same quantity of land to which the persons whom they represent would have been entitled."[389]

Since the deceased Icarians had remained in the colony for less than two months, it is not entirely clear whether or not they were entitled to the 320 acres they once believed they had secured. If no one had defended their heirs' claim, they certainly would have been forgotten.

Instead, John McCoy made claims on their behalf in November of 1853, and submitted "the proof required," to ensure that each would obtain a certificate for 320 acres.[390]

McCoy submitted a series of petitions to Chief Justice J.W. Latimer of Dallas County, appointing Gouhenant as the administrator of the estate for each deceased Icarian. The appointment was agreed upon before the county court.[391]

The impetus for Gouhenant's involvement is unknown. However, in 1853, Bourgeois, Drouard, and Gouhenant had renewed contact with their native country via family letters. In addition, Maxime Guillot—a relative of Pierre Guillot's, the first Icarian who died—was sailing back to France to marry Drouard's sister, whom he would bring back with him to Dallas. Perhaps some of the Icarians' heirs had learned of their potential heritage and they asked their fellow countryman in Texas to take the legal steps necessary to claim it. Given their relationship several years earlier, Gouhenant would have been the most likely candidate to serve in this capacity. In this last attempt to represent them, he may have seen the effort as a fraternal and ethical obligation, or on a more mundane level, he may have seen the appointment as an opportunity to make money, since the administrator was remunerated. In any case, becoming the administrator of the estates was a serious commitment since he had to sign a $500 bond for each, committing to "well and truly perform and discharge all the duties required of him by law under said appointment."[392]

By the summer of 1855, Gouhenant began auctioning off the deceased Icarians' land certificates. It did not take long for the transactions to end up in court. Only a few details are known for six of the eleven cases.[393]

A group of influential men that included Samuel B. Pryor, Trezevant C. Hawpe, Edward C. and Janing M. Browder, William W. Peak, and John J. Good, together purchased the land of Levi, Chauvin, Collet, Rovira, and Boissonnet. In July of 1855, they signed joint notes promising to pay Gouhenant twelve months later, but for whatever reason, they ultimately refused to pay. Gouhenant hired John Crockett as his new counsel and sued the men in July 1856. In total, there were six lawsuits, five of which had similar results: in January 1857 the five men were ordered to pay on their delinquent promissory notes. They appealed to the Texas Supreme Court, but no records of the corresponding judgments have been found. Whether or not the Supreme Court examined the case is unknown, but it appears from the probate case archives that the district court's decision was ultimately upheld.

Similarly, in September 1855, the Keen family, William H., John W., and A.M. Keen, agreed to pay $321.00 for Pierre Guillaume Guillot's land. Their promissory note was payable ten months later, and in July 1856, they also refused to pay. However, their rationale is documented:

> The consideration for which said note was given have totally failed for they say that the said Guillot was an alien and not entitled to hold land in the state of Texas; that he was not a settler in Peters' Colony and was not entitled to have land therein; but that the said plaintiff [Gouhenant] fraudulently obtained said certificate by representing that the said Guillot was entitled to a certificate as a colonist aforesaid, and sold the same to the defendants, with the design to defraud them, well knowing that said Guillot was not entitled as aforesaid and that said certificate was so obtained in fraud.[394]

The same argument was probably given in the other cases, and the parties involved were exploiting the ambiguous definition of a "settler."

Another act concerning the rights of aliens to hold land in Texas had been approved on February 13, 1854, stating, "Any alien, being a free white person, who shall become a resident of this State, and shall, in conformity with the naturalization laws of the United States, have declared his intention to become a citizen of the United States, shall have the right to acquire and hold real estate in this State, in the same manner as if he was a citizen of the United States."[395] It is not known whether the Icarians ever declared their intent to become citizens. The Keens' attorney may have argued that because they were still aliens, they were not entitled to the land. In any event, in July 1856, the district court found in favor of Gouhenant. The Keens appealed to the Texas Supreme Court and the judgment was confirmed in November of 1858.

Coincidentally, in Dallas County, the judge also heard arguments against Victor Considerant on the exact same day he heard Gouhenant's case against his adversaries in the Icarians' land dispute. Considerant was being sued by some of the La Réunion colonists. He did not appear in court however, having absconded from La Réunion the previous week.[396]

It was not until August of 1858—nearly five years after the original petitions were filed—that the arguments surrounding the Icarians' land were finally put to rest. A series of notices appeared in the newspaper under the heading, "Final Settlement," all making essentially the same proclamation,

> The State of Texas, County of Dallas. A. Gouhenant, Administrator of the estate of ...[Henry Levy...Ludwick...Chauvin, etc.] deceased, has filed in my office his final account current with said estate, together with this petition praying that said succession is finally closed. These are therefore to notify all persons interested to come forward at the next term of the Honorable County Court of Dallas County to be holden at the court house in the town of Dallas, on the last Monday in the month of August, 1858 and contest the same as they think proper.
>
> W.K. Masten[397]

The Keens, however, still refused to pay on Guillot's estate, and the outbreak of the war in 1861 would delay the final settlement even further. Finally, in June of 1863 the Keens were obligated by the 1858 judgment to pay their debt of $321, plus $169 interest. Once the settlement was published, it put an end to the legal entanglements of the eleven deceased Icarians.

The entire episode did not yield much profit for anyone. The sale of all the lands brought in a total of roughly $2500, which was shared almost equally between Gouhenant, his attorney, the Court, the land surveyor, and the heirs. In fact, the heirs' part of $500 was paid to the state treasurer and their actual share is unknown. In any case, their share would have been minimal, quite a small gain for the loss of their family members.[398] Gouhenant received $40 for each case except for Guillot's, for which he received $100, the court providing it for "services, time and expenses in attending on court etc., etc., as administrator of said estate from March 1854 up to final settlement."[399] A decade later, the land patents were scattered across Dallas, Tarrant, and Ellis Counties, and beyond. In only two cases was land located adjacent to each other: that of Jean Collet and Boissonnet, and that designated for heirs of Henri Levi and Henri Saugé.[400]

The Arts Saloon Dispute

Gouhenant v. Cockrell was perhaps the most contentious of all his legal disputes. At issue was the sale of the Arts Saloon.

In September of 1855, Gouhenant had left Dallas to go to Fort Worth, temporarily renting his Arts Saloon to Baer. Gouhenant was again accumulating debt. In March, he had begun to sell some of his assets to pay off those debts, and by September he had lost or sold three of the lots he owned in Dallas. The deadline to repay his $500 loan to Brisbane had passed in April, and Alexander Cockrell, another creditor, was also seeking repayment of a $100 loan.

Alexander Cockrell was born in Kentucky in the summer of 1820 and came to Texas in 1845, settling near what is now Mountain Creek Lake. He met Sarah Horton, his future wife, whose family had arrived from Virginia the year before.[401]

The following month, just after Gouhenant left Dallas, Cockrell sued him before the justice of the peace, a man named A. Beard. Beard ruled in favor of Cockrell; Gouhenant did not appear and the judgment was given by default, triggering a three-year court battle over Gouhenant's popular Arts Saloon.

The fact that he did not appear in court is odd. It is possible he never received the summons; communication between the two settlements was difficult. As Thomas F. Crutchfield, the postmaster of Dallas, testified, the only direct mail routes between Dallas and Tarrant County were to Johnson Station, about twenty miles west of Dallas and to Birdville, six miles northeast of Fort Worth.[402]

The judgment was disastrous for Gouhenant, precipitating a series of unfortunate consequences that were unrelenting over the next few years. Justice Beard commanded Dallas Sheriff Adam C. Haught to "make the sum" of $100 plus the interest and costs from "the goods, chattels, lands, tenements, moneys, credits and effects of A. Gouhenant."[403] In response, on February 6, Sheriff Haught sold two of Gouhenant's lots (Lots 5 and 6 in Block 27) at a public auction, but the sale did not bring enough to cover the debt, and so on March 13, Haught sold the Arts Saloon to William Turberville for a mere ninety-one dollars! The amount was ridiculously low. In fact, all the parties would later agree that the property was worth far more—the value was closer to about $1,000.

The Arts Saloon was not only a source of Gouhenant's livelihood, but his home in Dallas. It was the place he welcomed Major Arnold and the officers of Fort Worth, the place where he established his reputation as an artist, and the hub of culture for the burgeoning town. It was certainly his most valuable property in Dallas. He was trying to sell it on his own, but the sheriff's sale proved to be a terrible loss of potential income that he urgently needed.

Just one month prior to the sheriff's sale, Gouhenant had placed an ad in the Dallas paper and hired a man to haul two wagon loads of his daguerreotype and household possessions from Dallas.

The Arts Saloon for Sale or for Rent

This fine lot with very commodious buildings, situated in the most beautiful and business [*sic*] part of the town of Dallas is now for sale on the most reasonable terms. For particulars inquire of Crockett and Guess, Attorneys at law, Dallas, Texas. Or of the subscriber at Fort Worth, Tarrant County, Texas.

Adolphe Gouhenant

February 2, 1856 [404]

Gouhenant was completely unaware of the auction until it was too late and he was outraged to learn that his property had been sold. He immediately sued Cockrell in Dallas District Court, claiming that Cockrell, Sheriff Haught, and Turberville colluded to defraud him.[405] It seems that Cockrell was only one of Gouhenant's adversaries in this battle. Immediately after the sale, several actions occurred, but incomplete court records offer only a hint at the total picture. Although the highest bidder was Turberville, the deed was delivered to W.W. Peak, and soon after, it was sold to Cockrell for an unknown amount by the same group of men with whom Gouhenant was battling over the Icarians' land.

Gouhenant vs Cockrell was heard during the July 1856 term of the district court. During the trial, Alexander Cockrell declared that when they sold him the Art Saloon, Edward C. Browder, W.W. Peak, Samuel B. Pryor, and T.C. Hawpe promised him that he "should be at no trouble or expense in defending the title to said premises in the event a suit should be instituted against him."[406] Given Cockrell's declaration, the trial more closely resembled an ambush, and could almost be more accurately described as another Gouhenant versus Browder, Hawpe, Peak, and Pryor battle. Furthermore, Cockrell's lawyer was John J. Good, who was also involved in the Icarians' dispute.

Arguing on Gouhenant's behalf, John Crockett's goal was to convince the Court that the sale of the Arts Saloon was invalid. He argued that the price was too low, but even more to the point, he contended that the

Arts Saloon was Gouhenant's homestead, which would make it secure from any forced sale.

Arguing for Cockrell, John Good then tried to prove that Gouhenant had abandoned his home and left Dallas for good, and that the Art Saloon was no longer his homestead. Several men provided evidence that Gouhenant was now living permanently in Fort Worth. On July 19 a man named David Phillips testified, "sometime during last year he thinks in October or November he met Adolphe F. Gouhenant in Dallas and asked him where he had been living, Gouhenant said he was living at Fort Worth. That said Phillips had not seen said Gouhenant about Dallas for a month previous to the time of said conversation."[407] Another witness, Mathias L. Swing, was well acquainted with Gouhenant. In 1854 he had appraised the estates of all the deceased Icarians. His testimony was more evasive about the fact that Gouhenant had left Dallas for good, but he gave some details about Gouhenant's intent to sell his Art Saloon during that time,

> on the day of February [illegible] 1856 [Mathias Swing] was at the residence of Adolphe Gouhenant in the town of Fort Worth and county of Tarrant and the said Gouhenant told affiant he had moved to Fort Worth and he wished to sell or rent the arts saloon in the town of Dallas county of Dallas and state of Texas. Gouhenant requested affiant to sell the saloon at some price now forgotten by affiant. Affiant thought the price too much and told Gouhenant he could not sell it for the same. Gouhenant then requested affiant to rent the premises for him and gave particular directions [illegible]. Affiant agreed to do so if he could. In about ten days after the time of the above conversation, the arts saloon was sold to satisfy an execution in favor of Alexander Cockrell v. said Gouhenant.[408]

On July 20, Judge Nat. M. Burford summarized the case for the jury and asked them to rule on these two questions:

> The jury must determine from all the acts and declarations of the plaintiff as to whether or not he left Dallas with the intention of

still returning it as his home [*sic*], or for the purpose of changing his domicile Bona fidely to another place ....

If the Jury are satisfied from the evidence that the town lot in controversy was free from encumbrance and was of the value of one thousand dollars, and that the amount due on the execution when levies on the lot was in amount less than one hundred dollars, then the levy was excessive and the sale an absolute nullity.[409]

After deliberation, the jury found in favor of Gouhenant.

The following day, after the trial was over, Peak, Pryor, Hawpe, and Browder went to Judge Burford and declared, "that they made diligent inquiries of all such persons as they thought likely to know or probably knew any facts that would be of service to them as evidence in the defense of said Cockrell" and that those new facts would "produce a different verdict if a new trial [was] granted." Indeed, on behalf of the judge, the clerk of the district court, Ed C. Browder—one of the men who were fighting with Gouhenant in the Icarians' land cases—heard three witnesses: Walter Caruth, Wesley M. Chenault, and Samuel S. Jones all testified that Gouhenant told them he was leaving Dallas for good. Jones gave some details about his conversation with Gouhenant,

> about two or three days before Adolphe Gouhenant left Dallas for Fort Worth the last fall, the said Gouhenant was in the store of Gold and Donaldson at which place I then was and still am clerking and having heard of his intention to go to Fort Worth I asked him if he was going to leave us, Gouhenant said he was. I asked him if he was going to Fort Worth to live he said he was. I then asked him what he intended following then. He said he had land there and was going to Fort Worth to open a farm or improve his land. Affiant does not now recollect which.[410]

Judge Burford determined that there was sufficient evidence to grant a new trial.

Illustration 30. Daguerreotype of Samuel S. Jones, who testified at the *Gouhenant v. Cockrell* trial in 1856.

Sara Cockrell Collection, Dallas Historical Society. Used by permission.
The date of this photo is unknown but Jones was twenty-five years old in 1855, compatible with the age he appears to be in this portrait. The daguerreotype was thus likely made by Gouhenant. Jones married Louise Dusseau, the daughter of a French colonist of La Réunion in November 1855.

The third legal encounter in the *Gouhenant vs Cockrell* case was held about six months later in January of 1857. This time, John J. Good was ready to attack two of the main arguments John Crockett had used that had invalidated the sale in July and secured Gouhenant's victory over Cockrell. Not only had he and his friends found new witnesses who swore they heard Gouhenant claim he had left Dallas for good, but they were also determined to show that the low price for which the Arts Saloon had been sold was justified by the mortgages against it, especially the mortgage Albert Brisbane held.

On July 20 of the previous year—when the court sided with him—Gouhenant was still contesting the mortgage. It was only on July 23 that the District Court had ruled against him in *Brisbane v. Gouhenant*, and in November the Supreme Court confirmed the lower court's decision. Subsequently, it was legally proven in January of 1857 that the Arts Saloon was encumbered with Brisbane's mortgage, lessening its value. As a matter of fact, John Good notified Gouhenant that he would use all the records and papers in the *Brisbane v. Gouhenant* case as evidence in the new *Gouhenant v. Cockrell* case.

On December 5, 1856, in preparation for another trial in January 1857, three men provided depositions to A.M. Keen, the notary public in Tarrant County. The men, Julius Fields, Lawrence Steel, and David Mauck, all answered in similar fashion testifying that they knew Gouhenant and that he resided in Fort Worth. Mauck stated that Gouhenant approached him in the early part of the winter of 1856 to purchase land so he could build a two-story house and start a vineyard. When further questioned, they responded that they did not know whether or not he brought "household items and kitchen furniture" with him to Fort Worth, or whether he tried to sell the Arts Saloon. In response to inquiries about his accommodations in Fort Worth, Julius Fields stated that he rented a house. And both Steel and Mauck testified that indeed, he "lived with E.M. Daggett."[411] A.M. Keen also testified against Gouhenant, stating that he saw him in Fort Worth in August of 1856 participating in the local election. The testimony severely undermined the argument supporting the Arts Saloon as Gouhenant's homestead.

Gouhenant's attorney John Crockett fought back, producing his own set of witnesses. One witness claimed that when he had asked Gouhenant if he had left Dallas for good, he answered, "Oh no! I will be back." Another witness testified that Gouhenant told him he was going to Fort Worth to "raise some money and [would] return to Dallas and complete a new house which he had commenced erecting on the land in controversy." William Beeman testified that when Gouhenant was about to leave for Fort Forth, he said he was going there to help establish his nephew in his work, and would be back in a few months.

Furthermore, Gouhenant insisted on the fact he had already been absent from Dallas for long periods in pursuit of his activities as a painter and "dagueman," traveling once to Corsicana and Waxahachie for about three months, and then once to New York for six months, according to one document.[412]

Concerning the price at which the Arts Saloon was sold, John Good honored his promise to present the new evidence regarding the Brisbane mortgage and he placed before the court the judgment against Gouhenant. He also added that at the time of the sale, "there was a financial crisis in this country, the money was scarce and property of every kind and particularly the property in controversy commanded but a small sum in cash."[413]

Following closing arguments in the January trial, Judge Burford asked the jury the same two questions that he had in July, one question concerning his homestead, and the other regarding the price of the sale. By this time, the jury was convinced by Good's well-placed arguments and found against Gouhenant. The judgment was reversed and the sale of the Arts Saloon was once again determined to be legal.

The court subsequently upheld Judge Burford's earlier judgment to foreclose on Brisbane's mortgage of the Arts Saloon. So, it was sold once again in April of 1857 to John J. Good who bought it for $141.00. The sum was not sufficient to pay off the debt and the sheriff proceeded to sell the last two lots that Gouhenant still owned in Dallas, Lots 5 and 6 in Block 71. Rubbing even more salt in the wound, Good also bought both lots at the very low price of $30. It was still not enough, and Deputy Sheriff W.M. Moon sent a note to the Judge stating, "returned not satisfied. No more property to be found in this County belonging to Adolphe Gouhenant."[414]

Of course, Gouhenant could not bring himself to accept the critical financial loss and decided to appeal to the Supreme Court. During the November 1857 session of the Texas Supreme Court, Judge John Hemphill heard the case. (Charles DeMorse had thought very highly of Judge Hemphill and a few years earlier, in 1844, the *Northern Standard* vigorously advocated for Hemphill for the presidency of the Republic of Texas. Refusing to be considered because of ill health, the judge continued to focus his energy on jurisprudence, much to the advantage of Adolphe Gouhenant.)[415]

Ultimately, Judge Hemphill recorded his opinion. Curiously, Hemphill echoed the exact same phrase that had been proclaimed by the French judge back in 1843, referring to Gouhenant once again as "a wanderer."

> He was a daguerreotypist; a wanderer by vocation and it was proven that in pursuit of his business he had been absent on former occasions. When he left Dallas for Fort Worth, to all inquiries if he was leaving for good he replied in the negative that he would be back. There was no declaration of his at any time and especially at the time of his removal that he intended to abandon his residence in Dallas.
>
> The object of his temporary removal or residence was by the proof to settle a son or nephew in business. And by one witness, the carpenter employed by him, it was to raise means for the erection of a building on his homestead lot. That he boarded for some months after he went to Fort Worth with one of the nephews. And afterward rented a room and boarded himself ... and that if he could sell his Saloon (meaning his residency) in Dallas that

he would be able to put up a house and that if he should sell his Saloon in Dallas he would move to Fort Worth. That he had come up to settle his son in business, this evidence shows beyond a doubt that he had some purpose of removing from Dallas but that he would not return unless he could sell his house and quite over all causes all the other circumstances of the reverse such as voting for county officers being regarded at Fort Worth as a citizen, and that he employed two wagons to carry his plunder and it seems that most of that freight was his daguerroean apparatus.[416]

Judge Hemphill, reversing the decision of the lower court, found in favor of Gouhenant. Hemphill's ruling was monumental. Not only did Gouhenant win a much-needed legal victory, but the case also set a precedent for Texas homestead law and was subsequently cited as such in at least fifteen decisions, and well into the twentieth century.[417]

Despite the victory, Gouhenant dug his heels in and refused to call it quits in his battle with Cockrell and the others. Eventually, all the sales of the Arts Saloon, including the one in March 1856, as well as the subsequent one to John Good in April of 1857 were invalidated. But, the loss of revenue during the two-year period caused a severe shortage of cash. Gouhenant and his attorney sued Cockrell once again during the 1858 July term of the district court, claiming that he had "used and consumed the rents and profits of the town lot and the improvements thereon for a long space of time … to [Gouhenant's] damage one thousand dollars."

John Good, who was still Cockrell's counsel, was prepared to match Gouhenant's tenacity, and he had planned to tackle the homestead exemption argument again. Court documents contain an additional interrogatory of a Fort Worth citizen showing more questions that were intended to prove that Gouhenant had left Dallas for good in 1855.

Five months after the Supreme Court decision, an odd turn of events transpired. On April 3, 1858, in a dramatic and bloody spectacle, the town marshal, Andrew M. Moore, gunned down one of Dallas's most prominent citizens—Alexander Cockrell. According to the newspaper's report, Moore was trying to arrest him for "violating a corporation ordinance."

There may have been more to it than that. Moore was a carpenter and it seems that in 1855 he had purchased between $100 and $200 of lumber from Cockrell's mill but never paid him.[418]

In any event, both parties were armed. Moore shot Cockrell numerous times, hitting him mostly in his lower abdomen. Cockrell passed away an hour and a half later.[419]

Cockrell's wife Sarah called upon Gouhenant to bring his photography equipment and record the image of her husband in death.[420]

Three months after his arrest, Moore was brought to trial for Cockrell's murder. District Attorney John McCoy, with assistance from attorney George W. Guess, prosecuted Moore for Cockrell's death. The trial lasted three days from Thursday to Saturday and was conducted under "the burning rays of the fiery summer solstice" with temperatures reaching ninety-five degrees in the shade the week of the trial. After closing arguments, the court adjourned for supper and immediately after the meal the jury returned to the "breathless silence" of the courtroom to render a verdict of not guilty. For whatever reason, it was reported that the courtroom burst out into applause at the decision, the enthusiasm subsequently flowing out into the streets.[421]

The litigation briefly continued after Cockrell's death. Browder, Hawpe, Peak, and Pryor had become defendants in the case. Testimony was supposed to be heard at the July 1858 term of the district court, but probably because of the Cockrell's death, the trial was postponed, and ultimately the matter was closed by mutual agreement. The men had been sparring for more than two years. Perhaps they were tired of fighting or maybe Judge Burford convinced them it was time to bury the hatchet.

Illustration 31. Alexander Cockrell's portrait from a daguerreotype made by Gouhenant.

Sara Cockrell Collection, Dallas Historical Society. Used by permission.
The daguerreotype was taken after Cockrell's death, and the eyes were likely drawn after the image was taken.

In any event, each man signed a document in August of 1858: "All the said parties agree to stand towards each other and to the property in controversy just as they did before it was sold at the said sheriff's sale. And it is thereby agreed that all the matters in controversy in the suit are hereby settled, both parties relinquishing any and all claims against each other as regards the said property and all matters incident thereto or in any way growing out of the same."[422]

The battle for the Arts Saloon was over. Remarkably, at the very same time, the settlements of ten of the Icarians' estates were finalized. Gouhenant had won back his most valuable property and as the administrator of the estates, had finally been paid $400. However, his losses were severe. Five of his other lots in Dallas had been sold at prices far below their true market value to pay off some of his debts including the most significant, Brisbane's mortgage, which still had not been paid.

One year after Cockrell's death, Albert Brisbane and Adolphe Gouhenant apparently reconvened on the Arts Saloon issue. On March 8, 1859, five years after the initial loan agreement, the two men made a new deal, mortgaging the property for $656.66 with interest that would be due on, or before, January 1, 1860, and with the further understanding that the first mortgage from February 8, 1854, was "canceled, set aside and held for naught." Their new agreement directly stated,

> If the said Gouhenant shall not well and truly pay said sum with legal interest from this time, at the time above specified, then the said Brisbane need not foreclose this mortgage in court but he is authorized and empowered to advertise and sell said property at the court house door in the town of Dallas on the first Tuesday of any month after the said first day of January 1860, by giving twenty days' notice at three public places in the said County of Dallas.[423]

It appears that Gouhenant did not pay this debt when it came due. So, it is not clear why Brisbane did not sell the Arts Saloon at that time. One possible reason might be that Brisbane was wealthy and he was simply not in hurry to recover his money at the exact time it was due.

In 1855, after the first mortgage deadline, he had waited several months
to sue Gouhenant. This time a historic event would delay any attempt
to recover the debt for a long time, since both men would be separated
by the division created by the Civil War.

In May 1868, the Art Saloon finally passed from Gouhenant's hands
once and for all. Surprisingly, Brisbane did not sell it to recover his
mortgage. Instead, John McCoy acquired it from Gouhenant. He knew
the property was encumbered by a mortgage. Yet, he bought it for $1,000.
By then Gouhenant had long since left Dallas, the Arts Saloon having
closed its doors many years before. But the sale marked the official end
of Adolphe Gouhenant's artistic legacy in Dallas.[424]

Less than one year after McCoy bought the Arts Saloon, Brisbane
resurfaced. Although the Arts Saloon did not belong to Gouhenant
anymore, Brisbane was entitled to sell it by virtue of the 1859 mortgage,
and indeed he offered it up for auction in the spring of 1869. That year
the notice that appeared in the *Dallas Herald* was situated just below
Mr. Theodore Von Bellmont's invitation to patronize his new lager beer
saloon offering visitors a comfortable spot at his "fine new pigeon-hole
table." Brisbane's more banal ad offered a "Valuable Town Lot for Sale."[425]

The legal battles that transpired in this nascent community reflect the
nature of conflicts and relationships that occurred in Dallas's earliest
days. Fights could be fierce for a few acres of land, leading to trials
that burdened the courts and afforded lawyers plenty of opportunity to
practice their craft. It was certainly true in the Icarian Peters Colony
land conflicts. Reporting on the district court session of July 1858, the
Dallas Herald stated,

> The greater portion of the present week has been occupied in
> trying two or three tedious land cases. Two entire days were
> consumed in the trial of the cause of Horton v. Cockrell, which
> has been on the docket for years, and has been tried some half
> dozen times. Between five and ten acres of land only, being at
> controversy as to the true boundary between two surveys, were

originally involved, but costs have accumulated so as to make the result important in a pecuniary point of view. —The verdict was for the plaintiff, but the case will again go to the Supreme Court.[426]

ONE MORE CASE

One more court case is worth noting. Throughout 1856, the Arts Saloon disputes kept Gouhenant locked in a legal morass, but there was yet another fight brewing. Once the new year arrived there was no sign of things slowing down. By January, he was also battling with Joseph Anderson over two adjacent lots in Block 71, on Houston Street, just a few blocks south of the Arts Saloon. Anderson was a bricklayer from Illinois and Gouhenant claimed that he was making bricks on his property. He sued Anderson and charged that he had trespassed, erected a brickyard, and destroyed the improvements he had made to the lot. Gouhenant provided an affidavit affirming that he owned the property and improved it by paying "skillful and scientific" laborers $200.00 to plant vegetable and flower gardens on the property.

Anderson did not dispute Gouhenant's title to the property, but he did dispute the amount of damages and also the fact that Gouhenant did not show sufficient evidence to prove that he had damaged the property. Gouhenant claimed the land was worth a total of $500. Anderson claimed that he had Gouhenant's permission to use the land and that the lots were worth no more than $30.00 each. He further claimed that the district court had no jurisdiction in the matter and since the dispute was for such a small amount, it should have been tried before a justice of the peace. In response, the court had summoned some familiar names to testify— William Beeman, Charles Pryor, James W. Latimer, Alexander Cockrell, and others. Ultimately, Judge Burford granted Anderson's motion to dismiss and Gouhenant lost his battle. Not suprisingly, Gouhenant then appealed to the Supreme Court. He argued that the $500 claim for damage should have been within the court's jurisdiction. The Supreme Court held that the district court's ruling should stand, handing Gouhenant a less substantial, but nonetheless painful defeat.[427]

Gouhenant's struggles are a testament to his tenacity. His diligent pursuit of knowledge—languages, music, scientific exploration, politics, and human rights—never waned, nor did his goal to obtain financial prosperity. While his ambition was enormous and his spirit unyielding, true success seemed just beyond his grasp.

His lack of business acumen, or perhaps even chronic bad luck, hung over him like a dense black cloud and remained his biggest obstacle. Youthful energy may also have been a contributing factor to success on the frontier. By 1854, Gouhenant had turned fifty, an elder in terms of life expectancy in the nineteenth century. By contrast, his legal adversaries— the energetic and prosperous young entrepreneurs in Dallas—were all in their twenties and thirties. Whether or not they were targeting the old Frenchman, they were undoubtedly pursuing collective business interests, evidenced by the joint promissory note. Most of the men were fellow Masons from the same lodge and while they shared the same fraternal ideals, they were also not without ambition. The minutes from 1853 admonished members to respect each other and work together.

> We are BRETHREN, and among brothers there should be no strife except that glorious emulation, of who can best work and best agree. In the building of the Temple, there was not heard the sound of any tool of metal; but alas! the tongue is an unruly member. It is a tool of iron, whose harsh notes clash and resound in parts of our building that the spirit of peace seems well nigh ready to take its flight, and leave us no good designs on our trestle board — or rather that board, and its teachings, seem to be cast among rubbish, or overwhelmed by the ruins of the temple.[428]

By the end of the decade, Gouhenant's interests had turned away from the Arts Saloon, and even from Dallas, to points further north—Pilot Point to be exact, where he would join another Masonic lodge, embark on new adventures, and unexpectedly fall in love.

Chapter 15

A Painful Era

I put him beside the grave of Major Arnold, on a high point of my property[429]

Adolphe Gouhenant, November 1856

A Family Torn Apart: 1856

Ernest Humbert spent three interesting years in Dallas and Fort Worth. The poignant letters that he wrote to his family in Flagy have filled in a few lost passages of his Uncle Poupon's life. Even more significantly, Humbert had had a powerful impact on his uncle personally.

In May of 1857, Gouhenant received a letter from his sister, Marguerite, that she had written on March 3. In her note, she shared the news that their mother had passed away the year before. Heavy-hearted, he read her somber words. As he digested each thought, he realized that she had not seen his letter from the previous November. That important letter had contained disastrous information and he was quite distraught to learn that she had not received it. A deep melancholy gripped his body and permeated down to the depths of his soul, not only for his mother but for his nephew, Humbert. "I don't understand how you did not receive my letter from the 24th of November 1856. During the time of revolutionary troubles, I would have feared the government agents, but today? After 10 years of exile! Forgotten— completely lost to France, who could intercept my letters? It should have reached you because I brought it to the post office and paid for the stamp myself."[430] As he sat down to write her again, he attempted to reconstruct his thoughts from six months earlier. Taking pen in hand he wrote,

> I believe that sadness cannot be expressed, it is felt – it racks and crushes the heart. It dries the eyes after having flooded them. It spreads its burning fluid in the veins, then it paralyzes the tongue and all the other organs. Oh yes! My beloved sister. I understand your grief and that of my niece as deeply as I feel mine.

> Absorbed by sorrow, I postpone every day, hoping for some calmer ideas to dictate with phrases less distressing, the sad news of the death of your son.

> Poor Humbert looked strong, but he was not robust. He had a liver disease that he was unable to overcome. He probably would not have lived longer in Flagy than he lived here. Because I watched him, I nursed him, I counseled him... so assiduously, as tenderly as you would have done. To the point that everyone said I had a hundred times more respect and attention for my nephew than for my son! But my son was not jealous. He knew, and understood the situation.

> I had to take two home nurses to help me to treat him and to wake me up when, overwhelmed, I dozed off in my chair beside his bed. I also had the assistance of two of our best doctors around, and the continual visits of all our friends, ladies and gentlemen. He was well appreciated in Dallas and in Fort Worth. We shared our time between these two towns, having properties in both of them. We were obliged to visit them alternately. Humbert prefered the situation in Fort Worth because of its similarity to Flagy. We wanted to build a comfortable house there and to bring you

to live with us. The Supreme Regulator of our destinies decided differently.

Humbert was declining hour after hour.

He could not get up. You had to slide the chamber pot under him every moment. He made a slimy matter, reddish, indicating the breakdown of the liver. Finally on Monday, the eve of his death he had a rebound in his strength that revived my courage, my expectations.

At 4 o'clock he got up on his bed and said "Uncle, I am better. It seems to me that a glass of Malaga wine would render me my strength. Go get a bottle. You will choose better than anyone"

I went out immediately to appease him. I did not stay away more than fifteen to twenty minutes. When I returned, I found him near the fire, with his trunk overturned, burning books and papers and telling me all was useless. I had a great amount of trouble putting him back to bed.

The doctor came at that time.

I told him what had happened. He told me that it was an ominous sign. He was not mistaken. The next day at the same time, he took his last breath, without pain or agony, effortlessly, making the finest, most touching prayer that I've ever heard.

His face expressed heavenly bliss. His right hand pressed against mine, flooded with tears, I beseeched him with all my power, with all my heart, when suddenly he pulled away from my embraces, raised his arms skyward, staring in the same direction

Farewell my uncle ... oh ! My mother ... oh ! My sister ...

Farewell all you I love... I'll wait for you in heaven ...

Then his hands slowly fell on his chest and he was with the Angels...

I paid him funeral honors, with the greatest care, all desirable accommodations. Four gentlemen friends had stayed with him all night. And the next day until four o'clock, the funeral hour.

They dressed him in his best clothes, then wrapped him in a shroud of fine muslin, his head surrounded by a wide band of lace.

I laid him beside the grave of Major Arnold, on a high point of my property. His headstone is carved into a solid rock. This is where I want to be when our beloved Father will ring my last hour, if I am still here, which is quite probable, unless you manage to change my decision, by giving me a better and faster way for us to be together.

... I wanted to send a lock of Humbert's hair, but hoping to go to France, I will carry what I have kept from him myself.[431]

He ended his letter to Marguerite with a note about his own son. There is no description of the time they spent together or mention of any plans for the future, just a simple statement of fact: "My son came to visit me 15 days ago. He stayed only four days, then he left to go 150 miles from here. He works quite well. He earns enough to live decently and secure himself, but he doesn't save!"

Humbert had passed away in August of 1856, the same summer that Gouhenant was involved with all the legal proceedings in Dallas. So, he had not written his sister until November, putting off the unpleasant task as he was struggling to bring an end to the Arts Saloon chaos that was still occupying his time thirty miles east. Once he finally wrote with the tragic news, Marguerite must have also been devastated. She had lost her husband two years before, her mother just a few months prior to receiving Gouhenant's letter, and now she was learning in very vivid detail, that she had also lost her only son.

In describing Humbert's death, Gouhenant shares his sentiments for his beloved nephew, but also for the land he had come to know as home

—the spot where the Arnolds were buried, sitting on a bluff overlooking the West Fork of the Trinity River.

Gouhenant was despondent. Not only had he lost his only nephew, and learned that his sister had never received the news of her son's death, but his own son was living in another town. After nearly a decade of living in Texas, his family was again absent and Gouhenant was alone.

Humbert had signed a promissory note in April of 1856 to purchase Gouhenant's original land grant near the fort. Gouhenant deeded the land to his nephew for $2,500, but shortly after the transaction, the tragedy unfolded.[432]

After Humbert died, Gouhenant's friend Ephraim M. Daggett served as the administrator of the estate. Daggett thus claimed there were outstanding liabilities against Humbert's estate for $2,500, essentially his unpaid balance on Gouhenant's property. Daggett asked the court to sell the 160 acres of land. Subsequently, Gouhenant bid on the land paying $13 an acre buying back his own land. Since he was Humbert's creditor however, he only paid $78.70 in court costs.[433]

Recent events had worn him down and he longed for the support of his family. After all that had occurred, he was considering returning to France, and wrote to Marguerite to solicit her thoughts: "If I liquidate and sell everything, I could earn around thirty thousand francs. Do you think I could live in Flagy with this small fortune, or would you prefer to sell, and leave Flagy to join me? Discuss this together. I will do whatever you want in order to meet you." Court battles raged on and against the backdrop of his own personal sadness, there was a palpable anxiety in the air, a growing tension between the northern and southern states, and a fear that things were about to change.

"DOCTOR GOUNAH"

Three years after Humbert's death, Gouhenant's sister and niece had still not made the trip to America, and he had not traveled back to France. Putting the Arts Saloon business behind him, he had embarked upon a new chapter of his life treating the sick and practicing medicine!

On March 2, 1859, Gouhenant pulled into Dallas, arriving from Pleasant Run, a community about fifteen miles south of Dallas. The day was mild, although there had been a light frost the previous Friday. The last winter weather in Dallas was described as being delightful.[434] "The earlier fruit trees are putting forth their foliage, flowers are shedding their grateful fragrance; the peach plum and other fruit trees have flowered; gardeners have planted most of their seeds and everything announces that Spring is at hand."[435]

The notion that Gouhenant would choose to begin practicing medicine is puzzling, but not completely surprising. It seems that something may have touched him during the time he cared for Humbert that spurred him on to begin helping his fellow Texans. Another possible motive may have been sheer desperation after exhausting all other career opportunities.

In America, there is no record of him ever being involved in any kind of treatment for the sick, nor assisting with any medical procedures of any kind prior to Humbert's death. Yet, since his early days working as a drug seller in Lyon, Gouhenant had at least an elementary knowledge of the methods and remedies that would cure, or at least address the symptoms, of certain ailments. Now, he would apply the knowledge acquired in his younger days.

In France, the only indication that he received any kind of medical training, aside from his drug selling experience, was his exposure to the Raspail method. François-Vincent Raspail was a French socialist and also a physiologist and Gouhenant subscribed to his teachings. Raspail promoted a new medical approach, especially targeted to laborers, that focused on hygiene and prevention as well as self-medication. He wrote a manual explaining how to make medicines from a few basic ingredients such as camphor, aloe, roots of plants, and other types of natural remedies. Raspail was extremely successful and his method was well known to the Icarians. In August 1848 the Icarians wrote in their desperate letter, "It is deplorable that our pharmacy is very incomplete; several very useful medicines are missing, and especially the Raspail pharmacy, which in our opinion would have been a big help." Among the Icarian avant-garde, there is no mention of Gouhenant as a doctor; Charles Leclerc and Juan Rovira were the only physicians. Gouhenant's familiarity with Raspail medicine, coupled with his pharmaceutical skills from Lyon, would have made him somewhat of a specialist in natural medicine.[436]

When Gouhenant had written to his sister about Humbert's death, he had clearly stated, "I had to take two home nurses to help me to treat him" indicating that Humbert was under his care, while at the same time, he received support and "assistance from two of our best doctors around."

Gouhenant's competence as a practicing physician is questionable. There is no record of his successful interventions, but on at least one occasion, his actions led to drastic results. After arriving in Dallas in the spring of 1859, he walked over to the St. Nicholas Hotel, Sarah Cockrell's grand two-story building resplendent with chandeliers and wall tapestries, and signed the register with his usual flamboyant signature. The next day, he would be back in court once again, but this time suing a man named Solomon Brundage to claim his unpaid fee for treating Brundage's wife.[437]

Solomon Brundage and his wife, Juliette (Winny) Campbell had married in Illinois on December 12, 1848, and moved to Texas around 1856. They settled south of Dallas and started a farm. Four years later they were well established, with six horses, nine head of cattle including some milk cows, and a crop of corn. They had no children.[438]

Shortly after their arrival, Winny became ill. Gouhenant examined her and told her that he "thought he could effect a cure." Brundage asked how much Gouhenant would charge to take on his wife's case. Gouhenant told him that he was not sure of the exact price, but that it would be reasonable. He treated her from October 28 to November 29 of 1857 with all manner of contemporary medical remedies. His attempts to heal the thirty-two-year-old woman included prescribing stomach elixirs, applying poultices, and administering bowel and uterine injections.

He prescribed *angélique*, a plant known for medicinal and culinary applications that was among the standard pharmacopeia popular in the nineteenth century. *Eau d'angélique* was made with the root of the plant and used as a treatment for asthenia (lack of energy) and digestive diseases. For Mrs. Brundage, Gouhenant prescribed a regimen several times during her illness. His son Ernest, who seems to have joined his father during this time, delivered the prescriptions to their home. In spite of the treatments—or perhaps because of them —Mrs. Brundage was still in some pain and experiencing other undisclosed side effects under Gouhenant's care. The bill for supplies over the month-long treatment was $34.00. Her husband was not pleased with the outcome and refused to pay Gouhenant for his services.[439]

Gouhenant sued Brundage for $50.00 and Brundage subsequently countersued, testifying that he was incompetent as a physician. Brundage claimed that Gouhenant overcharged him for visits and medicines. In the lawsuit, he signed the following statement: "A. Gouhenant is unskillful and inefficient in the science of medicine and the treatment of the disease that the defendant's wife is laboring under. And the defendant further says that neither visits nor medicine of said Gouhenant done his wife any good but greatly damaged her to the amount of fifty dollars."[440]

The conflict with Brundage went on for a while. Gouhenant traveled to Dallas at least two more times that year. His second trip was only eight weeks after the first, and on April 28 he returned, arriving the day after Ernest; they both signed the hotel register coming from Pleasant Run. Gouhenant returned to Dallas again on August 3, this time arriving from presumably his new home in Pilot Point.[441]

When Gouhenant treated Mrs. Brundage with his medicinal concoctions, they may have produced dramatic results for the poor woman. The list of medical supplies introduced as court evidence covers two pages and includes treatments for a wide variety of conditions.

In *Gouhenant v. Brundage*, Justice of the Peace Archibald M. Lavindar found in favor of Gouhenant and ordered Brundage to pay him $29.40. Brundage appealed the decision to the district court arguing that Gouhenant had not proven he was a physician. Two physicians, Dr. A.B. Palmer and Dr. David King, then testified that indeed Gouhenant was not a doctor. Gouhenant asked for the case to be dismissed arguing that his status as a physician was irrelevant to the contract. Gouhenant's victory was upheld and whatever her ailment, Winny survived his attempts at doctoring and she lived several more years before passing away on August 2, 1863.[442]

In Gouhenant's defense, public health and medical treatment were only vague concepts in 1850s Texas. Doctors who treated injuries and ailments had little formal training. Further, there was no medical school in North Texas at the time. Prevention of illness sprang mostly from folk remedies. The cause of malaria was still unknown, and surgical procedures were just shy of torture. For medical treatment of pain, morphine was used as an anesthetic; the hypodermic needle was not even invented until 1853. Doctors did what they could to relieve the pain of ailments afflicting those on the frontier. It is certainly plausible that Gouhenant was acting in the best interests of his patients, and that the treatments he prescribed, based on Raspail medicine, were just as effective as the remedies of more academic medical treatments in many cases.

Furthermore, citizens of the area had few options when they fell ill. While there are references to several doctors working in Dallas in the 1850s, there was no official medical association to govern their practices and Gouhenant never promoted himself as a doctor in the local newspapers. From the mid- to late-1850s there were a handful of doctors and a dentist advertising their practices in Dallas. Frank A. Sayre opened the first drugstore in 1855, located on the west side of the square at the corner of Houston and Main, across from the Arts Saloon. Sayre advertised in the *Dallas Herald* as a druggist and chemist.[443]

La Réunion colonist Auguste Savardan was perhaps one of the most qualified physicians in the Dallas area. He was educated at the University of Paris and when he immigrated, he brought with him two boxes, one of drugs and the other of surgical supplies and instruments, as well as a significant amount of academic training.[444] Overall, the public health situation was bleak.

Sometime around the late 1850s to early 1860s, Gouhenant came to be known to many as "Dr. Gounah," with a spelling of his name that more closely matched the pronunciation. There is only one other known occurrence of him practicing medicine. According to family lore, Gouhenant was in Pilot Point when a young woman hurt her ankle in a buggy accident. Gouhenant was on hand to provide her care and as he nursed her back to health; they grew closer and a relationship developed between them.[445]

Still, the Brundage incident seems to be the only such case where a patient expressed sufficient malcontent to seek legal recourse. Certainly, he dispensed a fair amount of medical advice later in life, because once he moved to Pilot Point, he opened an apothecary and the citizens in his newly adopted town referred to him as "doctor." In one instance a letter from his old friend E.M. Daggett requested his assistance on a matter relating to collecting an outstanding debt and Daggett addressed his letter to Dr. Gouhenant using both his title and the original spelling of his surname. Daggett added a personal note that his own health was not as good as it usually was, and he wrote, "Hope you're doing well in your profession."[446]

Back in 1853, Humbert had written that his uncle was a "respected man" in Texas. Regardless of his lack of medical training, he was educated, and a self-taught healer who was likely trying to assist the local population by treating minor health ailments. Ultimately, he had acquired sufficient knowledge about chemistry and medicine to run a pharmacy and dispense cures to meet the local demand. Texans made a doctor of Adolphe Gouhenant.

PASSIONS IGNITE ON THE EVE OF CIVIL WAR

In July of 1860, with both the mercury and human temperaments on the rise, a series of fires broke out across North Texas. In Dallas, a blaze destroyed most of the buildings in the business district. Town leaders attributed the fires to "a combination of the exceedingly hot summer temperature (it was reportedly as hot as 110 degrees in Dallas on the afternoon of the fire) and the introduction into the stores of the new and volatile phosphorous matches."[447]

The office of the *Dallas Herald* burned down, so the incident was reported in other Texas papers.

> The flames had broken out in front of Peak's new drug store, which almost immediately enveloped the whole house. It was a two story frame, and filled with stores of all kinds. The fire then spread to Smith's warehouse, then to the *Herald* Office, from which nothing but the books could be removed. The *Herald* office was a total loss, four presses, material of every kind, clothing, in fact everything...

> The St. Nicholas Hotel, a large three-story frame-building, 100 feet front, by 100 feet back, is totally consumed. Smith & Murphy's brick store burnt. Shiek's new warehouse and store, with entire stock of goods; the Crutchfield House and all its furniture, including the Post office and the mail matter in it. Westin's corner, Simon's new building just framed; the old tavern, Saddler's shop, Hirch's large storehouse with entire lot of goods. Carr's new frame building...[448]

Amidst the suffering from scorching temperatures, there were also accusations of a Northern plot to devastate North Texas. Some men charged that white abolitionists had incited black arsonists to set the town ablaze. Several other suspicious fires had occurred about the same time in Denton, Pilot Point, Milford in Ellis County, and as far south as Austin.

Although no evidence was ever presented to prove anyone's guilt, some renegade Texans took justice into their own hands. In the melee, dozens of men were hanged to satisfy the vigilantes' thirst for retribution.[449]

Townspeople were becoming more and more anxious about the nation's growing political schism and public debates on secession occurred frequently. As tensions between the North and South were exploding, Dallas had become a bustling center of commerce. Since the first crop of cotton was planted in 1853, the town had mostly experienced sustained growth. By 1860, several stage lines were providing better means of transportation and the railroad lines were gradually approaching from the south. Some telegraph lines had already been strung along a few east Texas treetops, slowly inching their way to Dallas.

Curiously, in the late summer of that year, Samuel Morse himself wrote to Texas Governor Sam Houston rescinding his previous offer to provide the Republic of Texas with his telegraph. He left little doubt about where his Unionist sympathies lay as he fired off his thoughts: "I, therefore, now respectfully withdraw the offer then made, in 1838, the better to be in a position to benefit Texas, as well as the other States of the Union."[450] Morse sent his letter to Houston just a couple of months after Congress passed the Pacific Telegraph Act of 1860. The transcontinental telegraph line was completed in October the following year.

Just six months after Morse wrote to Sam Houston, delegates to the Texas state convention voted to support an ordinance separating Texas from the United States. In actuality, the act repealed the annexation ordinance of 1845 by which Texas had joined the Union. On February 23, 1861, voters ratified the passage of the secession ordinance, which became effective on March 2, the twenty-fifth anniversary of the state's Declaration of Independence from Mexico, and shortly thereafter a measure was adopted to join Texas with the Confederate States of America. Governor Houston, who had not supported secession, refused to take an oath of allegiance. His office was then declared vacant and Lt. Governor Edward Clark became the governor.[451]

A Unionist Minority and the Sixth Texas Cavalry

In the days leading up to the Civil War, sentiment in Texas was divided between the minority who supported the Federal cause, and those who supported secession. In North Texas, there was a substantial number who sided with the Union; seven counties actually voted *against* secession and in another six counties, over 40 percent of voters were against it. Neither Dallas nor Tarrant County fell into these categories, but neighboring Wise, Denton, Collin, and Hunt Counties did have large populations that openly opposed secession.[452]

In addition to the improved access to communication, the expanding transportation routes encouraged migration. Once the Overland Butterfield Mail route had opened, running from St. Louis, Missouri through Gainesville, Texas, it brought in new waves of settlers from the upper south and Midwest—and abolitionists from Kansas. Tensions between the two factions were high and sometimes stretched to the breaking point. In October of 1862, Unionist supporters in Gainesville were arrested, tried by a citizen jury, convicted, and finally hanged! The horrendous act of violence would later be called the "Great Gainesville Hanging." In the weeks following, Unionists were hanged in Grayson, Wise, and Denton Counties as well.[453]

> Several slaves and a northern Methodist minister were lynched in North Texas. Cooke and the surrounding counties voted against secession and thus focused the fears of planters on the nonslaveholders in the region. Rumors of Unionist alliances with Kansas Jayhawkers and Indians along the Red River, together with the petition of E. Junius Foster, editor of the *Sherman Patriot*, to separate North Texas as a new free state, brought emotions to a fever pitch. Actual opposition to the Confederacy in Cooke County began with the Conscription Acts of April 1862. Thirty men signed a petition protesting the exemption of large slaveholders from the draft and sent it to the Congress at Richmond.[454]

Unionist support was strongest in central Texas among the German immigrants, some of who had organized a Union Loyal League in 1862. Confederate leaders considered them subversive and as they were attempting to join up with Union forces, they were captured and executed.

Gouhenant's views on the war can be surmised with some confidence. His beliefs supporting workers' rights are indisputable. His revolutionary actions in France and his commitment to the Icarian principles in the 1840s leave his views on equality unquestioned. Although he was detached from Icarian philosophy and had become a part of a growing capitalist society, he had no stake in the cotton market, he owned no slaves, and even if his views had changed since arriving in Texas, it is hard to fathom that he would have supported the war. Despite the revolutionary tendencies of his younger years, he certainly would not have supported any government policy seeking to deny rights to a group of people.

Some of Gouhenant's colleagues however, were definitely standing with the Confederates and had clear pro-slavery positions. One of his fellow Masons, David Jones Eddleman, who lived in Pilot Point, wrote an unpublished autobiography in which he strongly advocated for slavery, even long after the end of the war. Eddleman described in a few words the tense climate felt by the pro-Union population in North Texas: "In 1860, after the burning of so many towns in Texas ... the lines became very strictly drawn, and if a man felt any free-soil sentiment he dared not express it. Nothing could have been more unpopular, and I presume, before the winter set in, that most of the free-soilers had left the State."[455] Had Gouhenant been opposed to slavery, he likely kept his thoughts to himself.

In the spring of 1861, the conflict at Fort Sumter sparked Confederate recruitment efforts and the first Texas Regiment was formed. It was not difficult to recruit Texans into Confederate service. Some aspects of local culture promoted the concept that Texans rarely needed an excuse to fight. In the twenty-five years preceding the Civil War, they had fought in the Texas Revolution and the Mexican-American War, and engaged in many battles with Native Americans, and even shot and killed each other in the streets of their own towns. Still, the generation that fought in the Civil War was quite removed from the realities of battle and expected that the war would last only a few months.[456]

Texans were keen on defending their honor, home, and family, and some perceived the war as a threat to all of these. When volunteers signed on for Confederate service, they were allowed to choose where they wanted to fight. Since many men had recently moved to Texas, or were only a generation removed from their home states of Tennessee, Virginia, or other Southern states, they were eager to defend those communities where their relatives still lived.[457] "Men who went off to camp were consumed with a fear that the war might actually be over before they got into action – an emotion which, a year later, they recalled with wry grins."[458]

It was easier to recruit men into the cavalry than the infantry; they were especially eager to fight if they could take their horses with them. Arthur Fremantle, a British soldier who observed the Confederate army during the Civil War, noted that "at the outbreak of the war it was found very difficult to raise infantry in Texas, as no Texan walks a yard if he can help it." Of the 25,000 men who were recruited in 1861, two-thirds served in cavalry regiments.[459]

A veteran soldier from the French army, Gouhenant's son Ernest volunteered for the Sixth Texas Calvary on September 12, 1861.[460] Ernest's motivation for serving is unclear. The Conscription Act would not be passed for another seven months. Possibly, he needed some kind of purpose or glory since he was probably living in his father's shadow. He certainly had no relatives in other Southern states, nor did he have a significant economic stake in the fight. Perhaps after being in Texas for seven years, he had become fully integrated into the culture and he was persuaded by Southern politics, or possibly he thought he would be ostracized had he not joined. Most likely he needed the salary that the military would provide. He had been known to drink and be reckless with his money. He had become a citizen of the United States on February 3, 1858. By the time he joined the Confederacy three and a half years later, he had fallen in love with a woman named Mary and they had started a family.

Mary Withers was born in 1841 to James and Luisa Withers of Missouri. James had brought his family to Texas in 1845 and they settled a Peters Colony grant on Hickory Creek, north of the Pritchett family farm—the same Pritchetts who offered Gouhenant a safe haven years before. James had died only a few years after arriving in Texas, but his widow patented 640 acres in the fall of 1855 and remained in Denton County. The fact that Ernest knew Mary indicates that Gouhenant was likely still in touch with the Pritchett and Withers families in Denton County.[461]

Ernest and Mary had a daughter, Emily Hortense. So he now had a family to support and he marched off to war when Emily was still a baby. At the age of twenty-nine, he was mustered into Company I. Upon enlistment, his personal belongings were valued at twenty dollars and his horse was worth one hundred and twenty dollars. Barton Warren Stone's regiment had ten companies, organized with 1,150 men from seven North Texas counties. Stone, an attorney who had come to Dallas in 1851, obtained the authority to raise a cavalry regiment for service under Benjamin McCulloch. His regiment was sworn in at Camp Bartow in Dallas County. Ernest had evidently inherited his father's talent for playing musical instruments and he enlisted as company bugler and would later be promoted to chief bugler.[462]

As chief bugler he performed a key role for the company, and as such, had more benefits and responsibilities than the average soldier. The chief bugler was usually a mature man who was responsible for the training, appearance, and performance of other company buglers, who were younger boys. The bugler was absolutely essential to the company giving voice to the commands that could not be shouted to soldiers half a mile away. Since the bugle's sound carried a few miles, it could easily be heard by thousands of men, even over the sound of gunfire. Ernest would have stayed near the commander at all times, transmitting his instructions to the men in the field.[463]

In addition to their utilitarian purpose, musical instruments were an important part of a soldier's life in the Civil War. Prior to the war, music had been an integral part of the American lifestyle and once the soldiers marched off, they took their music with them. Brass bands played a key role in keeping up morale and in the camps at night, it would be quite common to hear music written with a northern theme, played with southern words; there are numerous accounts of bands in adjacent Union and Confederate camps playing the same songs or echoing each other's songs in impromptu concerts or "battles of the bands." Hearing songs in the evening composed by Stephen Foster, Patrick Gilmore, H.S. Stanton, George Frederick Root, Henry Clay Work, and others would have been routine. Ernest likely joined in the musical diversions around the evening campfire.

In November 1861, just about six weeks after he enlisted, Ernest's unit was ordered to Fort Smith, Arkansas, to join General McCulloch's Army of the West. The Sixth was engaged in their first fight the day after Christmas at Chustenahlah, Indian Territory, on Battle Creek. Although it was a short fight, thirteen men were killed and thirty more injured. There were several reorganizations over the next few months and by March, the Sixth was absorbed into General Van Dorn's army. They were engaged at the Battle of Pea Ridge in Arkansas and were badly beaten.

In April 1862, the Sixth Cavalry was dismounted for infantry duty and had only 935 men left. They were sent to fight at Shiloh, but arrived after the battle was over. On April 16, just ten days after the bloody disaster at Shiloh, realizing that the war would not be won in a matter of months, the Confederate Congress passed a conscription law. That law would keep Ernest in the war much longer than his original twelve months, with just five months of his service remaining. Congress extended the enlistment terms of currently enrolled soldiers to three years from the date of original enlistment, effectively keeping all male citizens between the ages of eighteen to thirty-five under control of President Davis's Confederacy, and Ernest in the war until September of 1864.[464]

The same conscription law also extended the service of Newton Asbury Keen. Ernest's contemporary, Newton Keen was the nephew of Melvon Keen. Melvon, known as A.M. Keen, was the same man who had surveyed Gouhenant's land a few years earlier and who had reneged on the promissory note to Gouhenant for Pierre Guillaume Guillot's land in 1853—and for whom Newton worked briefly when he was fifteen. Newton Keen joined the Sixth Texas Cavalry and enlisted about a month earlier than Ernest. He was in Company C, composed of 110 men. Keen recorded his still-vivid memories more than thirty years after the war. The narrative of his terrifying experiences, including an episode of sickness and subsequent transport to a distant hospital resembles many similar descriptions of Confederate battle conditions and offers insight into the life he and Ernest experienced as soldiers serving in the Sixth.[465]

Four months after they had been dismounted, details were sent back to Texas to retrieve the men's horses, and bring them to Mississippi, but before they arrived, the Sixth was engaged at Corinth and suffered heavy losses, including some men who were taken prisoner. Keen recalls the horrific scene that transpired on Friday, October 3:

> In our company every commission officer, save 3 lieutenants was wounded and many of the soldiers killed. It was fearful charge through open Spanish and post oak timber. The trees were tumbling in every direction and the limbs fly through the air .... We formed just under the brow of the hill on which the battery was stationed. Sim Lindsey was killed at my side, his blood and brains being scattered all around. He told me that morning that he never would get out of the battle alive ....

> When the morning dawned a great line of battle stretched away to our left and the long line of flags were seen for more than a mile. A blast of trumpets was blown and the mighty charge of thousands was on. It was a grand sight. For over a mile down the line my eye could see every flag and regiment. What a sweep, what

a blast of noise and death... Some thirty thousand men engaged in fearful struggle for the victory. But fate—cruel fate decided against the Southern cause.[466]

The Sixth Calvary suffered heavy losses from deaths and also from the soldiers who were taken as prisoners. Muster rolls from 1861 showed over 1,150 soldiers in ten companies, Field and Staff. By the time the unit surrendered at Jackson, there were fewer than 200 men left from their brigade. Colonel Jack Wharton, the commander of the Sixth at the time, signed the surrender and the remaining men of the Sixth Texas Cavalry returned home via the USS *E.H. Fairchild*, disembarking at Natchitoches, Louisiana, and slowly making their way back to Texas.[467]

Newton Keen and Ernest Gouhenant had seen a tremendous amount of death and bloodshed. Physical wounds were inflicted upon the soldiers with a new generation of weapons that had made the task of killing much more efficient than in previous wars. Appalling conditions in the camps, combined with a lack of sufficient medical treatment, created too significant a barrier for most men to overcome. Emotional wounds were deep, too, and some men would never recover. Yet, miraculously, both Newton and Ernest survived.

GOING HOME TO TEXAS

Keen was taken prisoner in August of 1864 and transported to Camp Douglass in Chicago, and placed in overcrowded housing with several thousand men, many of whom had survived the war only to die in prison camp. He was released in June of 1865, after spending seven months in heinous conditions. Without a penny in his pocket, Keen made his way home to Texas, traveling by rail, wagon, and mule, and relying on strangers for food. Finally, he arrived at his grandfather's home, reuniting with his family, including his uncle, Reverend John W. Keen. After the war, Newton married, raised a family, and became a preacher.

Ernest and Newton's wartime experience ran along parallel paths for nearly four years. In all likelihood, Newton heard the shrill timbre of Ernest's bugle commands in camp or on the battlefield. Whether or not they knew each other before or during the war, or whether they ever had a conversation is unknown. Since they enlisted from the same area, and so few soldiers survived from their unit, they almost certainly crossed paths.

Ernest returned home to Denton County a decorated soldier. He resumed his life with his wife and daughter and within a year they had a son and named him Edgar.

Having served in the Confederate cavalry, and bearing witness to many horrifying scenes, Ernest was surely a battle-weary man by his mid-thirties. Not long after he returned, his domestic life with Mary would come to an end. By 1867, Mary Withers had died, leaving Ernest a widower with two small children.

The letters that Humbert left behind years earlier offer a brief glimpse into Gouhenant's life in Texas and also hint at his feelings about his cousin, but the dearth of personal information concerning the relationship between Gouhenant and his son Ernest offers no clues regarding either man's feelings about the war, or about each other. Gouhenant had left his family when his son was sixteen and had no communication with him from 1848 to 1853, leaving only speculation about their relationship. Ernest had visited his father every day while imprisoned in Toulouse and once Gouhenant left France, his wife Jeanne had lobbied unsuccessfully for Ernest to join his father in Texas. When they finally did reunite, it seems that Ernest worked with his father for a while before marrying Mary Withers. At some point, Gouhenant's relationship with his son became strained. Perhaps they were at odds over money, family matters, or the war. Gouhenant's imposing presence and his desire for his son's success in Texas may have also created some difficulties between them. Whatever the cause for their estrangement, after the war, both men went on with their separate lives.

CHAPTER 16

A WANDERER RESTS

[He] is a very intelligent gentleman, and not without honor in his own State, which recently appointed him to make a Geological survey of Texas...[468]

Missouri Weekly, 1871

PILOT POINT: THE FINAL CHAPTER

Adolphe Gouhenant wandered throughout his life. His adventures carried him from the provincial towns and crowded urban centers of France, where countless insurrections occurred in his wake, across the Atlantic to the United States. From New Orleans, he ventured up the Mississippi and Red Rivers, and across the sweeping plains and Cross Timbers of North Texas. Financial missteps in France served as his impetus to flee Lyon, and his pursuit of a new start with an evolving communist movement fueled his wanderlust for the untamed west. His documented social and economic ties to North Texas covered an area of roughly 2,000 square miles. Towards the end of his life, he would travel once again beyond Texas, to his final destination.

Prior to the Civil War, sometime in the late 1850s, Gouhenant was spending most of his time in Tarrant and Denton Counties. The City of Fort Worth was competing with Birdville (present-day Haltom City) and Johnson Station over which town would become the seat for Tarrant County. Townsmen thought that if Fort Worth were to thrive, it should be the county seat—not Birdville. The men of Fort Worth lobbied to hold a special election and in November 1856, Fort Worth won. The Birdville men tried to invalidate the outcome, and held another election. In an effort to boost Fort Worth's chances, more than three dozen men came forward and offered to pay for a permanent county courthouse if the seat of governance stayed in Fort Worth.

Gouhenant and some of his friends, including Middleton Tate Johnson and E.M. Daggett, signed a $2,700 bond guaranteeing the cost of construction. Gouhenant pledged $150.00, a large sum considering only two of the men pledged more at $200 a piece.[469]

Once the election was held again in the spring of 1860, Fort Worth was the clear winner. The citizens made good on their promise and construction soon began on the courthouse, although it would not be finished until after the war.[470]

Although his ties to Fort Worth remained strong, he eventually made a move that would close the circle on his frontier journey; Adolphe Gouhenant returned to Denton County to begin the final chapter of his life. In 1857 he was boarding with Thompson Smith, a forty-four-year-old farmer, his wife Mary, and their eight children on a farm in Denton County. He likely moved permanently to Pilot Point perhaps as early as 1858 or 1859, when the village was still the most populous in the county. The census describes Gouhenant as being a fifty-year-old physician, with real estate and personal property valued at $4,700. Curiously, he had not only become a doctor, he had miraculously deducted six years from his age.[471]

It had now been well over a decade since he had seen his wife, Jeanne. Ernest may have brought letters from his mother when he arrived in America, but more than likely, the marriage was completely dead. Gouhenant's hairline was receding to reveal an even broader forehead, and with his gray hair now overtaking a once magnificent blond beard, the enigmatic Frenchman married a second time.

Elizabeth Martin was his bride. Born in 1842, Elizabeth was the third child of Jacob and Susan Martin from Virginia and Ohio respectively. Jacob was a farmer and by the mid-1850s he had settled his family in Pilot Point. The town was platted in 1854 and a year later, it had a postmaster, and then a school and two churches, and would soon be a stop on the Butterfield Overland Mail stage route. By 1860, the Martins were well established and a few years later, Jacob would become postmaster. Elizabeth attended school, graduated in literature, and according to family accounts, the beautiful and tall young woman was a scholar and probably taught school herself for a while. She apparently met Gouhenant during a buggy mishap where she hurt her ankle. Gouhenant was there when the accident occurred and offered to assist, but while Elizabeth was initially not inclined to show her ankle to a stranger, she acquiesced and he nursed her back to health. The two were subsequently married, despite their nearly forty-year age difference—and despite the fact that there was no formal divorce from Gouhenant's first wife, Jeanne. The exact year of their marriage is not documented. However, in the summer of 1860, she was eighteen years old, still living with her parents on their farm, and she had attended school within the past year, so it likely occurred about 1860 or 1861.[472]

According to the census, fewer than one-third of the children between six and nineteen were attending school in the young village and the issue of education was a concern, especially among the town's educated Masons. In 1861, Gouhenant actively participated in founding a new lodge in Pilot Point. A co-founder, David J. Eddleman, left testimony about the settlement in his autobiography:

> When I first knew Pilot Point, it was a very small place, only two families, and three boarders no other house nearer than one mile

from the public square, this was in the fall of 1854, but the town grew rapidly. Then, there were only a few small farms opened, the citizens were mostly engaged in stock-raising, and farm lands were at a very small value. Good prairie land within one mile of the new town could be bought at twenty-five cents per acre; very soon new men came into the country and bought up some of the lands and put in farms, and the country improved, and the town built up, but there was no school house, nor house to preach in, so all the preaching that was done was at a school house some distance from the town.[473] Not many years had passed until the masons decided to organize a new lodge at Pilot Point, but there was no suitable house in which to their lodge meetings .... The masons proceeded to get a lot and raise money to build the lodge. My brother, Dr. Eddleman donated the lot, and the following list made up the masons subscribing to form the new lodge and build the house: Viz: J.F. Elmore; Nick Wilson; A.J. Miller.; T.W. Skinner; John Morgan; J.B. Self; Z. Lindsey; C. Yarbough; T.W. Dirickson; Ren McAdams; W. Noll; A. Gounah [Gouhenant]; A.W. McFarland and myself. We soon got together money enough to erect the house, lay the floors and make it habitable; at least the upstairs portion, the lower part so near finished that a school could be taught in it during warm weather, and preaching also.[474]

The Lodge received its charter on June 1862 and among its first officers, Adolphe Gouhenant was elected as Senior Warden.[475]

When Gouhenant had first settled in Dallas a decade earlier, he had quickly become an important character, but his Arts Saloon was relatively short-lived and his position in the community eventually waned. Dallas grew and expanded without him. It seemed that he was tired of fighting. Perhaps setting up his family in Fort Worth, the subsequent death of his nephew, and the volatile events leading up to the war, took their toll on the aging Gouhenant. He finally settled down in Pilot Point where he found peace and quiet, and an environment where he could prosper once again—better to be the head of a dog than the tail of a lion.[476]

Pilot Point was an isolated community. It would not be connected to the rest of the world via telegraph until 1877, and the railroad didn't arrive until 1880, but Adolphe and Elizabeth had made it their home in the 1860s, raised cattle, and grew their land holdings. A young man named William was working for them on the farm. By the fall of 1866 Gouhenant was again thriving, owning two apothecaries and two carriages.

In October of 1866, Albert Brisbane once again tried to establish contact with Gouhenant. Brisbane wrote a letter addressing the issue of the Arts Saloon mortgage, which was still pending, but his primary inquiry was of a more personal nature.

> Monsieur Gouhenant
>
> This letter will be delivered to you by my son, Dr. Charles F. Brisbane. He goes to Texas to seek a good climate, and exercise on horse for his health.
>
> I have authorized him to make any settlement practical in relation to the mortgage. If the warranty is still good, and everything in order, you can pay him. I am not in hurry for the money, and very likely you are.
>
> My son speaks French perfectly. I advised him to hunt in the Cross Timbers, and to live outdoors. Give him information on what he should do.[477]

Charles F. Brisbane was the eldest son of Albert. He was born to Adele LeBrun, a European lady whom Albert had met in the 1830s, during the same tour in which he had encountered the ideas of Charles Fourier. In 1834, Albert had become such a devoted Fourierist, he even named his first son after him—Charles Fourier Brisbane.[478] Charles was studying medicine when he became ill. During the war, he had enlisted in the Union army as an assistant surgeon. He was wounded (or got sick) in June of 1865, and he mustered out the following month. Charles did not recover after the end of the war. In the fall of 1866, probably on advice from his father, he decided to head for Texas, seeking a better climate than the one in New York. Surprisingly, his father turned to Gouhenant to help him.[479]

The first leg of his trip was to San Antonio, where Albert's old partner Victor Considerant had been living since the failure of La Réunion. The goal of the San Antonio trip was to investigate Considerant's future projects, and Albert wrote to his son: "Find out from Considerant what he intends or wants to do. See how he feels towards Fourier's ideas. Let me know all you can of his plans." It was Albert's intention that this would be just the first step for Charles before going north to Denton County. Albert wrote, "[Gouhenant] is in or near the Cross Timbers, and from February on, North Texas will be preferable to the South . ... I think Gouhenant will get board for you and furnish you with the means of hunting." However, Charles ultimately decided to remain in San Antonio, seemingly on Considerant's counsel. His father was furious and wrote him again in January 1867:

> Considerant's advice was very unwise, and you ought to have had judgment enough not to have remained in an expensive city, when you could have started on your way, and written me to send funds to Dallas, or some other point. Try and calculate your movements more wisely and do not spend twice as much money as is necessary. ... I think you had better go straight to Pilot Point, Denton Co. where Gouhenant is. Write him there and at Dallas to inquire where he is. Let him answer you at some point on your way.

It is likely Charles's health did not allow him to go further. The outdoor life his father recommended as a treatment came too late, and Charles died in San Antonio in March 1867, probably before he ever met Gouhenant.[480]

In his letters, Brisbane never alluded to any of Gouhenant's healing skills that he might have used to cure his son. When Brisbane had interacted with Gouhenant, he was still known mainly as an artist, and Brisbane probably did not know he was now known as "Doctor Gounah" in Pilot Point, where his practice was apparently thriving. In 1869, Gouhenant placed an advertisement in the Pilot Point *Vedette*. The listing read, "Dr. A. Gounah, practical chemist and physician, Pilot Point, Texas."[481] By 1870 Gouhenant's holdings were worth $15,000—making his family the thirteenth wealthiest of the 368 families who were living in the town—and he was still a self-described "Doctor of Medicine."[482]

It was likely around the time he married Elizabeth that Gouhenant changed the spelling of his last name to "Gounah," since before 1860, there is no record of him using that spelling. Perhaps it was Elizabeth who suggested using an Americanized version of his surname. In any event, the decision to do so seems to have been agreed upon by family consensus because Ernest also changed the spelling of his name. By the time he mustered out of the war, Ernest had seen multiple spellings of the family name. The revised spelling took root and was permanently carried down to his children, who passed it on to their children.

Illustration 32. A photograph of the north side of the square in Pilot Point.

From the Eddleman Collection, courtesy of Jay Melugin, Pilot Point, City Historian.
This photo shows how the town looked in 1872, the year following Gouhenant's death.

A Painful Accident

In 1872, the railroad was finally making its way to Dallas. By the end of the year, the population would double, making Dallas the hub of commercial markets for raw materials like cotton and grain that were being transported from the rural communities around the south. The city would experience unprecedented growth, emerging as a significant economic center at the dawn of the twentieth century. Unfortunately, Gouhenant would not live to see the railroad arrive in North Texas, nor the economic boom it brought with it.

In 1871, he was just as driven as he had been forty years earlier and he was also about to embark on a new assignment. On a windy day in April, he left his home, boarded a stagecoach, and headed to Missouri. He was planning to travel by rail to Washington, DC, to conduct business for the state, supposedly under some type of geological appointment.[483]

On Sunday evening, April 23, the train carrying Gouhenant north pulled into the newly built depot, the giant metal beast screeching to a halt. He left the train to have a bite to eat before continuing on his journey. This would be his last stop. On Thursday, the *Missouri Weekly Patriot* printed a chilling story under the headline, "A Painful Accident."[484]

> An elderly gentleman by the name of Dr. A. Gournah, from Pilot Point, near Sherman, Texas met with a serious accident at North Springfield, on Sunday evening last. He arrived on the evening train from Seneca, and while taking his supper the bell rang, and he and other passengers rushed out—thinking the train was leaving; seizing hold of the railing on the car platform, he stepped up with his right foot, and in attempting to raise his left foot, it was caught under the wheels and crushed, and under which too, his body would have been drawn had he not clung to the railing of the platform with a desperate grip. In this position, he was carried forty feet, when he was seized by an engineer, by name of J.M. Richardson, and wrenched from his agonizing and perilous position. He was taken up into a comfortable room in

the Ozark House, and amputation was performed at the ankle, by Drs. Robberson, Ross, and Hansford.

He is now doing well, and is kindly ministered unto by A.O. Fairchild, and other brethren of the "Mystic Tie," who supply as far as is possible the attentions and sympathy of his distant home.

Dr. Gournah is a very intelligent gentleman, and not without honor in his own State, which recently appointed him to make a Geological survey of Texas, and he was on his way to Washington to make arrangement for that important work, when he met with the sad accident related. He had in his possession quite a large sum of money, which has been prudently cared for, and deposited in the bank. The Dr. bears his afflictions with fortitude, and even cheerfulness. We trust he will soon be able to return to his family which has yet not been startled by the unwelcome news in store for them.

After the train crushed his foot, a group of men carried him over to the Ozark House where he spent seven long, agonizing days. His Masonic brothers attended to him, including E.T. Robberson, a local doctor, and J.M. Richardson, the engineer who had pulled him from the wheels of the train. A local silversmith, Artemis Fairchild, stayed with him day and night; others were also assisting. They did their best to care for his wound and make him comfortable, but since antibiotics had not yet been discovered, "unfavorable symptoms" manifested after the amputation, and infection set in. He knew the end was near. Putting his affairs in order, Gouhenant appointed Fairchild and Elizabeth's younger brother, attorney John Edward Martin, as executors of his will. He signed a document on April 29, 1871, stating that he was, "sick and weak in body, but of sound mind, memory, and understanding."[485]

A second article appeared in the paper the following week,

The advanced years and high, nervous organism of the patient aggravated the case so that despite the skill of the attending physicians and careful nursing of the Masonic brethren, it became apparent by Saturday to the deceased and his attendants—that the last great journey was surely approaching. With calmness and fortitude the Doctor prepared for his long journey. Mindful of the dear ones he was to leave behind, he executed the "last will and testament" on Saturday, making full and complete disposal of his large possessions. He directed that his remains should be laid in our cemetery. He quietly passed away on Sunday morning last.[486]

In his will, the sixty-seven-year-old left all his land to his beloved wife Elizabeth Gounah. Then, with one swift gesture, he left one dollar each to his son Ernest and to his daughter, Anastasie. He purposefully withheld from them what would otherwise have been a generous inheritance. However, to his two grandchildren, Emily and Edgar, he left the sum of two hundred dollars, to be held in trust by Elizabeth and to distribute as she would deem proper. All his remaining personal property went to Elizabeth. The will was witnessed by Richardson and three other men. He then signed it, "A. Gounah, M.D." There was no mention of Jeanne Durand.[487]

The morning after his death the men from the Solomon Lodge convened at the Masonic Hall. They formed a large and imposing procession, and with solemn music, marched two by two, wearing lambskin aprons, badges of mourning, and a small sprig of evergreen. At about ten o'clock the carriages in waiting began to roll forward, joining the Masons, winding their way through the streets, towards the cemetery to bury the remains of their deceased brother. Mason J.E. Tefft, who was also one of the first doctors in Springfield, conducted the graveside service and Rev. Haggerty said prayers of the Order. The Rev. Tuttle, a servant of the church, also prayed and the mourning brothers chanted the requiem. Masonic honors were given and the brothers passed over his grave one by one, each throwing the small evergreen, and a portion of the damp, fresh earth on top of the coffin. Adolphe Gouhenant, a wanderer, was finally laid to rest.[488]

A Death Shrouded in Mystery

When he died, Gouhenant had several items in his possession: a trunk, a ticket issued by the South Pacific Rail Road valid for travel from Springfield to St. Louis and valued at $11.85; he also had nearly $900 in currency and gold coins. He was billed posthumously for medical necessities incurred during his illness, including fifty dollars for "medical attention day and night," fifty dollars for "amputating foot," sixteen dollars paid to Artemis Fairchild for "nursing," and $1.75 for oranges and lemons. The cost of the coffin, hearse, and burial came to $35. Oliver Smith, the druggist on the south side of St. Louis Street, submitted two bills totaling about twenty dollars for various medical supplies that included alcohol, camphor, brandy, and whisky.[489]

There was one statement printed in the Missouri paper that is quite mysterious. The sentence states that Gouhenant was on his way to Washington because he had been "recently appointed to make a Geological survey of Texas." The item is strange and warrants some exploration.

There is nothing in Gouhenant's past to suggest that he had any education or formal training in geology, or in any other scientific studies whatsoever. He clearly had a passion for art, science, and politics, but the fact that he had no academic credentials is almost beyond doubt. The only references that even remotely link him to geology are from the early 1850s. Charles DeMorse had written about the fossils he observed at the Arts Saloon back in 1852. Then, in the summer of 1854, Gouhenant had sent a batch of cretaceous fossils that he collected in Dallas County, to the Academy of Natural Sciences of Philadelphia; the fossils may or may not have been from the same collection that he showed to DeMorse.[490]

In fact, during the 1860s and early 1870s the topic of the Texas geological survey was of intense interest to many people and the consideration for appointing a state geologist was political as well as scientific. A few years earlier, in 1858, the Texas legislature had passed a law authorizing a geological and agricultural survey to be made by a state geologist, an assistant state geologist, and a chemist; the applications were "as numerous as mosquitoes in the Brazos Bottom."[491]

Governor Hardin R. Runnels appointed Dr. Benjamin F. Schumard as the first state geologist. Schumard was an experienced man who had participated in the geological surveys of several states. On November 1860, Governor Sam Houston removed him and appointed Francis Moore, "an enthusiastic amateur geologist and old Texan."[492] The war interrupted the survey a few months later, and one of Schumard's collaborators— S.B. Buckley—left the South, "taking the notes of the survey" with him. Then, in 1866, Governor Throckmorton appointed S. B. Buckley to the position, despite Schumard's protests that "[Buckley] knows nothing of geology, is utterly incompetent to arrange and classify the collections at Austin, and anything he may write, would not command the respect of any scientific man."[493] Buckley held the position for less than a year.

During post-war Reconstruction era, Governor Edmund J. Davis,was appointed as provisional governor of Texas. Among his many initiatives, he established a bureau of geology that would provide a survey to showcase the abundant mineral riches that Texas possessed. In the 12th Texas Legislature, held in Austin on April 29, 1870, Davis proposed "a complete geological survey." He suggested the survey be under control of the General Land Office where it could be "systemized in a better and cheaper way in connection with surveys of the public lands."[494]

In late 1870, the Legislature authorized the survey. The position of state geologist was still highly coveted and it seems several men were lobbying for it. E.H. Bowman, surveyor of Fort Bliss, wrote to Governor Davis requesting that his son, Samuel, who at the time was the state geologist of Illinois, be appointed to the Texas post.[495] On April 10, 1871 —just two weeks prior to Gouhenant's accident—four Texas Senators, A.J. Fountain, G.T. Ruby, Thomas Baker, and W.H. Parsons— sent a note to Governor Davis, to "respectfully recommend the appointment of J.W. Glenn, esq. as state geologist."[496]

In March of 1873, John Wright Glenn was finally appointed. Years later, he sent a letter to renowned geologist Robert T. Hill, stating he had no predecessor. [497] Like Buckley, Glenn remained in the position for just a year, and when Richard Coke became governor in 1874, Glenn resigned in turn, and Buckley was appointed once again. [498]

None of Schumard's three successors were skilled geologists. It is possible that Davis could have envisioned appointing Gouhenant to such a position in 1870. Since no documentation of the appointment survives, one possibility is that Governor Davis's staff procrastinated on the paperwork, and if any record did exist, it was discarded after Gouhenant's death.[499]

There have been other vague references to the appointment. Almost thirty years after he died, a story appeared in *The Bohemian*, published in Fort Worth in 1900, which stated, "The doctor was appointed State Geologist of Texas and was killed... at Springfield, Mo., on his way to New York on business pertaining to the chemical and geological department."[500]

After his death, local lore altered his destination from Washington DC to New York. The appointment was seemingly referenced again in 1943 when an article written by Ephraim Daggett's daughter was published in a Fort Worth newspaper echoing the claim that he was appointed to the position.[501] "Dr. Gonnough was appointed state geologist of Texas. He married Elizabeth Martin, a sister of Judge J.E. Martin, in Denton County, and was killed in a railroad accident in Missouri while en route to New York on business pertaining to the chemical and geological affairs of the State." [502]

Whether or not the Springfield reporter got his facts right, one thing is clear—Gouhenant was headed east to fulfill some type of obligation. It is unlikely the reporter would have completely invented a story about the geological survey. Perhaps he did not understand what Gouhenant told him. Indeed, he was weak from his injury and his story may have been garbled. In any case, he was about to embark on one more phase of his incredible life, perhaps one that would marry his love of science and politics, and finally reward him with the elusive credentials he had sought his entire career. In the end, the misstep cost him his foot, his last hope of securing a political legacy, and ultimately his life, now extinguished like so many of his dreams before. [503]

François Ignace (Adolphe) Gouhenant marked each decade of his life with a significant milestone. He left his small village at the age of fifteen and struck out on his own, learning to paint and then making a living doing so, an accomplishment quite unusual for that era. In his twenties, he married and raised a family, and before his thirtieth birthday, he had built a one-hundred-foot high monument atop Fourvière hill. Despite going bankrupt, his tower survived. In his forties, he organized laborers to impact political change and emerged from imprisonment and subsequent trial, to be found innocent. He crossed the Atlantic, leading a group of passionate men to establish a new community based on equality. While the community failed, Gouhenant survived and returned to his roots as an artist to establish the first cultural and artistic establishment in Dallas. In his fifties, he married a much younger woman and settled into a quiet life raising cattle and running his apothecary business. He died prematurely, the result of a senseless accident at the age sixty-seven. Had he lived, he would no doubt have made another mark in his seventh decade.

In May of 1871, twenty years after the Arts Saloon opened, a small notice appeared in the Dallas Herald paper, tightly wedged between the editorials and advertisements, the last mention of Gouhenant for a very long time.

> **Death of Dr. Adolph Gounah:** The *Sherman Courier* of last Saturday learns that Dr. A. Gounah of Pilot Point, Denton County, died at Springfield, Missouri recently, from the effects of a wound received in attempting to get on a railroad car while in motion. The Doctor was formerly and for a number of years a resident of this city, and will be well remembered by all our old citizens.[504]

CHAPTER 17

EPILOGUE

A FAMILY LEGACY

François -Ignace Gouhenant has not been well remembered in the telling of North Texas History. His tale is usually reduced to a few brief sentences in books that herald the lives of other men—those men who made names for themselves, passed their fortunes or vast land acquisitions on to their heirs and have been well documented over the past century and a half. There are several reasons why Gouhenant's story has been overlooked.

First, although his name has appeared in many books, articles, and archival records, over two dozen misspellings have been found, probably due to the challenging and ambiguous pronunciation. Even in Haute-Saône—where the family name originates—the *he* syllable is silent and the name is pronounced as if it were written *Gounan*—in French the final *t* after *an* is always silent. Everywhere else in France, the usage is unknown and the name is pronounced *Goo-hey-nan*. Sometimes an acute accent has even been added on the *e* to force this pronunciation. [505] This inconsistency likely hampered research efforts where the thread from *Goonan* to *Gouhenant* could easily be lost.

Second, while the events of his trial in Toulouse are fairly well known among French Icarian scholars, few historians have traveled beyond that event to fish out details of his early years in Lyon. Once the first few clues were uncovered about his activities in Toulouse and Lyon, many pieces of the puzzle fell into place; his advocacy for workers' rights in southern France and his clandestine movements among the revolutionaries of the early 1840s had been nearly lost. His revolutionary exploits prior to the Toulouse trial, his efforts to build the tower in Lyon, and his imprisonment and subsequent trial reveal an outrageously complex character who wandered around grasping at the edges of a successful career, staking small claims along the way.

Third, adding to the lack of published materials, there is the question of missing artifacts; aside from the few early daguerreotypes that have been attributed to him, none of Gouhenant's art works have been found. Some of his religious paintings were exhibited during his lifetime in Toulouse and his name appears at least once in an exhibition catalogue from that era. An announcement for the auction of his work has also been located. However, research inquiries to French museums and Catholic dioceses have yielded no success in locating his lost paintings. There are almost surely paintings and other images that survived into the twentieth century both in France and the U.S. They may reside in church basements or private residences, but so far, surviving tangible art objects have eluded researchers. Conversations with some descendants have revealed that fires in family homes took their toll on historic treasures.[506]

Then, there is the issue of local folklore driving the propagation of erroneous information. Gouhenant reportedly kept a diary. More than twenty years after his death, a local historian and friend of Gouhenant's brother-in-law, Judge C.C. Cummings, wrote a wild story about Gouhenant in *The Bohemian* (Cummings had also corresponded with Simon Ferrar about the early days of Fort Worth). He wrote that Gouhenant had recorded a dream he had while en route to Missouri,[507]

Sleeping at the Kelly House in Sherman, he dreamed that he met with a railroad accident while boarding the cars at some Missouri town on the way of his journey north in the interest of his new office which resulted in his death. That after being injured he was taken charge of by the brothers of the "Mystic Tie," a branch of Masonry of which he was a member, of the highest standing, and was carried to the third story of some building there and was cared for and tenderly [nursed] by Sisters of Charity till his death, or, as he noted in his diary, "till he went up in light." [508]

The Missouri newspaper confirms the statement about the Mystic Tie, but there is no record of the Sisters of Charity being in Missouri during that time. According to Cummings, who arrived in Fort Worth two years after Gouhenant's death, "they happened to be there temporarily on a visit for some ulterior purpose of locating their order there." Cummings's narrative goes on to claim, "He arose in the night, lighted a lamp and noted it in full in his diary, which he kept for years before his death. He also noted that his wife came to his body as it laid [sic] in that room and wept over his remains the next day after his death... The notes of this incident was [sic] found in his diary after his death." Cummings does not note which of Gouhenant's two wives might have appeared to him in his dream. He never met Adolphe Gouhenant, but probably knew Elizabeth Gounah and he may have heard her tell the story, the accuracy of which must be questioned. In any event, it is certainly a romantic tale that Gouhenant would have relished.

His diary has likely vanished forever; his paintings are apparently lost, and according to Cummings, he also possessed a collection of books dedicated to the Swedenborgian faith. Where are those books now?

Finally, the absence of a more substantial telling of Gouhenant's story in local history, may also be due to the fact that he simply was not a local hero. He was complicated and misunderstood. His motives were sometimes unclear and his actions tested the limits of the law in both France and America. He advocated for workers' rights, but his reputation was tarnished by oral histories that perpetuated misleading details about his contribution to the failure of the Icarian settlement. His name was also attached to La Réunion, adding to confusion about his role with "the other North Texas socialist community." Even fictitious accounts were printed including an almost humorous item that appeared in an 1893 newspaper where Ernest Gouhenant reportedly claimed his father "resigned his position as a royal astronomer at Lyons to come to Texas."[509]

In spite of the fact that he was the first naturalized citizen in Dallas, artist in residence, and photographer of early citizens, his history was lost. He did not leave a legacy of Civil War accomplishments. He built no bridges, and he left no canvas to be exhibited at the Kimbell or Dallas Museum of Art. He ultimately left Dallas and Fort Worth behind to live a quiet life in Pilot Point, where more of his history might have been preserved, had he not departed this world prematurely.

Supposedly Gouhenant had been appointed to a state position. Had he fulfilled said duties, his life would likely have been better documented. Instead, a horrific accident kept him from reaching the pinnacle of his career. Although he had unfinished business to attend to when he died, Adolphe Gouhenant had already lived a life more robust than most men. Ultimately, he had left everything from France behind: his family, his citizenship, and even his name.

The site of the Arts Saloon, a North Texas beacon for art and culture, and an important token in one of Dallas's earliest homestead disputes, was gradually absorbed by the city's expansion, becoming no more than a faded memory of the earliest citizens. After Brisbane finally auctioned the property in the spring of 1869 the lot became home to several businesses throughout the 1870s and 1880s. The buildings in Block 7, which were among the town's original frame structures on the courthouse square, remained on maps until the late 1880s, perhaps up until after the turn of the century. They were eventually destroyed in the twentieth century and the site where his Arts Saloon stood, just south of the Old Red Museum, is now paved with cement. With the exception of a few red brick buildings in downtown's West End, and a handful of streets named Good-Latimer, Peak, Crockett, McCoy, Browder, Pryor, and a few others, there are few reminders left of nineteenth-century Dallas.

Gouhenant cemented his legacy simply by immigrating to North Texas and becoming one of Dallas's most colorful early citizens. He provided land for the burial of Major Ripley Arnold and his family in Fort Worth (prior to his land grant being divided) and the street that runs adjacent to the Pioneer Rest Cemetery is named "Gounah." He built a beautiful tower on Fourvière hill that in recent years has housed a restaurant offering a spectacular view overlooking the city of Lyon. In the midst of three cities—Lyon, Dallas, and Fort Worth—that share a common pride originating from numerous cultural and artistic achievements, François Ignace Gouhenant was a French revolutionary, expatriate, and charismatic pioneer whose story has finally been told.[510]

ICARIA AND THE COLONISTS

More than a hundred years after the Icarians left Denton County, the land they once occupied came to be owned by the Henry B. Taylor family. Taylor's 450 acres were at the heart of 32 half-sections of the land settled by the Icarians. According to Taylor, there was very little topsoil and it was not suitable for farming; the area was mostly gravel. (They farmed "a little bit of everything to get by" including wheat, maize, cotton, cattle, and hogs.) The story handed down to the Taylors was that the Icarians died suddenly and the survivors were too weak to dig graves. So, they buried the dead in a mass grave in a water well. Another old-time resident, Mrs. Mary Hodge, who came to Justin in 1889 after the Santa Fe Railroad built through the town, reiterates the local lore saying that her best recollection of the story was that the colonists died of yellow fever. More recent visits to the area in 2015 have yielded no results for any remnants of the short-lived community. [511]

In July 1849, *Le Populaire* published the fates of the men who made up the Icarian first avant-garde. Five men left the group as soon as they learned about the overthrow of Louis Philippe and six additional men abandoned the group a short time later. One man was killed by lightning at the new settlement and seven more died in Texas either at the site or during the retreat.[512] Six remained behind to work in Texas or New Orleans. Two men died in New Orleans from cholera. Six men were described as "hostile dissidents," one of whom committed suicide in New Orleans. Fourteen of the Icarians returned to France or remained in the U.S. to work elsewhere, but were not considered "hostile." Finally, there were twenty men who returned to New Orleans to convene in the communal house. According to the same report, "Gouhenant was expelled."[513]

The subsequent fate of most of these men after the retreat in September 1848, especially the ones who did not follow Cabet to Nauvoo, has not been documented. For a few, sparse information can be gathered here and there.

Bourgeois, Gouhenant, and Drouard had voted against the retreat from Peters Colony. In May of 1849, Bourgeois wrote to his parents: "I and one of my Icarian comrades, the brother Drouard from Angers, have decided to stay in Texas. We took possession of a one-mile plot. It is an area of about half a league."[514] Another year passed and Bourgeois wrote to his sister. In May of 1850,

> I have obtained the certificate attesting to my rights three weeks ago, it cost me $2.50 (12,5 francs) .... The parents of those who died in Icarie are entitled to half a section of ground for each man. I have a small house of 18 square foot in wood and with one floor .... I am convinced that all the projects of partial community will fail. I have felt so many disappointments among the icarians of the first avant garde, I have seen men I fully trusted cheating me so cruelly that I have decided to protect myself from any further deception.[515]

Bourgeois moved to Dallas, and when Victor Considerant first arrived there he helped La Réunion colonists get settled. In 1856 he joined them with his wife Louisa and served as a cook, according to Amédée Simonin, the accountant of La Réunion. Bourgeois died in 1885 and is buried in the Pioneer Cemetery adjacent to Dallas City Hall—the only original Icarian known to be buried in Dallas County.[516]

Drouard and Bourgeois were friends and they were both issued certificates for 320 acres on the same day in 1850 in Alton. Drouard was also associated with Maxime Guillot and a man named Laurent Fleury in Denton County in 1850, before Guillot left for Fort Worth. He died before 1862, when his land was patented and awarded to his heirs by the court. His parcel sits only a few miles north of the original Icarian site.[517]

The two physicians sailing with Gouhenant in 1848 were Charles Leclerc, who left the group in New Orleans almost immediately upon arriving, and Juan Rovira, who had been a member of the same group of Catalan Icarians as Abdon Terradas.[518] When he left the Icarian settlement after the disaster, Rovira went back to New Orleans, and was joined by his wife and child. He and Dubuisson—a member of the second avant-garde—led a group of dissident Icarians who were waiting for Cabet. When Cabet arrived in January of 1849, they accused him of having abandoned them and they sought to liquidate the community's assets, but Cabet wound up leading his followers to establish another community in Illinois. Rovira was completely distraught.[519] A New Orleans newspaper reported,

> Don Juan Rovira had committed suicide, by blowing out his brains with a large pistol, the fatal [weapon] lying alongside of his right arm, while with the left hand he grasped another loaded pistol ... two letters were found, setting forth that he had attained the age of 29 years, and that it had been his intention to live until he was 30, but having become quite tired of life, he could no longer endure his earthly existence. He hinted, also, that he had been a believer in the doctrines of Communism but had found out that they were not the panacea he imagined, and trusted that people

would no longer be led astray by such ideas, and that his blood would be the last to be shed in such a cause. [520]

Alfred Piquenard left the Icarians in Texas but later joined the Icarian community at Nauvoo, Illinois. Gaining notoriety as a meticulous and successful architect in the Midwest, he married Marie Denuzieras and they had four children, two of whom died as babies. He helped to build the (sixth) State Capitol in Springfield, Illinois, and also the Capitol in Des Moines, Iowa, which he was working on when he died in 1876, just a few weeks prior to his fiftieth birthday. [521]

ERNEST AND HIS CHILDREN

Ernest's story, less colorful perhaps than his father's, is nevertheless worth telling. He seems to have struggled throughout his life. At the impressionable age of eleven, he saw his father arrested, accused, imprisoned, and put on trial. When he was sixteen, Gouhenant left him behind to go to America, and Ernest did not see him again until just after his twenty-first birthday. Ernest seems to have inherited some of his father's artistic talent, working as a painter and playing the bugle. Unfortunately, his talents did not seem to include his father's tenacity or his inclination to rebound economically.

Ernest had married Mary Withers in 1857 or 1858, about the same time he became a U.S. citizen. The couple had a daughter, Emma (Emily) Hortense, born December 30, 1858. Emma was less than a year old when Ernest left home to enlist with the Confederate army. When the war was over, he returned to Denton County after an absence of three and a half years. Ernest and Mary then had a son, Edgar in 1866; Mary died the same year, leaving Ernest with two small children. [522]

Following the war, Ernest and Thomas Wisdom Daugherty were jointly selling retail liquor. The Daughertys were a prominent family in Denton and the Daugherty brothers held elected positions in the 1860s. They were half Cherokee and had settled in Denton County in 1851. Their sister Mary was allied to another prominent family in the county, since she was married to David J. Eddleman, one of the first settlers of Pilot Point and Gouhenant's Masonic brother. [523]

Two articles, the first most closely resembling small-town gossip, were published in the *Denton Monitor* in August 1868 and show that Ernest was well established in Denton: "A few days ago we noticed our friend Gounah dashing around town in every direction on a fine, newly-painted buggy, we supposed for the purpose of making some poor fellow's 'mouth water for it.'" [524]

The second story shows that Ernest did play a horn for musical enjoyment. It describes a theater exhibition where all the town had gathered and "the sweet notes of Miss Sue Battle's piano, attended by the symphonic voice of Mr. Gounah's brass pipe and Dr. Hughes' violin, rang out upon the darkling stillness with delicious thrill." [525]

In the summer of 1870, Emma and Edgar were living with their grandmother, Luisa, and her second husband, Benjamin Hardin, all still in Denton County. After Mary's death, Ernest seems to have drifted around Texas over a period of several years, moving to East Texas, where he continued to work as a painter. There, he met eighteen-year-old dressmaker, Sara Lorena (Sallie) Boyd and she became his second wife on October 2, 1870. From 1871 to 1880 the couple had five children: Edna, Ernest Jr., Julia, Boyd (Adolph), and Anna (Nannie). Tragically, Sallie died of consumption on May 20, 1880, several days after Nannie was born. Having fathered seven children, Ernest was now a widower for a second time. [526]

Five years after Gouhenant died, Ernest was back in Dallas, at least temporarily, to participate in Dallas's First Mardi Gras, held on February 24, 1876, which was reported to be a spectacular event attended by 20,000 people. Alfred Freeman photographed him with his son Ernest Jr., both dressed for the occasion and it is the only known photograph of Ernest.

Illustration 33. Photograph of Ernest Gouhenant with his son.

Copyright Paula Selzer.
This photo was taken by Alfred Freeman during the Dallas Mardi Gras in 1876.

By 1877, Ernest had moved again, this time settling in Palestine. He was still working as a painter, residing on Bluff Street, the first street east of the courthouse. By 1880, now in his late forties, he had moved to Cohen Street on the south side of the railroad tracks. A widower with spotty employment history, he had been out of work for six months that year. The children from his second marriage were all living with him, although he had some assistance from Sara's older sister, Julia Boyd Hubbard, who helped raise her nieces and nephews. [527] His children from his first marriage to Mary Withers had remained with their grandmother. By January of 1893, Ernest was sixty-one years old and he had been admitted to the Confederate Soldiers Home in Austin.

> Ernest Gounah, bugler of Ross' brigade, full of years and covered with glory, entered the confederate home at Austin last Sunday to fight over his battles with old comrades and await the inevitable says the Caldwell Chronicle.
>
> Ex-Gov. Ross says, in a letter to the writer, that the south had no braver or more faithful defender than this same Ernest Gounah. He enlisted in the beginning of the war, and was present in all the great battles fought by Texas troops. He messed with the staff of Gen. Ross at the headquarters and was acquainted with many of the great generals of our army. [528]

He was in the home only a few months and by the fall, had been dropped from their roster. Their records list his residence as Burleson, his religion as Catholic, his occupation as painter, and that he suffered from rheumatism. The date and location of Ernest's death is uncertain. One version of family lore claims he moved to New Orleans, sold wine, raised cattle, and made and lost a fortune several times. Another version claims that he died in Cloud Chief, Oklahoma, about 1900. His daughter Emma is thought to have died in Cloud Chief in 1898 and it is possible she brought her father to Oklahoma before he died. [529]

Adolphe Gouhenant had no other children in America, but his known descendants include seven generations of Americans who currently live in California, Colorado, Florida, Indiana, North Carolina, Oklahoma, Texas, and perhaps other states as well.

ANASTASIE (ANNA)

Gouhenant's daughter Anna remained in France for the rest of her life, and never saw her father again. In the mid-1850s, she and her husband, Charles Houry, were active in the artistic circles of Paris; it seems she too, had inherited her father's love of music. She was a talented pianist and singer, performing for friends, and in February of 1867, she was known to play during a society evening in Montmartre that was attended by several artists. [530]

She also wrote several compositions for piano and vocals that were published between the years of 1877 to 1883. In 1881 the journal *Beaumarchais* introduced one of her scores:

> We are glad to offer to the readers of the *Beaumarchais* the first publication of the melody composed by Madame Houry and sung by Madame Sallard of the Théâtre Lyrique, at the last artistic evening given by the painter and ceramist Charles Houry.

> We are confident this melody will have the same success with our readers as had with the privileged audience attending the workshop of the sympathetic artist, and who had the good fortune to applaud the composer and her performer at the same time. [531]

Like her father, Anna was also involved in politics and she supported the theories of Fourier and then Considerant. In the 1870s, she was a member of the *Société pour l'amélioration du sort de la femme et la revendication de ses droit*, an organization that advocated for women's equality. Along with several other women, Maria Deraisme, Anna Féresse-Deraisme, Hubertine Auclert and a few others, she sent a letter to Victor Hugo asking him to support the fight for women's emancipation. Hugo did respond in March of 1875, lending his verbal but vague support. [532]

In 1878, Anna attended the International Congress for the Rights of Women in Paris. In her speech, she passionately advocated for women's rights and for equal pay for equal work. Anna's speech was met with unanimous applause from the audience, who happened to include American notable, Julia Ward Howe, and surprisingly, Gouhenant's former colleague and sometimes nemesis Albert Brisbane! [533]

In the 1890s, the Hourys made a financial contribution for the creation of a statue to honor Charles Fourier and participated in the jury selection for the project in the studio of sculptor Émile Derré. [534] She attended the inauguration of the Fourier statue in 1899, and later supported the creation of Victor Considerant's statue, sculpted by Madame Gagneur.

In 1903, Anna published a text in the Fourierist journal *La Rénovation* calling for equal rights between men and women, and in particular, "truly universal suffrage, feminine as well as masculine." She further expressed her convictions in a pamphlet entitled, "A Mother of a Family," where she took exception to misogynistic remarks made by Alexandre Dumas. She passed away on November 12, 1906, and is buried with her husband and mother in Père Lachaise Cemetery in Paris.

JEANNE DURAND

Gouhenant's wife also remained in France. She seems to have been an educated woman and on October 26, 1852, she submitted a patent, "for a device able to prevent the fall of horses," This invention was described in the *Journal d'agriculture pratique*:

> In a communication recently given to the Society for the promotion of the national industry products, Madame Gouhenant proposed a very simple device that we must point out. It is made of rigid rods, in iron or wood, which are placed under the shafts, a little ahead of the back loops, near the girth .... We must congratulate Madame Gouhenant for her rare selflessness in the communication of her device: although she took a patent, she imposed to the workers who use it not to sell her rods for more than 20 to 25 francs. If

all the inventors followed this example, they would be doing a
big service... [535]

She was living in Paris with her daughter and her son-in-law when
she died on August 13, 1882, at the age of seventy-one.

ELIZABETH MARTIN GOUNAH AND JOHN EDWARD MARTIN

Elizabeth Martin was thirty-eight years younger than her husband.
They were likely married about ten years. After his accident, he left his
wife well off, with plenty of real estate in Tarrant and Denton Counties.

In the fall of 1874, she sold part of the original Gouhenant Peters
Colony grant that lay two miles south of Fort Worth to John B. Rector for
$1,100. (Ironically, John Peter Smith, the deputy surveyor who certified
the original field notes, notarized the deed twenty years later.) Less than
fifteen years after that, John Rector sold the land to James H. Raymond and
Company for $5,200. Today, the Berkeley Place neighborhood occupies
the former Gouhenant survey. [536]

In the spring of 1889, when Elizabeth was forty-seven, she must have
known the end was near. On May 18 she signed a will appointing her
older brother Newton as executor and leaving her property to her sister,
Harriett Martin. She passed away thirty-seven days later. Before she
died, she fulfilled Gouhenant's wishes regarding his estate and provided
a small inheritance to his granddaughter, Emily Hortense Baker. [537]

Elizabeth's younger brother was John Edward Martin, who had served
as the administrator of Gouhenant's estate and also played a key role in
preserving Gouhenant's history in Fort Worth. Martin had a great deal
of respect for his brother-in-law. He himself was a well-respected judge
and a local historian, described as being over six feet tall, slender, and
known to all as the "Judge." Elizabeth sold John part of the land she had
inherited near the fort for $600. Judge Martin moved his family to a home
just south of the cemetery. He practiced law, was in business with E.B.

Daggett (E.M. Daggett's son) at Daggett, Martin, and Company, and was also the editor of a weekly Fort Worth paper called *The Age of Progress.* He was also a "faithful contributor" to the *Bohemian.* [538]

After Elizabeth's death, he continued to advocate for issues that would have mattered to his sister and brother-in-law. A few weeks after her passing, Judge Martin seems to have been taking care of family business and filed an affidavit stating that "He was a brother-in-law of A. Gouhenant and that he pronounced his [name] Gannah. That the said Gouhenant was a Frenchman and that after he came to this country he spelled the name the way he pronounced it being Gannah." John Peter Smith signed a similar affidavit stating "he pronounced his name Gannah and that he is the A. Gouhenant to whom the Gouhenant survey in Tarrant County, Texas was patented." [539]

One of the legacies Gouhenant left to Fort Worth is his assumed donation of land to the city for Pioneers Rest Cemetery. An historical marker erected on the site in 1979 reads,

> This burial ground was started in the summer of 1850 upon the deaths of Sophie and Willis Arnold, children of Major Ripley A. Arnold (1817-1853), Commander of the troops at Ft. Worth. Arnold's friend, Dr. Adolphus Gouhenant, set aside a three-acre burial site at that time. In 1871, after a cemetery association was begun, Baldwin Samuels gave three adjoining acres. Many early Fort Worth settlers, including 75 Civil War veterans, are buried here. This site also contains the graves of Major Arnold and General Edward H. Tarrant (1799-1858), for whom Tarrant County was named.

The saga of the cemetery goes on. As stated, Gouhenant buried his family and friends on the land he originally claimed prior to a second survey that then put the graves on the Baugh Survey. He had written to his sister, "I laid him [Humbert] beside the grave of Major Arnold, on a high point of my property." [540]

At the time of the initial survey, Gouhenant and Middleton Tate Johnson both claimed the Mitchell Baugh Survey. Johnson had purchased the Baugh land and had it surveyed in 1854. The dispute resulted in Johnson getting the survey with the exception of twenty-five acres off the north end, which Johnson sold to Gouhenant as a compromise on April 15, 1856.

After Gouhenant's death, Elizabeth Martin donated the twenty-five acres to Fort Worth. Judge Martin assisted with the legal transaction. Then, in the fall of 1901, the U.S. Army was advocating to have Major Arnold's remains once again reinterred. Judge Martin responded by advocating not only for Major Arnold's final resting place, but defending his brother-in-law in the process.[541]

> To the Honorable Mayor and Gentlemen of the City Council:
>
> I have been informed that the War Department has ordered that the remains of Major Arnold be taken to San Antonio, where a monument will be erected to his honor and memory. As pioneer of this country and knowing the history and merits of Major Arnold, the founder of Fort Worth, in common with our citizens, I would not only regret but would feel mortified to see his remains removed from our city. My brother-in-law, Dr. Adolphus Gounah (who was the head of the Icarian colony), lived with Major Arnold at his quarters while the fort was kept here and furnished all the timber from his land to build the fort. Major Arnold then established Fort Graham and moved the army to that place and not a great while after the fort was moved to Graham, Major Arnold was shot and killed by an army surgeon and sometime thereafter Dr. Gounah had his remains moved to Fort Worth and buried on his land north of the town, which is now the old cemetery. Major Arnold was universally admired by all the old settlers of North Texas. He was continually vigilant in protecting their families and property against the Indians. He was a man of culture and military training and loved and admired by all, and I hope that some action will be taken by your honorable body to keep his remains here, and that a suitable monument will be built to the memory of the noble

man who protected those that first plowed the ground and cut the trees and burned the brush and paved the way for you to come.

Very respectively,

J.E. Martin[542]

Deputy Quartermaster General John L. Clem sent a letter, which was read at the town's meeting, that provided detailed instructions for disinterring the body. In his letter, Clem instructed Fort Worth leaders to "place the body in a 26x10x10 pine box with sufficient hay or straw to keep the bones from breaking, with name, rank, and regiment painted on top of the box with black paint and convey the box to the rail road station." Clem estimated that the cost to exhume the body, box and pack with straw, and transport to the nearest railroad station, should be about five dollars. Judge Martin's letter must have helped to persuade local leaders; Arnold's body remained in Fort Worth.[543]

In addition to removing Major Arnold's body, there was also an unsuccessful effort to move others from their permanent resting place. There was a move to abolish the cemetery. A letter from Judge Martin not only references the twenty-five acres and provides the provenance of the land in question, but also makes clear his brother-in-law's position on the cemetery.

> There is no question about the title. About half of the old cemetery is on the F.G. Mulligan [sic] survey and about half on the M. Baugh survey. The Mulligan survey was purchased by B.L. Samuels and the M. Baugh survey was owned by M.T. Johnson. Dr. Adolphus Gounah (Gouhenant, in French), purchased from M.T. Johnson twenty-five acres of the north end of the M. Baugh survey. My understanding is that Mr. Samuels donated to the city that portion of the cemetery on the Mulligan survey which is the north portion.

> Major Ripley Arnold, who located the federal post where Fort Worth is situated, and a particular friend of Dr. Gounah, was killed at Fort Graham, Texas. Mrs. Elizabeth Gounah was my sister. I had his will duly probated in this and other counties where the

estate was situated. He owned about three hundred and fifty acres of land in Fort Worth, 160 acres on the south side upon which is located the residences of Captain B.B. Paddock and the late J.C. Terrell, and 160 acres in the locality of the city waterworks, and 25 acres purchased from M.T. Johnson. The first two mentioned tracts were sold by Mrs. Gounah for a very low price, giving Fort Worth a chance to expand.

Dr. Gounah made no donation of that portion of his land covered by the old cemetery. He positively refused to do so. I think he would have done so if Fort Worth had built a monument to the memory of his friend Major Arnold, the founder of Fort Worth, whose grave till this day is only known by a large flat stone placed on the grave by Dr. Gounah.

Mrs. Gounah made a deed to Captain E.M. Daggett, an old particular friend of her husband, to all the Daggett grave lots on the land, and would not accept any consideration for the same. I am satisfied Captain Daggett recorded his deed. All I know about Mr. Samuels donating that portion of the graveyard on the Mulligan survey, is what he told me. He simply said, "I have given it to the people for a graveyard."

I purchased from Dr. Gounah one half of the twenty-five acres, which was ratified by his widow after his death. In August, 1877, I put the twenty-five acres into an addition to the city of Fort Worth, which is recorded and shows the number of feet of land in the old cemetery that belonged to Mrs. Elizabeth Gounah.

About 1878 the city council instructed the city attorney to investigate the title to the old cemetery, which he did, and reported that all of that portion on the M. Baugh survey belonged to Elizabeth Gounah. This action of the council was at the instance of John Q. St. Clair, who represented some people who had grave lots on the land. Mrs. Elizabeth Gounah departed this life some years ago, and the abstract of titles of the Fort Worth and Tarrant county abstract and land title office show no deed from her to that part of the old cemetery, and Major K.M. Van Zandt, who was connected with the old graveyard association, says she made no deed to that part of her land covered by the old cemetery.

It can clearly be seen that the title to all that portion of the M. Baugh survey covered by the old cemetery is in the heirs of Elizabeth Gounah, which are a sister residing in Denton county, myself, and the widow and children of a deceased brother, Reve. Newton Martin.[544]

Several years after he wrote the letter, Martin died on January 13, 1915, at his home in Fort Worth. An article appeared in the *Dallas Morning News*, "Interment will be in Pioneers' Rest, Fort Worth's first cemetery. The land for half of this cemetery was donated to the city by Mr. Martin and his sister, Mrs. Lizzie Gounah, now deceased."[545] His letters help put to rest the confusion about Gouhenant's role with the cemetery. It is also worth noting that a monument was finally erected to Major Arnold in June of 2014—more than one hundred and sixty years after his death and reinterment in Fort Worth. The statue sits on the bluff above the river within a few feet of the southern border of Gouhenant's survey.

Endnotes

Abbreviations Used in Notes:

AN: Archives Nationales de France (French National Archives)

BNF: Bibliothèque Nationale de France (French National Library)

AD Haute-Garonne: Archives Départementales de Haute-Garonne (Archives of the Haute-Garonne Department)

AD Haute-Saône: Archives Départementales de Haute-Saône (Archives of the Haute-Saône Department)

AD Rhône: Archives Départementales du Rhône (Archives of the Rhône Department)

AD Tarn-et-Garonne: Archives Départementales du Tarn-et-Garonne (Archives of the Tarn-et-Garonne Department)

AM Lyon: Archives Municipales de Lyon (Archives of the Town of Lyon)

1. Edmond F. Bates, *History and Reminiscences of Denton County,* 59, 72, 81-84.
2. Marie-Pierre Rey, *Un Tsar à Paris* (Paris: Flammarion, 2014), 62.
3. Francis Borrey, *La Franche-Comté en 1814* (Paris: Berger-Levrault, 1913), 252.
4. Ibid., 187.
5. AD Haute-Saône, Civil Registration Documents.
6. Jocelyne George, *Histoire des maires de 1789 à 1939* (Paris: Plon, 1989).
7. AD Haute-Saône, 2M 111.

8. Michel Fleury and Pierre Valmary, "Les progrès de l'instruction élémentaire de Louis XIV à Napoléon III, d'après l'étude de Louis Magiolo (1877-1879)," *Population*, no. 1 (1957): 71-92.

9. AD Haute-Saône, 235E Supp-1. Deliberation of the town council of Flagy.

10. AD Haute Saône, Successions.

11. A fragment of Gouhenant's letter to his mother was published by a descendant of Gouhenant's sister, Bernard Masson, in a self-published book: *Les Humbert-Caillier*. This book was kindly made available to Emmanuel Pécontal by Bernard Masson's son and granddaughter, Dominique Masson and Florence Ferraud-Masson. Unfortunately, the original letters quoted in this book have been lost.

12. AD Haute Saône, Military census table of 1824.

13. AD Rhône. 3E/11523.

14. Alexandre Dumas, *Nouvelles Impressions de Voyage – Midi de la France*, Vol. 1 (Bruxelles: Société Belge de Librairie, 1841), 46.

15. Fernand Rude, *Les révoltes des Canuts (1831-1834)* (Paris: la Découverte/Poche).

16. Joseph-Louis Crivelli, *Dictionnaire du droit civil, commercial, criminel et de procédure civile et criminelle* (Paris: A. Bavoux, 1825), 572.

17. Archives of the Lyon diocese.

18. AD Rhône, 1Q 323, 1Q 327. *Vente de biens nationaux—Bref de vente*. The name of Perreyve is not unknown to French Catholic scholars: he was the grandfather of Henry Perreyve, a figure of the social Catholic movement.

19. AD du Rhône, 6UP/1/1796. This reference contains all the information concerning the debts incurred by Gouhenant and the mortgages on his properties.

20. Henry Lyonnet, *Dictionnaire des comédiens français (ceux d'hier)*, *volume 2* (Bibliothèque de la Revue Universelle Internationale Illustrée, 1912), 67; Graziella Beting, "Au fil de la plume," doctoral thesis, University Panthéon-Assas, 2014, 54.

21. Chanut Jean-Marie, Heffer Jean, Mairesse Jacques and Postel-Vinay Gilles, "Les disparités de salaires en France au XIXe siècle," *Histoire & Mesure* 10, no. 3-4 (1995): 381-409

22. Louis Philippe was the previous Duke of Orleans until he became king in 1830. His son Ferdinand-Philippe was the incumbent.

23. Gouhenant refers to the aftermath of the Canuts' revolt.

24. AN F17-3160. This file contains Gouhenant's letter as well as the correspondence between the Duke of Orleans, the prefect of the Rhône department, and the Academy of Sciences, Art and Humanities of Lyon concerning the tower.

25. Archives de l'Académie des Sciences Belles Lettres et Arts de Lyon, Comptes rendus des séances de l'année 1832. This reference contains all the documents related to the interactions of Gouhenant with the academy as well as the reports on the tower and the deliberations of the academy on the project.

26. Unfortunately this drawing has not been kept.

27. Archives de l'Académie des Sciences Belles Lettres et Arts de Lyon, Report of the commission.

28. Archives de l'Académie des Sciences Belles Lettres et Arts de Lyon, Minutes of the sessions.

29. *Lyon vu de Fourvière* (Lyon: Chez L. Boitel, éditeur-imprimeur, 1833), 45-46.

30. Auguste Bonjour, "L'Observatoire de Fourvières" in *Nouvelles archives statistiques, historiques et littéraires du département du Rhône*. Vol. 1. Janvier 1832, 322-328.

31. *Morgenblatt für gebildete Leser*, November 17, 1838.

32. AM Lyon 480 WP 13, 480 WP 15.

33. Joseph Bard, 1839, "Notice sur Jean Pollet architecte" in *La revue du Lyonnais, série 1*, no. 10, 115-124. The Grand Théâtre is now known as the Opéra de Lyon and was heavily modernized in 1993 by one of the most renowned architects of the time, Jean Nouvel, who kept only the four monumental walls from the older structure.

34. The fireworks of July 29, 1832, are mentioned in the Lyon journal *Le Précurseur* of August 4. One of the entrance tickets to the tower has been kept in the Historical Museum of Lyon under the reference N.1217.1.

35. AD Rhône, 4Q/5/3787. This small building bore the sign "Café de l'Observatoire."

36. AD Rhône, 6UP/1/1796.

37. *Journal des annonces judiciaires du ressort du tribunal civil, affiches et avis divers de la ville de Lyon et du département du Rhône.* Saturday, February 2, 1833, p. 3.

38. AD Rhône, 4Q/5/3787.

39. Armand Pignel, *Conducteur ou guide du voyageur et du colon de Paris à Alger et dans l'Algérie*, (Paris: Imprimerie de E.J. Bailly et Cie, 1836) 35.

40. *La Gazette de Lyon*, December 9, 1852.

41. AD Rhône, *Vente par M. et Mme. Perreyve à la Commission de Fourvières*, 3E18729.

42. *Bibliographie de la France, XXIIe année* (Paris: Chez Pillet aîné, imprimeur-Libraire, 1833), 480.

43. Albert Shaw, *Icaria: A Chapter in the History of Communism* (Baltimore: Johns Hopkins University, June 1884), 5-7.

44. François Fourn, *Étienne Cabet ou le temps de l'Utopie* (Paris: Éditions Vendémiaire, 2014), 48-57.

45. Shaw, 10-19.

46. Shaw, 15-19.

47. *La Glaneuse, Journal populaire*, November 29, 1832.

48. *Grand Dictionnaire Universel Larousse, Tome 14* (Paris : Administration du grand dictionnaire universel, 1875), 283.

49. J.A. Faucher and A. Ricker, *Histoire de la franc-maçonnerie en France* (Paris: Éditions latines, 1967), 273.

50. *Le Précurseur*, September 7, 1829.

51. André Combes, *Histoire de la Franc-Maçonnerie à Lyon* (Brignais: Éditions des Traboules, 2006), 186.

52. Ibid., 191, 200.

53. A.G. Cesena and F.I. Gouhenant, *La Maçonnerie* (Lyon: Chez les principaux libraires, 1832).

54. As attested by the civil documents of this town.

55. This correspondence is kept in the archives of the history museum of Lyon.

56. *La Glaneuse*, October 11, 1832.

57. Marx and Engels, *Manifesto of the Communist Party: A Modern Edition* (London: Verso editions, 2012), 74-75.

58. His name appears in the directory of Swedenborgians in America published in the journals of the annual sessions of the General Conventions of the New Jerusalem in the United States of America up until 1876.

59. Cabet, *Procès du communisme à Toulouse* (Au bureau du Populaire, 1843), 44.

60. Cabet's papers, BNF NAF-18148, Letter to Gouhenant of April 29, 1843.

61. Karl-Erik Sjödén, "Swedenborg en France," *Acta Universitatis Stockholmiensis. Stockholm studies in history of literature* 27 (1985).

62. Ibid.

63. The French Swedenborgian church archives are now kept by Jean-François Mayer, a historian of the religions based in Fribourg, Switzerland.

64. Lucien De la Hodde, *Histoire des sociétés secrètes et du parti républicain de 1830 à 1848* (Bruxelles: Méline, Cans et Cie, libraires-éditeurs, 1850). De la Hodde's real name was Delahodde.

65. Gouhenant, like other artists, had his workshop in the circus of Toulouse, and was probably living there. The circus was a permanent building close to the center of the town. In the archives, Gouhenant's address is sometimes "Au cirque," or "Hôtel du Cirque." It is not known whether he worked for the circus or if

the owner of this establishment was renting rooms to the artists in town.

66. All this narrative is based on two reports of police informers found in the Archives Départementales de Haute Garonne in the file 1M 346.

67. Félix Ponteil, "Le Ministre des Finances Georges Humann et les émeutes antifiscales en 1841," *Revue Historique* 179 (1937): 311.

68. The spelling of Gouhenant's name is erroneous. The prefect says that he "recently arrived from Paris" but in fact, he had been living in Toulouse since at least May of 1840, evidenced by his signature on the birth certificate of Adolphe Mouynet's son, where his address is given as Rue Saint Aubin in Toulouse.

69. AD Haute Garonne 1M 346.

70. Dubedat, "Le procès des communistes à Toulouse," *Recueil de l'Académie de législation de Toulouse* 37 (1888-1889): 293.

71. *Journal de Toulouse*, August, 24 and 25, 1843.

72. Archives Départementales de Haute Garonne, U 1433.

73. Cabet, *Procès du communisme à Toulouse*, 75.

74. AD Haute Garonne 1M 346

75. The text of this speech, as well as the reactions of those attending the meetings, have survived through a report Gouhenant made to Laponneraye, a copy of which resides in the archives of the prefecture (AD Haute-Garonne 1M 346).

76. Charles Dupont, *Histoire d'un enfant du peuple* (Marseille: Imprimeries nouvelles Alfred Valz, 1886).

77. Gouhenant means the *compagnons*, workers organized in trades whose role will be discussed further.

78. AD Haute Garonne, 1M 346. Correspondence between the prefects of Haute-Garonne and Rhône dated November 1842.

79. In 1840, the revolutionary movement in Paris was weakened by the arrest of their main leaders, and Lyon had become the center of the political revolution. See Jean-Noël Tardy, *L'âge des ombres*.

Complots, conspirations et sociétés secrètes au XIXe siècle (Paris: Les Belles Lettres, 2015), 293-303.

80. AD Haute-Garonne, U 1433, First letter of the Lyon committee to Gouhenant.

81. De la Hodde. Delahodde's book should be read with some skepticism. Still, it contains some interesting information for any historian working on the political movements of that time.

82. De la Hodde, 252.

83. Ibid.

84. *Gazette des tribunaux*, September, 22, 1844.

85. De la Hodde, 139. Another source of Callès's participation in the riot of 1834 can be found in Albert Maurin, *Histoire de la chute des Bourbons*, vol. 5, 1851, 275, but Maurin had probably read Delahodde's book since his words are very similar.

86. AD Haute-Garonne, 1M 346.

87. "Torreno" was in fact Terradas, one of the leaders of the insurrection who would soon get in touch with the Toulouse revolutionaries.

88. *Le Censeur, journal de Lyon*, June 1, 1845.

89. Apart from the archive of the Toulouse prefect, there are few traces of Kersausie's stay in Catalonia but proof of his presence is cited in a report made during parliamentary debates in the French National Assembly in 1848, which shows that during the Catalan revolution of 1842, he actually had moved to Barcelona. See *Compte rendu des séances de l'Assemblée Nationale, tome cinquième* (Paris: Imprimerie de l'Assemblée nationale, 1850), 906.

90. Eugène Sue, *Une page de l'histoire de mes livres: Madame Solms dans l'exil* (Turin: Imprimerie de Joseph Favale et compagnie, 1857), 64.

91. Ian Birchall, "The Enigma of Kersausie: Engels in June 1848," *Revolutionary History* 8, no. 2, 25-50.

92. AD Toulouse, 1M 346.

93. Ibid., Report of the police informer dated January 5, 1843.

94. AD Haute-Garonne, U 1433, Second interview of Terradas.

95. AD Haute-Garonne, U 1433, Letter of Gouhenant to Terradas.

96. Thanks to the diary Stendhal kept during his travels in the south of France in 1838, it is possible to approximate the cost of the journeys. The coach from Agen to Toulouse cost him 11 francs, the hotel room, 1 franc per night, dinner 2.5 francs. Even if, being *compagnons*, Sagansan and Rolland were probably accommodated by their comrades, the trip alone cost them at least 20 francs to Agen which is 120 kilometers from Toulouse. This amount was about one month's salary for a worker. The trips to Pau (200 km) or Nimes (300 km) were even more expensive in proportion to the distance.

97. AD Haute-Garonne, 1M 346, Letter from the minister of interior to the prefect.

98. Ibid., Letter of Commissioner Boissonneau to the prefect.

99. This fact is quoted in a report of the police informer, but we also found the ad in the *Journal de Toulouse* on December 17 and 18.

100. AD Haute-Garonne, 1M 346, Reports of Commissioner Boissonneau, December 28 and 30, 1842.

101. Ibid., Report of Commissioner Boissonneau, January 11, 1843.

102. Ibid., Report of Commissioner Boissonneau, January 15, 1843; Report of the prefect's informer, January 14, 1843.

103. Karl Marx, *Neue Rheinische Zeitung Politisch-ökonomische Revue*, no. 4, 1850, in Marx and Engels, *Collected Works*, vol. 10 (London: Lawrence and Wishart, 1978), 311-325.

104. De la Hodde, 280.

105. Philippe Darriulat, "Albert Laponneraye journaliste et militant politique du premier XIXe siècle," PhD thesis, University of Paris 10, 1989.

106. Alain Maillard, "La génération communiste de 1840 et la mémoire de Gracchus Babeuf," *L'Homme et la société*, nos. 111-112 (1994): 89-100.

107. Louis-Gabriel Michaud, *Biographie universelle, ancienne et moderne,* vol. 23 (Paris: Chez Madame C. Desplaces, 1843), 241.

108. Eugène Fournière, "Le règne de Louis-Philippe" in *Histoire socialiste,* vol. 8 (Publications Jules Rouff et Cie), 372.

109. Joseph Benoit, *Confession d'un prolétaire* (Paris: Édition sociales, 1968), 59.

110. Jeanne Gilmore, *La République clandestine* (Paris: Aubier, 1997), 272.

111. Darriulat, 307; Fourn, 609.

112. Cabet, *Les masques arrachés* (Paris: Imprimeries Delanchy, 1844), 101.

113. AN, BB18 1395c, quoted in Johnson, *Utopian Communism in France, Cabet and the Icarians 1839-1851,* 131.

114. AD Haute Garonne, 1M 346, Report to the Minister of the Interior.

115. AD Haute Garonne, U 1433, Letters from Laponneraye to his sister and mother.

116. AD Haute-Garonne, 1M 346, Report of commissioner Aumont to the prefect, January 29 1843.

117. Proof of the timeline appears in a letter from the attorney general of Toulouse to the prefect of the department: "As for Gouhenant, mail left yesterday with the warrant issued by the investigating judge. Everything will then be normalized." AD Haute-Garonne. U 1433.

118. AD Haute-Garonne, U 1433, letter of the Lyon committee to Gouhenant, January 26, 1843.

119. AD Haute-Garonne, 1M 346, letter of the prefect of Rhône to the prefect of Haute-Garonne, February 3, 1843.

120. AD Haute-Garonne, 1M 346, letter from the prefect of Bouche du Rhône to the prefect of Haute-Garonne dated February 21, 1843.

121. See note 113.

122. AD Haute-Garonne, 1M 346.

123. AD Haute-Garonne, U 1433. Documents 10 and 11 from the inventory related to the court procedure.

124. AD Haute-Garonne U 1433, Fourth examination of Gouhenant, February 10, 1843.

125. AD Haute-Garonne, 1M 346, Report of commissionner Boissonneau, February 7, 1843.

126. AD Haute-Garone, 1M 346, Statement of commissionners Aumont and Boissonneau, February 23, 1843.

127. AD Haute-Garonne, U 1433, Third Examination of Dufaur and his confrontation with Piquemal and Gouhenant, March 1, 1843.

128. Even the most republican activists championed universal suffrage for males only. The advocates for true universal suffrage including women were a tiny minority.

129. This is the opinion of Henry Joly, a republican Member of Parliament and one of the defense lawyers at the trial, who, after the revolution of 1848, would become the government representative at the head of a vast region around Toulouse. Having learned in March 1848 that his commissioner in the department of Gers had appointed Dufaur deputy commissioner in Lombez, he strongly opposed this appointment by writing: "Today I learn that your deputy commissioner in Lombez is the citizen Dufaur, attorney, the same man who played such a sad role in the trial of the Communists in Toulouse. I have not forgotten that inspired by his uncles, one sub-prefect, the other investigating judge, he sheltered himself behind a system of treason against his political co-religionists in order to save himself." Letter from Joly to the commissioner of Gers. AD Haute-Garonne, 1M 366.

130. AD Haute-Garonne, U 1433, Statement of Henry Dufaur.

131. Ibid., Fourth Examination of Gouhenant.

132. French National Archives, 10 AS 28(9), Manuscript text of Considerant relating his meeting with Gouhenant.

133. AD Haute-Garonne 1M 346, Letter of Gouhenant to the investigating judge, February 11, 1843.

134. Ibid., Report of commissioner Boissonneau, February 25, 1843.

178. AD Lot-et-Garonne, 1K 2, Electoral Lists 1831-1857.

179. AD Lot-et-Garonne, 3U3-159.

180. Jyotsna Sreenivasan, *Utopias in American History* (Santa Barbara, CA: ABC-CLIO, Inc., 2008), xii-xiii.

181. John Ludlow, *The Autobiography of a Christian Socialist,* edited by A.D. Murray (London: Frank Cass and Company Limited, 2005), 136-137.

182. *The Movement and Anti-Persecution Gazette,* No. 29, p. 230.

183. John Ludlow, "Some of the Christian Socialists of 1848 and the Following Years," *The Economic Review* 4 (1894): 36-37.

184. The negotiations with Pellegrini were revealed by Cabet in *Défense et Acquittement de Cabet, accusé d'escroquerie au sujet de l'émigration Icarienne* (Paris: Au bureau du Républicain, Octobre 1851), 199.

185. Robert A. Calvert and Arnoldo De León, *The History of Texas,* 2nd ed. (Wheeling, IL: Harlan Davidson, 1996), 56. Also, Seymour V. Conners, *The Peters Colony of Texas* (Austin: The Texas State Historical Association, 1959), Chapter 1. The Peters contract was complicated throughout its four iterations; it was based on the Mexican Empresario system. The authors enthusiastically attempt to summarize it in a few sentences.

186. Johnson, 237-239; Harry E. Wade, "PETERS COLONY," *Handbook of Texas Online,* accessed May 07, 2019, http://www.tshaonline.org/handbook/online/articles/uep02. Uploaded on June 15, 2010. Modified on February 5, 2019. Published by the Texas State Historical Association.

187. Raymond Walters, *Stephen Foster, Youth's Golden Gleam: A Sketch of His Life and Background in Cincinnati 1846-1850* (London: H. Milford, Oxford University Press, 1936), 12-23, 69-77. Also, James T. Lloyd and Benjamin F. Klein, *Lloyd's Steamboat Directory and Disasters on the Western Waters* (Cincinnati: Young and Klein, 1979), 349, and *Stephen Foster Chronology from 1800.* http://www.pitt.edu/~amerimus/FosterChronology1800.html

188. Fourn, 177.

189. Denise Rocher, "Aux origines de l'associationnisme français. Images d'Étienne Cabet dans les Archives Parisiennes" in *Communautés, Archives Internationales de Sociologie de la Coopération et du Développement* 28 (1970), 25-55. The man proposed by Berrier-Fontaine to join Sully was Emile-Auguste Caillié, whose application letter is in Cabet's papers in Bibliothèque Nationale de France, NAF-18148.

190. Rocher, 47.

191. Shaw, 23-24. Primary Source: *Le Populaire,* January 16, 1848.

192. Johnson, 239-245.

193. *Défense du Citoyen Cabet, accusé d'escroquerie devant la Cour d'appel de Paris (11 décembre 1850)* (Paris: Bureau du Populaire, January 1851), 8. Note that this reference is different from the one cited in note 184, although the titles are almost the same. In both of them Cabet defends himself from any responsibility in the fiasco of Icaria in Texas. It is worth noting that the argument cited here appears only in the first edition of the book, and was removed in the second one.

194. *Défense et acquittement de Cabet, accusé d'escroquerie au sujet de l'émigration icarienne,* 200.

195. Cabet's papers, BNF NAF-18148, Printed prospectus entitled "Emigration to Texas— Peters' grant" signed by Richard Coad, European agent of the Texas Emigration and Land Company.

196. *Le Populaire,* no. 31, October 31, 1847.

197. *Défense et acquittement de Cabet, accusé d'escroquerie au sujet de l'émigration icarienne,* 199.

198. *The Galveston News,* April 27, 1848.

199. *Le Populaire,* Feb. 20, 1848.

200. Robert P. Sutton, *Les Icariens: The Utopian Dream in Europe and America* (Urbana: University of Illinois Press, 1994), 50.

201. Obituary of Robert P. Manson, "Sketch of the Veteran and Esteemed Shipmaster," *Bath Daily Times,* December 8, 1894.

202. Shaw, 24.

203. *Le Populaire*, January 30, 1848. This is an adaptation of a famous French revolutionary song.

204. *Le Populaire*, August, 13, 1848. The presence of the two Icarian men, Senez and Herqué, and their families, explains why in some reports there are 75 instead of 69 Icarians.

205. From the ship's manifest/passenger list dated March 27, 1848. Quarterly Abstracts of Passenger Lists of Vessels Arriving at New Orleans, Louisiana, 1820–1875. M272, 17 rolls. Records of the U.S. Customs Service, Record Group. Two men from the avant-garde— Rougier and Van den Eden— were not mentioned in the manifest although they were definitely on board, based on the letters and those of the other Icarians written to their families and published in *Le Populaire* in 1848. The spelling of the Icarians' names fluctuated from one source to another. The authors have kept the spelling from the manifest, except for the men whose names were quoted several times in *Le Populaire* with different spellings.

206. In the Icarians' letters, Waucherpfenig is always mentioned under his francized name Voquefen or Woquefen.

207. *Le Populaire*, August 20, 1848.

208. These journals were published in *Le Populaire*, May 11, 1848, August 13, 1848, and August 20, 1848.

209. Louisiana Division, New Orleans Public Library. "Yellow Fever Deaths in New Orleans, 1817-1905" Accessed May 23, 2018. http://nutrias.org/facts/feverdeaths.htm. Original source: George Augustin's *History of Yellow Fever* (New Orleans, 1909), a thick volume that chronicles the year-by-year yellow fever numbers for the Crescent City—and for the rest of the world as well.

210. Rebecca Burlend, Edward Quaife, and Milo Milton, eds., *A True Picture of Emigration* (Chicago: Lakeside Press, R.R. Donnelley & Sons, 1936), 33-34.

211. Cabet's papers, BNF NAF-18148, Report of Sully to Cabet.

212. Sutton, 56-57; Shaw, 29.

213. *The Daily Picayune*, March 28, 1848.

214. Gouhenant's journal, *Le Populaire*, Aug. 20, 1848.

215. Ibid.

216. *Réalisation d'Icarie, Nouvelles de Nauvoo* (Paris, July 14, 1849), 19.

217. Leclerc went back to France and ultimately died in China in February 1857 (as attested by the remarriage act of his widow in Paris, 1st arrondissement, November 29, 1860). His application letter was published in *Le Populaire*, December 5, 1847.

218. *Le Populaire*, July 1, 1849.

219. Gouhenant's journal.

220. Gouhenant's journal; "Arrivée de Sully à la Nouvelle-Orléans," *Le Populaire*, March 16, 1848; *Défense et acquittement de Cabet*, 196.

221. *Le Populaire*, Aug. 20, 1848.

222. William Becknell's details can be found in "The world of Hannah Chribbs Evans" Accessed May 23, 2018 https://chribbs.wordpress.com/

223. Sutton, 57.

224. Cabet's papers, BNF NAF-18148, Instructions about Sulphur Prairie.

225. *Clarksville Northern Standard*, April 22, 1848.

226. Cabet's papers, BNF NAF-18148, Report of Sully to Cabet; Texas General Land Office, accessed May 29, 2018. https://cgis.glo.texas.gov/cfGIS/glomapjs/basefile.cfm?SDENUM=483871435. The geographic coordinates of Sulphur Prairie are 33°22'27" N and 95°13'32" W.

227. Letter from Sully to Cabet dated February 19, 1848, *Le Populaire*, April 23, 1848.

228. Fourn, 206-237.

229. Ibid.

230. W. B. Parker, *Through Unexplored Texas* (Austin: Texas State Historical Association, 1990), 84-85. Originally published as *Notes Taken during the Expedition Commanded by Capt. R.B. Marcy, U.S.A. Through Unexplored Texas in the Summer and Fall of 1854.*

231. Jane Dupree Begos, "Document: Henri Levi's 'The perilous Voyage to Icaria,'" *Communal Societies* 3 (1983): 147-157. Levi's account was originally published in *Le Populaire*.

232. Census of Shreveport of 1850; Elliott Ashkenazi, *The Business of Jews in Louisiana, 1840-1875* (Tuscaloosa: University of Alabama Press, 1988), 110-112; "Collective Letter from the Icarians Remaining in Sulphur Prairie," dated May 13, 1848, *Le Populaire*, July 11, 1848.

233. *Clarksville Northern Standard*, April 22, 1848, page 2. Then on May 18 another article appeared in the *Democratic Telegraph and Texas Register* that cites the *Northern Standard* as the source of information on the 50-60 colonists who stayed in Titus County.

234. Ibid.

235. Cabet's Papers, BNF NAF-18148, Letter dated 1848, August 9 to Caudron, the leader of a commission sent to bring money and to inform the Icarians about the situation in France.

236. *Democratic Telegraph and Texas Register* (Houston, TX), May 4, 1848. The article quotes the *Caddo Gazette* from March 15 (not available). The article states, "A writer in the *Caddo Gazette* of the 15th March speaking of the arrival of a company of these emigrants at that port says..." The date is incorrect in the article since the avant-garde did not arrive in New Orleans until March 27, 1848.

237. Collective letter from the Icarians to Cabet, *Le Populaire*, July 11, 1848.

238. Letter from Grillas to his wife, *Le Populaire*, July 11, 1848.

239. Letter from Marchand to his brother, *Le Populaire*, Aug. 20, 1848.

240. Letter of Therme to the Icarians of Vienne, *Le Populaire*, Aug. 20, 1848.

241. *Défense et acquittement de Cabet*, 173.

242. One dollar in 1848 would be the equivalent of about $30 in today's currency according to http://www.davemanuel.com/inflation-calculator.php, the inflation calculator website. The website was accessed June 3, 2018.

243. Cabet's papers, BNF NAF-18148, Explication de Gouhenant.

244. Ibid., Notes by Sully.

245. *Le Populaire*, July 11, 1848.

246. *The Northern Standard* (Clarksville, TX) June 10, 1848. The article did not appear in publication until most of the Icarians had arrived in Denton County.

247. Dupree Begos, 147-157.

248. Cabet's papers BNF NAF-18151, Correspondence between Jeanne Gouhenant and Cabet.

249. Cabet says in *Le Populaire* of December 17, 1848, that "Gouhenant, at the time of the Toulouse trial in 1843, offered to sell himself to the Prefect for 200,000 francs." However, as pointed out by Fourn in *Étienne Cabet ou le temps de l'utopie*: "the accusation is absurd. If Gouhenant asked for so much money from the Prefect of Haute-Garonne, the amount requested can only be seen as insolence or an act of rebellion."

250. Gouhenant's claim that a half section is equal to one square mile is erroneous; it is in fact half a square mile. The Icarians had then secured 16 square miles, more than 10,000 acres.

251. *Le Populaire*, October 1, 1848.

252. *Le Populaire*, August 20, 1848.

253. Letter from Therme to his father dated August 15, 1848, *Le Populaire*, December 17, 1848.

254. *Le Populaire*, December 3, 1848.

255. *Le Populaire*, December 17, 1848.

256. *Le Populaire*, December 17, 1848; August 27, 1848.

257. *Le Populaire*, December 17, 1848.

258. Ibid.

259. *Le Populaire*, August 27, 1848.

260. *Le Populaire*, September 10, 1848.

261. *Le Populaire*, December 3, 1848.

262. Cabet's papers BNF NAF-18148, Letter from Cabet to Favard dated May 30, 1848.

263. For the claim that the second avant-garde was sent to control Gouhenant, see *Procès et acquittement du citoyen Cabet*, 68.

264. *Le Populaire*, December 17, 1848.

265. Cabet's papers BNF NAF-18148, Confidential instructions concerning Gouhenant.

266. *Procès et acquittement du citoyen Cabet*, 69.

267. *Défense et Acquittement de Cabet*, 185.

268. *Dallas Morning News*, January 25, 1891. The authors could not locate any record of Gouhenant being a bookkeeper for the colony. However, his son later had some interaction with the La Réunion colonists.

269. Edmond F. Bates, *History and Reminiscences of Denton County* (Denton, TX: McNitzky Printing Company, 1918), 81-84. Bates quotes an article written by Alex W. Robertson and published in the *Denton Record-Chronicle* on May 12, 1894.

270. Manuscript text of Considerant relating his meeting with Gouhenant. Op. cit.

271. Shaw, 43-44.

272. Gluntz's letter published in *Le Populaire*, July 1, 1849; Ludlow, *The Autobiography of a Christian Socialist*.

273. *The Northern Standard* (Clarksville, Tex.), Saturday, January 20, 1849, as "Extracted from the Caddo Gazette relative to the French Colony in the Cross Timbers." In fact the first time this letter was published was in a New-Orleans journal in French, *Le Courrier de la Louisiane* of 1848, November 23.

274. *The Bohemian*, 1900, page 20, states Gouhenant "made his home at the residence of Samuel Pritchett, a colonist and Ranger." Considerant mentioned the fact that Gouhenant stayed at the Pritchetts' farm in his letter of 1855.

275. The 1850 census lists all the Pritchett siblings living together with Samuel on the farm. According to Texas General Land Office

records, Edley Pritchett and Samuel Pritchett both had land grants. Edley's land was patented in 1855 and 1860. Samuel's land was patented in 1855 and 1871. Samuel's land was surveyed in an "L" shape at the current junction of I-35W and 2449. Edley's land was in two sections, one north of where Loop 288 runs through Denton County. The other section is south of Justin sitting due west of Argyle and just north of road 1830. Samuel's and Edley's land were both only a few miles from the junction of Denton and Oliver Creeks. It is presumed that Gouhenant went to Samuel's farm. See also: Texas Ranger Hall of Fame muster rolls, and *The History of Dallas County, Texas from 1837 to 1887* by John Henry Brown, page 50. Also Ancestry.com was consulted for genealogy of the Pritchett family.

276. Manuscript text of Considerant relating his meeting with Gouhenant. Op. cit.

277. Kathryn Julia Garrett, *Fort Worth: A Frontier Triumph* (Fort Worth: Texas Christian University Press, 1996). Originally, Encino Press, 1972, 63-64. Garrett had earned her PhD and taught in Fort Worth for years. She wrote *Fort Worth: A Frontier Triumph*, the result of a lifetime of research. According to the Texas State Historical Association, the book was written "in a graceful prose style that helps make the book a definitive work on the subject." In doing so, she intentionally chose not to use footnotes in her book, making it difficult to track down the original sources—although her bibliography is extensive.

278. "The Old French Colony," *Dallas Morning News*, January 25, 1891. The article mentions some of the original settlers from the La Réunion French colony, who were still living in Dallas at the time of publication. It should be noted that most of the information about Gouhenant in the article is wrong, including the spelling of his name. He was never a bookkeeper for the La Réunion settlement, did not deliberately lead the Icarians into the wilderness, "so [they] might perish," and he was never in the employ of the French government.

279. Richard Selcer with drawings by William B. Potter, *The Fort that Became a City: An Illustrated Reconstruction of Fort Worth, Texas,*

1849-1853 (Fort Worth: Texas Christian University Press, 1995), 93. See also Samuel Henry Starr Papers, 1848-1930, Sam H. Starr to Mrs. Starr January 18, 1850. Starr Papers, Dolph Briscoe Center for American History, University of Texas, UT Austin. Starr writes on that date that he had been living in a tent since his arrival nearly three weeks previously.

280. *Texas in 1840 or the Emigrant's Guide to the new Republic* (New York: William W. Allen, 1840), 35.

281. Frederick Law Olmsted, *A Journey Through Texas or a Saddle-Trip on the Southwestern Frontier* (Lincoln: University of Nebraska Press, 2004). Originally published, New York: Dix, Edwards, 1857, 36.

282. Garrett, 109. The first federal census taken in Tarrant County in 1850 documented less than 700 white men and their families and only 82 dwellings in the entire county.

283. Samuel Henry Starr Papers, 1848-1930. Letters dated January 6, 18, and 25, 1850. Starr may have been a bit off on the ages of the Arnold children. The census taken in November of that year shows the children's ages as Florida, age 10, Katherine, age 7, and Sophia age 1. (It is also possible there are errors in the census.) The same census shows Starr's daughter, also named Kate, to be 7 years old.

284. Garrett, 79. The original source for this statement is unknown. Richard Selcer states that the men in Fort Worth did not carry sabers, but it is possible that some officers possessed swords that could have been used in demonstrations.

285. There were about 94 soldiers and four officers at Fort Worth according to the 1850 census. In addition, Middleton Tate Johnson, Archibald Robinson, Major Arnold's and Lt. Starr's families were at the fort.

286. Eliza Starr to Catherine Arnold, November 27, 1852, Samuel Henry Starr Papers, Box 3P46.

287. Gouhenant's original 160-acre section lies neatly along the boundaries of Forest Park Boulevard on the west, just slightly above Windsor Place on the north, along 8th Avenue to the east, and roughly below Park Hill Way on the south.

288. From Tarrant County Archive File Deed Records. A notation on the document states, "Recorded in Book A page 676 Surveyors office Tarrant County, Texas. On April 15, 1850, he obtained a certificate." See also article on John Peter Smith at https://tshaonline.org/handbook/online/articles/fsm29. Accessed May 24, 2018. Keen's father, A.M. Keen, was also surveyor for Dallas County and was believed to have been part of the original Peters Colony surveyors. He donated land where the First United Methodist Church now stands. The Keens are scattered throughout North Texas.

289. *Dallas Morning News*, Sunday July 28, 1889, 11.

290. Texas General Land Office Archival Records, land grant files for Mitchell Baugh, Felix Mulliken, Adolphe Gouhenant, and Archibald Robinson. Found online at http://www.glo.texas.gov/. See additional details about Pioneers Rest Cemetery in the Epilogue.

291. A.C. Greene, *Dallas: The Deciding Years* (Austin: Encino Press, 1973), 11.

292. *Colonel John C. McCoy: The Lone Star State Magazine* 1, no. 7 (June 1887). Edited by Mrs. Lou S. Bedfore, Dallas, Texas. (From Dallas County Historical Society, McCoy Papers, Folder A84.42). Also, Cecil Harper, Jr., "MCCOY, JOHN CALVIN" *Handbook of Texas Online.* http://www.tshaonline.org/handbook/online/articles/fmc29, accessed May 30, 2015. Uploaded on June 15, 2010. Modified on November 26, 2014. Published by the Texas State Historical Association.

293. John Henry Brown, *History of Dallas County, Texas: From 1837 to 1887* (Dallas: The Aldredge Book Store, 1966), 25; Joan Jenkins Perez, "Burford, Nathaniel Macon," *Handbook of Texas Online*, accessed June 05, 2018, http://www.tshaonline.org/handbook/online/articles/fbu27. Uploaded on June 12, 2010. Published by the Texas State Historical Association.

294. John Alan Hord, "CROCKETT, JOHN MCCLANNAHAN," *Handbook of Texas Online* (http://www.tshaonline.org/handbook/online/articles/fcr25), accessed May 30, 2015. Uploaded on June 12, 2010. Published by the Texas State Historical Association.

295. Bruce Roche, "LATIMER, JAMES WELLINGTON" *Handbook of Texas Online*, http://www.tshaonline.org/handbook/online/articles/fla47, accessed May 30, 2015. Uploaded on June 15, 2010. Published by the Texas State Historical Association.

296. Register of the Tannehill Lodge, A.F. and A.M. 1849-1882 (Dallas, TX: Dorsey Printing Co.,1960), 247-249. In Masonic records, he is listed as "Adolf Gouhenant Mechanic, born in France, residence, Dallas." He joined in August 1850 and withdrew August 25, 1860. This record is included in the second volume of Early Dallas Records compiled by James Campbell Chapter of the Daughters of the American Revolution. The transcripts of three documents make up this volume. In addition to the Records of the Tannehill Lodge No. 52, Isaac Webb's Diary 1802-1857, and the Records of the First Presbyterian Church, 1861-1876 were also reviewed. The authors also referenced a pdf file entitled, "History of Tannehill Lodge" posted on the lodge website at https://www.masonsofdallas.org. The file has since been removed, but permission to use the source was granted by The Grand Lodge of Texas, Ancient Free and Accepted Masons, January 2018. Also consulted; The Mackey Encyclopedia which provides the definition of the "Tyler." Gouhenant was a Master Mason as listed in the *Proceedings of the Grand Lodge of Texas from its organization in the city of Houston, Dec. A.D. 1837, A.L. 5837, to the close of the grand annual communication held at Palestine, January 19, A.D. 1857*, Vol 2, page 238 (texashistory.unt.edu/ark:/67531/metapth29777/: Accessed September 15, 2017), University of North Texas Libraries, The Portal to Texas History, texashistory.unt.edu; crediting Star of the Republic Museum. His name appears "A Gouchenant."

297. Gouhenant's Masonic path in Paris and Marseille is briefly summarized in the Bossu file of French Freemasonry at the French National Library (FM fichier Bossu (316)).

298. *History of the Tannehill Lodge*, 4-6, see note 296.

299. *The WPA Dallas Guide and History*, 48.

300. Ibid.

301. Robert T. Gill, "Cross-file of Grantors and Grantees of Town Property in the First Ten Years of the Town of Dallas, 1846-1856," *The Quarterly: A Bulletin of the Local History and Genealogical Society* 12, no. 1 (1966): 1-35.

302. Margaret Denton Smith and Mary Louise Tucker, *Photography in New Orleans* (Baton Rouge: Louisiana State University Press, 1982), 61-65.

303. Walters, 12-23.

304. *The Photographic and Fine Art Journal*, vol. 7, p. 339; vol. 8, pp. 32, 52, 344; vol. 10, p. 169. The origin of the word "saloon" is from the Italian, *salone*, or *sala* large hall. In French it was *salon*. http:// www.dictionary.com/browse/saloon (accessed: April 4, 2018).

305. Smith and Tucker, 50 (Original source is the *New Orleans Pictorial Advisor*, 1849); Advertisement in *Dallas Times Herald*, February 16, 1856, page 2.

306. Samuel Morse, Letter to the editor, *New York Observer*, April 20, 1839.

307. Beaumont Newhall, *The History of Photography, from 1839 to the Present Day* (New York: The Museum of Modern Art, 1964), 13-15. The camera obscura (Latin: *dark chamber*) is an optical device that had been used for centuries by artists and scientists to perform experiments in light and physics and is considered the most basic form of photography.

308. Beaumont Newhall, *The Daguerreotype in America* 3rd ed. (New York: Dover, 1961, 1976), 15-34; David McCullough, *The Greater Journey: Americans in Paris* (New York: Simon and Schuster, 2011), 148-159.

309. Lewis Coe, *The Telegraph: A History of Morse's Invention and Its Predecessors in the United States* (Jefferson, NC: McFarland and Company, 1911), 32.

310. Peter E. Palmquist and Thomas R. Kailbourn, *Pioneer Photographers from the Mississippi to the Continental Divide. A Biographical Dictionary, 1839-1865* (Stanford: Stanford University Press, 2005), 601-602. For the contacts between Vassallo and Gouhenant, see

Dallas County Court Records, No 389: Gouhenant v. Cockrell; No 96: Brisbane v. Gouhenant.

311. *Northern Standard*, Saturday, July 21, 1849.

312. Greene, 53. Original image is lost. The reproduction is from *Our City—Dallas* by Justin Kimbell, Dallas Public Library Historical Archives. The first brick courthouse was built in 1857 and was torn down in 1871. Depending upon the orientation of this courthouse, the photograph may have been taken from across Houston street. However, no one knows for certain. See also, Darwin Payne, *Dynamic Dallas: An Illustrated History* (Carlsbad, CA: Heritage Media Corp., 2002), 22.

313. The image of the Arnolds is from the Tarrant County Archives. (Ownership was in transition during publication of this book.) Their collection contains more than two dozen daguerreotypes of Fort Worth, Major Arnold, and Arnold's extended family. It is presumed that Gouhenant photographed the Arnolds, but there is no solid evidence the portrait is of the Arnolds. However, one of these daguerreotypes was used to design the statue of Major Arnold that was erected in 2014 in Fort Worth.

314. Gary W. Clark, *Cased Images and Tintypes Kwik Guide: A Guide to Identifying and Dating Daguerreotypes, Ambrotypes, and Tintypes.* Phototree.com. 2013, 13-16; Interview with Shirley and Marvin Applewhite, September 16, 2014, Dallas, Texas, and Dawn Youngblood at Tarrant County Archives, Fort Worth, on January 31, 2019; correspondence with Richard Selcer, January 30, 2019.

315. *The WPA Dallas Guide and History*, 49.

316. *Dallas Morning News*, July 28, 1889.

317. J.O. Crutchfield was mistaken about one thing in his recollections. In the full article, he goes on to state that Gouhenant, "had come over with Victor Considerant, Mr. Cantagrel, and their associates." In fact, those men came to Texas as La Réunion colonists about three years after Gouhenant was well established in Dallas.

318. *First Half Dozen Years: Dallas County Texas as Seen Through the Commissioner's Court Minutes*, Compiled and Published by Helen M. Lu and Gwen B. Neumann (1982), 71. Green, 11; *The WPA Dallas*

Guide and History, page 48 cites the date of rental as 1850, but is incorrect since the minutes from the Commissioner's Court list the date as 1852. The *WPA Guide* also states that this was the first courthouse in Dallas while other sources would make this the second courthouse in Dallas. The third courthouse is the two-story structure that Gouhenant photographed.

319. Joyce Martin Murray, "Martin, Bennett H.," *Handbook of Texas Online,* accessed July 9, 2017, http://www.tshaonline.org/handbook/online/articles/fmaec Uploaded on June 15, 2010. Published by the Texas State Historical Association. Clarksville *Northern Standard,* July 10, 1852. The judge mentioned by DeMorse is Bennet H. Martin. J. According to the Portal to Texas History Online, Pinckney Henderson, the first governor of Texas after annexation, appointed Martin judge of the Ninth Judicial District of Texas (Grayson, Collin, Denton, Dallas, Kaufman, Henderson, Anderson, Houston, and Van Zandt Counties). "He traveled by horseback over great distances and held court sessions under trees, in small log courthouses, and in private homes. Many stories tell of his compassion, practical approaches to justice, and his sense of humor. He died of typhoid fever at his home near Palestine, on September 7, 1852." His death occurred just 5 months after his visit to the Arts Saloon. See also: Historical List of Elected Officials: Dallas County 1846-Present, Partial Listing. Revised January, 2013, Prepared by the District Clerk's Office, Gary Fitzsimmons, District Clerk, Dallas, Texas. http://docplayer.net/6109417-Historical-list-of-elected-officials-dallas-county-1846-present-partial-listing-revised-january-2013-prepared-by-the-district-clerk-s-office.html

320. The article appeared in *The Northern Standard* (Clarksville, Texas), July 10, 1852, under "Editorial Correspondence" and is dated Dallas, April 5, 1852.

321. *The Northern Standard* (Clarksville, Texas), July 17, 1852.

322. Tannehill Lodge History, minutes of a Masonic ceremony for the Saint John of 1852, page 66.

323. "Editorial Correspondence, Dickson's Near Gainesville, Cooke County, April 9th, 1852," *The Northern Standard* (Clarksville, Texas), Saturday, July 24, 1852.

324. Selcer, 141-142; Julia Kathryn Garrett, 128.

325. C.C. Cummings in *The Bohemian*, Easter 1900, 21.

326. Charles David Grear, *Why Texans Fought in the Civil War* (College Station: Texas A&M University Press, 2010), 191-197. Original source is from *The Vedette* (Washington) as told by eyewitness Dr. D. Wooster in "Santa Anna... A Reminiscence of the Mexican War," 1896.

327. Victor Considerant, *Au Texas* (Paris: à la librairie Phalanstérienne, 1854), 59.

328. W. Clytes Anderson Cullar and Lawrence Elie Guillot, *French Carriages on the Trinity: The Guillot Family of Dallas* (Wolfe City, TX: Henington Publishing Company, 1986), 1-10; *WPA Dallas Guide and History*, 176. Guillot had arrived in New Orleans in February of 1850, but he stayed for only three months before heading out to Shreveport with three other men in search of work. As he made his way across North Texas, he met up with Elie Drouard, one of the Icarian *avant garde*. The Guillot family history also states that Gouhenant attended the first Catholic mass held in Guillot's home in the summer of 1859, but no records have been found to confirm this. In a second religious reference, the *WPA Guide to Dallas* also states that in 1853, Presbyterianism was introduced to Dallas and services were held in a Saloon owned by a Frenchman. The latter seems more probable.

329. *The Northern Standard* (Clarksville, Texas), May 21, 1853.

330. *Dallas Herald,* September 27, 1856, and August 14, 1858; Greene, 11.

331. Considerant, 42.

332. Additional details about Anastasie's life are addressed in the Epilogue.

333. Oath of Citizenship, Dallas Public Library, County Court Records, Civil Minutes Volume A page 343, May 16, 1853.

334. Ibid.; Gouhenant signed his oath "Adolphe F.I. Gouhenant." According to Cullar and Guillot, Maxime Guillot filed his papers on May 14, 1853 (page 4 of Cullar and Guillot references Civil Court Minutes Vol. A, page 339). Gouhenant's "intent" was filed prior to taking the oath.

335. U.S. Citizen and Immigration Services, Department of Homeland Security. Accessed May 25, 2018. http://www.uscis.gov/history-and-genealogy/our-history/historians-mailbox/whos-1. According to the Department of Homeland Security, "the federal government did not begin overseeing naturalizations until September 27, 1906. Prior to that date the nation's courts had sole control over naturalization. In practice this meant that between March 26, 1790, when congress passed the first Naturalization Act and September 26, 1906, when the federal government began collecting and filing naturalization records, thousands of individual local, state, and federal courts independently performed naturalizations. Each court had its own practices and each kept separate sets of records of varied quality and detail."

336. Viktor Bracht, translated by Charles Frank Schmidt, *Texas in 1848* (San Antonio: Naylor Printing Company, 1931), 141-142.

337. Ibid., 104.

338. Pierre Mercklé, "Le Phalanstère," charlesfourier.fr, rubrique "Découvrir Fourier," March 2006, online, accessed June 14, 2017: http://www.charlesfourier.fr/spip.php?article328

339. Redelia Brisbane, *Albert Brisbane: A Mental Biography with a Character Study* (1893; repr., New York: Burt Franklin, 1969), 51.

340. Ibid., 190.

341. *Le Populaire*, 1849, April 15.

342. Jonathan Beecher, *Victor Considerant and the Rise and Fall of French Romantic Socialism* (Berkeley: University of California Press, 2001), 290-291; Redelia Brisbane, 296-299.

343. Beecher, 295-315.

344. Based on this statement, it can be surmised that Gouhenant would have been with them from August/September 1848 to near the end of 1849.

345. Manuscript text of Considerant relating his meeting with Gouhenant.

346. Ibid.; Beecher, 309.

347. The item Gouhenant mentions is from *The Northern Standard* (Clarksville, Texas), May 21, 1853. The small article states, "A Socialist Colony—Albert Brisbane and Victor Considerant, two of the most eminent living Socialists, of the Fourier school, were in Cincinnati on the 5th last. Both of these gentlemen are able popular advocates of the Phalansterian system of the great French associationists above named. They are on the way to Northern Texas and the Red River country, for the purpose of selecting from twelve to fifteen thousand acres of good land, with a view to the importation of a colony of French and American Socialists—Picayune."

348. Beecher, 309.

349. Manuscript text of Considerant relating his meeting with Gouhenant.

350. There were in fact 69 men. For the discrepancy, see endnote 204 above.

351. Beecher, 506. In footnote 41 Beecher cites Considerant's manuscript relating his meeting with Gouhenant.

352. Considerant, 190.

353. Beecher, 295-315.

354. Selcer, 147.

355. Clay Perkins, *The Fort in Fort Worth* (Keller, TX: Cross-Timbers Heritage Publishing Company, 2001), 157. (Original source cited as: "Testimony of William Slade, 10 September 1853. Recorded by C. Brooks, Justice of the Peace, Hill, County, Texas. NA Microfilm in Confederate Research Center, Hill College.")

356. Selcer, 147. See Selcer's endnote on page 184 which cites original source as the "recollections of Mrs. W.H. Thompson, Maj.

Arnold's granddaughter" and "[Interview with Ruby] Schmidt to Selcer"; Thomas W. Cutrer, "ARNOLD, RIPLEY ALLEN," *Handbook of Texas Online,* http://www.tshaonline.org/handbook/online/articles/far16, accessed March 9, 2013. Published by the Texas State Historical Association; Gouhenant wrote a letter to his sister, Marguerite, in 1856 referencing another burial, "on [his] land next to Major Arnold." The source of the letter is discussed in detail in Chapter 15.

357. *Texas State Gazette,* June 30, 1855.

358. Masson, *Les Humbert-Caillier,* 45.

359. Dallas Historical Society. Accessed May 25, 2018. https://web.archive.org/web/20060422183559/http://www.dallashistory.org/ history/dallas/dallas_history.htm; *Handbook of Texas Online,* Curtis Bishop and L. R. Wilcox, "TELEGRAPH SERVICE," accessed February 03, 2019, http://www.tshaonline.org/handbook/online/articles/egt01.

360. Cullar and Guillot, 2.

361. Masson, *Les Humbert-Caillier,* 41; Gouhenant's letters, as well as his nephew's, which are quoted in this chapter, were published in *Les Humbert-Caillier* and in another self-published book by the same author *L'aventure américaine d'Ernest Humbert.*

362. The pipe manufacturing company closed, but the addresses in Besançon are the same. See http://tobaccopipeartistory.blogspot.com/2015/12/saillard-aine-catalog-1843.html Accessed May 25, 2018.

363. Humbert writes, "At last I am in Dallas. I arrived there with my cousin the 29th of December." Gouhenant's story remains consistent whether he is telling the Icarian brothers, Considerant, or his nephew about his affiliation with the Icarians and the accusations from his countrymen.

364. Gouhenant was known at times as "Poupon" among his family, and that nickname is also listed in his military file from the Archives Départementales de Haute-Saône. In French, the name means "little baby" or "baby doll."

365. Gill.

366. Lot 2, Block 7 was two lots over from the Arts Saloon, which sat at Lot 4, Block 7.

367. Dallas County Court Records, Dallas Public Library. Deed from Adolphe Gouhenant to Daniel Cornwell for Lot 2, Block 68 dated March 19, 1855. No amount of money is mentioned in this deed.

368. Gill. On June 14, 1853, Gouhenant sold Lot 4 in Block 7 to John McCoy for $1.00. From Dallas County Court documents.

369. Masson, *L'Aventure Américaine d'Ernest Humbert*; see also Selcer, 93. Selcer's notes reference an interview with Fort Worth historian Ruby Schmidt. Schmidt also states that Gouhenant built the Frenchman's well, a well-known Fort Worth landmark for decades, and she also claims that he was appointed a geological surveyor for the state.

370. Dallas County Court Records. Dallas Public Library. *Brisbane v. Gouhenant,* Case #96.

371. Considerant, 41.

372. V.E. Gibbens, "Lawrie's Trip to Northeast Texas, 1854-1855," *Southwestern Historical Quarterly* 48 (October 1944): 238-253. Their trip began October 27, 1854. Lawrie's biographic information compiled from Ancestry.com.

373. Craig H. Miner, *The St. Louis-San Francisco Transcontinental Railroad: The Thirty-Fifth Parallel Project 1853-1890* (Lawrence: University Press of Kansas, 1972), 1.

374. Evelyn Foster Morneweck, *Chronicles of Stephen Foster's Family,* vol. 2 (Pittsburgh, PA: University of Pittsburgh Press, 1944), 469-471.

375. Michel Cordillot, *La Sociale en Amérique. Dictionnaire biographique du movement social francophone aux États-Unis 1844-1922* (Paris: Les éditions de l'Atelier, 2002), 65; Auguste Savardan, *Un naufrage au Texas* (Paris: Garnier frères, libraires-éditeurs, 1858) 25; Gibbens, 248.

376. Savardan, *Un naufrage au Texas*, 30-31.

377. Texas General Land Office records of land grants, surveys, and patents of Adolphe Gouhenant. Abstract 582 surveyed in April 1855 by A.M. Keen.

378. Beecher, 328.

379. Gibbens, 238-253. Lawrie kept diaries about his trip to Texas from December 4, 1854, to January 20, 1855. In the spring of 1855 Cantagrel purchased land for La Réunion.

380. William L. McDonald, *Dallas Rediscovered: A Photographic Chronicle of Urban Expansion 1870-1925* (Dallas: The Dallas Historical Society, 1978).

381. Savardan, 97.

382. Dallas County Court Records, Dallas Public Library, *Gouhenant v. Cockrell.*

383. "Present on May 16, 1855," Réunion, Texas, manuscript table, Fonds Considerant, ENS, Ref. 2/13/2.

384. Beecher, 345.

385. Texas, Supreme Court, Reports of cases argued and decided in the Supreme Court of the State of Texas, during Austin session, 1857, and part of Galveston session, 1858. Volume 20, book, 1882; St. Louis, Mo. (texashistory.unt.edu/ark:/67531/metapth28554/m1/108/: accessed May 25, 2018), University of North Texas Libraries, The Portal to Texas History, texashistory.unt.edu.

386. There is a deed of conveyance in the county court files dated April 8, 1854. The actual court case with Brisbane seems to have occurred in 1856 and 1857.

387. Dallas Public Library, Dallas County Court Records. Gouhenant v. McPherson.

388. The petitions are inserted in the Texas General Land Office survey files of each deceased Icarian: Barroux (file #2944), Berson (file #2511), Boissonnet (file #2507), Chauvin (file #2898), Collet (file #2506), Guérin (file #4566), Lévy (file #2508), Ludwig (file #2897), Rovira (file #2899) and Saugé (file #2512).

389. *Laws of Texas,* vol. 3 (Austin, TX: Gammel's Inc., 1898), 489.

390. Texas General Land Office. See note 389.

391. Dallas County, Texas Probate Cases. Cases Number 79, 81, 133, 138, 217, 223, 258, 352, 552, 591, Microfilmed by the Dallas Genealogical Society.

392. Ibid.

393. The court case documents for only six corresponding trials are located in Dallas County Court archives at the Dallas Public Library. However, the probate case files show that all the 11 transactions ended up in court and had similar outcomes. See also note number 400 below.

394. Dallas Court case papers: 405 (*Gouhenant v. Keen and Keen*), Dallas Public Library.

395. George W. Paschal, *A Digest of the Laws of Texas* (Galveston: S.S. Nichols, 1866), 106.

396. The reference to Considerant is taken from the Dallas County Court Records. Minutes from 1856 civil court cases. The date of his departure from La Réunion is July 7, 1856. See Beecher, 345.

397. *Dallas Herald*, August 7, 1858, and *Dallas Herald*, June 10, 1863.

398. Dallas County, Texas, Probate cases number 79, 81, 133, 138, 217, 223, 258, 352, 552, 591.

399. Ibid.

400. See General Land Office of Texas map of original land grants. http://www.glo.texas.gov/

401. Ibid.; *Handbook of Texas Online*, Joan Jenkins Perez, "Cockrell, Alexander," accessed June 07, 2018, http://www.tshaonline.org/handbook/online/articles/fco09; Elizabeth York Enstam, "The Frontier Woman as City Worker: Women's Occupations in Dallas, Texas, 1856-1880," *East Texas Historical Journal* 18, no. 1 (1980).

402. Dallas Court case papers: 389 (*Gouhenant v Cockrell*).

403. Ibid.

404. *Dallas Herald*, February 9, 1856.

405. Dallas Court case papers: 389.

406. Ibid.

407. Ibid.

408. Ibid.

409. Ibid.

410. Ibid.

411. Ibid.

412. Ibid.

413. Ibid.

414. Dallas Court case papers: 389 and 96 (Brisbane vs Gouhenant).

415. Wallace, 74; Handbook of Texas Online, Thomas W. Cutrer, "Hemphill, John," accessed July 30, 2016, http://www.tshaonline.org/handbook/online/articles/fhe13. Uploaded on June 15, 2010. Published by the Texas State Historical Association.

416. Texas Supreme Court, Reports of cases argued and decided in the Supreme Court of the State of Texas, during Austin session, 1857, and part of Galveston session, 1858. Volume 20., book, 1882; St. Louis, Mo. (texashistory.unt.edu/ark:/67531/metapth28554/m1/108/: accessed May 25, 2018), University of North Texas Libraries, The Portal to Texas History, texashistory.unt.edu.

417. Court records dated December 4, 1857. Hemphill was later noted for shaping the precedents for Texas homestead exemption law; The Handbook of Texas Online, Thomas W. Cutrer, "Hemphill, John," accessed July 30, 2016, http://www.tshaonline.org/handbook/online/articles/fhe13, Uploaded on June 15, 2010. Published by the Texas State Historical Association.

418. Michael Philips, *White, Metropolis: Race, Ethnicity, and Religion in Dallas, 1841-2001* (Austin: University of Texas Press, 2006), 24.

419. Rogers, page 74. The newspaper article from the *Herald* is printed in its entirety. The date of publication is unknown.

420. Payne, 24. Lists original source in footnote: "The photograph is in the possession of Ruth Melton of Dallas, whose father, Joseph M. Wilson, wrote in the 1970s an unpublished family history from

which some of the details in this account are taken. It is entitled 'Seven Generations in Dallas.'" Sources provide documentation that Gouhenant was still making photographs as late as 1858.
Not only that, but Cockrell's portrait has had some artistic modifications; it is possible that Gouhenant painted his eyes over the
eyelids since they were likely closed after his death.

421. *Dallas Herald,* July 31, 1858. The actual dates of the trial are not
listed ("Thursday last" seems to refer to July 22. the "summer
Solstice" seems to have been poetic license in this case.)

422. Dallas Court case papers, 389, August 1858.

423. Dallas County Court Records, Mortgage and Deed of Trust by A.
Gouhenant to A. Brisbane, March 8, 1869.

424. Adolphe Gouhenant research collection of Alexander Troup,
University of Texas at Arlington, original source is from the Dallas
County Deed Records.

425. *Dallas Herald,* March 6, 1869.

426. *Dallas Herald,* July 24, 1858.

427. Oliver Cromwell Hartley, and R. K. Hartley. *Reports of Cases
Argued and Decided in the Supreme Court of the State of
Texas, During Austin Session, 1857, and Part of Galveston
Session, 1858.* Volume 20., Book, 1882. 459-461 (1857) (http://
texashistory.unt.edu/ark:/67531/metapth28554/ Accessed May 2,
2015, University of North Texas Libraries, The Portal to Texas
History, http://texashistory.unt.edu; crediting UNT Libraries,
Denton, Texas. Pages 492-494. (*Gouhenant v. Anderson* was significant, cited as a precedent at least 5 times from 1851 to 1885.) Also
of note: According to the Texas General Land Office Records, there
was another legal dispute involving Gouhenant and Archibald
Robinson in Fort Worth; although not nearly as significant as his
other battles, it is worth noting. Robinson had a certificate for a
land grant which he located directly south of Gouhenant's acres.
On May 2, 1854, Robinson had filed a suit against Gouhenant and a
man named Joseph P. Philpot for trespassing. The dispute seems to
have evolved from the general confusion associated with locating
Peters Colony land grants mid-century. It seems to have been

resolved amicably, with Gouhenant disclaiming "all right, title, and interest to the land." He had the land surveyed about a year later on April 20, 1855. Another year passed and the land was finally patented April 14, 1856, just about two months after he first tried to sell the Arts Saloon.

428. Tannehill Lodge History.

429. Masson, *L'aventure américaine d'Ernest Humbert.*

430. Ibid.

431. Ibid.

432. Tarrant County Archives: Deed dated February 5, 1856, filed April 7, 1856 in Book A, page 309. The document lists Adolph Gouhenant as "Grantor" and Ernest Humbert as the "Grantee." Under Description and Remarks, it states, "160 acres of land in Tarrant County, Texas being the A. Gouhenant survey Patent No. 1152, vol. 12."

433. Tarrant County Archives: Oath of office as administrator signed by E.M. Daggett and sworn to by him October 25, 1858, filed on same day; Petition for sale of 160 acres of land belonging to the estate of E. Humbert, filed on November 29, 1858; Final report of sale of 160 acres of land, filed on June 27, 1859.

434. In the mid 1850s, there were two small communities in North Texas named Pleasant Run. One is now Colleyville, about fifteen miles northeast of Fort Worth. The other was close to Lancaster, about fifteen miles due south of Dallas. All the occurrences of the name Pleasant Run found in the *Dallas Herald* between 1850 and 1860 concern the community south of Dallas near Lancaster, and in all likelihood, this is the one from which Gouhenant was coming when he arrived in Dallas.

435. *Dallas Herald*, March 9, 1859, page 3.

436. McCullough. Pages 103-136 provide background for the practice of medicine in Paris.

437. *Dallas Herald*, March 2, 1859, page 3, and *Dallas Herald*, March 9, 1859; *WPA Guide and History*, 1992 for description of the hotel, page 276.

438. June Anderson Shipley, *Lancaster, A History 1845-1945* (Lancaster, TX: Lancaster Historical Society, 1978), 26. Winny is likely a nickname for Juliette; they seem to be the same person. There is only one Solomon Brundage in the Lancaster census from 1860 and he was married to Julia at that time. Texas Wills and Probate Records, 1833-1974 for Solomon Brundage, packets 2555-2640.

439. Receipt from Dallas County Court files in the collection at the Dallas Public Library.

440. Philip Lindsley, *A History of Greater Dallas and Vicinity*, vol. 2 (Chicago: Lewis Publishing Company, 1909); http://texashistory.unt.edu/ark:/67531/metapth21071/ accessed May 09, 2015, University of North Texas Libraries, The Portal to Texas History, http://texashistory.unt.edu UNT Libraries, Denton, Texas. Page 319; Federal census from 1860; member information from Ancestry.com.

441. *Dallas Herald*, May 4, 1859; *Dallas Herald*, August 10, 1859. Early Dallas Hotels, William Adair transcriptions.

442. Dallas Public Library, Dallas County Court Records; Dallas County (Tex.). *Dallas County Probate Case 85: Brundage, Julia (Deceased)*. The Portal to Texas History. http://texashistory.unt.edu/ark:/67531/metapth598070/. Accessed May 10, 2015.

443. Marie Louise Giles, "The Early History of Medicine in Dallas, 1841-1900," Master's Thesis, University of Texas, June 1951, 28-29. Original source, Frank Marion Cockrell, *History of Early Dallas* (Collection at the DeGolyer Library, Southern Methodist University, Dallas).

444. Giles, 48-49. She cites Eloise Santerre's *Reunion: A Translation of Dr. Savardan's Un Naufrage au Texas* (Masters Thesis, SMU, 1935), 77.

445. From an Interview with Paula Baker. The details of this encounter are given in chapter 16.

446. Letter from E.M. Daggett to Gouhenant dated July (year illegible) at Pilot Point. From Fort Worth Public Library, Mary Daggett Lake

Files, Folder labeled, Daggett, E.M – Correspondence 1853-1882, Box 1, 1:1:8

447. *Handbook of Texas Online*, Donald E. Reynolds, "Texas Troubles," accessed June 8, 2018, https://tshaonline.org/handbook/online/articles/vetbr. Uploaded June 15, 2010. Modified on July 12, 2016. Published by the Texas State Historical Association.

448. *New York Times*, July 3, 1860.

449. *Handbook of Texas Online*, Donald E. Reynolds, "Texas Troubles"; "The Late Fire at Dallas, Texas; Extraordinary Developments Alleged Abolitionist Plan for Devastation Northern Texas," *New York Times*, July 26, 1860.

450. Samuel F. B. Morse to Governor Sam Houston, Texas State Library and Archives Commission. Accessed May 25, 2018 https://www.tsl.texas.gov/treasures/giants/houston-morse.html. The letter was written August 9, 1860 in Poughkeepsie, New York.

451. Ralph A. Wooster, *Civil War Texas: A History and Guide* (Austin: Texas State Historical Association, 1999), 1-5.

452. Wooster and Grear, 29.

453. Wooster, 42-43.

454. Wooster, 41-43 and Richard B. McCaslin, "GREAT HANGING AT GAINSVILLE," *Handbook of Texas Online* (http://www.tshaonline.org/handbook/online/articles/jig01), accessed August 29, 2015. Uploaded on June 15, 2010. Published by the Texas State Historical Association.

455. UNT Library, David Jones Eddleman Collection, 1854-1955, Box 1810.

456. Grear; Wooster; see also Bruce Catton, *The Civil War* (Boston: Houghton Mifflin Company, 1960).

457. Grear, 2.

458. Catton, 143.

459. Wooster, 5.

460. Confederate Military Record for Ernest Gounah, National Archives and Records Administration.

461. General Land Office of Texas county abstract data.

462. Joan Jenkins Perez, "Stone Barton Warren Jr." Accessed May 25, 2018, https://tshaonline.org/handbook/online/articles/fst63

463. *Soldier's Life: Bugle Calls from "Reveille" to "Taps,"* https://fas.org/man/dod-101/sys/land/bugle.htm; "Bugler's call has historical origins," http://www.irontontribune.com/2011/04/24/bugler%E2%80%99s-call-has-historical-origins/#sthash.t7Yk1l8w.dpuf; *Civil War Re-enacting for the Bugler,* http://tapsbugler.com/civil-war-re-enacting-for-the-bugler/.

464. Library of Congress: *Civil War Conscription Laws,* Blog by Margaret Wood, November, 15, 2012. Accessed May 25, 2018, http://blogs.loc.gov/law/2012/11/civil-war-conscription-laws/; *Under the Rebel Flag, Life in Texas during the Civil War,* Texas State Library and Archives Commission, accessed May 25, 2018 https://www.tsl.texas.gov/exhibits/civilwar/1862_1.html; Catton, 206.

465. Newton A. Keen, *Living and Fighting with the Texas 6th Cavalry* (Gaithersburg: Butternut Press, 1886), 1-4, and 18; The 1850 Census for Dallas County. A.M. Keen was living with his parents in 1850 and was listed as a surveyor. He was 21. He was probably named Abner Melvon. He was one of eight sons and three daughters born to Abner and Susan Keen.

466. Ibid., 37-40.

467. *Fiery Trial Part I,* general information about Texas in the Civil War from the Texas State Library and Archives Commission, Jennifer Bridges, https://www.tsl.texas.gov/exhibits/civilwar/1862_1.html; *Sixth Texas Cavalry,* Handbook of Texas Online, accessed October 09, 2015. Uploaded on April 8, 2011. Published by the Texas State Historical Association, https://tshaonline.org/handbook/online/articles/qks13; John Henry Brown, 96; 6th Texas Cavalry Regiment, http://

www.rosstexascavalrybrigade.com/6thtexascavalryregiment/index6.html, accessed June 17, 2018.

468. *The Missouri Weekly*, Thursday, May 4, 1871. "Sunday evening last" refers to Sunday, April 24, 1871.

469. Oliver Knight, *Fort Worth: Outpost on the Trinity* (Fort Worth: Texas Christian University Press, 1990), 38. (Original source cited as a book by B.B. Paddock, ed., *A Twentieth Century History and Bibliographical Record of North and West Texas*). Gouhenant was one of the citizens who signed a bond to build the court-house; *Dallas Herald*, April 18, 1860; Garrett, 158, lists the amounts pledged by each citizen who signed the bond.

470. Knight, 37-39.

471. Federal Census of 1860 for Denton County shows him living in Pilot Point that year. In addition, when he came to Dallas in 1859 for court proceedings, he signed the hotel register as being from Pilot Point for that year as well. Also, his voter registration from Denton County documents that on August 10, 1867, he had been in Denton County for nine years, placing him in Pilot Point as early as 1858. Ancestry.com. *Texas, Voter Registration Lists, 1867-1869* (database on-line). Provo, UT, USA: Ancestry.com Operations, Inc., 2011. Original data: 1867 Voter Registration Lists. Microfilm, 12 rolls. Texas State Library and Archives Commission, Austin, Texas.

472. Compiled from census data for 1860 and 1870 and family records from Ancestry.com. Marriages were not recorded at the state level until well into the middle of the twentieth century. The story about Gouhenant and Elizabeth meeting and her background is from Baker family history. Paula Selzer interviewed Paula Baker, whose husband was a descendent of Judge Martin Edward (Elizabeth's brother) on July 1, 2017, Fort Worth, Texas.

473. Eddleman states there was no school in the early days (1854) and references a school outside of town where preaching occurred. It is worth noting that according to the National Register of Historic Places registration form that was submitted to the United States Department of the Interior in June 2007, the first school in Pilot Point was built in 1856 by Alphius Knight, "a New Yorker,

[who] built a frame school house on the northwest corner of Liberty and Hill street. Known as 'Yankee Knight's' school, it was a 'subscription school' as there were no free schools at this time." In 1872, Dr. M.B. Franklin and Mr. Greene consolidated two schools (which were possibly the Knight school and the school then meeting at the Masonic lodge) and founded the Pilot Point Seminary, a subscription school that offered education from first grade to college. In 1884, the school obtained a charter and the name was changed to Franklin College. Pilot Point began offering free public schools in 1894 and Franklin College enrollment dwindled, until it finally closed in 1900. https://atlas.thc.state.tx.us/NR/pdfs/07000893/07000893.pdf

474. UNT Library, David Jones Eddleman Collection, 1854-1955, Box 1810.

475. Resolution Celebrating the 150 Years of the Ford Lodge No. 270 A.F. & A.M. of Pilot Point, Texas. Accessed May 25, 2018, http://dentoncounty.granicus.com/MetaViewer.php?view_id=26&clip_id=270&meta_id=48717

476. According to 1860 census records, the population of Pilot Point was very young. The average age was 19 years. Gouhenant was 56 at that time and was among the oldest 4 percent in the village.

477. AN 10 AS 28(9). A microfilmed version is available at The State Historical Society of Missouri.

478. Ibid.

479. Ibid.

480. *The Medical and Surgical Reporter* 17 (1867): 22.

481. *Record and Chronicle* (Denton, Tex.), June 2, 1910, newspaper, June 2, 1910; Denton, Texas. (texashistory.unt.edu/ark:/67531/metapth505025/: accessed June 30, 2017), University of North Texas Libraries, The Portal to Texas History, texashistory.unt.edu; crediting Abilene Library Consortium. The *Denton Record Chronicle* published some items from the *Vedette*, a publication of Pilot Point. It was thought that no editions of the *Vedette* remained until

a copy of the six-column single sheet newspaper was found by family members among some older papers of Judge F.E. Piner.

482. Census from 1870 for Denton County and National Archives. District 3, Annual, Monthly and Special lists, December 1865-Dec.1866. Microfilm series M791, Roll 2. Found online at Ancestry.com; Letter from Fort Worth historian Pat Crowley, whose family descended from Peters colonists, to Carolyn Selzer; Handbook of Texas Online, Lisa C. Maxwell, "Pilot Point, TX," accessed November 12, 2016, http://www.tshaonline.org/handbook/online/articles/hgp04 Uploaded on June 15, 2010. Published by the Texas State Historical Association.

483. *The Missouri Weekly*, Springfield, Missouri, April 27, 1871.

484. Miner, 71; *The Missouri Weekly*, Springfield, Missouri. Thursday, April 27, 1871. The first train arrived in Springfield on May 5, 1870. At the time of his accident, the South Pacific Railroad had just recently arrived in North Springfield; the depot and hotel had been there less than a year.

485. *Record of Wills, 1840-1916*. Author: *Missouri. Probate Court (Greene County)*. Probate Place: *Greene, Missouri*. Notes: *Wills, Vol A-B, 1840-1883*. Ancestry.com. *Missouri, Wills and Probate Records, 1766-1988* (database on-line). Provo, UT, USA: Ancestry.com Operations, Inc., 2015. Original data: Missouri, County, District and Probate Courts.

486. *The Missouri Weekly*, Thursday, May 4, 1871. He died April 30, 1871.

487. The typed will is from the Tarrant County Archive, but the original seems to have been filed April 7, 1888, and recorded in Book 54 page 113 in the office of the County Clerk of Tarrant County, Texas records of deeds.

488. *The Missouri Weekly*, Thursday, May 4, 1871.

489. Eleven dollars and eighty-five cents was a hefty sum to pay for a railroad ticket in 1871. The reason for the exorbitant cost was that in 1871 a ticket between those two towns cost about three dollars more than it did at points one hundred miles to the west where there was more competition for fares.

490. Samuel Wood Geiser, *Men of Science in Texas 1820-1880* (Dallas: Southern Methodist University Press, 1958-59), 23-24; History of the Academy of Natural Science, accessed May 28, 2018. http://www.ansp.org/about/academy-history/. On July 1, 2011, John Sime, curatorial assistant and student research associate confirmed that it is listed in the Donations to the Museum in their August 1, 1854, report.

491. S.W. Geiser, "John Wright Glenn (1836-92), Early State Geologist of Texas," *Field and Laboratory* 13 (July 1945): 66.

492. Ibid.

493. A.R. Roesler, *Reply to the Charges Made by S.B. Buckley, State Geologist of Texas in his Official Report of 1874 against Dr. B.F. Shumard and A.R. Roesler*, 1875, 6.

494. *First [fourth] Annual Report of the Geological Survey of Texas*, 1889 by Edwin T. Dumble, state geologist 1890. Published in Austin by the State Printing Office, 1890. Pages 241-245. https://archive.org/details/firstfourthannua01geol ; *First Annual Report of the Geological and Agricultural Survery of Texas* by S.B. Buckley, A.M., Ph. D, state Geologist, Houston: A.C. Gray, State Printer, 1874, page 6.

495. Texas State Archives, Governor Edmund Davis Files, Box 2014/110-13 Folder 183, April 19-25, 1871. Bowman wrote to the governor on April 22; the note on the file states that he was sent an answer on May 15, 1871.

496. Texas State Archives, Governor Edmund Davis Files Box 2014/110-13 April 8-12, 1871.

497. Robert T. Hill, "The Present Condition of Knowledge of the Geology of Texas," *Bulletin of the United States geological survey*, no. 45, 1887, 39.

498. Geiser, 69.

499. Texas State Archives. Governor Edmund Davis Files Box 2014/110-13 April 8-12, 1871.

500. *The Bohemian*, 1900, 20-21.

501. Mary Daggett Lake, "French Communists Who Sought Utopia in Texas Succumbed to Frontier Trials," *Fort Worth Star-Telegram*, June 13, 1943.

502. Pat Crowley letter to Carolyn Selzer, March 27, 2002. Crowley's personal notes to Carolyn Selzer state that Lt. Starr's daughter was able to influence the appointment.

503. *Dallas Herald*, May 20, 1871.

504. The authors have recorded no fewer than 24 different spellings of his name (not to mention the instances with the French acute accent on the *e*): Gouhenant, Gouhenans, Gougenant, Gouhenaut, Gouhnaut, Gouchenant, Gochenant, Goualand, Gounant, Gonant, Gouhenaught, Goughnant, Goughanant, Gounah, Goumah, Gournah, Gornah, Gorenah, Gohnor, Ganar, Goonan, Goumah, Gonnough and Ganaugh. A poll of Facebook users named Gouhenant provided the following results: Among 14 persons who answered our questions, all the 7 who are still living in Haute-Saône pronounce their name *Gounan*, and all 7 whose family have left this department generations ago pronounce it *Goo-hey-nan*. In the 1835 Lyon census, his name is spelled Gounant, probably reflecting the fact that the census agent wrote the name as he heard it. Finally, there is a little town in Haute-Saône called Gouhenans, which the locals also pronounce *Gounan*. There is thus a good level of confidence to assume that Gouhenant pronounced his name Gounan. In Texas, descendants pronounce the name Gounah with a decidedly drawn out second syllable.

505. *Exposition des produits des Beaux-Arts et de l'industrie à Toulouse Dans les Galeries du Capitole le 25 juin 1845* (Toulouse: Imprimerie de J. DUPIN, rue de la Pomme, 14), 17.

506. For Judge Cumming's biography see Geneology Magazine online. Accessed 28 May 2018 https://www.genealogymagazine.com/judge-c-c-cummings-biography/. It is taken from the original notes of B. B. Paddock, *History and Biographical Record of North and West Texas* (Chicago: Lewis Publishing Co., 1906), 1: 206.

507. *Bohemian*, Easter 1900, 22.

508. *Brenham Daily Banner*, January 8, 1893.

509. Maxime Guillot filed a statement of intent to become a US citizen on May 14, 1853. Gouhenant took an oath of citizenship on May 17, 1853. Civil Court Minutes Vol. A, page 339, Dallas Public Library.

510. Ernest G. Fischer, *Marxists and Utopias in Texas* (Burnet, TX: Eakin Press, 1980), Chapter IV only.

511. Begos, 8.

512. *Le Populaire*, July 1, 1849.

513. *Le Populaire*, December 1849.

514. *Le Populaire*, August 1850.

515. Cordillot, 65; Jim Forster, *La Reunion Remembered: 150th Anniversary 1855-2005* (Self published, 2005).

516. Begos, 7; Cullar and Guillot, 1.

517. *Le Populaire*, February 13, 1850.

518. Sutton, 56.

519. *The New Orleans Bee,* February 6, 1849 page 1 column 3.

520. Lillian M. Snyder, *Communal Societies,* published by the Communal Studies Association. Volume 6, 1986. The Contribution of Icarian, Alfred Piquenard to Architecture in Iowa and Illinois. Snyder, 164-165. The *Rome's* manifest shows Piquenard's age as 40. He was actually about 22 years old since the ship arrived in New Orleans in 1848 and Piquenard was born in 1826.

521. He was registered to vote in July of 1867. Ancestry.com. Texas, Voter Registration Lists, 1867-1869 [database on-line]. Provo, UT, USA: Ancestry.com Operations, Inc., 2011. 1880 Census for June shows Emily being months old. Original data: 1867 Voter Registration Lists. Microfilm, 12 rolls. Texas State Library and Archives Commission, Austin, Texas. Also Gounah Family Bible, and correspondence with Anita Trotter, a descendant by marriage. See also 1860 and 1880 census records.

522. Nita Thurman and Weldon Lucas, *150 Years of Denton County Sheriffs, 1846-1996* (Denton, TX: Old Alton Press, 1998); *Denton Monitor,* Saturday, May 30, 1968, "Official Directory"; Legislative Refer-

ence Library of Texas, accessed May 12, 2018, https://lrl.texas.gov/mobile/memberDisplay.cfm?memberID=4905;

523. *Denton Monitor*, August 15, 1868.

524. *Denton Monitor*, August 22, 1868.

525. Mary Withers was born in 1841 in Missouri to James W. and Louisa (Luisa) E. Withers. Sources: Family records; 1870 Census for Denton County (There is no last name provided for Emily, but the letter "G" appears before her name.); Early Texas Birth Records (Sumner) and Family Bible. 1880 Census for Anderson County. Also of note is the fact that Ernest had been unemployed for six months and had the responsibility for five children: Edna, age 9, Ernest Jr. age 7, Julia, age 5, Adolph (Boyd) age 2, and Anna who had been born the previous month; http://files.usgwarchives.net/tx/anderson/history/1877dir.txt 1877 Palestine City Directory. Anderson County, TX - 1877 Palestine City Directory, contributed for use in the USGenWeb by: East Texas Genealogical Society. USGenWeb Archives.

526. 1880 Census Anderson County, Texas; Roll: 1288; Family History Film: 1255288; Page: 10C; Enumeration District: 001, Ancestry.com; Original data: Tenth Census of the United States, 1880. (NARA microfilm publication T9, 1,454 rolls). Records of the Bureau of the Census, Record Group 29. National Archives, Washington, D.C.

527. *Brenham Daily Banner*, January 8, 1893, reprinted from a Burleson newspaper. texashistory.unt.edu/ark:/67531/metapth486557/: accessed June 30, 2017, University of North Texas Libraries, The Portal to Texas History, texashistory.unt.edu.

528. Flora B. Ratchford's letter to Carolyn Selzer, October 20, 1984. If Emma died in 1889 (the date of her death is unknown) Ernest may have not gone to Oklahoma. The French family records (Masson, *L'aventure américaine d'Ernest Humbert*) provide another version of his life. They state that Ernest was a livestock breeder in Louisiana and that he amassed a fortune several times, each time losing what he had earned, and that he was living in Jefferson, Texas, widowed, with two children.

529. *La Comédie*, February 17, 1867.

530. *Beaumarchais. Journal satirique, littéraire et financier,* December 25, 1881, 4.

531. Victor Hugo, *Actes et paroles: III Depuis l'exil 1870-1885* (Paris: Albin Michel, 1940), 177.

532. "Discours de Mme Houry" in *Congrès international des droits des femmes ouvert à Paris le 25 juillet 1878, clos le 9 août suivant. Compte-rendu des séances plénières* (Paris: Auguste Ghio, 1878), 74-75.

533. All the information concerning Anna Houry's Fourierist activities are from Bernard Desmard, "Houry (née Gouhenant), Anastasie, dite Anna," *Dictionnaire biographique du fouriérisme,* notice mise en ligne en janvier 2017 : http://www.charlesfourier.fr/spip.php? article1836 (accessed July 24, 2017)

534. *Journal d'agriculture pratique, de jardinage et d'économie domestique.* 1853/01 - 1853/06. p. 182.

535. Tarrant County Archives. Originally filed October 16, 1874 and recorded in the Book A-3, page 498 deed records of Tarrant County.

536. Texas Wills and Probate Records, 1833-1974. *Probate Minutes, Vol C-E, 1887-1892.* Ancestry.com. *Texas, Wills and Probate Records, 1833-1974* [database on-line]. Provo, UT, USA: Ancestry.com Operations, Inc., 2015. Original data: Texas County, District and Probate Courts.

537. *Dallas Morning News,* January 14, 1915, page 13. "Judge J.E. Martin Dead: Was Pioneer Fort Worth Layer and Body Will Be Buried in Plot He Gave City." Also, interview with Paula Baker, Baker family records; Van Zandt County History Book Committee, *The History of Van Zandt County Texas* (Wills Point, TX: Van Zandt County Genealogical Society, 1984), 339.

538. Tarrant County Archives, Record of Deeds. Abstract number 54970. Affidavit of J.E. Martin, filed on May 29, 1905 and recorded in Book 198 page 604 in the office of the County Clerk of Tarrant County, Texas records of deeds and also Archives document filed

on May 29, 1905 and recorded in Book 199 page 564 in the office of the County Clerk of Tarrant County, Texas records of deeds.

539. Masson, *L'aventure américaine d'Ernest Humbert.*

540. Pat Crowley letter to Carolyn Selzer, March 27, 2002. She quotes Chapter XVI of *Fort Worth's First Cemetery.*

541. "Major Arnold's Remains: Communication Relative to Their Removal Read to the Council," *Dallas Morning News*, September 22, 1901, 8.

542. Ibid.

543. "Title Claim May Block Park Plan: Removal of Bodies from Samuels Avenue Cemetery Confronts New Obstacle," *Fort Worth Star Telegram*, Archival newspaper clipping located in the folder entitled, "Samuels Avenue Area Research—Pioneer Rest Cemetery Research by Dee Barker Cemetery File," Tarrant County Archives. The article is undated but references that are also included in the file indicate Judge Martin's words may have been published November 10, 1909.

544. "Judge Martin Dead," *Dallas Morning News,* January 14, 1915, page 13; family biographical notes and news clippings of Judge Martin provided by Paula Baker in interview on July 1, 2017.

Bibliography

Archival Sources

France
Archives Nationales

F17 Series: Education.

BB18 Series: Minister of Justice – General correspondence of the criminal division.

10 AS 28(9): Manuscript of Considerant relating his meeting with Gouhenant; Letters of Brisbane to Gouhenant.

Bibliothèque Nationale de France

NAF 18146-18166: Cabet's papers.

Fichier Bossu: List of the French Freemasons.

Archives Départementales de Haute Garonne

1M Series: Administration of the Department.

U1433: Communists Trial in 1843.

Archives Départementales de Haute Saône

2M Series: Administrative Personnel.

E Series: Communal Archives.

3Q Series: Estate.

Archives Départementales du Lot-et-Garonne

1K 2 Series: Electoral lists 1831-1857.

3U Series: Civilian Justice.

Archives Départementales du Rhône

1Q Series: National Goods.

3E Series: Notarial Archives.

4Q Series: Mortgages.

UCIV Series: Civilian Justice.

6UP Series: Bankruptcies.

Archives Municipales de Lyon

480WP Series: Cultural Institutions.

Archives de l'Académie des Sciences Belles Lettres et Arts.

This archive has no standardized classification. It contains the report of the committee who visited the tower, as well as the letter of Gouhenant to the committee and the minutes of the academy sessions.

Archives du Musée d'Histoire de Lyon

Contains items relative to the tower erected by Gouhenant in Lyon.

United States (Texas)

Dallas Public Library

County Court Records: Civil minutes; Deed records; Probate Records; Dallas County Court.

Fort Worth Public Library

Mary Daggett Lake Files.

Tarrant County Archive

Deed Records, Pioneer Rest Cemetery File.

Texas General Land Office

Archival Records: Land grants, surveys and patents.

Texas State Library and Archives

Governor Edmund Davis Files.

University of North Texas Library

David Jones Eddleman Collection

University of Texas Briscoe Center for American History

Samuel Starr Papers

Greene County Archives and Record Center (Missouri)

Probate Court: Record of Wills.

Books

Ashkenazi, Eliott. *The Business of Jews in Louisiana, 1840-1875.* Tuscaloosa: University of Alabama Press, 1988.

Bates, Edmond F. *History and Reminiscences of Denton County.* Denton, TX: McNitzky Printing Company, 1918.

Beecher, Jonathan. *Victor Considerant and the Rise and Fall of French Romantic Socialism.* Berkeley: University of California Press, 2001.

Benoit, Joseph. *Confession d'un prolétaire.* Paris : Édition sociales, 1968.

Borrey, Francis. *La Franche-Comté en 1814.* Paris: Berger-Levrault, 1913.

Bracht, Viktor. *Texas in 1848.* San Antonio, TX: Naylor Printing Company, 1931.

Brisbane, Redelia. *Albert Brisbane: A Mental Biography with a Character Study.* New York: Burt Franklin, 1969.

Brown, John Henry. *History of Dallas County, Texas: From 1837 to 1887.* Dallas, TX: The Aldredge Book Store, 1966.

Buckley, Samuel Butsford. *First Annual Report of the Geological and Agricultural Survey of Texas.* Austin: A.C. Gray, State Printer, 1874.

Burlend, Rebecca, and Edward Burlend, edited by Milo Milton Quaife. *A True Picture of Emigration.* Chicago: Lakeside Press, R.R. Donnelley & Sons, 1936.

Cabet, Étienne. *Défense du Citoyen Cabet, accusé d'escroquerie devant la Cour d'appel de Paris (11 décembre 1850).* Paris: Bureau du Populaire, Janvier 1851.

Cabet, Étienne. *Défense et Acquittement de Cabet, accusé d'escroquerie au sujet de l'émigration Icarienne.* Paris: bureau du Républicain, October 1851.

Cabet, Étienne. *Les masques arrachés.* Paris: imprimeries Delanchy, 1844.

Cabet, Étienne. *Procès du communisme à Toulouse.* Paris : bureau du Populaire, 1843.

Calvert, Robert A. and Arnoldo De León. *The History of Texas,* 2nd ed. Wheeling, IL: Harlan Davidson, Inc., 1996.

Catton, Bruce. *The Civil War.* Boston: Houghton Mifflin Company, 1960.

Cesena, Amédée G., and François Ignace Gouhenant. *La Maçonnerie.* À Lyon: Chez les principaux libraires, 1832.

Clark, Gary W. *Cased Images and Tintypes Kwik Guide: A Guide to Identifying and Dating Daguerreotypes, Ambrotypes, and Tintypes.* Phototree.com. 2013. (hardcopy)

Cockrell, Frank Marion. *History of Early Dallas.* Chicago: Dallas Historical Society, 1944.

Coe, Lewis. *The Telegraph: A History of Morse's Invention and Its Predecessors in the United States.* Jefferson, NC: McFarland and Company, 1911.

Combes, André. *Histoire de la Franc-Maçonnerie à Lyon.* Brignais, France: Éditions des Traboules, 2006.

Conners, Seymour V. *The Peters Colony of Texas.* Austin: Texas State Historical Association, 1959.

Considerant, Victor. *Au Texas.* Paris: Librairie phalanstérienne, 1854.

Cordillot, Michel. *La Sociale en Amérique. Dictionnaire biographique du mouvement social francophone aux États-Unis 1844-1922.* Paris: Les éditions de l'Atelier, 2002.

Crivelli, Joseph-Louis. *Dictionnaire du droit civil, commercial, criminel et de procédure civile et criminelle.* Paris : A. Bavoux, 1825.

Cullar, W. Clytes Anderson, and Lawrence Elie Guillot. *French Carriages on the Trinity: The Guillot Family of Dallas.* Wolfe City, TX: Henington Publishing Company, 1986.

Daughters of the American Revolution, James Campbell Chapter. *Transcripts of Early Dallas Church and Lodge Records and the Diary of an Early Settler.* Dallas, TX: Dorsey Printing Co., 1960.

De la Hodde, Lucien. *Histoire des sociétés secrètes et du parti républicain de 1830 à 1848.* Brussels: Méline, Cans et Cie, libraires-éditeurs, 1850.

Dumas, Alexandre. *Nouvelles Impressions de voyage – Midi de la France.* Brussels: Société Belge de librairie, 1841.

Dumble, Edwin T. *First [fourth] Annual Report of the Geological Survey of Texas, 1889.* Austin: State Printing Office, 1890.

Dupont, Charles. *Histoire d'un enfant du peuple.* Marseille: Imprimeries nouvelles Alfred Valz, 1886.

Faucher, J.A., and A. Ricker. *Histoire de la franc-maçonnerie en France.* Paris : Nouvelles éditions latines, 1967.

Fischer, Ernest G. *Marxists and Utopias in Texas.* Burnet, TX: Eakin Press, 1980.

Forster, Jim. *La Reunion Remembered: 150th Anniversary 1855-2005.* Self published, 2005.

Fourn, François. *Étienne Cabet ou le temps de l'Utopie.* Paris: Éditions Vendémiaire, 2014.

Fournière, Eugène. *Histoire socialiste. 8, Le règne de Louis-Philippe.* Paris: Jules Rouff, 1901.

Garrett, Julia Kathryn. *Fort Worth: A Frontier Triumph.* Fort Worth: Texas Christian University Press, 1996.

Geiser, Samuel Wood. *Men of Science in Texas 1820-1880.* Dallas: Southern Methodist University Press, 1958-59.

George, Jocelyne. *Histoire des maires de 1789 à 1939.* Paris: Plon, 1989.

Gilmore, Jeanne. *La République clandestine.* Paris, Aubier 1997.

Grear, Charles David. *Why Texans Fought in the Civil War.* College Station: Texas A&M University Press, 2010.

Greene, A.C. *Dallas: The Deciding Years.* Austin: Encino Press, 1973.

Hartley, Oliver Cromwell. *Reports of Cases Argued and Decided in the Supreme Court of the State of Texas, Austin Session, 1857, and Part of Galveston Session, 1858. Vol. XX.* St. Louis, MO: The Gilbert Book Company 1882. Originally printed in 1858.

Hugo, Victor, *Actes et paroles. III Depuis l'exil 1870-1885.* Paris: Albin Michel, 1940.

Johnson, Christopher. *Utopian Communism in France, Cabet and the Icarians, 1839-1851.* Ithaca: Cornell University Press, 1974.

Keen, Newton A. *Living and Fighting with the Texas 6th Cavalary.* Gaithersburg: Butternut Press, 1886.

Knight, Oliver. *Fort Worth: Outpost on the Trinity.* Fort Worth: Texas Christian University Press, 1990.

Lloyd, James T. and Benjamin F. Klein. *Lloyd's Steamboat Directory and Disasters on the Western Waters.* Cincinnati: Young and Klein, 1979.

Lindsley, Philip. *A History of Greater Dallas and Vicinity.* Chicago: The Lewis Publishing Company, 1909.

Lu, Helen M., and Gwen B. Neumann. *First Half Dozen Years: Dallas County Texas as Seen Through the Commissioner's Court Minutes.* Self-published, 1982.

Ludlow, John. *The Autobiography of a Christian Socialist,* edited by A.D. Murray. London: Frank Cass and Company Limited, 2005.

Lyonnet, Henry. *Dictionnaire des comédiens français (ceux d'hier).* Geneva : Bibliothèque de la Revue Universelle Internationale Illustrée, 1912.

Marx, Karl, and Friedrich Engels. *Collected Works.* London: Lawrence and Wishart, 1978.

Marx, Karl, and Friedrich Engels. *Manifesto of the Communist Party: A Modern Edition.* London: Verso Editions, 2012.

Masson, Bernard. *L'aventure américaine d'Ernest Humbert.* Montpellier, France: Self-published, 1989.

Masson, Bernard. *Les Humbert-Caillier.* Montpellier, France: Self-published, 1992.

Maurin, Albert. *Histoire de la chute des Bourbons.* Paris: Bureau de la Société des travailleurs réunis. 1851.

McCullough, David. *The Greater Journey: Americans in Paris.* New York: Simon and Schuster, 2011.

McDonald, William L. *Dallas Rediscovered: A Photographic Chronicle of Urban Expansion 1870-1925.* Dallas, TX: Dallas Historical Society, 1978.

Michaud, Louis-Gabriel. *Biographie universelle, ancienne et moderne.* Paris: Chez Madame C. Desplaces, 1843.

Miner, Craig H. *The St. Louis-San Francisco Transcontinental Railroad: The Thirty-fifth Parallel Project, 1853-1890.* Lawrence: The University Press of Kansas, 1972.

Morneweck, Evelyn Foster. *Chronicles of Stephen Foster's Family, Volume II.* Pittsburgh: University of Pittsburgh Press, 1944.

Newhall, Beaumont. *The Daguerreotype in America.* 1961. 3rd ed. New York: Dover, 1976.

Newhall, Beaumont. *The History of Photography, from 1839 to the Present Day.* New York: The Museum of Modern Art, 1964.

Olmsted, Frederick Law. *A Journey Through Texas: Or a Saddle-Trip on the Southwestern Frontier.* Lincoln: University of Nebraska Press, 2004.

Paddock, Buckley B. *A Twentieth Century History and Biographical Record of North and West Texas.* Chicago: Lewis Publishing Co., 1906.

Palmquist, Peter E. and Thomas R. Kailbourn. *Pioneer Photographers from the Mississippi to the Continental Divide: A Biographical Dictionary, 1839-1865.* Stanford University Press, 2005.

Parker, W. B. *Through Unexplored Texas.* Austin: Texas State Historical Association, 1990.

Paschal, George W. *A Digest of the Laws of Texas.* Galveston: S.S. Nichols, 1866.

Pratt, James. "Our European Heritage: The Diverse Contributions of La Reunion," in *Dallas Reconsidered: Essays in Local History,* edited by Michael V. Hazel. Dallas: Three Forks Press, 1995.

Payne, Darwin. *Dynamic Dallas: An Illustrated History.* Carlsbad, CA: Heritage Media Corp. 2002.

Perkins, Clay. *The Fort in Fort Worth.* Keller, TX: Cross-Timbers Heritage Publishing Company, 2001.

Philips, Michael. *White, Metropolis: Race, Ethnicity, and Religion in Dallas, 1841-2001.* Austin: University of Texas Press, 2006.

Pignel, Armand. *Conducteur ou guide du voyageur et du colon de Paris à Alger et dans l'Algérie.* Paris: Imprimerie de E.J. Bailly et Cie, 1836.

Rey, Marie-Pierre. *Un Tsar à Paris.* Paris: Flammarion, 2014.

Roesler, A.R. *Reply to the Charges Made by S.B. Buckley, State Geologist of Texas in His Official Report of 1874 against Dr. B.F. Shumard and A.R. Roesler.* Self-published, 1875.

Rude, Fernand. *Les révoltes des Canuts (1831-1834).* Paris: La Découverte/Poche, 2007.

Savardan, Auguste. *Un naufrage au Texas.* Paris: Garnier frères, libraires-éditeurs, 1858.

Selcer, Richard, and William B. Potter. *The Fort that Became a City: An Illustrated Reconstruction of Fort Worth, Texas, 1849-1853.* Fort Worth: Texas Christian University Press, 1995.

Shaw, Albert. *Icaria: A Chapter in the History of Communism.* Baltimore: Johns Hopkins University, June 1884.

Shipley, June Anderson. *Lancaster: A History 1845-1945.* Lancaster, TX: Lancaster Historical Society, 1978.

Smith, Margaret Denton, and Mary Louise Tucker. *Photography in New Orleans: The Early Years, 1840-1865.* Baton Rouge: Louisiana State University Press, 1982.

Sreenivasan, Jyotsna, *Utopias in American History,* ABC-CLIO, Inc.

Sue, Eugène. *Une page de l'histoire de mes livres: Madame Solms dans l'exil.* Turin: imprimerie de Joseph Favale et compagnie. 1857.

Sutton, Robert P. *Les Icariens: The Utopian Dream in Europe and America.* Urbana: University of Illinois Press, 1994.

Tardy, Jean-Noël. *L'âge des ombres. Complots, conspirations et sociétés secrètes au XIXe siècle.* Paris: Les Belles Lettres, 2015.

Thurman, Nita, and Weldon Lucas. *150 Years of Denton County Sheriffs, 1846-1996.* Denton, TX: Old Alton Press, 1998.

Van Zandt County History Book Committee. *The History of Van Zandt County Texas.* Wills Point, TX: Van Zandt County Genealogical Society, 1984.

Wallace, Ernest. *Charles DeMorse: Pioneer Editor and Statesman.* Lubbock: Texas Tech University Press, 1943.

Walters, Raymond. *Stephen Foster, Youth's Golden Gleam: A Sketch of His Life and Background in Cincinnati 1846-1850.* Princeton: Princeton University Press, 1936.

Wooster, Ralph A. *Civil War Texas: A History and Guide.* Austin: Texas State Historical Association, 1999.

ONLINE BOOKS AND WEBSITES

Association d'études fouriéristes. "Charlesfourier.fr" accessed July 24, 2017.

Dallas Public Library and University of North Texas Press. "The WPA Dallas Guide and History." Accessed August 29, 2018.

Hancks, Gregory. "The world of Hannah Chribbs Evans." Accessed May 23, 2018.

The Portal to Texas History, https://texashistory.unt.edu

Texas State Historical Association. "The Handbook of Texas." Accessed August 29, 2018. https://tshaonline.org/handbook/online.

MONOGRAPHS AND DISSERTATIONS

Beting, Graziella. "Au fil de la plume." Doctoral thesis of the University Panthéon-Assas, 2014.

Darriulat, Philippe. "Albert Laponneraye journaliste et militant politique du premier XIXe siècle." Doctoral thesis, University Paris 10, 1989.

Giles, Marie Louise. "The Early History of Medicine in Dallas, 1841-1900." MA Thesis, University of Texas, 1951.

Santerre, Eloise, "Reunion, A Translation of Dr. Savardan's Un Naufrage au Texas." Master's Thesis, SMU, 1935.

JOURNAL ARTICLES

Birchall, Ian. "The Enigma of Kersausie: Engels in June 1848." *Revolutionary History* 8, no. 2, 25-50.

Caron, Jean-Claude. "La Société des Amis du Peuple." *Romantisme* 10, no. 28,# 169-179.

Chanut Jean-Marie, Heffer Jean, Mairesse Jacques and Postel-Vinay Gilles. "Les disparités de salaires en France au XIXe siècle." *Histoire & Mesure* 10, no. 3-4 (1995): 381-409.

Dubedat, Jean baptiste. "Le procès des communistes à Toulouse." *Recueil de l'Académie de législation de Toulouse* 37 (1888-1889): 293.

DuPree Begos, Jane. "Henri Levi's The Perilous Voyage to Icaria (1848)." *Communal Societies* 3 (1983): 147-157.

Enstam, Elizabeth York. "The Frontier Woman as City Worker: Women's Occupations in Dallas, Texas, 1856-1880." *East Texas Historical Journal* 18, no. 1 (1980).

Fleury, Michel, and Valmary Pierre. "Les progrès de l'instruction élémentaire de Louis XIV à Napoléon III, d'après l'étude de Louis Magiolo (1877-1879)." *Population,* no. 1 (1957): 71-92.

Geiser, Samuel Wood. "John Wright Glenn (1836-92), Early State Geologist of Texas." *Field and Laboratory* 13 (July 1945): 66.

Gibbens, V.E. "Lawrie's Trip to Northeast Texas, 1854-1855." *Southwestern Historical Quarterly* 48 (October 1944): 238-253.

Gill, Rocert T. "Cross-file of Grantors and Grantees of Town Property in the First Ten Years of the Town of Dallas, 1846-1856." *The Quarterly: A Bulletin of the Local History and Genealogical Society* 12, no. 1 (1966):1-35.

Hill, Robert T. "The Present Condition of Knowledge of the Geology of Texas." *Bulletin of the United States Geological Survey*, no. 45 (1887): 39.

Ludlow, John. "Some of the Christian Socialists of 1848 and the Following Years." *The Economic Review* 4 (1894): 36-37.

Maillard, Alain. "La génération communiste de 1840 et la mémoire de Gracchus Babeuf." *L'Homme et la société*, nos 111-112 (1994): 89-100.

Ponteil, Félix. "Le Ministre des Finances Georges Humann et les émeutes antifiscales en 1841." *Revue Historique* 179 (1937): 311.

Rocher, Denise. "Aux origines de l'associationnisme français. Images d'Étienne Cabet dans les Archives Parisiennes." *Communautés, Archives Internationales de Sociologie de la Coopération et du développement* 28 (1970): 25-55.

Sjödén, Karl-Erik. "Swedenborg en France." *Acta Universitatis Stockholmiensis. Stockholm Studies in History of Literature* 27 (1985).

Snyder, Lillian M. "The Contribution of Icarian, Alfred Piquenard to Architecture in Iowa and Illinois." *Communal Societies. Published by the Communal Studies Association* 6 (1986).

CONFERENCES

Congrès international des droits des femmes ouvert à Paris le 25 juillet 1878, clos le 9 août suivant. Compte-rendu des séances plénières (Paris, Auguste Ghio, 1878).

NEWSPAPERS/PERIODICALS

USA

The Bath Daily Times

The Bohemian (Fort Worth)

Brenham Daily Banner

Daily Picayune

Dallas Herald

Dallas Morning News

Denton Monitor

Denton Record and Chronicle

Democratic Telegraph and Texas Register

Fort Worth Star-Telegram

Missouri Weekly

The New Orleans Bee

The New York Times

New-York Observer

The Northern Standard (Clarksville, Texas)

Photographic and Fine Art Journal (New York)

The Texas State Gazette

France

Beaumarchais. Journal satirique, littéraire et financier (Paris)

La Comédie (Paris)

L'Émancipation (Toulouse)

La Gazette de Lyon

La Gazette des Tribunaux (Paris)

La Glaneuse (Lyon)

Journal d'agriculture pratique, de jardinage et d'économie domestique (Paris)

Journal du Lyonnais

Le Journal de Toulouse

Nouvelles archives statistiques, historiques et littéraires du département du Rhône (Lyon)

Le Populaire (Paris)

Le Précurseur (Lyon)

Réalisation d'Icarie. Nouvelles de Nauvoo

Revue du Lyonnais

Other European Countries

The Movement and Anti-Persecution Gazette. London, UK.

Morgenblatt für gebildete Leser. Heidelberg, Germany.

INTERVIEWS BY AUTHORS

Dawn Youngblood, February 1, 2019

Paula Baker, July 1, 2017. Baker's husband, James Clifford, was Judge J.E. Martin's great grandson.

Shirley and Marvin Applewhite, September 16, 2014, Dallas, Texas.

Index